Jacquetta Hawkes grew up i[...]and attended Newnham College. She has been United Kingdo[...] Secretary to UNESCO, and archaeological correspondent first of the *Observer* and then of the *Sunday Times*. Her many publications include *The Archaeology of Jersey*, *Early Britain*, *Prehistoric Britain* (with Christopher Hawkes) and a volume of poetry called *A Land*. She wrote the first part of the UNESCO *History of Mankind*, and edited a massive anthology, *The Worlds of the Past*. In 1968 she published her study of the beginnings of European history, *Dawn of the Gods*.

Jacquetta Hawkes

A GUIDE TO THE PREHISTORIC AND ROMAN MONUMENTS IN ENGLAND AND WALES

EPSOM COLLEGE
LIBRARY

First published in Great Britain
by Chatto & Windus Ltd 1951
Revised edition published in 1973
Copyright © Jacquetta Hawkes 1951, 1973

Published by Sphere Books Ltd
30/32 Gray's Inn Road, London WC1X 8JL
(under the CARDINAL imprint) 1973, reprinted 1975
This ABACUS edition published
by Sphere Books Ltd 1978

This book is sold subject to the condition that it shall
not, by way of trade or otherwise, be lent, re-sold,
hired out or otherwise circulated without the pub-
lisher's prior consent in any form of binding or cover
other than that in which it is published and without a
similar condition including this condition being imposed on the subsequent purchaser

Set in Monotype Times Roman

*Printed in Great Britain by Hazell Watson & Viney Ltd,
Aylesbury, Bucks*

CONTENTS

CONTENTS

ILLUSTRATIONS

Black and White Illustrations

Photographs and illustrations were supplied by and are reproduced by kind permission of the following: I, VII, VIII, Picturepoint; III, IV, 18, A. F. Kersting; V, VI, XIV, C. M. Dixon; XIII, Michael Holford; 1, 6, Aerofilms; 3, 4, Ashmolean Museum, Oxford; 7, 8, 12, 13, 14, 16, 22, Barnaby's Picture Library; 17, 21, Camera Press; X, Sussex Archaeological Trust, photographed by C. M. Dixon; II, IX, XII, XV, XVI, 2, 5, 9. 10, 11, 15, 19, 20, 23, 24, Crown copyright – reproduced with the permission of the Controller of Her Majesty's Stationery Office.

MAPS

(*Drawn by K. C. Jordan*).

PREFACE

SINCE this book was first published in 1951 interest in the remains of our past has probably increased. Certainly far more visitors go to see the ancient places for themselves. That is why it has seemed worth while to revise the old Guide in the light of the excavation and research of the last twenty years. On the whole it has stood the test of time remarkably well, and the arrangement based on itineraries of an informal kind has, I believe, recommended it to tourists. With the additions that have now been made, I hope that it will help a new generation of explorers to find and appreciate the wonderfully wide range of field monuments that survive in so many regions of England and Wales.

Although great stretches of countryside have been engulfed by modern development of all kinds and the threat to archaeological sites is so great that organisations such as *Rescue* have been set up to protect or explore them, it is encouraging to know that the type of monument described here, those that, I said before, 'the eye and the imagination can still enjoy', have hardly suffered. Many minor earthworks have gone, or have been spoiled by the ploughing of what used to be open downland, but the finer, better preserved monuments figuring in this Guide have been well looked after.

For this reason revision has not meant removing names from the itineraries or the gazetteer, but only expanding or correcting the histories of sites excavated since 1951 and adding new discoveries. There have not been many additions so spectacular as the great Roman palace of Fishbourne, but anyone who cares to check will find quite a number of interesting new entries. The gazetteer has also been brought up to date by substituting letter references to the O.S.100 km. squares in place of the number system that prevailed until 1953.

In my original Preface I made the usual thanks to several people who had been helpful in various ways. Now I want to concentrate my gratitude on one person: Dr. Julie Hanson. She undertook all the basic work of revision, carrying it out with exceptional efficiency and despatch. I was left with little to do beyond the application of stylistic oil to ease the additions into my own text. It is not often that one gets such faultless collaboration as hers.

JACQUETTA HAWKES

A Guide to the
Prehistoric and Roman Monuments
in England and Wales

TYPES OF PREHISTORIC AND ROMAN REMAINS TO BE SEEN IN ENGLAND AND WALES

A. DOMESTIC, AGRICULTURAL AND CIVIC SITES

Caves

Natural caves are the only class of site, normally visible, which can be associated with the hunting peoples of the Old and Middle Stone Ages. They rarely show any kind of structural additions and there are no cave paintings or engravings in Britain; they are distinguished only by the litter of flint implements and bones which accumulated on the floors.

Although cave dwellings can properly be regarded as characteristic of the early Stone Ages, caves were sporadically occupied throughout prehistoric and Roman times.

Huts, Farmsteads and Villages

The foundations of ancient settlements, often with protecting banks, walls and ditches, survive in many parts of the country. On chalk down-land, where they are often marked on Ordnance Survey Maps as 'British Settlement', little more is visible of them than low irregularities in the turf. These sometimes mark the sites of hamlets, sometimes of single farm-steads with out-buildings. A few date from the late Bronze Age, but the great majority belong to the Iron Age or to Romano-British times. Far more spectacular, and therefore more often mentioned in this *Guide,* are their counterparts in the stone country of the west and north. These consist mainly of the so-called hut-circles, which are in fact the stone foundation walls of circular huts roofed with branches and turf; the pair of large jamb-stones at the entrance is usually the most conspicuous feature. Often a cluster of such hut-circles is enclosed within a low stone wall, which on Dartmoor is sometimes known as a pound. These settlements can be seen in most moorland areas; they date from the Bronze and Iron Ages. Comparable but architecturally more advanced villages are known in Wales, most notably in Anglesey (p. 233 ff.) where the majority seem to be native settlements of the Roman period.

Another, much rarer variety is the compact village of 'courtyard houses' found in Cornwall (p. 179); in this type of dwelling, rooms and small

17

cells constructed in the thickness of the wall open on to an unroofed central court.

Although many of the hill-forts described below were used only in times of emergency, some were permanently occupied. In forts on the chalk, the floors of huts or storage pits may show as small circular depressions; in stone country, tumbled circular walls are sometimes visible (pp. 228–9).

Embanked Enclosures

The earliest form of enclosure is found in the causewayed camps which survive, though largely eroded away, across the south of England from Sussex to Devon. They consist of two or more concentric rings of banks and ditches with a considerable space between them. The ditches are never continuous, but broken into sections by causeways of undisturbed ground; it was formerly held that these causeways led to corresponding gaps in the banks to make large numbers of possible entrances, but it is now believed that the banks were continuous and that the causeways had no practical purpose. If this proves to be true the name places a false emphasis on an unimportant feature. Although there is often plenty of food, bones and other occupation rubbish in the inner ditches, only one causewayed camp (p. 148) has so far been proved to contain a hut site. It is thought that they may have served as tribal meeting places. The enclosures date back to early phases of the New Stone Age.

A second type of embanked enclosure, also possibly mainly pastoral in purpose, is of much later date. This is the relatively small, rectangular form of which a few examples, too insignificant-looking to win a place in the Guide, have been noticed in Wessex. They date from the late Bronze Age.

Roman Villas

These range in size and dignity from large 'country houses' to quite modest farm-houses. They were most numerous and prosperous in the Home Counties, but frequent enough right across southern England, with noticeable concentrations in Hampshire, the Isle of Wight and the Cotswolds. The most elaborate villas were built round a courtyard; others had a main block with wings, very many consisted only of a single block with rooms opening on to an arcaded corridor. Their remains often include foundations of brick or stone walls, mosaic floors, small column bases, hypocaust columns from the central-heating system, and, of course, the usual Roman litter of bricks, tiles and potsherds. The buildings seem often to have been enclosed within an outer boundary ditch or wall, and the estates attached to them must sometimes have been extensive.

Roman Towns

A very large proportion of the towns which the Roman conquerors established in Britain have been overlain and partly obliterated by modern towns and cities. All were at one time laid out on a more or less regular grid street system; very often, however, the 'blocks' or *insulae* were not completely filled with houses; the amount of garden space must have been considerable. Among the regulation public buildings, there was the central market or forum with the arcaded basilica or 'town hall' running along one side of it, the public baths, and the amphitheatre, generally built on the outskirts. True theatres were rare. The walls and gates, which are frequently the principal surviving remains, were usually later additions to the towns and as a result may show an irregular outline contrasting with the rectangular plan of the military forts and camps. The cemeteries normally lay along the roads outside the gates.

Although town life seems never to have been as popular in Roman Britain as in other western provinces, a number of Romano-British towns, especially in those areas protected from the full force of the first incursions of the Angles and Saxons, survived into the fifth century. Notable among these survivals are *Isca Silurum* (Caerwent), *Verulamium* (St. Albans) and *Uriconium* (Wroxeter), where excavation has proved that the Romano-Britons fought a long but inevitably futile battle to preserve their urbanised existence.

B. MILITARY WORKS AND BOUNDARIES

Hill-Forts

One of the commonest and most striking types of prehistoric monument is the fort; because very many of them are built on summits, the whole class is often loosely known as the hill-fort. These strongholds are abundant among the southern chalk lands and also among the hills of the west and north. Very many date from the Iron Age, though in parts of Wales and the far north they might still be occupied in Roman times and later.

There are many varieties of hill-fort to be distinguished. A characteristic which is, however, common to most of them is that the ramparts follow the natural contours of the hill-top; care was generally taken to avoid leaving any 'dead ground' where attackers could approach unseen. In Cornwall (pp. 175–8) the so-called ring-forts are distinguished by regularly planned circular ramparts. Another variant is the promontory fort in which a coastal headland or steep-sided spur of hill is defended only by ramparts running across the neck. Occasionally forts lie on level plateaux, and there, in the absence of determining contours, the usual plan is a roughly rounded one.

All these variants may have single, double or multiple lines of rampart and ditch. It can generally be assumed that a fort with only one line dates from the first half of the Iron Age, say between 450 and 150 B.C., while those with two or more have been either constructed or elaborated during the second half—from 150 B.C. to the Roman conquest.

Although the plans are similar in the two regions, the forts of the chalk and those of the stone country are very unlike one another in appearance. The chalk ramparts and ditches are often imposing, but they show as mild, turf-grown banks; the stone-built walls, on the other hand, have usually tumbled in a rocky confusion, overgrown with heather and bracken. In the single, early forts the chalk ramparts were commonly given almost vertical faces by revetment of timber boards and uprights; in the multiple forms they often stood as simple banks, though sometimes bonded with timber. Timber bonding was employed also in some of the stone forts, and slots may still sometimes be seen marking the position of the beams; it is doubtful, however, whether in our area any of these forts ever possessed the full elaboration of the stone and wood *murus Gallicus* which Julius Caesar saw and recorded in Gaul.

Our prehistoric forts often have horn-works, baffles and other devices for protecting the entrances; another protective device was to bend the rampart ends inwards and set the main gate at the inmost extremity in such a way that it could only be reached by an easily defended alley between the inturned walls. Guard-chambers were sometimes built within the angle of these inturned entrances.

Dykes or Linear Earthworks

The word dyke is used archaeologically to describe any considerable stretch of bank and ditch. Such linear earthworks range in length from small cross-ridge dykes intended to command some upland thoroughfare to such monsters as Wansdyke (p. 113) and Offa's Dyke (p. 238). There may be one, two or several lines of bank and ditch, but the longer dykes are usually single.

Of their nature dykes can hardly be regarded as defensible; rather they are boundaries, often they are true political boundaries, marking the limits of estates, territories, kingdoms. A few, however, were more strictly military in purpose, being designed to defend a limited area—like those near Colchester which ran from stream to stream protecting the Belgic capital of *Camulodunum* (p. 251). To-day linear earthworks often appear to come to an abrupt and meaningless end; the explanation is that when they were built these ends rested on dense forest or swamp which made their continuation both impossible and unnecessary.

Dykes other than the small cross-ridge type are not earlier than the end of prehistoric times. The Belgae were the first considerable builders; the next period was the late Roman and sub-Roman (p. 129) and the last Anglo-Saxon (p. 247). There are no structural differences to distinguish the works of these periods.

In a sense the Roman frontier of Hadrian's Wall (p. 284) can be recognized as a sophisticated version of the linear earthwork; it probably helped to inspire Offa's tremendous conception of his frontier against the Welsh.

Roman Forts, Camps, and Signal Stations

During their conquest and throughout the four centuries that they occupied Britain, the Roman armies built large numbers of military strong points, ranging in size from signal stations and look-out towers to legionary fortresses, and in permanence from marching camps occupied only for one night to great military bases held for hundreds of years. All were laid out to military textbook design with only minor variations to suit local conditions. Roman forts and camps can readily be distinguished from prehistoric earthworks by their regularity of plan—usually quadrilateral with four gates and neatly rounded corners. The Forts of the Saxon Shore show massive stone and brick walls with bastions.

Of temporary marching camps, nothing can be expected to be visible beyond the earth ramparts, but the remains of permanent or semi-permanent forts are often far more extensive. In the earlier years of the occupation even these forts had no more than earthen ramparts and wooden buildings, but during the first half of the second century very many of them were rebuilt in stone. In these the masonry foundations of gates and walls often survive, and inside may be seen the monotonous lines of barracks and granaries. In addition to these dreary buildings, normal forts were also provided with a commandant's house, and a regimental headquarters with shrine and treasury occupying a position corresponding to that of the forum in a civil town.

A few of the marching camps raised during the conquest can be seen in the English lowlands, but most Roman military remains belong to the west and north where the frontier garrisons had to be maintained, or to the Saxon Shore in the south-east.

C. INDUSTRIAL

Flint-Mines

These are limited to the chalk country where shafts could be sunk to reach the natural beds of flint nodules. Apart from the famous centre at Grimes Graves in Norfolk (p. 248) most mining was carried out along the South Downs (pp. 82–3) and in Wiltshire. The mined flint was used for axes, adzes and hoes which were manufactured on the spot, workshops sometimes being established at the top of abandoned and refilled shafts. Unexcavated mining areas show as a rash of turf-grown mounds and hollows.

Stone-Axe Factories

In the mountain country the equivalent of the flint-mine was the quarry where hard, tough rocks were cut and shaped into implements. Few are known (p. 235) and they can be detected in the field only by a scatter of unfinished and broken products lying on or near the surface.

Copper, Tin, Lead and Iron Mines

Tin-mining in Cornwall and copper-mining in Wales were important industries during prehistoric times; the iron of the Forest of Dean and the Kent and Sussex Weald was exploited in the Iron Age and Roman period, while lead-mining was strongly developed by the Romans in the Mendips and the north of England. Yet visible remains which can confidently be attributed to these ancient industries are scanty (p. 155). Of them all only the iron-mine at Lydney (p. 204) is complete enough to give some idea of the methods employed. The mining of metals has left far less striking remains than the earlier flint-mining partly because it was mainly on the surface, partly because the sites might be exploited continuously into historic times.

D. COMMUNICATIONS

Ancient Tracks

It is impossible to point to any existing trackway and say that it is prehistoric, yet many follow routes which we know to have been in use in prehistoric times. Most of the long upland ridges were established thoroughfares, but they were not artificially improved. Many of them, too, remained in use in the Middle Ages and even up to the eighteenth century (for example the Salisbury-Shaftesbury coach road, p. 126). Famous thoroughfares certainly established before the Roman conquest are the Icknield Way, the Berkshire Ridgeway and the Pilgrims' Way along the North Downs.

It should be noticed that where medieval drove roads have to climb steep hills they often break out into large numbers of tracks running side by side. This was caused by slight changes of course made when the old way became deeply worn and therefore wet or rough. The same thing must often have happened with prehistoric trackways.

Roman Roads

Roman roads are usually well marked on Ordnance Survey maps which indicate them even when, as so commonly occurs, they have been buried below a modern highway. Few ancient monuments present a more exciting spectacle than a major Roman road running across open country. Often only the strongly cambered central *agger* is visible, but sometimes flanking ditches and low banks are preserved. Minor roads, of which there must have been many, are more difficult to detect, but enthusiasts become skilful at following them by the lines of old lanes and parish boundaries, raised hedge banks and other clues.

In the south the metalling of the *agger* was normally made up merely of compacted chalk, gravel or small stones; stone paving is found in the north (p. 276), and there are good examples with stone culverts (pp. 268, 279).

Bridges are rare (p. 286) as fords were the common form of river crossing.

Roadside burial was a Roman practice and graves with or without some visible monument may be expected near centres of population.

Roman Canals

Canals cut by the Romans to link natural waterways in the Cambridgeshire and Lincolnshire fens show as a shallow groove between low-flanking banks. The drainage system was almost certainly undertaken by a central authority and was started towards the end of the first century A.D. and remained in use until the fifth century. The most famous canal of all, the Car Dyke, was probably cut in the time of Hadrian. As well as helping to drain the land the canal system was important as a means of transport and it was possible to travel by inland waterways from the Fen district as far north as Brough-on-Humber or York thus linking one of the important agricultural areas of the province with the military zone.

E. RELIGIOUS AND SEPULCHRAL MONUMENTS

Embanked Sanctuaries

Sanctuaries with settings of stone or timber, enclosed within a circular bank, usually with internal ditch, form a distinct class of sacred sites, but one with many variations. The embankment may be as relatively insignificant as it is at Stonehenge, or as imposing as at Avebury, and it may have one, two or four entrances; the inner settings may be of wood or stone, they may consist of concentric circles, of circles set side by side, of horseshoe-shaped forms or of combinations of circle with horseshoe.

Most of these sanctuaries date from the earlier part of the Bronze Age; Stonehenge has an exceptional long history (p. 123). There is a current opinion that the type with a single entrance originated with the native peoples of the New Stone Age, while the other varieties were inspired by the invaders of the early Bronze Age; evidence for this division is at present quite insufficient.

Though some of the least imposing and supposedly the earliest of these structures may have been designed for the reception of burials, this is certainly not true of the fully developed forms. They must have served ritual and ceremonial purposes, and only the most austere authorities object to them being called temples. A great deal of doubtful and indeed crazy theorizing has been devoted to astronomical interpretations of the lay-out of the sanctuaries, particularly of Avebury and Stonehenge. It need not be doubted, however, that at least some of them are significantly orientated in relation to the movements of the sun and perhaps of other heavenly bodies.

Stone Circles

Rings of standing stones without external earthworks are to be distinguished from the embanked sanctuaries and have a very different distribution (pp. 172–3, 212, 282). They cover a wide range both in size and in number of stones; occasionally the bases of the stones are set in very slightly raised banks (p. 230), but more usually the sites are level. There are some instances of groups of circles (p. 150), but far more commonly they are isolated.

Not many rings have been dated; probably they all belong to the late New Stone and earlier Bronze Age, tending to be rather later than the embanked class. If the word cromlech is used at all, it should be reserved for these free-standing stone circles.

Stone Rows

Single and double lines of standing stones are characteristic of Dartmoor and occur occasionally in other areas (pp. 109, 222). They seem sometimes to be significantly related to stone circles, and may indeed be linked by way of an intermediate form (p. 150) with the Avenues of Stonehenge and Avebury. Some of the Dartmoor examples have stone burial-cists on their course.

Very little is known about our stone rows, but probably they cover much the same period as the stone circles.

Standing Stones or Menhirs

Single standing stones are found throughout most of the moorland country of the west and north. Some of them may be the relics of more extensive monuments, but unquestionably the majority were designed as single uprights, with what intention is unknown. There are several instances of a menhir standing as an outlier of a circle—the most famous being the Heel Stone at Stonehenge.

Cursus

These mysterious and inconspicuous monuments are best represented by the Stonehenge cursus (p. 124); there are a few others in Wessex and (now visible only from the air), on flat gravel spreads in the Thames and several other river valleys. They consist of a very long narrow strip enclosed between banks. They usually date from a late phase of the New Stone Age.

Megalithic Tombs

This is a very large, varied and important class of monument, and one which offers some of the most striking and imaginatively stirring spectacles of all our ancient remains. Every properly named megalithic tomb is walled and often roofed with massive stone blocks or slabs; the space between these is characteristically packed with small stones, a kind of dry-walling, while the roofs are occasionally corbelled. These burial chambers were hidden below a long or round cairn or barrow; it has been claimed that some of the small dolmens (see below) were never completely covered, but this must be regarded as not proven.

In a theoretical classification applicable to the megaliths of all western and northern Europe, two main divisions are recognized. One, the passage grave, has a rounded or polygonal chamber approached by a much narrower passage. The second, the gallery grave, has no distinct passage but instead consists of a single parallel-sided grave, sometimes divided internally into ante-chamber and main chamber; in some areas it is broken up into segments by low cross slabs or by pairs of stones projecting from the walls, and in others furnished with side cells.

In England and Wales, however, the classic passage grave is represented solely by Bryn-Celli-Ddu and another much mutilated example also in Anglesey (p. 231). It is impossible here to enumerate all the supposed variants of the gallery grave, but the most important group is that of the so-called Cotswold-Severn chambered long barrows—a group centred on the Bristol Channel but extending westwards into Breconshire (pp. 207–210, 217) and eastwards as far as the Berkshire Downs (p. 105).

The simplest and most widespread forms of megalithic tombs, generally held to be degenerate and relatively late, show a rectangular or polygonal chamber built of a few very large blocks and normally roofed with a single huge capstone. These can usefully be distinguished as dolmens; in our area they are commonest in Cornwall and south-west and north-west Wales.

These tombs were intended to receive many bodies, and although the entrances were carefully blocked, they were certainly sometimes unsealed to allow successive burials over a considerable period of time. They are characteristic of the New Stone Age.

The distribution of megaliths is conspicuously western and coastal and this form of funerary architecture must have been introduced by immigrants seeking their way by sea up our Atlantic coasts. The single exception is the small group in Kent (pp. 68–70).

Long Barrows

Long burial-mounds without megalithic chambers are characteristic of Wessex and Sussex, but their builders pushed along the chalk into East Anglia (pp. 245–6) and also northwards into Lincolnshire and Yorkshire (p. 268). They may be several hundred feet in length and are both broader and higher at one end than the other; there is a tendency for the larger end, containing the main sepulchre, to point in an easterly direction. Most long barrows now appear as simple turf-grown mounds of chalk, but originally many, and probably all, of them were given greater formality by façades and containing walls of timber or turf. It was also certainly normal for them to enclose a wooden or turf-built burial compartment; a large number of bodies might be interred, but there is at present no evidence to show that the burials could be made successively as in the megalithic tombs.

Long barrows are a feature of the New Stone Age and have never yielded metal grave-goods.

Round Barrows

The round burial-mounds and cairns still often marked on the Ordnance maps as *tumuli* complete with hill-forts as the commonest and most noticeable of all survivals from the prehistoric past. These mounds were raised over a single main burial—a rite sharply distinct from the communal burial of the long barrows and megalithic tombs. At first the burial was by inhumation, the body being laid in a crouched position in a pit cut into the surface of the ground; cremation later became general and the barrow was raised over urns which might or might not be sunk below ground surface. Careful excavation has shown that barrows might be raised over a miniature 'house of the dead' rings of posts, and even over a real house— doubtless that of the dead man.

The simple form introduced by the early Bronze Age invaders is known as the bowl barrow; it is a pudding-shaped mound immediately encircled by a ditch. Later in the Bronze Age the Wessex chieftains (p. 50) introduced other forms, many fine examples of which occur in the vicinity of Stonehenge. These include (*a*) Bell barrows, in which a wide level berm was left between the edge of the mound and the ditch. The material of the mound having slipped slightly to slope over the berm, a profile results which suggests a flanged bell. (*b*) Disk barrows in which a very accurately cut ditch with a low bank on its outer rim is the most important feature, the burial-mound within being reduced to a small tump. Occasional freakish double forms are known (p. 120). (*c*) Pond barrows, which are really not barrows at all, but just the reverse—saucer-shaped depressions in the level surface of the ground. The depressions do, however, contain burials, and it has been suggested that they were designed to receive libations poured to the dead.

Cairns of small stones are the counterpart of the bowl barrow in stone country; very often in them the place of the sunken pit is taken by a slab cist above ground level.

Barrows and cairns are often found in more or less dense concentrations. In Yorkshire there are the cairn cemeteries, vast numbers of tiny cairns (pp. 263, 270) which have been found to cover the burials of the Iron Age Celts who invaded the region during the third century B.C.

It may generally be assumed that any ordinary-looking round barrow or cairn dates from the Bronze Age, and from the early or middle part of it. In a few areas a low-pitched form was built to receive a number of crema- tion urns and these tend to be later. Nevertheless it should be remembered that *tumuli* were occasionally raised as burial monuments by the Roman Britons and by the Anglo-Saxons. The Roman variety may be distinguished by its conical form with very steeply pitched sides (p. 246). There are also small square mounds dating from the Roman period; they may perhaps be recognized as the base of some rustic version of the pyramidal or obelisk monuments fashionable in other parts of the Empire.

Rock Carvings

In a few localities Bronze Age peoples carved the surface of boulders and exposed rock. The commonest designs are known as cup-and-ring mark- ings: small cup-shaped pits surrounded with incised rings and not in- frequently approached by radial lines. The two important centres for these rock carvings within our area are the West Riding of Yorkshire (p. 277) and on the slopes of the Cheviots in Northumberland (pp. 287, 288).

The function and meaning of these symbols are quite unknown, but they clearly had some magico-religious significance.

CHRONOLOGICAL DIVISION
OF ANTIQUITIES

The field monuments described below can be assigned to their periods as follows:

Old and Middle Stone Ages.   Cave dwellings.

New Stone Age or Neolithic.   c. 3500–1900 B.C.
'Causewayed Camps'; Megalithic Tombs; Long Barrows; Flint-Mines; Stone-Axe Factories; The early Embanked Sanctuaries and Stone Circles.

Early to Middle Bronze Age.   1900–1000 B.C.
Embanked Sanctuaries; Stone Circles; Stone Rows; Menhirs; Round Barrows and Cairns; some Hut Circles and Pounds; some Flint-Mines.

Late Bronze Age.   c. 1000–500 B.C.
Rectangular Embanked Enclosures; some Hut Circles and Pounds; Settled Farmsteads.

Iron Age.   c. 500 B.C. to 43 A.D.
Hill-Forts and Related Types of Fort; Farmsteads; Villages and Hamlets; Dykes; Cairn Cemeteries (local).

Roman Period.   43 A.D. to early fifth century.
Towns; Amphitheatres; Theatres; Villas; Forts; Camps; Signal Stations; Roads; Frontier Works (Hadrian's Wall, etc.); Dykes; Canals; Round Barrows and Square Mounds (both rare).

THE PAST: AN INTRODUCTION

THERE can be no human being, I believe, who is not stirred by the places of his childhood. Perhaps those who have moved away from them in later life feel this emotional attachment even more strongly, or more consciously, than those who settle in the place where they were born. Nostalgia is relieved by an uprising of love when they return to see a room, a gate, ancient tree roots, a bend in the lane, a street corner with its lamp, any of those things which the associations of childhood have given an intimacy never to be shared by any of the scenes or possessions of adult life. There is a corresponding pang, a sense of utter loss, if the early home is destroyed or its familiar surroundings completely changed.

These emotions can be strong even in those whose memories are all of city houses and streets, but they are usually far stronger in the country-born. Men are still half aware of a relationship with the land which has nourished them and their ancestors, and from which, accepting the longest perspectives, all forms of life have emerged. This more universal sense of kinship raises personal attachment to a greater intensity than anything likely to be experienced in the wholly man-made world of a town.

It is here, among the riches of our ancestral inheritance, that the monuments of antiquity have their significance. They belong not to individual childhood but to the early years of our nation. A Stone Age burial-mound, a sanctuary of the Bronze Age, the earthen ramparts of a fortress of the Celtic Iron Age proclaim how deeply-rooted our culture is in the past.

This is not a false or sentimental response, nor one without importance in contemporary life. Anyone who has travelled in the Middle West of America must have felt the desolation which seems to rise like a fog from territories mauled by man but lacking any of the attributes of history. Territories that have taken shape since man ceased to battle with and court the land and began instead a loveless exploitation. It is not only that the visible remains of antiquity are lacking, the countryside itself is quite without the forms of slow growth and maturity—the sure but sensitive line with which lanes, farms, cottages, lead up to the great house or country town; the delicate precision with which this pattern of human settlement is related to the natural features of the land. There in the Middle West the

31

straight roads and scattered shacks have been imposed by the motor-car and their design is as lifeless and mechanical.

It is always mistaken to think of the surviving relics of prehistoric times in isolation, for in truth the whole of an ancient countryside is the slow creation of the thousands of years of its cultivation. Some three hundred generations have shaped the landscapes of Britain from a primeval island of mists and oak forests. The handiwork of the earliest is incorporated in that of all succeeding generations.

Admittedly, however, while the creation of a land is continuous, human handiwork lapses. No houses more than nine hundred years old are still inhabited, no building of any kind which is still in use, still a living part of our inheritance, is older than the few Saxon churches of the seventh century. Several Roman buildings are still standing, motor traffic flows under the Newport Arch at Lincoln—but they are not functioning and cannot be said to be incorporated in our contemporary life.

This distinction does indeed seem to cut us off from remains of prehistoric houses, sacred buildings, military works and burial-places. They are sites to be visited and not used; they have been left behind. Yet there is another sense in which these deserted ruins of the past have been brought back into use among us. Thousands of people read about them, visit them; a few hundred people devote their whole lives or all their spare time to their study and interpretation. Men do only what seems needful to them, whether the needs are material, emotional or intellectual. It is plain that we have now reached a stage in our development, in our decay perhaps, at which a knowledge of our origins, an ability to re-identify ourselves with them, has come to satisfy an emotional and intellectual need. The relics of our past, therefore, by which in part the need is satisfied have been drawn back into the current of life and are as much a feature of contemporary life as the stuffed hare and greyhounds that rush round an arena to gratify a longing for excitement. Indeed, they are more up to date, for they satisfy a very recently developed appetite possible only to highly civilized men, while the hare and hounds run in response to desires already implanted in mankind long before the oldest monuments were built.

So the present has secured itself by re-absorbing the past, and can never now exist without it. To maintain their sense of unity with their origins and to confirm it in a simple way, many people like to visit ancient sites, to stand again where they know remote ancestors have stood, to touch stones which ancestral hands have shaped. Even if we are satisfied by a less imaginative approach, antiquities make an objective for excursions into the country, often leading to the discovery of remote and lovely places. Only let all travellers to the past remember that its monument is to be found not only in these relics themselves, but in a whole countryside which has been cleared, cultivated, matured and embellished through the service of three hundred generations.

Chapter One

THE LAND OF BRITAIN

IF it can be claimed that the whole of our country and not only its surviving antiquities should be seen as the creation of past generations, it is legitimate to go much further, to penetrate below the surface of pasture, arable, woodland and waste and to see the whole substance of the island as one continuous creation. Through milliards of years it has been built and shaped; sometimes lying as a part of a vast continent embracing what is now the Atlantic and North-America, sometimes part of the sea-bed of equally vast oceans. Tropical, desert, and arctic climates have played over it.

So, side by side with the evolution of life, the land of Britain was brought into being; the remodelling of its surface by man belongs to this continuous and still rapidly developing process. Before the emergence of the creative force of imagination and intellect, life could leave its mark only in the physical remains of its creatures. In this it was prodigal. Often layers of rock may be largely composed of the remains of reptiles, fish, corals, molluscs, plants and many other living forms. There are, for example, the famous Purbeck marbles made through the accumulation of the bodies of water-snails on the floor of a long-forgotten lake; there are the Ludlow bone-beds where fragments of innumerable fish have been swept together and cemented into a rocky mass. Sometimes men have used these organic formations for their buildings and works of art, and so we see a curious interplay between lowly forms of life and the creative imagination achieved by its highest forms. The product of the slow processes of inorganic nature, of life and of mind, is the familiar landscape of contemporary Britain.

The folding of our area of the earth's crust has determined that the most ancient rocks are exposed in the north and west of the island and slope consistently downwards towards the south and east, until in the region of the capital they lie many miles below the feet of Londoners. On them the younger formations rest, layer upon layer, like a tilted pack of cards, the youngest of all—as it were the top cards—forming the surface in some parts of our southern and south-eastern counties. By travelling from East Anglia across country to North Wales one is travelling back and back into time. Starting from sands and gravels laid down when humans of a kind

35

were already hunting with well-made stone implements, the traveller crosses first the chalk and then the limestone belt deposited during the rise and fall of the dinosaurs and other great reptilian monsters, and passes on to the Old Red Sandstone whose formation coincided with the dominance of strange fishes in tropical seas. So at last he reaches the country which the immense hardness of the ancient rocks makes mountainous, the North Welsh ranges whose schists, shales and slates were deposited grain by grain in seas where the most primitive forms of life—jelly-fish, worms and crustaceans—were evolving with unimaginable slowness. Finally, if he crosses the Menai Straits, he will find Anglesey an island much of whose substance is older than life itself.

Man now feels himself to be master of all these formations and he uses all the variety which natural history has given them to serve the diversity of his own purposes. But even now the geology of Britain and the differences of climate caused by the conflicting influences of the Atlantic and the continental land mass of Europe and Asia do much to determine how and where the human population must live. While there are the innumerable local differences determined by the presence of minerals such as iron and coal, or of good and bad farming land, of pasture and arable, there are also the more general contrasts imposed by mountains and moorland on the one hand and the softer more genial English lowlands on the other. In the lowlands, after a prolonged struggle against the forest, man has in the end had it all his own way, the whole surface landscape is of his creation. The mountains are not to be tamed; they still dominate the people who live among them, asserting some positive being of their own, from which emanates the grandeur, solitude and tranquillity which Wordsworth sought and celebrated.

Even after the Industrial Revolution the structure and climate of Britain still partially control the manner of our life in the island; during the four thousand years between the earliest cultivation of the land and the beginning of the Revolution the control was, of course, far more tyrannical.

In later chapters, England and Wales will be anatomized, examined part by part as the traveller must visit them. Before this dissection, the country should be viewed as a whole so that it is possible to see the larger features which determined both the movement and the settlement of prehistoric peoples. To the peoples themselves this structure must long have remained unknown or only dimly guessed. It is doubtful whether any man, however gifted, would have been able to make even a rough sketch of the country sooner than the Late Bronze Age, when travelling bronze merchants must have been able to form a more or less coherent picture both of the island itself and of its relation to the Continent. Nevertheless, though they could not visualize the map, the land controlled the way in which successive invaders and their descendants penetrated and settled Britain and the lines of trade and communication which, however tenuously at first, linked the scattered and largely self-sufficient settlements.

To understand in greater detail how in practice the land guided the destinies of its inhabitants, it is best to consider England and Wales in those two bold divisions which geographers have now made familiar. One of them is the English lowlands, all that part of the country which we have recognized as being comparatively youthful, with none of its visible features more than two hundred million years old. The other is the mountain and moorland country or highlands starting in the south-western peninsula with the moors of Cornwall, Devon and Somerset, then including the Mendips and the whole mountain stronghold of the Welsh principality with its bastions projecting into the English border country. After the gap of the Cheshire plain we are in highland territory again with the Pennines and north Yorkshire moorlands and all the rocky country to the north and west of them—Durham, Northumberland and the mountains of Cumberland and Westmorland. It was once thought that prehistoric settlement was almost entirely limited to these uplands. Now, however, largely as a result of the skilled use of air surveys and photography, it has been discovered that river valleys where spreads of sands and gravels discouraged the growth of dense forest also supported flourishing communities.

Untold millions of years have made the highland rocks immensely hard, and two distinct periods of early folding have rucked them up into intricate patterns of ridge and valley; there is little soil and much of what there is has been washed down into valley bottoms. The coasts of the highlands, battered and gnawed by the Atlantic, are generally precipitous rocky cliffs, arched, pillared and fissured, accessible only to the sea-birds. Yet it is rare to find many miles of cliff unbroken by a river-mouth or a bay where boats can be beached, and in some stretches there are extensive coastal plains and wide estuaries where low-lying, cultiviable land edges the mountain and moorland behind.

Apart from those regions, usually on the margins of the greater mountain masses, where iron, coal and other minerals have brought industrialization, the ancient rocks have guarded something of the wildness of the past, a world utterly remote from the domesticity of rural England, a world of crags and boulders, of heather and peat-bogs, and clear, swift streams and rivers. The moors and mountains have their natural population of grouse, blackgame, curlew, merlin and buzzard; the rivers their salmon and trout and the plump dippers that fish from their boulders and nest behind their waterfalls.

Away from the industrial areas most of the human population live by small-scale dairy farming and running mountain sheep or by fishing. The fishing villages grow on bays and inlets with ready landing places; small towns sometimes develop at the mouths of valleys while above them the villages grow smaller and smaller towards the narrow valley heads; isolated farms stand high up in the side valleys where there may be just enough soil and grazing for the support of a single family. Each bay, each valley is commonly cut off from the next by bleak promontories and ridges and so the people living in them are isolated, divided into small communities.

For the rest the highland country has become a resort for visitors, a region which, having held the Industrial Revolution at bay, offers wildness to a people exhausted by city life or a little wearied by the mild charms of the English countryside. There the rich go to indulge the passion for hunting that has been an upper-class prerogative since the Bronze Age, while the poor walk, climb, and visit antiquities.

Along almost the whole of their frontier the division between highland and lowland is sharply drawn; the mountain scarp shows as a wall rising abruptly above the mildly undulating lowland; seen from the scarp the lowlands flow away like a sea below lofty cliffs. They are two confronted and contrasting worlds. Except for scattered outcrops such as Charnwood Forest where the jagged edges of ancient rocks thrust through the softer ground, the youthful lowlands lack age-hardened rocks with the strength to maintain heights and sharp outlines against the endless forces of denudation. Yet no one could think of them as a featureless expanse of undulating plain and level fen. They have their own pattern of uplands, a pattern already made familiar in the schoolroom by those relief maps in painted plaster which show the low-lying country in sleek spreads of green, and the uplands, embossed at twice their natural height, as crinkled ridges of fawn and brown. With this emphasis the upland pattern reveals itself at once as a radiate one; a series of ridges running out from the wide central plateau of Salisbury Plain and the adjacent chalk downland. In nature, without the influence of cartographer's licence, these hills are of very moderate height, rarely passing a thousand feet, yet anyone who has travelled the English countryside knows how delightfully they diversify the landscape. In almost any cross-country journey lines of hill and down succeed one another giving form and significance even to the surrounding plains.

These uplands provide much of the scenery which all over the globe is remembered as most characteristically English. The Cotswolds with their manor houses and farms, their villages and venerable towns, all built from their own grey or golden limestone; the drowsy villages of Wessex folded in the mild chalkland valleys; the Sussex Downs and the white cliffs of Dover themselves.

The great part of the hill system is built of limestone and chalk, and while enjoying the domesticated scenery—men ploughing, the flocks of plump sheep—travellers may like to reflect that the stuff of these hil's was formed when the reptiles, unchallenged masters of water, land and air, were achieving their grossest and most fantastic forms. Ichthyosaurs slashing through the seas, armour-plated dinosaurs carrying their tons of flesh on dry land, pterodactyls launching themselves from cliffs to float and wheel above the waves on their colossal leather wings.

The oldest and in many stretches the boldest of the upland ridges is the limestone belt which makes the noble scarp of the Cotswolds, then runs across Oxfordshire to Northamptonshire, where it dwindles only to emerge again in the narrow, sharply-defined line of Lincoln Edge. This belt ends in the sandstone which forms the rugged country of the north Yorkshire moors. To the east of it runs the longest of all the chalk ridges; leaving the White Horse Hills at the Chilterns it tapers away through Cambridge and Norfolk as the East Anglian Heights (including the famous Gogmagog hills outside Cambridge) and Norfolk Edge. It is cut by the Wash but rises again boldly to the north in the Lincolnshire and Yorkshire wolds.

Continuing to follow these spokes of the wheel of the hills, the next is already to the south of the Thames Valley; leaving Salisbury Plain by the Hampshire Downs the chalk thrusts one long finger, the North Downs, to the sea at Dover, while the shorter one forms the beautiful line of the South Downs. The South Downs extend behind a chain of seaside resorts and finally reach the sea, breaking off in the tremendous white bastion of Beachy Head, a sheer drop of cliffs far nobler than their more famous counterpart at Dover.

A short southern spur of upland is formed by the Western Downs which extend to the Channel coast between the two pleasant resorts of Lyme Regis and Weymouth. At Lyme the lofty but crumbling cliffs of the Blue Lias are so crowded with fossils, from the slender spikes of belemnites and coiled formality of ammonites to ichthyosaurs and other marine monsters, that to hunt them is a recognized sport for visitors. Finally the radial pattern is completed on the western side by the fine ridge of the Mendips, but these hills, of more ancient formation, belong geologically to the highlands.

To-day if one looks down on the Kent and Sussex Weald from the North or South Downs, or on the Severn Valley from the Cotswolds, it is still easy to feel that one is looking from an open onto a forest country. When seen from no great height all the trees which farmers leave standing by streams, roads and in their hedges, all the small patches of woodland, merge together to give this forested appearance to what is in fact fully cultivated agricultural land. This picture represents an undoubted historical truth; the scattered trees are the memory of great forests. When, well after the final retreat of the ice-sheets, Britain assumed approximately its present geographical form, much of the low-lying land was not only hidden below a close canopy of trees but made almost impassable by a tangle of thorn, bramble and other undergrowth. In contrast the uplands, though they did not show the bare tops of our present landscape, were relatively open; the tree growth was light enough to allow passage and encourage clearance. Given these contrasting conditions it was inevitable that from the time of the arrival of the earliest farming people over five thousand years ago, wave after wave of the prehistoric invaders who sailed to our southern and eastern coasts made their way on to the uplands and lived there islanded above the forests. These chalk and limestone hills offered pasture for the cattle and sheep that were their main support, and a light soil suitable to tillage with the hoe and digging-stick, which for long remained the only agricultural equipment. There they lived, clearing the woodland, tilling small patches of ground and treading out trackways along the ridges to serve them for trade, petty migration and war. There, too, they built the cattle enclosures, the forts and entrenched settlements, the burial-mounds, chambered tombs and sanctuaries whose ruins survive as their chief memorial.

Because the upland ridges and their roads converged on the central chalk massif of Wiltshire that region became the richest and probably the most thickly populated area in England, a pre-eminence clearly shown by the large number and distinction of monuments we shall find there—culminating in the temples of Stonehenge and Avebury that have a good claim to be the finest remains of prehistoric Europe. Salisbury Plain has been recognized as the metropolitan area of prehistoric Britain, and in this sense it is interesting to compare it with the modern Metropolis. The Plain is the hub of a radiate pattern which is raised, in relief, while since its foundation in Roman times London has become the centre of a wheel of roads, canals, railways, which so far as possible follow valleys and so represent as it were an incised or recessive pattern. While the herdsmen, warriors, bronze-

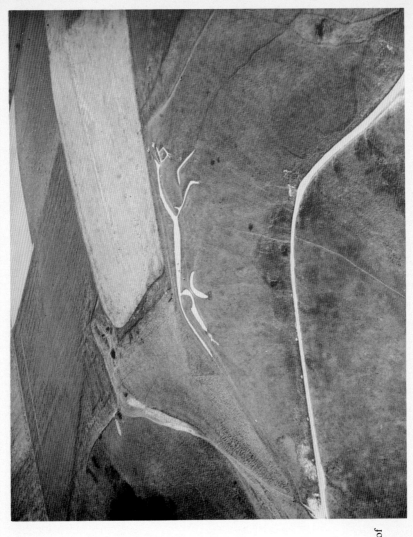

1. The White Horse of Uffington, on the Berkshire Downs.

2. Wayland's Smithy, a megalithic chambered long barrow on the Ridgeway of the Berkshire Downs.

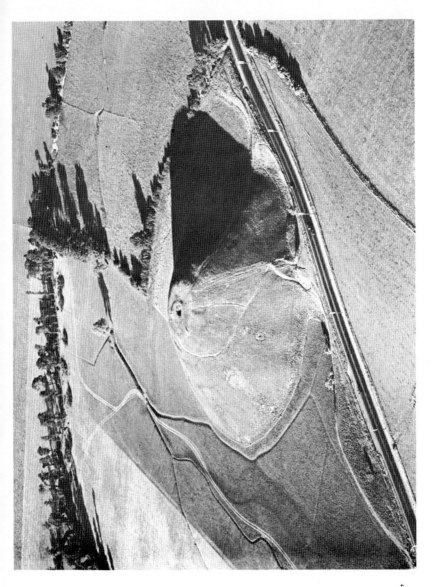

3. Silbury Hill, Wiltshire.

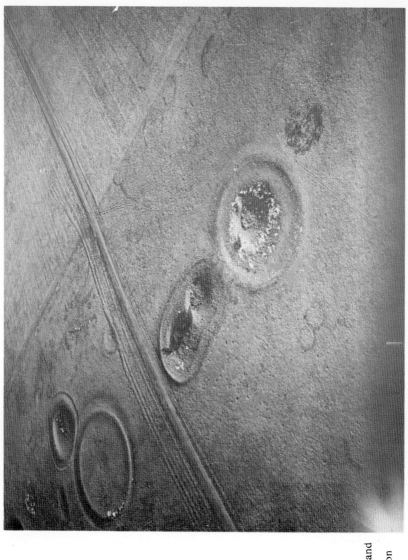

4. Disk, Bowl, Bell and Double Bell Round Barrows: Normanton Down, Wiltshire.

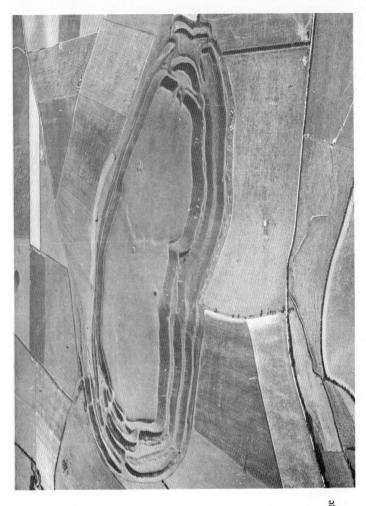

5. The great Iron Age hill-fort of Maiden Castle, Dorset.

6. The Cerne Abbas Giant, with the rectangular enclosure of the Frying Pan above his left hand.

7. One of the Bronze Age dwellings within a walled enclosure at Grimspound, on Dartmoor.

8. Chun Quoit in Cornwall, a closed dolmen with its capstone still in position.

workers and merchants came to the Plain for their various purposes by upland tracks from which as they trudged or rode they looked down across mile after mile of tree-tops, all those travellers who have come to London during the last nineteen hundred years have usually approached the city either by water or by valley roads from which, if the trees did not crowd too closely, they could look up at the hills which rose above them or filled a distant horizon.

The change from Salisbury Plain to London as the centre of England's thoroughfares and of its prosperity, represents the shift in the relationship between human settlement and the land which began late in prehistoric times, made some slight progress under the Romans, and was pushed rapidly towards completion by the Anglo-Saxons. This was, of course, the spread of population from the uplands to the valleys and plains which became possible with the clearing of forests. A thousand years later there was to be another equally great migration when the Industrial Revolution led men to swarm round the mineral deposits of the island; but for the Saxons the economic magnet was the richer soil with its sure promise of abundant harvests. The once populous hills are to-day relatively thinly settled and may even show as islands of uncultivated land in our rural landscape. Just because of the swing of population to the richer soils, the English uplands and the moors and mountains to the west have in many areas been little cultivated from late Saxon times until our own. Turf and heather were allowed to grow over prehistoric fields, houses, forts, temples and graves and they survived secure from the ploughman and builder, whose age-long energy has destroyed so much where settlement has been continuous.

Certainly it is a happy state of affairs for the seeker of antiquity. To-day the regions where prehistoric remains are abundant and fine are often also regions of great and untarnished natural beauty. It may be a Celtic hill-fort, its banks riding serenely on a swelling chalk crest, all war-like spirit gone from it with its people, but still lording it over the villages strung along the valley at its foot. It may be a stone burial-chamber gaunt among the heather on some Atlantic promontory, emptied even of its charnel bones but still waiting above the seaway which once carried these vanished dead. To go to them equally open to the timelessness of the natural scene and the poignancy of the human past: it is rare for any purely intellectual experience to bring a comparable delight.

Chapter Two

THE PEOPLE AND THEIR MONUMENTS

AFTER the present chapter this book will be devoted to a description of the traces of prehistoric man still to be seen in the countryside of England and Wales. They must be described region by region as the traveller is likely to visit them. Just as I wanted to give some account of the whole country before dismembering it, so now I want to tell as a continuous narrative the history of the various peoples who left these remains behind them. When visiting a region all its monuments of whatever age must be looked at together; here I wish to arrange them in due order in their historical setting.

Very many people take it for granted that by scrutinizing a building, whether it is a cathedral, castle or cottage, they will be able to judge within a century or so when and in what conditions it was built. So, too, though with much wider margins of error, it is possible to date the more remote antiquities, the part of our inheritance which has fallen into disuse, and to understand something of the ways of life which produced them. It is perhaps the greatest wonder of human life to be always changing; ants have been unshaken conservatives for many millions of years, men change everything they do, everything they make from year to year and millennium to millennium. Because of this restlessness, this perennial dissatisfaction with things as they are, it is always possible to distinguish between the products of every age.

No doubt there are plenty of people, and intelligent ones, who believe the present thirst for factual knowledge to be misguided, holding it to be much better to enjoy birds and flowers without asking all their names, to feel the awe inspired by ancestral monuments without wishing to assign them to precise dates or peoples. I myself have always given delighted approval to Shakespeare's eternal condemnation:

> These earthly godfathers of heaven's lights
> That give a name to every fixed star
> Have no more profit of their shining nights
> Than those that walk and wot not what they are.
> Too much to know is to know nought but fame;
> And every godfather can give a name.

42

Nevertheless few of us are always in that mood, and I know that I have sometimes enjoyed my shining nights the more for being able to name some of the stars and constellations, and my country days the more when I could distinguish chiffchaff from willow warbler and wild bryony from old man's beard. So, too, while a general sense of the past is exciting, as it excited the eighteenth century, most people find it more satisfying if they can give it sharper definition through factual knowledge. They like to picture it with the perspective given by chronology, and with the colour that intensifies with our understanding of the quality and character of life at different times and among different peoples.

One of the pleasures of historical associations we shall have to forswear in our excursions into prehistory. St. Thomas à Becket adds something to Canterbury Cathedral, there is Wordsworth at Dove Cottage and on Westminster Bridge, and even the least credulous look with an added appreciation at all the beds dinted by Queen Elizabeth or the lacy gloves worn by Charles I on the scaffold at Whitehall. The first individuals to emerge in British history, Cassivellaunus, Cunobelin, Caractacus and the other princes of the Belgic royal house ruling just before and after the beginning of our era, suggest that there must have been plenty of strong personalities among their prehistoric forbears; Boudicca shows that they need not always have belonged to men. But they have been forgotten for ever. Without the written letters which Celts, Anglo-Saxons, Danes were so understandably to regard as magical, there was nothing to hold their names or their exploits in the flux of time. It is a grievous loss. I personally feel sure that behind every monument of outstanding character and originality—Stonehenge and Avebury, Silbury Hill, Maiden Castle and the White Horse— we can assume the inspiration, the ruthlessness perhaps, of some individual of extraordinary vitality and imagination.

I am writing now for the traveller who has no desire to make an expert study of field archaeology but wishes to flavour his enjoyment of the countryside by visiting its antiquities, or who may even be inclined to make special pilgrimages to prehistoric sites just as he would to famous cathedrals, castles and mansions. It may always happen, I cannot promise it will not, that a few of these carefree dilettanti will become so infected by by such visits that they will begin to study field archaeology in earnest, to survey and make discoveries. For this is one of the delights of the subject— it still offers opportunity to amateurs; though some regions have been thoroughly worked, others, having failed in the past to produce their local historians, remain almost uncharted.

Though it may help to ensnare them, this book will be of no help to those who wish to undertake original work, for it will include only monuments too conspicuous to have escaped general attention. I shall confine my descriptions to sites striking enough either in themselves or in their situation to rouse the imagination and to repay, if need be, a walk across a ploughed field or wet grass, a bitter conflict with brambles or nettles. I shall not send my readers to those faint shadows or tussocks, those dubious piles of stone or dark depressions in gravel-pits which rouse the enthusiasm of the true addict.

The first human inhabitants of Britain have left no visible monuments. As hunters and gatherers of wild foods, the Old Stone Age (Palaeolithic) peoples had neither leisure nor social organization to dig or build on the scale necessary to leave any mark after the passage of at least ten thousand years. Their relics cannot be visited but must be sought after with patient and expert care. Their stone implements are found in the gravel terraces of some of our rivers, particularly in the south of England; many of these must have been lost on hunting expeditions, sometimes perhaps carried off by wounded animals, sometimes thrown and lost among the riverside vegetation.

Patient collectors may acquire these implements by years of watching in gravel-diggings, where they may also find the bones of the elephants, hippopotami, mammoths, bears and other great beasts that lived in England during the alternating warm and arctic phases of the Ice Age. Very rarely such watchers may find bones of another species among the gravels, human fragments which give a sudden clue to the appearance of the Old Stone Age hunters and the evolutionary history of *Homo sapiens*.

Not very many years ago the skull fragments of Swanscombe Man, the second oldest European, were found by a dentist who for long had given his spare time to collecting implements and fossil fauna in the huge gravel-pits of the Thames estuary. Such adventures are not for ordinary visitors, though they may care to vary a journey by persuading the passing scenery to revert to what it was when the hunters knew it—seeing either a landscape of grey, scrub-grown tundra with an edge of ice in the wind, or, with the abrupt transition allowed only to the inner eye, a lush, semi-tropical jungle.

The only places associated with the Old Stone Age which reward a visit are the natural caves where the hunting families took shelter during the winter months when they could not be out, following the trail of the game herds. There on the floor they left a litter of food bones, lost or discarded implements and flint chippings, and occasionally their own bodies. Such cave dwellings are rare in England and Wales, but we shall find a few of them in

Devon and Somerset, South Wales, Derbyshire and Yorkshire. Most of these were occupied only towards the very end of the Old Stone Age or in the succeeding Middle Stone Age, but two or three were already inhabited before the last cold phase of the Ice Age when the Neanderthal type of man was dominant in Europe.

Apart from the caves there are no Middle Stone Age sites, either, which are worthy of a visit. This was the time when milder weather allowed first pine and then oak forests to spread across Europe and when the native peoples, still dependent on wild foods, often lived by the sea shore or river bank where they could supplement their diet with substantial quantities of fish and molluscs. Such a way of life could hardly produce lasting monuments, and in fact we know only of a few huts and marsh-side dwellings of a kind which can be excavated but not preserved.

During the Middle Stone Age (Mesolithic), about eight thousand years ago, Britain began to assume its present familiar shape as the North Sea broke through to the Channel and turned what had been a West European peninsula into an island. This was an event whose future significance for human history could hardly have been appreciated by the fishers and fowlers who gradually settled the new coast-lines, struggling with their primitive nets and hooks, their bows and arrows, to win a livelihood from a damp and still chilly land.

It was when men began to raise their own food supplies that they developed the power to construct substantially, so to cut about the land on which they lived as to leave enduring scars. The first farming peoples were crossing to Britain over five thousand years ago; they not only themselves practised husbandry but their example taught its rudiments to the native Middle Stone Age hunters. Though they still had no more than stone tools, immediately, if slowly, the newcomers made their mark on the countryside. Inevitably they changed its natural face by a clearance of trees on the uplands and other light soils, by the cultivation of corn plots and the pasturing of large flocks and herds. But beyond this, the New Stone Age farmers built for their practical life and, far more nobly, for their religious life; they were responsible, too, for the earliest industrial litter.

They have left four principal kinds of remains behind them—ditched and banked enclosures, flint-mines, earthen burial-mounds, and tombs with sepulchral chambers built of massive stones.

The first three of these were all the work of invaders most of whom crossed from France and the Low Countries to our south and south-east coasts bringing with them domestic cattle, sheep and pigs and the seed grain of wheat and barley. Probably their earliest building enterprise, and the earliest in Britain on a scale larger than that of wattle huts and animal traps, were the embanked compounds which have sometimes been called 'causewayed camps'. These enclosures have been identified in some numbers between Sussex and Devonshire, but they are generally inconspicuous, so much worn away by time as to be hardly deserving of a visit. Of them all only the enclosure crowning Windmill Hill above the Bronze Age sanctuary of Avebury has been excavated in such a way that the ditches remain open, and even here they are overgrown and forlorn. Nevertheless as our first buildings they have a claim on our interest.

These compounds are roughly circular, with from one to four rings of ditches which are not dug continuously but interrupted at frequent intervals by causeways. When they were in commission the banks behind the ditches may possibly have been reinforced with light stockades or thorn hedges, and some at least of the causeways were fitted with wooden gates.

There is nothing to suggest that the causewayed camps were in fact built for military purposes—indeed their builders may have been the most peaceable people this country has ever known. Unlike later hill-forts, these earthworks are not always planned to take advantage of easily defensible slopes or to avoid leaving dead ground for attackers. The ditches were often allowed to fill with silt and rubbish soon after they had been dug.

On the other hand, available evidence is against causewayed camps ever having held permanent villages. Only Hembury (pp. 148–9) has so far produced the remains of a substantial hut. Yet food bones, representing mainly beef but also mutton, pork and goat flesh, had sometimes been thrown into the ditches in such a way as to suggest that they could be the left-overs of communal feasts. Pottery, flint implements and tools used for the preparation of skins have also been found in the camps, and at Windmill Hill (p. 112) young pigs and goats had been buried whole, quite possibly as religious sacrifices.

It used to be said that a very large proportion of the cattle and sheep bones came from young animals, and the accepted explanation was that the enclosures were resorted to in autumn when the young stock had to be slaughtered at the approach of winter. With one of the sudden changes in supposedly factual evidence that are more frequent than they should be in archaeological science, it has been proved that most of the slaughtered beasts were in fact mature. The interpretation of causewayed camps as tribal rallying places is now preferred. According to this, tribesmen living in scattered groups over a wide area would have come together at appointed times from spring to early autumn for such purposes as initiation ceremonies, the arrangement of marriages, barter and perhaps religious rites.

It must be admitted, however, that the purpose of these, our oldest large enclosures, remains obscure.

Flint-mining is the industrial enterprise of the New Stone Age which has left noticeable if unattractive traces behind it—most frequent on the chalk downs of southern England. In one place only, at Grimes Graves in Norfolk, an excavated shaft has been kept open and there visitors are able to gain a most lively impression of a highly specialized aspect of Stone Age life. The greatest practical need of the farmers of the time was for good axes for forest clearance, and for making the fences and more advanced works of carpentry of which we know they were capable. For axe-manufacture the nodules of fresh flint to be found bedded in layers in the chalk were greatly superior to surface flint, and that was why these primitive engineers were ready to sink shafts through the chalk and often to tunnel along the seams with antler picks and bone shovels and with no stronger source of light than a moss wick floating in animal fat. When the flint was exhausted, or the galleries had become so long that hauling out the nodules was becoming burdensome (need I say when the mine was becoming uneconomic?), a new shaft was sunk, the rubble from it being thrown into the old one. As anyone who has experience of refilling holes could guess, not all of the up-cast could be got back into the ground and so chalk dumps were formed, miniature white counterparts of the mountainous slag-heaps of our own coal-mines. After a time, too, the filling of the old shafts subsided leaving hollows at their mouths.

In many areas the mines still throve in the earlier part of the Bronze Age when metal remained scarce, but as gradually they were abandoned, grass and weeds grew over the broken chalk and thickened into turf, until these first industrial scars were softened into the mounds and hollows which are all that show to-day.

The remains of cattle-pounds and flint-mines are, then, the most ancient imprint of human economic activity left on the face of this country. Both are feeble imprints, mere unevenness of the turf unless excavated; exactly the kind of antiquity which should make any sane visitor forswear his interest in the past. Yet there are monuments of the New Stone Age capable of exciting the eye and quickening the imagination. In most of our towns and villages the religious buildings still dominate houses and even factories. We take this for granted, yet since in the nineteenth century we allowed ourselves to be caught up in an insane passion for the production of material goods, we simultaneously assume that art, ritual and the religious life are minor concerns on the fringe of real life. The small funds spent on such things are the first to be subjected to economy cuts by a State which spends thousands of millions on material ends. This assessment of values is exceptional in human history. Most societies from the most primitive to the most highly civilized have chosen to devote wealth, labour and genius to the service of their ritual life. In this our earliest agricultural population certainly conformed. For them the ritual centre of each community was the sepulchre built for its dead. In the south and east of England these tombs took the form of the long mounds or 'barrows' which are still to be seen lying on or just below the crest of the chalk downs. They were far more impressive when newly built they stood contained within wooden or turf walls with flanking ditches magnifying their apparent height. One can imagine, too, that they may have had near them the strange magical furnishings and religious symbols which so often accompany primitive ritual.

Even more impressive were the tombs raised by distinct, though probably related, peoples who came not across the narrow seas from France and the Low Countries but made far longer voyages right up our rocky western coasts from Cornwall to the Orkneys. Their burial-chambers were built with large stone slabs and hidden by long or round cairns. In our area the finest examples of this megalithic architecture occur in the south-western peninsula, in the Cotswolds and round the coasts of Wales. There are outlying tombs in Wiltshire, and even a little isolated group in Kent. Abroad these megaliths find parallels in Brittany, Spain and Portugal and even in the eastern Mediterranean—though here very often the chambers are not megalithic but hewn in the solid limestone. Like our own family vaults, the burial-chambers might be used again and again for successive generations. Occasionally they have been found containing large numbers of skeletons and with clear signs that old corpses have been pushed aside to make room for new ones.

These tombs were far more than burial-places. It is interesting to speculate how much a future excavator of Christian churches might overestimate the importance of the churchyard and tombs. Comparison is hardly just, for the megalithic chambers were opened only to receive the dead, yet on the other hand, there is little doubt that the monuments must have served as religious meeting-places, the scenes of the seasonal festivities of a simple agricultural people. This becomes more acceptable when it is remembered that the cult associated with the tombs seems to have been no cult of the dead of a necrophilous kind but on the contrary one very much concerned with ideas of rebirth. In Britain we do not find the sculptured goddesses and female symbols which occur in some French megaliths, but all cult objects belonging to our New Stone Age are female figurines and phalli, both surely attributable to the Earth-Mother and her fertility rites. I do not think it is allowing the imagination too great liberty to say that the faith, for it is very truly a faith, which made the New Stone Age communities labour to drag, raise, pile thousands of tons of stone and earth, was in resurrection, the resurrection of their corn and beasts, of themselves. They laid their dead in the dark, earth-enclosed chamber with something of the same conviction with which they cast the seed corn into the soil.

In the character of the visible remains left in the countryside the break between the New Stone Age and the ensuing Bronze Age is almost complete. The causewayed camps were no longer dug, and megalithic funerary architecture and long barrows soon went out of fashion. Such an abrupt change in the remains of both secular and religious life is the material expression of the history of those days. After some fifteen hundred years, the New Stone Age was brought to an end in about 1900 B.C. by the arrival of fresh invaders who steered their boats to good landing-places all along our southern and eastern coasts. In contrast with the New Stone Age peoples these invaders appear from the first to have introduced a martial tradition, which was indeed already characteristic of their continental ancestors. They were powerful bowmen, and though in early days when bronze was hard to get their chief metal weapons were small daggers, the British bronzesmiths in time developed a powerful armoury of halberds, rapiers and spears.

In my younger days these powerful invaders, often called Beaker people after the decorated drinking vessels they used, were the recognized heralds of the Bronze Age. More recently, because they still used many stone implements and were often found mingling with the native populations, it has been the custom to assign them to the final New Stone Age. As their coming made so sharp a break in the archaeological record, as they from the first used copper and were interested in the exploitation of metals, the change appears to me ill-judged and I shall refer the beaker-using peoples (they formed several distinct groups) to the opening of the Bronze Age.

It was sometimes well-armed and richly-dressed chiefs, the embodiment of a warlike ideal, who were buried under the round barrows which took the place of the long burial-mounds of the New Stone Age. These round barrows are by far the most widespread, abundant and characteristic of the Bronze Age contributions to our landscape. It is a remarkable fact that until late in the period when a new form of agriculture was introduced, there are practically no traces of settlements or indeed of any substantial remains connected with everyday life. A few flimsy huts of the earlier part

of the Bronze Age have been detected by excavation, while a small proportion of the moorland hut-circles in the south-west and in Yorkshire may
have been built in the middle and later phases. Otherwise there is nothing,
and it has been suggested that these invaders with traditions inherited in
part from the European and Asiatic steppes may often have used the skin
or felt tents characteristic of nomadic pastoralists. The light frameworks
of such tents and the thorn hedges or other transient defences would have
left no mark that we could expect to see after the passage of well over three
thousand years. On the other hand some round barrows have been found
to cover ritual houses of the dead which suggest a more substantial
architecture.

There is no doubt, at least, about the solidity and durability of the round
barrows piled for the dead; they are immensely common both on the
English uplands and the moors of the west and north. It is hardly surprising
that they should be so numerous, for they remained the usual form of grave
for more than a millennium of steadily mounting population. Then, too, they
were normally raised over one or two bodies, other burials might occasionally be added in the material of the mound, but there was never the
communal burial associated with megaliths and long barrows.

The first invaders introduced the simplest kind of round barrow, a
pudding-shaped mound often closely surrounded by a ditch, and in many
parts of the country this form lasted almost as long as the Bronze Age.
These barrows may remain as lofty and steep-sided as the fine specimen
many visitors have noticed on their way into Maiden Castle near Dorchester,
or they may be reduced to no more than a faint swelling in a ploughed field—
a swelling which in chalk country is usually emphasized by a scatter of
white chips. In stone country the smooth contours of the chalk mounds
are replaced by the roughness of a naked or heather-covered cairn.

In the downland areas of Dorset, Wiltshire and Hampshire, which is
conveniently described by the title of the later Anglo-Saxon kingdom of
Wessex, a further foreign influence made itself felt after about 1500 B.C.
This was of great significance for the Bronze Age monuments of the area,
for the Wessex chieftains patronized a new and more sophisticated form
of funerary architecture. These can still be classified as round barrows, but
one of the two main innovations is very distinctive. This is the so-called
disk barrow in which a circular ditch with a small external bank is the
most conspicuous feature; inside this ring the burial is usually covered by
a tump hardly larger than an ambitious ant-heap; occasionally there are
two or even three of these little mounds. The second new type is more like
the ordinary round barrow, except that the mound does not run right to

the edge of the ditch but is separated from it by a level platform. It would be more accurate to say 'was originally separated' for in the course of time the central pile has normally slipped and splayed out over the platform: the resulting shape has given this variety the name of bell barrow. Both the disk and the bell barrows of Wessex are distinguished by a remarkable perfection in their building; seen from the air the geometrical precision of mound, bank and ditch makes them stand out sharply—an assertion of the human mind among the natural curves of the downland.

Any observer of these graves, whether they lie beside one of the broad green ridgeways which make walking on the downs so pleasurable, whether they are seen, more substantial but functionless among shooting-butts on the moors, or are briefly noticed from motor-car or train, may ask what is likely to lie concealed below their smooth or broken domes. The answer is that only rarely are they undisturbed. Relatively few have been scientifically excavated, but during the eighteenth and nineteenth centuries barrow-digging became a gentlemanly pastime. Landowners who did not want to hunt the fox might instead enjoy the milder excitement of hunting their forbears. The usual method was to set some stout gamekeepers or labourers to work with spades while the gentry picknicked *al fresco*. The sole object was to reach the burial, assumed to be at the centre of the mound, and to remove the urns and weapons, ornaments and other grave-goods which might lie beside the dead. Very many barrows still show an irregular dent in their crowns as the results of these forays, but most of the plunder seems to have vanished, often no doubt thrown away by reforming widows, or even at spring cleanings, when the objects had grown dusty and lost the glamour of new discovery.

Although, after the recent assaults of romance and science, few of the dead still lie in their graves, we have learnt what structures and what forms of burial the mounds originally covered, and were able to preserve through thousands of years of quiet, uncurious peasant life. The earlier Bronze Age conquerors did not burn their corpses, but dug pits in the chalk or constructed boxes of stone slabs in which they were laid with knees drawn up towards the chin. The dead, whether men or women, were buried fully dressed and wearing their ornaments which among the wealthy might be of gold, amber or jet. Women had their hair properly dressed, the prevailing fashion being to fasten it on the back of the head with a long bone pin. Warriors might be furnished with bow and arrows, a flint or bronze dagger and a heavy axe of polished stone. It was also customary to stand beside the dead pottery vessels containing food and drink.

In the middle of the Bronze Age, after about 1500 B.C., this simple conception of burying the dead as they had lived and supplying them with the needs of physical existence was completely changed. More than half the round barrows were raised over cremation burials, after a funeral at which the body was burned on a huge pyre of faggots, and the ashes placed in a clay urn. The practice of urn-burial brought to an end the old custom of provisioning the grave and furnishing it with possessions. So the traveller must accept the improbability of any barrow he passes containing a rich burial. If it has escaped the various threats of man and nature, the chances are it covers only an earthenware urn full of charred bones. Yet of course there is always a possibility, however slight, that the remains of some nobleman of the Early Bronze Age are waiting there in the earth, the gold bright but unseen, bronze staining the soil with green, and roots pushing and twining round the skeleton.

If round barrows and cairns are the most characteristic and common of the Bronze Age features in our rural landscape, there is another type of monument which can be far more imposing. This is the embanked sanctuary or temple, an architectural form which includes two of our most famous prehistoric sites, Avebury and Stonehenge. These sancturies can be recognized by a circular enclosing bank and ditch, usually with one or two entrances and with the bank placed outside the ditch—an arrangement unthinkable in a military or defensive work. Inside this ring, which presumably marked off the sacred area, the temple consisted of settings of upright stones or massive wooden posts arranged either in circles or on the horseshoe plan so splendidly represented by the gigantic inner trilithons at Stonehenge. Occasionally the sanctuary may be approached by an avenue or holy way; at Stonehenge the course of such a way is defined only by an inconspicuous bank and ditch, but at Avebury we shall find an impressive avenue of standing stones.

Although of their nature these monuments could not be very numerous, they are remarkably widespread; in England we shall encounter them as far apart as in Somerset, Norfolk and Derbyshire, while fine examples exist as far north as the Orkney Islands. Some, like Avebury and Durrington Walls, covered twenty acres and more and their construction must have demanded a tremendous co-ordinated effort. It has been calculated that Durrington would have taken nearly a million man hours, Avebury over a million and a half—to use terms that would have seemed strange indeed to the actual builders. Evidence supports the obvious probability that these outsize sanctuaries attracted participants from quite distant regions. It is now appreciated that some henges with rings of wooden posts may have contained not, as was thought, free-standing posts but circular wooden buildings, perhaps usually with a centre court open to the sky. Such buildings serve to link true embanked henges with a site such as the Overton Sanctuary which has no enclosing earthwork.

Henges are an exclusively British monumental form. They seem first to have been constructed by native communities of the late New Stone Age round about four thousand years ago. The part played in their development by the beaker-using invaders at the end of the New Stone times is obscure. Many authorities make little of it, but to me it seems overwhelmingly likely that the elitist domination they exercized for a considerable time must have contributed greatly to the ambitious architectural development of henges, particularly at Avebury and Stonehenge. That these sanctuaries kept their power long after their main building is proved not only by finds on the spot, but more surely by the fact that still in the middle phase of the Bronze Age wealthy rulers liked to be buried within sight of them.

As their tombs were for earlier New Stone Age communities, these sanctuaries must have been the centres of religious life for the peoples of the succeeding centuries. The fact that they are larger, fewer and more widely spaced suggests that they served much more extensive social groups. Beyond that, it is a kind of penance for the imagination to look at them, so impossible is it to recreate for oneself any satisfying picture of what went on in them. We are grown so rational (in some directions) that the vast irrational imaginative creations of peoples living for their emotions and intuitions elude our understanding. We watch films of modern primitives performing their dances; we read about or look at pictures of the gorgeous cruelties of the Aztecs and Incas, but we do so as anthropologists, as historians, and cannot participate. Indeed, few of us can any longer truly participate in the rituals of Christianity. Yet if nearly two thousand years later the Druids, a philosophical priesthood, could still cram great wicker effigies with living animals and men and set fire to them, we should avoid English moderation in thinking of what may have been enacted among those sarsen stones which now stand so quiet and grey in our temperate countryside.

Round barrows and sanctuaries, together with the simple forms of stone circle and avenue which lack the sanctuary enclosures, are the only conspicuous marks of their presence left by the increasingly prosperous generations who lived in Britain for the thousand years of the Bronze Age between about 1900 and 900 B.C. They followed their flocks and herds, they raised a little corn, became increasingly skilful as metallurgists; they traded and fought. Yet none of these activities has left a lasting impression on their land. The results are to be seen in museum cases, but not in our fields or on our hills. Even more than in the New Stone Age, it was the energy generated by transcendental presentiments that was great enough to move earth and stone into enduring forms.

The end of the Bronze Age and the beginning of the Iron Age were of great importance in our prehistory. It was then that group after group of Celtic-speaking immigrants made a solid contribution to our racial stock and probably introduced a language parental to the Gaelic now spoken by millions of Scots and Irishmen. It was then, too, that these Celtic settlers began revolutionary changes in agriculture which affected the relationship between the people and the land, and their whole way of life. Regular and permanent fields cultivated with ox-drawn ploughs now took the place of the shifting corn plots turned by hand with hoe or digging-stick. From this change it followed that the farmers and their households gave up their partially nomadic life to settle beside their fields, living sometimes in clusters of huts, sometimes in relatively spacious single farmsteads. The improvement in agriculture and all the associated crafts of carpentry, building and the making of farm implements, was greatly helped at this same period by an increase in the available supplies of metal. At first the production of bronze mounted sharply, probably because the trade in copper and tin was better organized; then, in about 450 B.C., iron began to be worked in Britain and very rapidly outstripped bronze. It appears that the earliest mining was in the Forest of Dean, but it has left no certain traces; the earliest striking remains of what was to become one of our greatest industries are in the Sussex Weald where we shall find a system of roads largely surfaced with iron slag from the mines which they served.

I have said that cheap metal encouraged the manufacture of more and better-designed tools for the use of craftsmen; this was certainly so, but at the same time, then as to-day, this technological advance went together with a lavish expense of resources on instruments of war. In the Late Bronze Age, from about 900 to 500 B.C., more bronze was used for making swords, spears and fine shields than went into axes, sickles, gouges and saws, while in the Iron Age long swords were the finest product of the blacksmith. The Celtic peoples were already showing the passion for fighting which in the end was to bring about their subjection.

The beginnings of military architecture are, indeed, the only noticeable remains of the later Bronze and earliest Iron Ages, and even these are still very modest in scale. Of all periods in British prehistory since the first introduction of farming, it has left least that is worth seeing out of doors. No great ceremonial seems to have been allowed to death; urn-burial in flat cemeteries was the common practice. Nor, evidently, did other religious rites demand elaborate or substantial settings; the building of stone circles and sacred enclosures came to an end.

Some of the huts, walled plots and enclosures on Dartmoor and other moorlands in the south-west date from these centuries of transition from the Bronze to the Iron Age, and there are traces of settled farms of the same age on the Sussex Downs. In the stone country of the north, too, there are Late Bronze Age huts and other remains among the many antiquities scattered over the north Yorkshire moors. But these sites are both local and unremarkable.

The earliest military architecture of the Iron Age is represented by a number of simple earthworks in the south of England; the crown of a hill was defended by a single line of bank and ditch following along the natural contour; often this was no more than a trench with a stockade which would have disappeared but for the fact that they were sometimes covered by the massive ramparts of the later Iron Age and can be recovered by excavation.

Very few of the monuments of the period from 1000 B.C. to 300 B.C. are of even the second rank as spectacles and not many of them will be found to deserve mention in later chapters. When set beside the great megalithic tombs, barrows, long and round, Silbury Hill, Stonehenge, Avebury, and all the other fine monuments of earlier times, the survivals from this age are paltry indeed. Perhaps our conclusion should be that such momentous works are only created when human imagination is unbalanced, run riot after one aim so that men are happy to fling a disproportionate amount of effort into its service.

It has already appeared how in early days the imagination and its creative powers had been engaged in religious enthusiasm, but now, as the Celtic Iron Age progressed, it found a new obsession, a new madness, to divert it alike from religion and from the dull sensible pursuit of economic well-being. This obsession was war. From about 250 B.C. there were continued Celtic immigrations into various parts of the island, among the most important being those which affected Yorkshire and the south-west—where the trade in Cornish tin was always a powerful lure. These later invaders, like their immediate precursors, spoke the Celtic tongue which has survived in Welsh and Cornish. As conquerors imposing themselves upon the less vigorous, less well armed and equipped natives they remained in many regions as a warrior aristocracy. In Yorkshire, for example, small barrows were found to cover the graves of such fighting chiefs, some of whom had been buried with their weapons and their battle chariots in a fashion well known in their homelands in northern France. Both the new leadership itself and the effort to resist the invaders served to heighten the warlike qualities of the Celts. All historical records of this virile and gifted people both on the Continent and in Britain itself show them as prone to inter-tribal warfare and dynastic feuds. From petty cattle raiding to struggles between the princes of powerful royal families, we see them squandering their force in an endless competitiveness.

Without the testimony of history, there is striking evidence of the military spirit of the Celts to be found among the hills and mountains of Britain. No class of prehistoric monument is at once so numerous, widespread and conspicuous as the forts of the Celtic Iron Age whose ramparts show against the sky on many downland summits, and on the more jagged crests of the mountain country. Whether the ramparts were of chalk rammed behind wooden palisades or of rough stone masonry (sometimes bonded with timber) they were both more massive and far more elaborate than the embankments and stockades of the earlier Iron Age. Often there were two, three or even four lines of rampart, and outworks and other devices for the defence of the gates.

Taking the country at large, the bulk of chalk laboriously dug, shovelled into baskets, carried and piled, the tonnage of stone blocks lifted and built, the vast number of trees felled and baulks of timber shaped, make a staggering total of human effort. It is remarkable proof of the fertility of the island even at a time when so much of the richest land was still forested that enough grain and meat could be raised to support the labourers—in addition to the riches, time and human life sacrificed to war itself.

Some of the forts were built against invaders, being rushed up in a spirit of emergency akin to that of 1940. Others were built as tribal strongholds, places of retreat where cattle and other property could be defended in time of danger, whether the threat was a raid from a neighbouring tribe or one of military conquest. Others again were more or less permanently occupied. Some, like Badbury Castle and Danebury, can even be called hill towns.

In Cornwall the promontory forts whose strong ramparts run from cliff to cliff to fortify a headland, as well as perfectly circular forts such as Chun Castle, were probably built by invaders who, as I have said, came to the peninsula to control the tin trade with the Continent. Some of the most striking of the Wessex forts, on the other hand, including the final elaboration of the extraordinary maze of ramparts at Maiden Castle, Dorchester, are believed to have been the work of the Venetic Celts of Brittany, who fled to Britain after their utter rout on land and sea by Julius Caesar.

We can imagine disorganized parties of refugees fleeing across the

Channel in their shallow-draft, leather-sailed ships and dropping anchor off the Dorset beaches. The Veneti were famous for their skill as slingers, and it may have been as a defence against this long-range weapon that they had devised and adopted the type of fort with many lines of rampart. At Maiden Castle itself over twenty thousand slingstones were found in a single arsenal, all of them natural pebbles brought from Chesil Beach.

There were other movements into Britain during this restless time at the close of our prehistoric era which led to yet more fort-building and to a widespread refurbishing of neglected defences. As we know from his own mention of it in the *Gallic War* there had been an invasion of south-eastern England from Gaul not very many years before Ceasar's expeditions to this island in 55 and 54 B.C. We now understand that a second, lesser, invasion followed soon after. Both movements were of Belgic tribes, a stock of mixed Celtic and Teutonic origin coming from the territories round the lower Rhine which still form the borderland between these two great peoples. That the Belgae were at least as martial in their ideals as any of their Celtic precursors in Britain is shown accurately enough by the name of their most powerful tribe. The opposition to Caesar, and later to the legions of Claudius was led by the princes of the Catuvellauni, a title which may be translated Mighty Warriors. The Mighty Warriors called their capital *Camulodunum* after Camulos, god of War. After their conquest and settlement in the south-east and south, the Belgae began to fight their way westward, and their ruthless campaigning led to the strengthening of fortifications both by and against them. When we reach Wessex we shall encounter a line of very strong hill forts which held the Belgic advance for a number of years; we shall also meet the relics of the destruction wrought when the advance went on—for example in the storming and reduction of the fort on Bredon Hill.

It is not to be expected that the arrival of such a people as the Belgae would reduce the preponderance of martial remains among the monuments of the Iron Age. We do know of some most remarkable burial-vaults where the dead, though their bodies were cremated, were buried with the complete furnishings for a luxurious feast by a rite which recalls the graves of Early Bronze Age warriors more closely than those of the intervening centuries. However, these vaults have been closed and the traveller will generally look in vain for remains left by the Belgae other than their fortifications. On the other hand they began an agricultural revolution which was to transform the landscape of Britain. Coming themselves from heavily forested country on the Continent, their first contingents found it natural to use the river valleys of south-east England for their lines of communication and to begin their clearance and cultivation. In short it was the Belgae who were the pioneers in the movement down from the hills and on to the rich but hitherto heavily encumbered lowland soils which was described at the end of the last chapter.

They, therefore, have left the oldest monuments to survive on these heavier soils. To the west of modern Colchester we shall presently discover the lines of massive banks and ditches, many miles long, with which they defended their capital of *Camulodunum*—a scattered settlement occupying a gravel promontory between two rivers. There is another, much smaller dyke system just outside the Roman town of *Verulamium*, but more significant, if they are indeed Belgic, are the similar dykes on the Sussex coastal plain near Chichester. These Sussex earthworks are more significant because they may be an instance of a direct movement down from the hills. The old Celtic tribal stronghold of the Regni had been the fort now known as the Trundle near the Goodwood racecourse; the Belgic conquerors destroyed the place and shifted the capital down to the neighbourhood of Chichester, protecting it, perhaps, with these dykes and giving it the title of *Noviomagus*—the New Settlement on the Plain.

It must have been noticed how in this account of the later Iron Age the names of peoples, places and at last even of individuals have begun to assert their definite shapes against the vast anonymity of prehistoric times. This last century before our era is in fact the period of transition when the literacy which was spreading west and north with the soldiers and traders of Rome first begins to cast a few sparks of historical light as far as this island.

There had been the visit of the Greek traveller Pytheas in the fourth century B.C., but apart from tantalizing scraps of his story which are all that survive, we owe our first news of ourselves to the Romans. The earliest invaders whose tribal name we have been able to identify are the Parisii of Yorkshire, the earliest name of an individual, Cassivellaunus. As for literacy in Britain itself, the oldest lettering is found on Belgic coins, the oldest handwriting is scratched on potsherds from the quayside at *Camulodunum*. So words begin to assert their authority beside the evidence of things, and the archaeologist must work in co-operation with the historian.

After the successful conquest which began in 43 A.D., England and Wales were, of course, drawn within the limits of a fully historic Empire and their prehistory was brought at least temporarily to an end. There is no need for me to recall in detail the familiar story of that conquest. The Roman armies had little trouble in subduing the English lowlands; the open country was itself vulnerable and its peoples betrayed one another through inter-tribal feuds. When, however, the human resistance was stiffened by the highland rocks, by the ancient hills and mountains of west and north, the advance was slowed. Wales and the north gave trouble, and meanwhile Queen Boudicca had raised her savage forces, her infantry and chariots, and sacked the new towns at Colchester, London and St. Albans, before she herself was killed and her rebellion most brutally put down. It is worth remarking that this fiery, tragic and finally unsuccessful woman is the only native of Britain before King Alfred to have made a deep enough impression on the imagination of the more recent population to have been honoured by a statue. At the end of Westminster Bridge traffic passes within a few feet of the forehoofs of her horses; decorously and even voluminously dressed she is driving her chariot towards Parliament Square. Although not allowed the protection of a work of art, this Victorian rendering of an indomitable and virtuous, if bloodthirsty, queen survived all the bombs aimed at Westminster and Whitehall.

The rebellion was nearly the end of resistance in England, and the Province of Britannia may be said to have reached stability when by the early second century Wales was easily controlled from Caerleon and Chester, while Hadrian's Wall had just been built from the Tyne to the Solway, to hold the untamed northern barbarians at bay. The Wall, one of our most commanding relics of antiquity, stands as a fine achievement of rational planning and of orthodox military engineering to set beside the strange imaginative creations of Avebury and Stonehenge.

In this it clearly exemplifies the change which all travellers will expect to find when they turn from prehistoric remains to those of Roman Britain. They represent the first surviving marks on the face of Britain of intellectual planning imposed from a distant centre of control. The like is hardly to be seen again before the eighteenth century. First there are the roads, primarily military in purpose, and the lightly built marching camps of the Roman army; then the more substantial garrison forts and the big legionary fortresses of the permanent military areas of the west and north. There is Hadrian's Wall itself. It is certainly true to say that in spite of the *Pax Romana* military monuments are still dominant.

We shall, however, come across plentiful reminders of Roman civil life: the towns that were founded and at first carefully fostered as a part of the Imperial policy for romanization of the native Britons, and the villas where the successfully romanized aristocrats of the Province lived in comfort on their well-cultivated estates. The towns were of various kinds; tribal capitals, smaller country towns and the *coloniae* where retired soldiers were settled and given small holdings. There were certain semi-military centres, the chief being York, and there was London, the trading emporium which after Boudicca's revolt seems to have become the capital of the Province. Even in the towns the remains of the civic architecture—the forum with its basilica and other public buildings, the bath-houses and amphitheatres—have hardly survived so well as the military defences. Though generally unwalled in the earlier years, by the third century most of the towns had secured themselves behind stout walls and gateways. It is their massive masonry, often stripped of its smooth stone facings, which we shall find standing in many of our modern towns, sometimes clear to see, sometimes incorporated in the medieval walls. Here and there, when exceptionally the sites were not chosen for later towns, we shall see their ruins looking still a little incongruous in the rural landscape. The most famous of these urban ghosts is at Silchester in Hampshire where the complete circuit of the city walls still stands—enclosing arable fields and a diminutive parish church.

For many people the most characteristic remains of Roman Britain are the villas, often thought of only as representing the country houses of the wealthy and thoroughly romanized upper classes of the Province. Although some were indeed luxurious, villas as a whole reveal a remarkable variety in size and standards of comfort and the majority were the homes of working farmers. But whether working farms or country houses the barbarian raiders had no more understanding of the way of life represented by these villas than they had for urban living. The villas were destroyed, either directly or by the neglect which followed upon the collapse of the world to which they belonged.

When the Roman Province began to be seriously threatened by raids from barbarian pirates in the Channel and North Sea, the authorities responded vigorously. They built the so-called Forts of the Saxon Shore to protect the whole eastern angle of England from the Wash to the Solent. These forts, of which nearly a dozen survive, are the latest buildings with which I am properly concerned; their long curtain walls and projecting bastions have endured remarkably well. All were originally on the sea, but several we shall find now to be standing among fields well away from the water, a reminder of how greatly silt has accumulated round the Kentish and Sussex coasts

The Forts of the Saxon Shore symbolize the impossibility of turning back the great tides of history. The Empire was crumbling; it lacked the vitality to hold out for long against the violently fluctuating yet persistent pressure of the northern peoples who for so many centuries had lived as free barbarians in the prehistoric darkness beyond the Roman frontiers.

The Anglo-Saxon invasions soon swept round these forts leaving them at once as the empty shells which we ourselves have inherited.

For a time after the withdrawal of the Romans in the fifth century, Britain returned to what were virtually prehistoric conditions. Yet it was in truth a very brief relapse into darkness. With extraordinary speed the roving bands of freebooters turned into settlers—clearers of the land, builders of strong kingdoms—until in less than two hundred years after the legions sailed away to Rome St. Augustine was returning from the holy city, and a Christian England was in sight. Soon we shall find that the monuments are no longer deserted antiquities but still a functioning part of our national life. Bradford-on-Avon and many less excellent examples of Saxon churches still serve their congregations and indeed in most villages if we cannot see any traces of the pre-Norman church, it is because the existing one is built upon it. The present pattern of rural England, its villages, country towns and even many of its county divisions, was already established before the Normans came; very many of the names now marked on Ordnance Survey maps are to be identified in Domesday Book. Saxon life has been wholly absorbed into our own.

Already I have gone too far in this narrative, for in the following chapters I shall guide visitors to no monument later than Roman, unless, like some Saxon dykes, they thrust themselves on the eye in forms that might well be prehistoric. Yet I wanted to bring my summary account of early history and its material evidences to this point at the threshold of the Middle Ages. To have stopped with the Roman exodus might have left a sense of a break in continuity, while my purpose is to show how the early shaping of the countryside brings us gradually into our present scene, our contemporary landscape. It is this slow shaping by hands which brings to any countryside a sense of rightness, peace and finality, a quality of holiness. Every ancient man-made landscape has this numinous quality, something created by the passing generations with their labour and their imagination.

Chapter Three

THE SOUTH-EAST

A. Surrey and Kent
B. The South Downs

I ought to begin with London. Now, as in Roman times, our system of communications is designed to make every traveller start from London, and perhaps one ought not to leave a place without first looking at it. Nevertheless, I am chiefly concerned to guide those who wish to enjoy the remains of the prehistoric past in the countryside, and although I shall never ignore Roman antiquities when they are encountered, it is hardly part of my purpose to seek them out from under the accumulation of modern cities. A few words, then, about *Londinium,* and I shall feel free to leave the capital behind.

Although the Thames made one of the most-used thoroughfares all through prehistoric times, again and again giving immigrants access to the heart of the country, its lower reaches were too closely hemmed in by forest to be attractive for settlement. There were prehistoric waterside dwellings, but nothing which has left visible structural remains.

It was not until Roman times and the beginning of the shift from the hills that the importance of this lowest crossing-place of the Thames could develop. Merchants began to settle there immediately after the conquest, and, after Boudicca's bloodthirsty revolt had destroyed both towns, the capital seems to have been shifted there from Colchester. The stone walls, however, were not added until after the middle of the second century; they were built of Kentish Ragstone with bonding courses of the characteristic thin red bricks of the Romans; there was a stone plinth at the base projecting on both inner and outer faces. They enclosed some 326 acres with an external ditch running at a distance of about twelve yards from the foot of the wall. These walls are almost all that remains to be seen outside museums and are therefore all that concern us now. The trading city, which nearly two thousand years later was for a time to be the commercial capital of the world, was first built on two small gravel-topped hills separated by Walbrook and immediately to the east of the Fleet. The walls raised round it continued to contain London throughout medieval times, though constantly altered and raised as the ground level crept up with the mounting rubbish of the centuries. Even now the heart of the City of London lies within their lines. The names of Newgate, Aldersgate, Cripplegate, Bishopsgate and Aldgate still mark the Roman gateways. Moorgate may have been another. The roads entering from the south crossed a bridge rather to the east of the present London Bridge. Material remains are pathetically meagre and sometimes unattractive; large parts of the walls were pulled down in the eighteenth century by the Commissioner of Sewers and very much more has gone since. Part of the original wall can, however, be seen at the Tower of London where a short stretch is visible behind the ruin of the Wardrobe Tower and a more impressive section of wall, preserved in a sunken garden, can be visited to the north of the Tower on the opposite side of Tower Hill. One relic of particular interest, set into a modern wall in the car park behind Tower House, is a reproduction of the inscription from the tomb of a Roman Procurator of Britain, C. Julius Alpinus Classicianus. Classicianus deserves to be remembered, for it was his intervention that halted the brutal policy of retribution against the native population after the Boudiccan rebellion.

With determination and a map it is possible to trace the circuit of the Roman wall catching occasional glimpses of the original structure in Cooper's Row, Trinity Square, No. 1 Crutched Friars, 36 Jewry Street, Sir John Cass College, the underground car park at the west end of London Wall, and St. Alphage's Churchyard. In several places the wall is preserved only at basement level, sometimes on private property, and as such is not generally on view to the public unless permission has been obtained beforehand. At Cripplegate and below the building of the General Post Office in King Edward Street bastions survive, the massive semicircular towers that were added to the walls at various times against the threat of barbarian raids. Indeed their very composition reflects the emergency of the time, for those on the east were roughly built with fragments of demolished buildings, broken statuary, tiles, tombstones and other waste materials—a reminder of urban life in decay.

As for the great public buildings and the private houses of the Roman capital, although their foundations are often struck at depths between ten and twenty feet below the modern ground level, practically nothing remains to be seen. The most important of them, the basilica or town hall, centre of *Londinium's* civic life, lies partly under Leadenhall Market; the best-known private house was found in Lower Thames Street where part of the walls and central heating system are preserved in the basement of the Coal Exchange.

A more recent find was that of the Temple of Mithras excavated in 1954 on the west bank of the Walbrook. This startling discovery of a temple dedicated to a deity more usually associated with soldiers and military sites, was made the more exciting by the presence of a series of fine sculptures of gods and goddesses associated with the temple. These appear to have been hastily buried on the site by adherents of Mithras in the fourth century when the Christian religion, by now powerful and officially recognized, was intent on exterminating all rivals. Although it proved impossible to preserve the remains of the temple on the actual site where it was excavated the foundations of the building have been re-erected outside Temple Court, 11 Queen Victoria Street, only some sixty yards from where they were discovered. Two more prosaic remains, in the form of mosiac pavements, can be seen in the basement of Selborne House in Ironmonger Lane (which is on private property) and in the hall of the Bank of England.

A surprising discovery was made during excavations in the bombed areas. It was found that a rectangular fort had stood in the projecting angle of the walls at Cripplegate. It had been built in about 100 A.D. while *Londinium* was still an open city; when the walls were added, they incorporated the north and west sides of the fort, and the west gateway has been preserved and is open to the public. Many treasures from Roman London are in the British, London and Guildhall Museums.

We are now free to set out into the country, and all good reasons make it necessary to begin with Kent and Surrey. I do so reluctantly. The region was too thickly forested in prehistoric times to be at all populous, and now so much of it is neither town nor country, disfigured as it is by the suburbs, the dormitory centres, the villas and country houses which have sprawled out from that tiny nucleus of ancient *Londinium*. It is not until we reach the South Downs that we shall find prehistoric monuments both numerous and fine enough, and in sufficiently undisturbed country, to be fully enjoyed and understood.

The main structure of the south-eastern angle of Britain depends, as I have already described, on the two long chalk ridges of the North and South Downs which run out from the main chalk uplands to end at Dover and at Beachy Head. These ridges are, in fact, all that remains of a great spread of chalk which was gradually humped up into a dome with its centre over northern Sussex. This dome then cracked, broke, and was carried away leaving only the rim of its base—like a soap-bubble, which when it bursts will leave a ring behind it. That is why the steep broken edge of the North Downs faces southward, and that of the South Downs northward towards the Weald, while each slopes gently on its other side. The chalk dome when it broke exposed the layers of sand and clay which lay beneath it, and of these the soft clays have dissolved away to leave the level expanses of the Kent and Sussex Weald, while harder beds of sand have survived as mild ridges. The oldest and the highest of these rises along the centre on the line of Ashdown Forest, others, rather younger, are the Greensand belts which lie immediately inside both the North and South Downs.

Among these various territories, we shall find proof that the South Downs were most thickly and prosperously inhabited by prehistoric man, while on the North Downs settlement was to some extent discouraged by the growth of trees; the Greensand, particularly in Surrey, was well settled in the Iron Age, but many parts of the Weald were hardly penetrated, except perhaps for hunting, until they become a centre of iron smelting at the very end of the Iron Age and during Roman times.

I will begin, rather fitfully, in the north-west part of Surrey keeping the chalk ridge of the downs as the guiding line and making excursion from it on either side. The first site, suitably enough in this country, is already engulfed in a housing estate, but it can readily be traced in gardens and other open spaces. This is the Iron Age fort on the southern end of St. George's Hill, Weybridge, not far from Brooklands. The ramparts are roughly rectangular in outline, single on the north, double on the south-west where the approach is easiest and where the main entrance was situated. The chief interest of St. George's Hill (apart from the surprise of finding Iron Age military architecture in suburban back gardens) is its strategic position commanding fords across the Wey and the Mole.

Moving still closer to London we find the so-called 'Caesar's Camp' on Wimbledon Common—it was once more honestly called Bensbury, or the Rounds, but thin breezes of culture blowing from the capital attached Caesar's name to a number of earthworks in north Surrey. The circular fort lies in the western part of the Common where the fairways of the golf course pass across it. For this and other reasons the banks, originally double with a ditch between, are everywhere greatly lowered and sometimes totally destroyed. There are still a number of round barrows on the Common, probably all dating from the Middle Bronze Age, but the visitor may have difficulty in discovering their generally battered forms among the bunkers and other features of a public recreation ground.

We now have to cross the North Downs to reach a line of three more forts, all of them on the Greensand escarpment. The first, Hascombe Hill, occupies the highest ground in the heathy country south of Godalming. Indeed the hill is so steep and the promontory selected so narrow that the designers of the fortifications seem to have limited themselves to increasing the drop on the three steep sides by artificial scarping, while throwing their rampart across the narrow neck on the northern side. Hascombe Hill is in fact a promontory fort, with a single entrance through the northern defences. It appears to have been built in the Belgic Iron Age.

The second of our three is prehaps the best known, for it crowns Holmbury Hill in one of the prettiest and relatively least spoilt parts of the Surrey countryside. The hill, itself characteristically clad in pine and bracken, has a sweeping view southward across the Weald, and eastward looks on to Leith Hill and the lesser hillocks that lead up to it, all sufficiently wooded to hide the city men's houses, the institutions for further education or weekend conferences, which lie among them. It is typical sand country, this, with its dark pine and fir woods and occasional heaths, and a quality in the light totally different from that of the chalk hills with which we shall soon be more familiar. As an honest guide, I must say at once that Holmbury fort is difficult to distinguish, so greatly has it been cut about by sand and gravel diggings. Nevertheless with patience and a cool head it is possible to distinguish a strong triple line of defences on the northern and western sides—the central bank still high and well preserved. On the south and east the hill is steep and the defences must always have been slighter. Trial excavation has shown the fort to have been occupied by Belgic peoples towards the end of the Iron Age.

Before passing on to the third of the hill-forts in this area it is worth making an excursion to Abinger Common, just north of Holmbury, where are preserved the rare remains of a Mesolithic pit dwelling which was excavated in the 1950's. On the site can also be seen a small museum containing finds associated with this discovery.

From Holmbury we can almost see our next destination, for it is Anstiebury, just hidden from view on the east side of Leith Hill. This fort in many ways resembles its neighbour; here again the southern side is naturally steep and the strongest earthworks are to be seen on the north and west where there are three lines of bank and ditch. The whole place was planted with trees in the eighteenth century. The line of the Roman Stane Street passes within half a mile (p. 84), and this is perhaps the best place to mention the minor Roman roads of the Kent and Sussex Weald. After the Roman conquest, the Weald became one of the chief iron-smelting centres in the Province. A number of small roads and tracks were made to carry the products of the furnaces northward to the London markets and southward to the coast for foreign export. Most of them are now difficult to trace, but at Holtye, south of Edenbridge, a stretch of such a road which ran from London to Lewes has been excavated and kept open for all to see. The metalling is largely composed of slag from the furnaces and its surface is deeply grooved by the passage of heavily-laden carts.

We can now return to the North Downs, though there is little enough to see on them before they enter Kent. There are traces of a fort in the grounds of a house, White Hill, Caterham; it is now largely destroyed and perhaps hardly so precious for itself as for Aubrey's description: 'In this Parish are many pleasant little Vallies, stor'd with wild Thyme, sweet Marjoram, Barnell, Boscage and Beeches. At a place called War Copice is a Camp or Fortification on the Top of a Hill'. Such was the happy state of Surrey and the English language in the seventeenth century. A little further on, keeping to the line of the ancient thoroughfare which follows the southern side of the Downs to Canterbury and is usually known as the Pilgrims' Way, we come to the Roman villa between Titsey and Limpsfield. It was dug nearly a century ago, but is still kept open and makes an agreeable visit, for it is ringed with trees, prettily overgrown with moss, and generally conveys the atmosphere of a gentlemanly antiquarianism.

Nearby in Squerry's Park at Westerham is yet another hill-fort which, when excavated in 1961-2, was shown to have been occupied in the first century B.C., while a small detour to the north, to Lullingstone near Eynsford, makes possible a visit to one more villa in this area so well provided with such remains. The Lullingstone villa, however, is famous not only for its mosaics, one of which depicts the Rape of Europa and has a couplet drawn from Virgil's *Aeneid*, but also for its associations with Christianity. Included in the fourth-century layout of the villa was a small Christian chapel decorated with murals incorporating the Christian Chi-Rho symbol. Such specific evidence for the practice of Christianity in Roman Britain is surprizingly scarce, although excavations at another villa site, at Hinton St. Mary in Dorset, have recently brought to light a mosaic which has, in one of its panels, the earliest portrayal of Christ yet known in Britain.

At Wrotham it is well worth while to make another short southern excursion to Oldbury Hill near Ightham, a large part of the top of which is enclosed by Belgic Iron Age ramparts—well preserved but overgrown with trees. What, however, makes Oldbury Hill of unique interest is the existence of two shallow caves or rock shelters, one of them now unhappily partly quarried away, which were inhabited in the Old Stone Age, probably at a period well before the last main glacial phase of the Ice Age. Caves, dwellings or shelters of this very early age, perhaps two hundred thousand years ago, are exeedingly rare in Britain, and it is certainly unexpected to find two on this Kentish hill, side by side with villas of a speculative builder.

After Wrotham the Pilgrims' Way emerges from the modern road and for some distance runs as an unmetalled track. On the slopes to the south of it, and again on the far side of the Medway, the traveller will be rewarded by what are deservedly the best-known prehistoric monuments in this part of the country. This is the isolated group of megalithic tombs already mentioned—a curious and so far unexplained pocket of the late New Stone Age architecture far removed from its main centres along our western coasts and in the Cotswolds. Some authorities believe that these Kentish tombs are only indirectly to be connected with those of the west and that they were built by a small band of invaders, or missionaries, from Holland or north Germany where rather similar megaliths are found. I myself do not agree with this, but prefer to think that some of the western tomb-builders, perhaps after dynastic struggle or religious schism, broke away and came here either along the Thames or by way of the North Downs. For a time, perhaps for a few centuries, they were able to maintain their burial practice and whatever ritual forms went with it, here in the Medway valley between the two faces of the Kentish Downs. We should certainly know more if nearly all the chambers had not been plundered in the days before scientific excavation, and their contents lost. Most of these megaliths are set among woods and fields in the pleasant unspectacular Kentish countryside, and to go from one to another makes an enjoyable pilgrimage, though it necessitates going south to cross the river at Aylesford.

Approaching first from the downs on the west side of the Medway, the traveller should leave the Pilgrims' Way at a turning due south of Harvel and in a quarter of a mile he will find the Coldrum Stones immediately on the right of the track. This is a good monument to visit first, for it at once makes clear the general character of all the rest. Coldrum plainly consists of a closed burial-chamber towards the eastern end of a rectangular setting of stones which once enclosed a long mound, now much reduced in size. Unfortunately the huge capstone which should roof the chamber has been lost—but at Kit's Coty we shall be able to see another example still in position. This chamber was re-excavated in 1910, and the bones found in it were for a time almost the only surviving relics from any of these Kentish graves; in 1940 the museum of the Royal College of Surgeons in which most of them lay was completely destroyed by a bomb. The remains of many individuals, including babies, were identified; one skull, belonging either to the most important or the most recently buried corpse, was found resting on a stone shelf supported by two blocks of ironstone. The skeletons were recognized as belonging to a small, long-headed people of the kind which in the past it was permissible to call Mediterranean. Nowadays one has to be more cautious.

Following the lane past Trottiscliffe church and then turning left towards Addington one first passes a megalith, known as the 'Chestnuts'. This monument was extensively robbed in the Middle Ages and remained in a very ruinous state until 1957 when the site was excavated and the monument restored. Excavation revealed continuous settlement in the area from Mesolithic times, although the megalithic tomb itself was not constructed until the latter part of the New Stone Age and continued in use into the Bronze Age. Within fifty yards of the 'Chestnuts' in a paddock not far from Addington church, is a second and much less damaged tomb. Unfortunately the road divides it into two parts; on the north-east side of it are large stones representing either a portal or a complete chamber, while on the south-west two lines of blocks represent the rest of the retaining wall of the mound, similiar to that at Coldrum but relatively longer and narrower.

Making the detour by the bridge at Aylesford the traveller may like to reflect that he is near the place of a celebrated instance of urn-burial, though one unknown to Sir Thomas Browne. Just north of the church a cemetery was discovered which could readily be attributed to the Belgae of the Late Iron Age from the peculiar form of the pedestalled urns in which the cremated bones were contained. One very richly furnished grave contained several urns with their burnt bones, a bronze-bound bucket also containing ashes, together with three brooches, a bronze flagon and a bronze saucepan or skillet. In drawings of the find the group is always made to look like a tasteful display at an Ideal Homes Exhibition, and it is a bizarre thought that it may perhaps indeed represent a family, each member a handful of dust in his or her elegant urn.

Taking the road towards Chatham, in a little over a mile we reach a group of fallen megaliths with the appearance of a small shoal of stranded whales. These are the Countless Stones, marked on old Ordnance maps as a stone circle, but in fact certainly another ruined tomb. The name refers to a legend almost as common and widespread as those that identify standing stones with Sabbath-breakers—the notion that magic prevents the stones from ever being correctly counted. We are now within five hundred yards of Kit's Coty House, the most famous of these Kentish tombs—and indeed one of the best-known prehistoric monuments in the whole country. It was already famous enough in Pepys's day for him to break a journey from Chatham to Maidstone to see it. He noted 'three great stones standing upright and a great round one lying on them, of great bigness, although not so big as those on Salisbury Plain. But certainly it is a thing of great antiquity, and I am mightily glad to see it'. It still has the appearance Pepys describes, but now, alas, the House has to be protected by the usual hideous iron fence. When William Stukeley made a drawing in the early eighteenth century a mound ran westward from the chamber, clearly the remains of a long barrow. This still shows very faintly but is almost ploughed down. The three upright stones are arranged like an H, which might be interpreted as one of the 'false portals' which we shall meet elsewhere (pp. 189–197), on the other hand, some words of Camden's suggest that in the sixteenth century there were several capstones, suggesting a true chamber.

Like Wayland's Smithy on the Berkshire Downs, there is no doubt that Kit's Coty House owes much of its fame and popularity to its name. The 'House' is a modern redundancy, an addition made since it has been forgotten that Coty stands for Cote or Cot, Old English for a little house. As for Kit, there are several stories; the more pretentious identify him with Catigern, son of Vortimer, who fell in single combat against no less a person than Horsa, and was buried in the monument 'now vulgarly called Kit's Cothouse', while a simpler and more pleasing version says that he was Christopher, a humble shepherd who occupied whichever side of the H happened to be sheltered from the wind.

There are some odd stones in the neighbourhood—the Coffin and White Horse Stones for example—but some of them may be no more than blocks of sarsen weathered out of deposits which once overlaid the chalk—the natural sarsen, in fact, from which all the tombs have been built. Further east, at Chilham, a long mound called Julliberrie's Grave is accepted as a long barrow; nothing about it is so attractive as its name, and I propose now to move eastward towards Canterbury and the coast. Any traveller who has been following the North Downs will wish to remain in the footsteps of Chaucer's company on the Pilgrims' Way, but others, the motorists, will prefer Roman engineering and keep to the highroad from Rochester to Canterbury which follows exactly the line of Watling Street.

The Pilgrims' Way approaches the ancient city very agreeably over Harbledown, and here, about three miles west of Canterbury, it runs right through the defended settlement of Bigbury, a rectangular earthwork now severely damaged but which has yielded an unusual number of finds, particularly iron cart-tyres, horseshoes, bits, plough coulters, sickles, adzes, which show it to have been occupied by a Belgic farming community of the Late Iron Age.

Canterbury is a city of such profound and distinguished association in

English history and with such superb monuments to this historical past that it seems ridiculous to pick out from among them the few remains of the Roman *Durovernum Cantiacorum*. These amount to little more than some masonry in the south side of the castle wall, Roman material re-used in many places, including St. Mildred's and St. Martin's, some of the base of the City Wall, and the conspicuous burial-mound now known as the Dane John.

Excavations near the junction of Watling Street and St. Margaret's Street uncovered the foundations of a large theatre in classical style, similar to the one at *Verulamium*. Only a fragment is now visible. In Butchery Lane, somewhat incongruously preserved below the level of a modern shopping precinct, are the remains of a Roman house complete with hypocaust.

Durovernum, is the right centre from which to consider the Roman coastal forts of Kent, with all of which it was linked by roads. This country, where the Roman conquerors themselves had landed and which must always remain most vulnerable to attack, was protected by no less than four of the Forts of the Saxon Shore (p. 60) built to withstand the first on-slaughts of our Anglo-Saxon forefathers in the late third and fourth centuries. It must appear to us now that the Romans were struggling against the irresistible tides of history, but resistance is never unimportant or without result, and these forts, standing often in lonely places on our shores, are still a moving symbol of the Roman struggle to maintain their frontiers, the lighted space of civilization, against what seemed to them to be the hopeless catastrophe of barbarian invasion. The four Kentish Forts of the Saxon Shore are Reculver (*Regulbium*) near Herne Bay; Richborough (*Portus Rutupis*) at the mouth of the Stour between Ramsgate and Sandwich, Dover (*Dubris*), and Stutfall Castle (*Lemanis*) at Lympne on the northern edge of Romney Marsh. The present position of all the forts except Dover reveals changes in the coastline since Roman times; Reculver has been half carried away by the sea which on the north has advanced a quarter of a mile since the sixteenth century; on the other hand, both Reculver itself and Richborough have been affected in an opposite way by the silting up of the Wantsum Channel which once made Thanet an island; Stutfall has been similarly stranded by the silting of Lympne Haven which used to give it direct access to the sea.

Reculver is worth visiting, for although half the fort has been lost and the other half was ruined and much eroded before further encroachment was checked, it is a romantic place with the twin towers of a ruined medieval church standing within its walls, crowned with wooden lanterns and still maintained by Trinity House as a landmark, though lights, I think, are no longer lit in them. *Regulbium* was more like Brancaster in Norfolk (p. 251) than like the other Kentish sites: a square enclosure with rounded corners and without bastions, it may perhaps be early among the Forts of the Saxon Shore.

While *Regulbium* commanded the northern entrance to the Wantsum Channel, *Rutupiae* stood on an island within it, protecting an important anchorage at the southern entry. Richborough is one of the most interesting Roman sites in the whole country. The Fort of the Saxon Shore is remarkably complete, its walls in places standing twenty-five feet high, while large-scale excavation has revealed much of the earlier history of the place. Learning from the experience of Julius Caesar, the invading forces of Claudius landed not far from here in 43 A.D., and a Claudian entrenched fort was established on the site. This makes it all the more probable that the massive cruciform platform which excavation has uncovered and which seems to have been constructed at the end of the first century is in truth the base of an ornate monument to the Roman conquest of our island. Whatever it was this foundation supported some exceptional building, for we know it to have been faced with Italian marbles and to have been ornamented with pillars, mouldings and bronze statuary.

After the military occupation of the first century Richborough developed as a commercial centre, continuing as the main port of entry into the province for visitors and traders from the Continent. The stone foundations of an inn, probably for the use of official visitors, can be seen at the site. In the middle of the third century, as the Saxon threat developed, Richborough reverted to a military role; an earthen fort was soon replaced by the great stone stronghold so much of which still survives. The rectangular walls of the stone fort supported projecting turrets and there were heavy circular towers or bastions at the corners; the main gateways were probably on the east and west with posterns in the other two walls. Ironically, although *Rutupiae* has been left high and dry by the sea, the river Stour has cut away its north-eastern wall; the railway now runs approximately on its line between the Stour and the surviving part of the fort. A vast collection of finds from Richborough is well displayed in the museum on the site.

Dover has been too continuously prosperous for much of its Roman foundations to have remained; not only the fort but the harbour itself are now buried below the modern town. There is, however, one building, unique, and to my mind more affecting than most relics of Roman power. This is the lighthouse tower which stands inside the castle, clearly visible from the deck of cross-Channel steamers in the harbour. It is polygonal outside, square within, and still stands forty feet high and with its original windows—the door is Norman. I like to lean on the rails of a boat looking at the town, a harbour on and off for two thousand years, curled in this vast, slightly grimy yet awe-inspiring chalk arena; and while the sea-gulls maintain the continuity of their screams, to think of the *pharos* with flames leaping from its head, a longed-for sight to navigators British, Gaulish, Italian, who were making for port in their small ships after crossings more horrible than the worst I need contemplate.

Stutfall, the westernmost of the Kentish Forts of the Saxon Shore, stands on a hillside overlooking Romney Marsh, half a mile below the village of Lympne; when it was built it was reached by an arm of the sea on the line of the present military canal, but continuous silting has separated it from the coast by two miles of marshland. The walls have been thrown into hopeless confusion by landslides—helped by streams, the Greensand of which the hill is composed is liable to slip on the underlying clays. Those who can trace their line will find that the fort was unusual in being five-sided instead of rectangular. There is not much to say about *Lemanis* but I will give the history of a single find made there, 'a mutilated altar which had been used in the foundations of the main gate evidently without any care for its religious significance. It was dedicated probably to Neptune, god of the sea and water, by Gaius Aufidius Pantera, an admiral of the British fleet. Although the fleet is not heard of very much before the usurpation of Carausius in A.D. 286, it was of much earlier foundation, and Gaius may have been in command just before the middle of the second century.' It adds something to one's reflections on the Dover *pharos*.

Although they are small beer after the Forts of the Saxon Shore, I ought to mention two Roman villas at Folkestone, if only because they are unusually accessible. They stand on the cliff-edge above East Wear Bay, so close to it indeed that half of one villa has already gone over the edge. This one seems to have been built in about 100 A.D., while the other, which has short wings projecting towards the sea, was remodelled at a later date.

B. *The South Downs*

All holiday-makers escaping southward from London welcome the first sight of the South Downs, for then they know that the sea and the watering-place which is their chosen refuge cannot be far off. Whether they are heading for the hotels and neatly ranked boarding-houses of Eastbourne, for a dinghy at Hayling Island or any of the other resorts and attractions between these two extremities, they must find themselves approaching the sober and sage-coloured wall of the Downs rising strongly from the mild undulations of the Sussex Weald. From afar off the wall seems unbroken and the traveller may think that his train or car will have to climb over a formidable barrier, but on a nearer approach he is likely to find that a gap is opening before him, a gap cut long ago by a southward-flowing river on its way to the sea. The Brighton road mounts high on to the rounded crest of the hills while nearby the railway must resort to a tunnel, but elsewhere four easy passages are offered by the Cuckmere, the Ouse, the Adur and the Arun—all of them rivers which traverse the Weald and then flow in tranquil valleys through the Downs, bringing lush water-meadows and such luxuriant plants as kingcups and purple loosestrife right to the foot of uplands whose dry austerity encourages nothing larger than violet, rock-rose and wild thyme.

This approach from the north now so customary for the English was, of course, quite impossible for their remote ancestors who made their way on to the chalk in prehistoric times. Then the rich farming land of the Weald was choked with oak forest and the place of city men was taken by wild bears and wolves. To-day a few foreign visitors and returning travellers find themselves approaching England by way of Newhaven, and they it is who come nearest to following in the wake of the earliest colonists of the South Downs. There is no doubt that many of the New Stone Age farmers and pastoralists, whose long burial-mounds and causewayed enclosures we shall see on the hills, did cross the Channel and use the Sussex rivers as points of entry offering a road to the uplands behind. The hills themselves would have shown from the sea as relatively open country, attractive for adventurers looking for some grazing for the beasts on which they so largely depended. Over their eastern half where they approach most closely to the sea, the South Downs have little of the clay and other glacial deposits which encouraged the growth of woodland on the North Downs; the thin soil overlying the chalk summits cannot have supported more than a light vegetation

While throughout prehistoric times invaders came to the Downs from across the Channel, the population was also recruited from further west in Britain. During the first half of the Bronze Age, in particular, tribesmen were pushing eastward along the ridgeways leading from the central chalk uplands of Hampshire and Wiltshire. As their memorials we shall find bell and disk barrows, identical with those raised over chieftains in Wessex.

I want now to move along the South Downs from their eastern end where they break off in the splendid cliffs of Beachy Head. Because in my childhood I once lay at the top of these cliffs looking down on to the lovely sharp magpie cleanliness of the lighthouse and watching the sea-gulls, as small as sparrows, weaving in and out below, for me this and not Dover is the scene of Edgar's speech in *King Lear*. Although it is full of things of medieval interest (to say nothing of 1066 and the battle of Hastings), there are no prehistoric remains of note in the country between this end of the South Downs and the North Downs where we left them at Stutfall Castle; here, as so often, we find ourselves passing from upland to upland. Before continuing along the chalk, however, I want to describe a Roman site just to the north-east of Eastbourne. This is Pevensey Castle, the next Fort of the Saxon Shore after Stutfall, and the only one within the boundaries of Sussex. This fort of *Anderida* was built towards the end of the third century on a spit of well-drained land projecting into low-lying wastes of Pevensey Levels, at that time open to the sea. Probably it would be best to go there in spring or autumn; I cannot pretend that my summer memories of the place are attractive. I recall fields of rank grass bordered with brambles, little houses running up to the limits of the castle and a railway line not much further off. On the other hand, the ruins are themselves very striking; there are still ten of the characteristic bastions, and the curtain walls stand twenty feet high, enclosing an oval of about eight acres. Inside are the towers and walls of a strong Norman castle, built, one may like to reflect, almost exactly half-way in time between the foundation of *Anderida* and our own day. The fort itself had a dramatic end of which, exceptionally, we know something certain. It is recorded in the Anglo-Saxon Chronicle that in 491 it was subjected to a ferocious siege by Aelle, the leader of the South Saxons, who afterwards massacred the remnants of the Roman Britons who had been sheltering there.

Entering now on to the fifty-mile journey from the east to the west end of the Downs we mount first on to the short, broad segment between Beachy Head and the Cuckmere Valley. At once on following the pleasant way up from Eastbourne to the village of Jevington, which lies comfortably sheltered among trees between the bare summits, the track passes a number of round barrows, some of them of the bell variety which must have been built for Bronze Age colonists from Wessex. Round barrows, often plundered by man and then riddled with rabbit burrows, are so common a sight on the South Downs that I shall only notice the largest and best preserved. Close by Jevington on Coombe Hill is one of the relatively rare New Stone Age causewayed camps; it has at least two concentric circles of bank and ditch; they have been cut by a quarry but are not hard to distinguish on the ground. A hundred or so feet to the east of the outer ditch is a fine bell barrow which is of interest as an example of the long-continued sanctity of prehistoric burial-places. Four bronze axes of a kind which is roughly contemporary with the building of the barrow were found below the turf, three of them deliberately snapped across as though they had been ritually 'killed' before being buried as votive offerings to the dead. Yet round and in the same mound there were coins and pots of the Roman period which must have been buried about fifteen hundred years later.

About two and a half miles to the east of Coombe Hill and its New Stone Age earthwork there is a long barrow of the same period while two more, smaller in size, lie to the east again, at Alfriston and Litlington. When compared with Wessex, long barrows are uncommon on the South Downs and tend to be smaller in size; out of the dozen examples, two are over two hundred feet long, but many are much less than one hundred. Most of them are clustered here at the eastern tip of the range, but we shall reach a small group of three barrows at the west end near the Hampshire border; in the central region between these two groups there is not a single example

From Coombe Hill one can walk by greensward tracks to Windover Hill above the valley of the Cuckmere. Here already is the true South Down country; walking over the firm convolutions of the chalk, the traveller can feel that he has climbed to a new, exalted world, spacious in feeling and clear in atmosphere. The combes with their smoothly rounded hollows lined with juniper and yew seem mysterious and wholly alien in the green English countryside.

Windover Hill has provided the canvas for the famous Long Man of Wilmington, a colossal outline figure cut in the chalk of its steep northern face. The Long Man is certainly attenuated when seen in the flat, a poor characterless creature standing slackly with a rod in either hand, but seen from the Weald the foreshortening makes him stalwart enough. His present feebly naturalistic form may not be the original one, for it is known that it was altered in the late nineteenth century when the faint, overgrown outline was recut and filled with bricks. This work of renovation was carried out by a local antiquary who first went to study the construction of the Cerne Abbas giant; he had difficulty, so he says, in overcoming his reluctance to inspect this more virile effigy and it is likely that anyone with such excessive moral delicacy may have enfeebled the drawing of the Wilmington figure. The date of the Long Man is uncertain and probably will always remain so. At one time he was generally held to be medieval and connected with the Benedictine priory of Wilmington, but the recent discovery of a strikingly similar being on the bronze plaques of the Sutton

Hoo helmet (p. 253) gives some support for a Saxon date. In earlier and more spacious days when antiquarian speculation enjoyed greater freedom, the anonymity of the Long Man provoked his identification with Baldur the Beautiful, Beowulf, Woden, Thor, Varuna, Boötes, Apollo, Mercury, Mohammed and St. Paul; other less precise suggestions favoured an ancient British surveyor, a Roman soldier, a Saxon haymaker or an astronomical clock. Through the haze of speculation the giant has remained calm and impassive, staring out over the Weald.

If the Long Man of Wilmington is not himself of very great antiquity there are prehistoric sites clustered about him. Above his left, or western, hand there is a supposed long barrow; a round barrow stands almost directly above his head while away beyond his right hand there are mounds and hollows which have been recognized as flint-mines. Far below his feet is one of the dew-ponds which, though they are now known not to be ancient, still seem venerable in their simplicity and effectiveness. About a quarter of a mile further east along the scarp, the site marked on Ordnance maps as *Hunters Burgh* is a fairly well preserved long barrow.

The next natural block of downland is delimited by the valleys of the Cuckmere and Ouse, the splendid ridge of the northern scarp bending in a slight bow between the two rivers. Immediately on the other side of the Cuckmere from Windover Hill is the pretty, perhaps indeed rather too consciously picturesque, village of Alfriston. From there the track up on to the ridgeway passes between two long barrows, first one on the left with its flanking ditches very conspicuous and then one on the right of the way just above Winton chalk-pit. From this point up to the long summit of Firle Beacon is as fine a stretch as any on the north scarp of the Downs; on the left gentle undulations and spines slope gradually down to the sea while on the right the abrupt drop to the Weald, here very low and watery, makes it easy to throw the memory back a few hundred million years and realize that this grassy path is indeed following the broken base of a vanished chalk dome.

The commanding quality of the place evidently appealed to the local Bronze Age tribesmen, for they raised round barrows all along the ridge of Firle and beyond as well as on the lateral ridges to the south. On the longest of these, which carries a track from Firle to Seaford, there are several bowl barrows including the Five Lords Burgh, a landmark which was taken as the meeting point of five parish boundaries. Those who follow this way as far as the sea will find a strong Iron Age fort between Seaford and the mouth of the Cuckmere, the ramparts forming an elbow with the ends resting on lofty cliffs. This is one of the Sussex sites which has the distinction of having been excavated by General Pitt-Rivers in the 1870's during the apprenticeship of that great field archaeologist. His work suggested that the fort was a place of refuge never permanently occupied. From the western end of the Firle range the antiquarian traveller should resist the temptation to drop down to the Ouse at Southease, surely a lotus-eating haunt, and instead cross the little Glynde tributary to the detached block of hills immediately to the east of Lewes. This is a piece of country which has been made familiar to thousands by the Glyndebourne Opera House, but most of these visitors have arrived in evening dress and have seen no more than the sun setting deliciously behind the hills, a golden foretaste of Mozart, as they drove to their musical feast. More strenuous daylight visitors may find other goals. Quite close to Glynde village is the important hill-fort of Mount Caburn, originally a single roughly circular rampart and ditch which during the course of the Iron Age was strengthened by an additional line of fortifications on the northern side. The enclosed space has been excavated and found to have been continuously occupied through some three centuries of the Celtic Iron Age and until Roman times. There were huts, evidently of clay and wattle, furnished with the deep pits which were cut into the chalk to store corn against the winter. Although the houses might be thought to have been too flimsy, they had doors stout enough to be fastened with latches which had to be raised with an iron key or lifter. Although the excavators' estimate of a population of two or three hundred is probably exaggerated, there is no doubt that, in the Iron Age, this now bare hilltop supported a substantial village community, and possibly even the headquarters of a petty chief. Careful study of the evidence has suggested that the stronghold on Mount Caburn together with those we shall find further west at Cissbury, the Trundle, Old Winchester Hill and St. Catharine's Hill were small tribal capitals, the centres of clearly defined downland territories. The Caburn itself may have dominated an exceptionally large area—the whole extent of the Downs east of the Adur—where it seems to have no rival during the later part of the Iron Age.

Before leaving this island of hills between the Glynde and the Ouse it is worth noticing a long barrow on the slopes of Cliffe Hill above Lewes. Anyone going into the charming old town of Lewes should visit the museum of the Sussex Archaeological Society in Barbican House, where there is an admirable display of finds collected from every kind of prehistoric and Roman site up and down the country.

West of Lewes and the Ouse Valley there follows the broad belt of downland culminating in Ditchling Beacon which lies at the back of Brighton—that resort with its unique combination of Regency distinction and fantasy with modern hurly-burly. Although the northern scarp is sown with *tumuli* and minor earthworks, the main archaeological interest of this part of the downland is to be found on the southern slopes. The most westerly of the eastern group of long barrows lie near Piddinghoe and Rottingdean while a third New Stone Age monument of very great note is Whitehawk Camp on the eastern outskirts of Brighton.

Whitehawk is an example of the 'causewayed camp' considerably larger than the one on Coombe Hill, Jevington, and with as many as four rings of bank and ditch, widely separated. I cannot pretend that it is a pleasant site to visit; the neighbourhood is seedy—allotments and straggling suburban roads cover some of the camp while the pull-up beyond the grandstand of the Brighton race-course cuts right across it. Nevertheless it is just possible to trace the ditches and excavation has provided some most remarkable news about life in this settlement four thousand years before the Prince Regent founded the fortunes of the resort and built his pavilion about a mile away. It showed, first of all, the structural fact that these enclosures might have fences along the top of the banks and that the causeways were sometimes fitted with solid wooden gates. Of far greater interest were the 'startling revelations' provided by the litter in some of the ditches. In one, the burial of a young woman and her new-born baby lay close to a living-site, while in another the corpse of a woman appeared to have been thrown in anyhow with the rubbish. Most startling of all, in the ashes, broken pottery and food bones surrounding a hearth were found fragments of the brain-pans of five human beings, all of them young, some of them small children. Two of the pieces of skull had been charred in the fire and the general appearance of the whole scene left very little doubt that the Whitehawk people had been thoroughgoing cannibals. There are two other earthworks close to Brighton, both of them dating from the Iron Age. One of these, the fort of Hollingbury, stands on the north side of the town at the end of a long lateral ridge running down from Ditchling Beacon. This hilltop was very lightly fortified at the beginning of the Iron Age, then strengthened a little later only to be left unoccupied during the greater part of the Iron Age—from about 250 B.C. onwards. The special interest of the single strong rampart and ditch is due only to its excavators who were able to detect the precise structure of the timber framework which had supported the chalk ramparts. Hollingbury is, indeed, one of the classic sites where this study has been carried on and where we have learnt that the Celtic forts whose grass-grown banks now have so peaceful an air were often originally made formidable by deep, steep-sided ditches and ramparts with vertical faces of timber carried well above the summit to make breastworks for the defenders. At this fort a section of the rampart was restored, old telegraph poles taking the place of the six-inch posts used by its Celtic architects; the wood is now rotting and the chalk crumbling—there is in fact a repetition of the decay of over two thousand years ago—but it is still possible to get a fair idea of the construction.

The second Iron Age earthwork in the Brighton neighbourhood is the one known as the Devil's Dyke Camp, familiar to sightseers who have used the miniature Dyke pleasure railway to get up on to the Downs on the northern scarp about Poynings. This camp, which lies a mile to the north of the terminus of the Dyke station, is oval in plan with a well-preserved rampart; these have not been dated, but it is known that a village lying half in and round them was occupied in the Belgic period at the end of the Iron Age.

While in the area of Brighton the Bronze Age settlement site at Itford Hill, Beddingham, repays a visit. The outlines of the banks and enclosures of some thirteen round huts, dating to about 1000 B.C., are still visible.

Having used the railway (formerly known as the *London & Brighton and South Coast Railway, Brighton and the Dyke Branch*) to get back on to the northern ridge, we can push rapidly on through a region with little of more note than round barrows to cross the Adur Valley by way of Beeding, Bramber and Steyning. In this section of the South Downs between the Adur and the Arun the slight northerly trend of the hills and southerly trend of the coast results in the two parting company for the first time and leaving a coastal plain which widens steadily as far as Selsey Bill. Thus in the resorts of Worthing, Littlehampton, Felpham and Bognor it is no longer possible to turn equally easily towards the sea or the Downs. With this excuse of having mentioned the name, I cannot resist the recollection that William Blake came down to Felpham in 1800 and stayed there for nearly three years. On his first arrival he wrote of it enraptured: 'If I should ever build a Palace it would only be my cottage enlarged. . . . My Wife and sister are both courting Neptune for an embrace whose terrors this morning made them afraid, but whose mildness is often Equal to his terrors. The villagers of Felpham are not mere rustics; they are polite and modest. Meat is cheaper than in London, but the sweet air and the voices of winds, trees and birds, and the odours of the happy ground, makes it a dwelling for Immortals. . . the People are Genuine Saxons, handsomer than the people about London.'

In this part of the Downs there begin to be more trees, although it is not nearly so much wooded as in the regions west of the Arun where the chalk is heavily overlain with glacial drifts. In particular there are 'hangers' or steeply dropping woods of beech on the northern scarp. No feature of the chalk is more delightful than these woods; the prevailing sage green and white of the Downs are peculiarly adapted to the silvery grey beech trunks, to the copper carpet of fallen leaves and the pale, brilliant green of the new foliage. They seem so very much a part of the downlands that it is as well to remember that the beech did not flourish in Britain in earlier prehistoric times; it seems to have spread about the island only during the Bronze Age.

Beeches do much to enhance the beauty and fame of the best-known monument in all this part of the downland—Chanctonbury Ring. The rampart and ditch of this little circular fort standing on the scarp above the village of Washington are quite inconspicuous, but some eighteenth century landscape gardener planted the interior with beech-trees and now the clump, sleek and smoothly rounded as a sleeping cat, is a landmark showing for miles alike from the Weald and from distant points on the Downs. When as a child I first stepped across the Iron Age rampart among the slender beech-trunks, I felt that I had left the sun for a strange shadowy cage, a world entirely of its own. Although I did not know that the foundations of a Romano-Celtic temple (dedicated probably to some local Celtic divinity) were buried beneath my feet, I was possessed by a most potent sense of natural sanctity; the tree-trunks through which I could see the bright world of the Downs on one side and the swooning distances of the Weald on the other were themselves the pillars of a temple. In this tense and fragile atmosphere, a chaffinch burst abruptly into song, that spate of notes which is so full of vitality yet not of light-hearted joy. It seemed to me that here was the guardian spirit of the place and the moment of its spell sank into the depths of my consciousness. As these words themselves testify, I have never lost the memory and it still seems to me that Chanctonbury Ring is one of those places where the past lives with some peculiar power.

From Chanctonbury there is a choice of pleasant paths to Cissbury, the second famous monument in this part of the Downs. (The foolish and facetious with literary prejudices may like to notice that one of them passes by the placid contours of an eminence known as Middle Brow.) Cissbury lies on the highest point of a long southern spur about two miles inland from Worthing; it is one of the largest Iron Age forts in the country, its single stout bank and ditch enclosing an oval of sixty acres and themselves engrossing another eighteen. There seems no doubt that as the Caburn was the principal stronghold of the eastern hills, this huge fort was the local capital of the tribe holding the thirty-five square miles of territory between the Adur and Arun. The amount of labour they put into its building was prodigious, and I should like to quote a precise estimate. 'As first designed the ramparts contained about 35,000 cubic yards of chalk which weigh some 60,000 tons, and all this had to be raised from a ditch 11 feet deep. Then the revetment along must have required from 8,000 to 12,000 straight timbers, from 6 to 9 inches in diameter and at least 15 feet long.' Thinking of these weights and numbers in relation to the small population and primitive equipment of the Iron Age, brings home the contention that obsessional madness along can inspire the stupendous efforts of certain ages of history. The main fortification of Cissbury was probably carried out in about 260 B.C. and the occupation lasted for two centuries. After the middle of the last century B.C., it was deserted and the walls allowed to fall into decay, while under the *Pax Romana* its military importance was so far forgotten that the sixty acres of the interior were ploughed, the outlines of the small fields still being clearly visible. This was not the end, however. Excavation has shown that some restoration of the defences was hastily improvised, a turf wall being built to raise the denuded ramparts and the ditch extended on either side of both entrances. These panic measures have not been exactly dated, but it seems overwhelmingly probable that they were the work of Roman Britons trying to save themselves against the kind of Saxon raid which we know ended so bloodily at *Anderida* (p. 75). It is even supposed that the small rectangular enclosures visible below the turf at the northern end mark the wooden hutments of these unfortunate refugees.

At the western end of the fort and again outside the southern entrance the turf is heavily pocked with bumps and hollows, some of very considerable size. After Grimes Graves in Norfolk, this is perhaps the most famous group of flint-mines in this country and the first to be recognized. Here again the youthful General Pitt-Rivers (who, rather bafflingly, was then Colonel Lane-Fox) was the excavator, conducting two vigorous campaigns in the 1860's and '70's. Some of the pits proved to be without lateral galleries, but others showed an intricate pattern of tunnels set so close together that one would hardly think the piers strong enough to support the roof. One shaft proved to be an exceptionally large one, well over forty-two feet deep and tapping no less than six seams of flint. Pitt-Rivers describes one macabre adventure. He was crawling along a gallery when he reached the base of another shaft and began to dig into its chalk blocking. 'Presently a well-formed and perfect human jaw fell down from above, and on looking up we could perceive the remainder of the skull fixed with the base downwards, and the face towards the west, between two pieces of chalk rubble.' The head proved to have belonged to a young woman who had either fallen head-first down the shaft and been killed or whose dead body had been flung in as unwanted rubbish when the shaft was being filled; there was no suggestion of sacrifice.

All the Cissbury mines appear to have been worked in the New Stone Age and had therefore been forgotten for some two thousand years when the camp was built round and above them. The mining equipment of the period was touchingly simple; it consisted of picks made from the beam and brow tine of red-deer antlers and shovels from the shoulder-blade of ox, deer or pig. Occasionally the shovel might be neatly fitted to a T-shaped antler handle. In many of the shorter galleries the miners could work by a faint reflected daylight, but in long ones the predecessor of the Davy lamp seems to have been a small bowl carved from a lump of chalk and probably holding animal fat and a moss wick.

All those who have known it say that few experiences are more dramatic or bring more intimate contact with the prehistoric past than the first entry into the undisturbed gallery of a flint-mine. The explorer must go in as the last miner came out—on hands and knees, and there in the white tunnel with its chunky walls and roof he may come upon a scene which has waited there in all its small carelessness for four thousand years. Perhaps picks and a shovel left lying on the floor or leaning against the wall, the handles sometimes still carrying chalky finger-prints; marks of lamp black in startling contrast with the white roof on which the smoky flame has played; some ashes knocked from a torch; lines of wedge-holes driven into the chalk in preparation for prising out a block which then by some chance of personal history has been left for ever in place.

This region of the South Downs was perhaps the most important centre of the flint-mining industry in Britain, and its products must have been freely traded at least throughout southern England. Within half a dozen miles of Cissbury there are three more groups of mines; one immediately to the west on Church Hill, Findon, and the others further west again on a pair of eminences, Harrow and Blackpatch Hills, which lie about half-way between Storrington on the edge of the Weald and Patching on the edge of the coastal plain. Of these, Harrow Hill is best worth inspection for here the clustering remains of shafts and dumps are cut across by a neat little rectangular earthwork, probably of Late Bronze or Iron Age date. The hill is, too, of great natural beauty with a fine prospect towards the sea. These other groups of mines seem, like those at Cissbury, to have been worked mainly during the New Stone Age, but the Findon group was certainly still active in the Bronze Age.

The winding course of the Arun has opened a wide passage through the Downs, a peaceful stretch of reed-beds and water-meadows in perfect harmony with the gentle name of Amberley, the village guarding the entrance of the river between the hills. It is pure delight to drop down from the sober colours and severe curves of the downs to cross the Arun by the footpath and ferry of Amberley, a footpath which, if seasonably followed, will take the traveller through most verdant fields, dissected by little dykes brilliant with kingcups and the blue and white marbling of sky and cloud. Some may prefer the southern crossing with its view of Arundel Castle well set in its parkland, but I would always choose the quiet Amberley way—and indeed the village itself is not unworthy of its name. It is the better route for those who seek antiquities for it leads very easily to Bignor and what is certainly one of the best known of our Roman villas. I have spoken disparagingly of Roman villas as a class, and there is nothing at Bignor to change my judgement, yet for those who admire mosaics, this villa has some finely executed examples and the frieze of little cupids dressed as gladiators is representative enough of the upper class taste of the time. Perhaps the best thing about Bignor is the view it commands of the bold line of Roman Stane Street crossing the scarp of the Downs by Halnaker Hill on its way from Chichester to London. This prospect makes it inevitable to recall the days when this was a thriving country house standing beside one of the great trunk roads of the Province, its occupants well used to seeing merchants, officials, occasional troops, pass its gates and either disappear into the forest of the Weald or, as distant specks, climb slowly up the road towards the crest of the scarp.

Stane Street still offers a way to lead the traveller back on to the hills, and a way which takes him almost immediately to a prehistoric site—the small causewayed camp of the New Stone Age which can just be distinguished on Barkhale Down, a spur of Bignor Hill. It lies close to the south-east of Stane Street among a maze of tracks and *tumuli*.

The changed geological conditions of this more westerly portion of the South Downs at once make themselves felt in the far greater extent of woodland. The scarp is sometimes hung with superb beech-woods, but on the seaward slopes there are big areas of more mixed and tangled growth. The ridgeway along the northern scarp itself runs between hangers and woodland, but along its open corridor there is room for many round barrows. Particularly notable groups occur on Graffham and Heyshott Downs and further west again on Monkton Down near Treyford Hill where there is a group of six bell barrows known as the Devil's Jumps; one of them still standing sixteen feet is the highest barrow in the county.

Here again as in the Adur-Arun section, the most interesting monuments lie away from the scarp on the southern spurs. Of these the most conspicuous, attractive and at the same time the most historically interesting is the Trundle, a fort crowning a six-hundred-foot crest of the Down due north from Chichester. It is an earthwork which has been seen, consciously or unconsciously, by thousands of people devoted to an ancient sport but not to ancient remains; it stands immediately above the beautiful race-course of Goodwood and its graceful girdle of beech-woods.

The single strong circular rampart and ditch to which the fort owes its name—for Trundle means 'hoop'—dates from the Iron Age when, as we have seen, it was probably the principal stronghold of a local tribe, a tribe of some power and standing. I have also described in an earlier chapter (p. 57) how this is one of the few places where the shift of population to lower ground which was such an important part of the history of the Belgic Iron Age can be precisely observed. Whether or not the Belgae actually stormed and dismantled the Trundle, there is no doubt that it was abandoned after about 50 B.C. and that there was a considerable Belgic occupation of the coastal plain including the headland of Selsey Bill. On the plain to the north of Chichester there is a series of linear earthworks (long straight lines of bank and ditch, or dykes) closely comparable to those built by the Belgae to defend their great capital of *Camulodunum:* it is generally accepted that Belgic conquest led to the evacuation of the old hill-top fort and the foundation in its place of a new tribal capital at Chichester. Its Roman name of *Noviomagus,* the New Town on the Plain, certainly strengthens this interpretation of the events of the last prehistoric century. Standing on the bare, turf-covered summit of the Trundle and looking down to the place where Chichester lies gathered about its cathedral the visitor can feel close to those events, to the great change in the pattern of human settlement which made its modest beginning in Belgic times. All over the South Downs and Wessex the outlines of the little squarish Celtic fields survive, and their presence like scars beneath the skin of turf still commemorates the time when the Britons grew their wheat and barley on the hills and left the richer soils untroubled beneath their forest mantle.

To the west of Chichester lies the famous Roman palace of Fishbourne, the largest and most splendid Roman dwelling house in the country. What makes it still more remarkable is that it belongs to an early phase of the Roman occupation. From the first days of the conquest the site served as a depot for stores being shipped from the adjacent harbour to a military camp at Chichester. When the army moved on, the ground was taken over for a villa—which by 75 A.D. was being developed into the palatial building that is the chief attraction at Fishbourne today.

Most visitors of those times would have come from Chichester, where a new capital town for the tribe of the Regenses was now established. The king of the Regenses, Cogidubnus, was on the best of terms with the Roman conquerors. It is certain that any native Briton would have been amazed by the size of the place and the formal dignity of its architecture. The road led to an entrance hall with pediment and columns, through which could be seen a pool, well laid out gardens, and another equally grandiose reception hall on the opposite side of the great colonnaded courtyard. The interior decoration had been done by Continental craftsmen; the rooms had elegantly painted friezes and mosaics that were probably the first ever to be laid in Britain.

It was a palace comparable to those of Rome itself. For whom had it been built? There is no direct evidence, but it seems very probable indeed that it was for King Cogidubnus, by then a man growing old in the honours and prosperity accruing from his pro-Roman policies.

A fine museum has been built at Fishbourne where the whole history of the palace and the finds made during its excavation are excellently displayed.

Returning to the Trundle, it is worth noticing the two entrances where the banks are inturned to make a long, narrow way in—a passage closed by pairs of double gates and readily enfiladed by the defenders on the ramparts. These inturned entrances with their varying structure of gates, guard-chambers and turrets are frequently found in our Iron Age forts and must be regarded as typical of much Celtic military architecture.

The history of the human occupation of this hill is very much longer than the Iron Age, for its rounded summit had already attracted the farmers of the New Stone Age. The ditches of the causewayed camp which they established there can be seen very faintly on the ground inside the Trundle, particularly in the northern quadrant. From the air, when the light is favourable, they show up quite plainly, and in this they differ from the two other sites where Iron Age earthworks overlie causewayed camps—Maiden Castle, Dorset, and Hembury in Devon—where the older enclosures were quite invisible before excavation.

There is one other place in this Chichester region of the South Downs to which I should like to lure all travellers even though it has no prehistoric sites of grandeur or importance. This is Bow Hill, a bold ridge thrusting down to the coastal plain about five miles north-west of the city, and the combe of Kingley Vale which bites into its southern tip. Hill and vale together express the ancient, hoary spirit of the Downs at its strangest and most subtle. The bold convexities of the hill are heavily encrusted with juniper bushes, as silver-grey as Mediterranean olives-groves; the hollows of the combe are given an added shadow by yew-trees, large and old, each seeming to reign there as a prince of darkness. I have liked to fancy that the name Kingley Vale came into being to celebrate the regal presence of the yews. It is probable that the impression of immense antiquity made by this low-toned landscape is in no way misleading, that the juniper scrub and yew-groves are in fact a survival of the kind of scenery which the Stone Age peoples found when they first drove their beasts on to the uplands.

Bow Hill shows many marks of early human activity. The most striking is the fine group of four round barrows on the crest; all date from the first half of the Bronze Age but two are of the ordinary bowl type, two of the rarer Wessex bell variety. Their popular name—the Devil's Humps—links them in a slightly humorous fashion with the Treyford Devil's Jumps which lie only a few miles to the north. Another conspicuous monument of a form exceedingly rare away from Salisbury Plain stands on a western spur of Bow Hill; this is a pair of funerary mounds of the bell-barrow kind standing on a platform enclosed by a single oval ditch. Unfortunately we know nothing of the social, dynastic or family causes prompting this intimate association.

Other Bow Hill remains are flint-mines (a little uncertain, these), embanked hut sites probably dating from the Late Bronze Age, and a well-marked network of Celtic fields spread over the spur at the head of Kingley Vale.

Here, too, we have reached the point where long barrows begin again after the wide hiatus of central Sussex; there are two small examples on Stoughton Down within the western arc of Bow Hill and a third, known as Bavere's Thumb, a little further north on Telegraph Hill. These three together comprise the small western group of Sussex long barrows; they may perhaps have been the burial-places of peoples using the causewayed enclosures of Barkhale Down and the Trundle, just as the larger eastern group must surely have some connection with the Jevington and Whitehawk enclosures. So far as the New Stone Age is concerned the central area may be said to have been reserved as an industrial zone—for it contains nothing but flint-mines.

Now, close to the country boundary of Sussex and Hampshire, we have reached an intermediate territory where the long finger of the South Downs is broadening for its junction with the wide palm of the Wessex chalklands. The great ridge which we have followed for so many miles above the Weald begins to break up and diversify, just as after Petersfield the Weald itself breaks against the edge of the Hampshire Downs. If there is to be a fixed point for the termination of the South Downs I would choose Butser Hill which rises above the London-Portsmouth road a few miles south-west of Petersfield. It is well worth climbing its eight hundred and ninety feet, for this massive nob of chalk with many ridges running up to it from all sides like wheel-spokes, is a noble creation of nature and one not without many traces of the creations of man. Butser is scattered with round barrows, while lines of entrenchment run across the western neck as though to cut off the whole hill with its radial ridges as one colossal stronghold. The view from the top is in itself a sufficient reward. To the north and west the traveller looks back on the Weald with Hindhead and Blackdown jutting from it like islands; in the opposite direction he can see the hills of the Isle of Wight, and due west a broken expanse of woods and Downs—the beginning of Wessex.

The way into Wessex and towards its ancient capital of Winchester is indeed open. From Butser Hill an exceptionally lovely ridgeway, following the line of a prehistoric track, leads directly towards Old Winchester Hill with its Iron Age fort commanding the Meon Valley. The river Meon curves round to flow into the Solent and can be said to mark the true boundary of Wessex. The fort of Old Winchester Hill has an outline like one of those very narrow pears, with entrances, both of them inturned, at the points corresponding to the stalk and the mark of the blossom; the rampart is a single one. The hilltop already had its ancient monuments when the Celtic tribesmen threw up the wall of their stronghold, for there are groups of rather poor round barrows outside both entrances while a line of three better-preserved bowl barrows runs down the centre of the fort.

To reach the Meon I have already overstepped the end of the South Downs, and now, with the knowledge of their long, slender line stretching away behind us to Beachy Head, I must step back to survey the far larger and less easily manageable territories of Wessex.

Chapter Four

WESSEX

WESSEX is the core and propelling heart of the whole of prehistoric Britain away from the highland country. The North Downs, the South Downs and and the other upland regions to be covered in later chapters, for all their store of antiquity, are tributary to the wide central plain on which they converge. This has, I believe, already been made plain both geographically and historically, and it now only remains to explore this wide expanse of chalk upland so heavily scarred by the activites of early man. They are so abundant, the remains of life, death and religion, that inevitably they must receive less than their fair share of attention. Fair shares are not always fair; a bird or a tree in London must be more enjoyed, more admired, than in the country—a monument of the past in countryside where there are few of them will receive more consideration than in regions where every hill has a settlement, fort or temple, ancient fields or tombs. It is more fair to celebrate the whole of the richly endowed region as a single monument but of this I am scarcely capable. Although in Wessex there is no sense of the immense age of the land itself comparable with that aroused by the highland rocks, there is an even stronger awareness of a long, instinctive, and profitable relationship between man and the land. In a country where farms, villages, country towns and cathedral cities still fit harmoniously into the pattern of downland and valley, and where the graceful remains of remote ancestors are still everywhere conspicuous, the numinous quality of a man-made landscape is at its highest and most penetrating. Wessex, beyond all, is such a country.

In deciding where to draw its boundaries, the one difficult problem concerns the north: should the sweep of downland north of the Vales of Pewsey and Kennet and variously known as the Marlborough, Berkshire or White

Horse Downs be included or does it belong more properly in the Thames basin together with the Chilterns? I think very probably that geographers would give these hills to the Thames, but for early human history I find it better, ignoring Pewsey and Kennet, to unite them with the wide chalk massif to the south. Taken at this widest extent Wessex can be seen as a gigantic white meat dish lying on the shore tilted towards one end, and with this end (the southern) broken off far enough to allow some sand to silt in, and even for water to flow across the largest break. If we wish to elaborate this rather fantastic comparison we can see the many dissecting river valleys as cracks—a notion which would certainly suggest the plate had received a sharp blow at the point of Salisbury—and the woodland as a stencilled green pattern almost worn off on the western half but still making a cheerful show on the other.

Unwinding the analogy, the greater part of the chalk dish is, of course, made up of the Hampshire and Berkshire Downs, the huge fragment of Salisbury Plain, Cranborne Chase and the Western Downs of Dorset. The southern rim broken off and tipped up is formed by the Purbeck Hills and the edge of the chalk running across the Isle of Wight; the silted sand is the Tertiary gravel and other infertile soils now covered by the New Forest, the influx of water represents Spithead (with Southampton Water) the Solent and the stretch of sea which has broken the chalk ridge between the Isle of Purbeck and the Needles. It is appropriate that all round the circumference the chalk scarp faces outward, its abrupt drop representing the rim, while it shelves gently inwards and towards the south.

A. *Hampshire*

Having defined Wessex, that predominantly upland region which in so many works of geography and archaeology has been described as the *hub,* the *nodal point,* the *palm of the hand* of the whole hill system of lowland England, it remains to choose one of the many lines of approach to this hub, this node, this broad palm. For the very reason that it is so wide an upland area and one so immensely rich in antiquities, it will unfortunately be necessary to make several distinct approaches and retreats before the whole territory has been described. There can be no route simple and direct like that along the South Downs in Sussex. I propose, however, to make my first approach by continuing along this route, picking it up again on the Hampshire side of the Meon Valley from the point where we left it at Old Winchester Hill.

Once over the Meon the traveller can certainly feel that he is in Wessex proper, and he is indeed already approaching its ancient capital, the Winchester of King Alfred, which, as *Venta Belgarum,* was already an important city and road centre in Roman times. The way along this southern ridge of the Hampshire chalk still follows an ancient road; it is one of the chalk thoroughfares where the walker feels he is on the roof-beam of the world. Yet apart from the track itself there are no antiquities of note until the way turns slightly to the south to reach the full, rounded dome of St. Catharine's Hill which rises above the Itchen just to the south of Winchester. It seems that this rather than the summit above the Meon deserves the name of Old Winchester Hill, for the fort which crowns it probably bore a parental relationship to Winchester comparable with that of the Trundle to Chichester.

This stronghold has a single rampart and ditch, oval in plan, with a well-marked entrance on the north-east side. The entrance is inturned and was originally stoutly reveted with timber and flanked by a pair of wooden guard-chambers. The defences are not exceptionally powerful, but so smooth is the dome of the hill and so fine the position above the river, that they attract the eye even from a distance—helped, it is true, by the sloping clump of beech-trees on the highest point. After a long occupation and more than one reconstruction of the defences, particularly of the entrance works, the fort on St. Catharine's Hill was sacked about the middle of the last century B.C., falling, no doubt, at the hands of the Belgae who were then pushing their victorious campaigns to the west country. Although there is nothing like the Chichester Dykes (p. 85) to suggest an early Belgic capital on the site of modern Winchester, the Belgae certainly did establish themselves there by the river at the spot which was to become *Venta Belgarum,* while the old fortress on the hill was left deserted. We are, in fact, again seeing something of the movement down from the hills in which the Belgae led the way.

The clump of trees on the crown of the hill is rooted in the foundations of the little medieval chapel of St. Catharine which gave the place its name. Between it and the entrance to the hill-fort there is a maze cut in the turf which dates at least to the early eighteenth century and may be much older. It is, indeed, one of 'the quaint mazes in the wanton green', but this one has never become indistinguishable and is now kept well trodden by the boys of Winchester College who show their sound classical background by calling it 'Labyrinth'. There is a very close connection between the college and St. Catharine's Hill, and although the scholars no longer process up here two by two for games, as they were already doing in the reign of Queen Elizabeth I, they still frequent the hill during their free time. Here, running on the slopes and ramparts, lurking among the beech-trees or bird-nesting in the thickets on the lower slopes, I have seen the boys looking as out of place as rooks on the snow in the long black gowns they have inherited from the Middle Ages.

From Winchester I propose to swing north, following the Roman road to Silchester, a road which must once have carried the officials, the tax-gatherers, the merchants and the ordinary citizens who wished to visit between the district capitals of *Venta Belgarum* and *Calleva Atrebatum.* Just to the south-west of Basingstoke the Roman road crosses the still older track known as the Harroway, part of one of the main east-west thorough-fares of prehistoric times. If followed further east the Harroway leads off the chalk to the sandy country round Aldershot where, as so often, too, on Salisbury Plain we find military works of the Iron Age among the stranger constructions of our modern army. At Caesar's Camp, Aldershot, a strong cross-rampart cuts off a promontory of a gravel plateau; the double bank and ditch seen here on the neck are continued on a smaller scale on the south-east side but on the other sides the natural fall of the hill is steep enough to have made defences unnecessary. This plateau, which must always have been relatively open heathland, was evidently occupied before the Iron Age, for a group of seven round barrows lies on the neck about half a mile from the earthwork. The boundary between Surrey and Hamp-shire runs right across Caesar's Camp and we are here back within hailing distance of our earlier starting-place at Weybridge (p. 65).

This, however, has been no more than a tentative and doubtfully rewarding excursion; back on the Winchester-Silchester road we find it crossing the main ridge of the North Hampshire Downs just to the west of Winklebury, a much-damaged fort standing above Basingstoke. The Roman way drops quickly down from the chalk to heavy, low-lying country still thickly wooded and once undoubtedly covered with forest. This makes it all the more unexpected to find in the parish of Bramley and about two miles east of the road the strongly fortified site of Bullsdown. The three ramparts, destroyed for a short section to the north, but elsewhere in good preservation, enclose ten acres of woodland on a gentle rise hardly more than twenty feet above the surrounding country. It is easier here than on the bald crests of the chalk to liken this stronghold to the Celtic *oppida* described by Caesar: fortresses deep in the forest which his enemies defend-ed against him by felling large trees across all the approaches. Even now Bullsdown is protected on three sides by brooks and swampy ground.

In another two miles the Roman road reaches its destination. Silchester, one of the very few Roman towns which now stand desolate, is to my mind one of the most fascinating of our Roman sites. Its failure as a city is the source of its potency as a monument of antiquity. The setting is propitious. The country has here risen to sandy heath with a wide common of gorse and heather and dark pinewoods; I have been told, how truthfully I do not know, that the villagers are all the descendants of gypsies who in the course of time have forsaken their caravans for cottages.

To-day *Calleva Atrebatum* survives only in the complete circuit of its walls, polygonal in plan and built in flint bonded with limestone blocks. The whole of the one hundred and twenty acres which they enclose is level ploughland, with a picturesque timbered farm-house and a diminutive medieval church standing close to the former gateway on the eastern side. A single massive bank and ditch surround the stone walls at a distance— most conspicuously on the north-west, and in Rampiers Copse to the south-west. Outside against the sharp eastern angle of the wall is the small empty oval of an amphitheatre. There is something in this emptiness, this walled-in void which is curiously moving; all lost cities are moving, but this one buried not in sand but in the English countryside has a quality of its own. Its mute rusticity seems to make it easier for the imagination to repopulate the place, to call back its former citizens, to set bears and men fighting in the amphitheatre.

There is a peculiar pleasure, too, in the fact that archaeology has made this silent ruin reveal the most detailed account of its history, of the centuries when it knew a slender prosperity as a provincial capital of Roman Britain.

One of the earliest records of British history has associated with *Calleva Atrebatum* the Belgic leader Commius who escaped to Britain from Gaul in the middle of the last century B.C. Excavation has shown that Commius did in fact set up his capital at Silchester. Then with one of those strange quirks of fate that enliven history, Tincommius, the son who succeeded him in about 25–20 B.C., soon re-established friendly relations with Rome. The coins he issued were the work of Roman die-cutters and quantities of pottery, glass and wine were imported from the Empire during this period. The earliest post-conquest relics of the Roman town of *Calleva Atrebatum*, however, were those left by a party employed on raising the outer bank, defences which certainly date from the first century A.D. and which may have been thrown up after the Boudiccan revolt in 61 A.D. Before and after this time town houses were being built as well as public buildings that included a forum and handsome public baths. The middle of the second century saw the imposition of a town-planning scheme, when the lay-out of this country town was made to conform to a grid system of roads which divided it into regular *insulae*. During this period *Calleva* extended up to the outer earthen walls although only in a loose and very partially developed fashion. During the second half of the second century, however, a smaller earth rampart and ditch were built approximately on the lines of the later stone walls and can still be detected lying below them. Finally, it was in about 200 A.D. that these walls were themselves added, the builders using local flint and a Bathstone possibly brought from the Chippenham quarries. The history of *Calleva* during those subsequent centuries when town life was declining throughout the Western Empire is made remarkable for us by the building of a small Christian church not far from the forum. Its foundations, laid bare during the excavations of seventy years ago, represent the oldest Christian sanctuary known in this country.

A rich collection of finds, the property of the late citizens of *Calleva Atrebatum,* is now housed in the municipal museum at Reading.

Since I have lingered so long at Silchester, I will stay a little longer and recall a curious piece of litigation. Not long ago, the local folk fought their landlord, the Duke of Wellington, for a right of way across the walls. During the proceedings some of the oldest villagers came to court and gave their reminiscences as evidence against the Duke. Some spoke of farmers and pastors who had regularly driven their gigs along the disputed track, while others remembered how they themselves and their friends of fifty and sixty years ago had often sauntered that way as courting couples. I wish I could have been present to hear them; even reading the account of the action gave an enchanting impression of nineteenth-century rustic life moving across this deserted Roman stage.

To return to the scarp of the Downs, it is possible to follow the line of the Roman road to Old Sarum, joining the downland ridgeway near Hannington. If we then pursue this ancient track westward for about four miles we reach another small centre of antiquity close by the point where the ridgeway crosses the high road and the Didcot-Southampton railway. At this crossing-place are the Seven Barrows (and for once they really are seven in number) which give their name to the adjoining down. They are fine, large, Bronze Age round barrows and are said to have been a well known mark on the high road in coaching days; now, however, their unity has been spoiled by the railway line which isolated one barrow from the other half-dozen.

Northward from this spot, on the scarp of the Downs above Kingsclere and Burghclere, are two notable Iron Age hill-forts. The more westerly of the two is Ladle Hill, a site of peculiar interest. Some chance of history, probably the passing of a sudden threat, caused work on this fort to be stopped short, leaving the incomplete defences as a unique demonstration of methods of construction. The single rampart still stands in disjointed sections; each, probably, had been the responsibility of a gang of workers; just inside it are the shallow scoops from which chalk has been taken, and the heaps of top soil waiting (waiting now for over two thousand years) to be thrown up onto the rampart.

A mile further west the double banks of the fort of Beacon Hill fit firmly round the contours of a fine bare head of chalk, a landmark over a wide stretch of Hampshire. These contours have enforced a waisted, hour-glass plan and in the south-east corner adjoining the ridge there is a notable entrance with inturned ramparts and projecting horn-works. Scattered throughout the inside of the fort are shallow depressions of very varying size, probably marking the site of circular huts. In days before telegraphy this hill of 842 feet was an important beacon, taking up the signals from Beacon Hill, Bulford, and possibly passing them on as far as the Chilterns. It is, indeed, widely known as the Berkshire Beacon.

Both Ladle Hill and Beacon Hill lie to the north of the ancient track-way which we left at Seven Barrows, but it can be rejoined by walking through the woods on Siddown Hill and meeting it by the parkland of the Highclere estate. From here the six-mile walk westward to Walbury is a magnificent one, with prospects over the Kennet Valley and the beach hangers of the downland slopes; gradually the track climbs up towards the rounded crest of Combe Hill whose summit is one of the highest points which the chalk attains anywhere in Britain. The fort which has the distinction of enclosing this summit is appropriately large, the defended area being as great as eighty-two acres, but is not otherwise remarkable. Perhaps the best feature is the entrance in the north-west angle, and it is interesting to notice how the prehistoric track which we have been following runs straight across the fort from the weaker south-eastern entrance to this one. Formerly this track marked the line of the county boundary, but now Combe Hill falls within the curious little appendix to the south-western angle of Berkshire. The track goes on steadily, running now due east and west, for the line of the scarp has swung southwards. If he follows it across the Hungerford road the traveller will be confronted by a sight as startlingly unexpected to him as it would have been commonplace to his great-grandfather. This is Combe Gibbet, put up in the seventeenth century to hang a man and woman who had murdered two unwanted children and thrown their bodies in a nearby pond. To raise the criminals as high as possible the executioners stood the gibbet on a convenient mound, and that mound is, as it happens, a long barrow; it is over sixty yards long and shows the characteristic increase in height and breadth towards the east end. Just below Combe Gibbet, Inkpen lies in the Kennet Valley and close beside it begins the most easterly extension of Wansdyke, the great linear earthwork to be described where it reaches the Marlborough Downs (p. 114).

The track curves gradually in a more southerly direction as the hills bend towards the upper waters of the Bourne, and then, near Tidcombe village, joins the Roman road from Cirencester to Winchester just where it makes a curious bend in its otherwise straight track—probably in order to follow the line of a well-established prehistoric route. South of Tidcombe and at the beginning of this bend, the road passes Tidcombe long barrow, an impressive monument with a mound rising as much as nine feet above well-defined ditches, and with four recumbent sarsen blocks proving the existence of a megalithic chamber. There is a record that it was dug into in the eighteenth century by country people who found a skeleton in a chamber formed by two uprights and two roofing slabs. It has been assumed that the sarsens are the remnants of this cell. Tidcombe is merely the most interesting of a small group of long barrows in this area, the others being Fairmile Down, Tow Barrow, Botley Copse and Smay Down.

Further round the bow of the Roman road, to the north of Chute, there is another curious megalith of a type so unexpected that its identification seems still uncertain. This is a recumbent slab, lying to the left of the road, which may or may not be the 'Kenward-stone' from which the local Hundred took its name. The slab is ornamented with wavy lines of a type generally associated only with megalithic architecture much further west, particularly in Wales and Ireland (p. 232). The traveller will be excused, and indeed honoured, if he finds the view from the Kenward stone more remarkable than the antiquity itself. On a clear day it is possible to see from the Chilterns on the one hand to the Isle of Wight on the other, a span of some eighty miles and a great section of the map of southern England. To the south-west the observer can follow the continuation of the Roman road by which he stands as it passes Andover to reach Winchester; rather more than half-way along this course it crosses the Test, whose steep and marshy valley curving right across the Hampshire Downs makes a strong natural frontier.

In the stretch of country between our present viewpoint and Winchester there are some nine hill-forts on either side of the Test Valley, though not all of them are equally strong.

The most westerly of them, Quarley Hill, is as much as eight miles from the river, but it commands an ancient track which runs on to Danebury and crosses the Test at Longstock. It also lies close to the same Roman road, the Port Way, from Silchester to Old Sarum, which we used to mount on to the Northern Downs near Ladle Hill (p. 92). Quarley Hill fort has a single line of defences, pear-shaped in plan and following the contours of an oval hill crowned with a meagre, wind-torn clump of firs. It was built in the pre-Belgic Iron Age. I have an intimate personal affection for Quarley Hill for my husband and I were excavating there during the very hot summer in which our son was a year old. At tea-time it was a pleasurable moment when looking over the rampart I could see his nursemaid, very young and pink in her crisp uniform, carrying the child through the harsh and ancient juniper bushes whose hoary grey forms grew thickly on the lower slopes. When I saw them climbing towards me, I would bound over the defences and down the hill and bear him up again for rides along the rampart-top in a clumsy wheelbarrow, thick with the chalk of our excavations.

The three forts which make a line only about two miles west of the river frontier are Baulkesbury, Bury Hill and Danebury. Baulkesbury, in the area of suburban development just west of Andover, is not worth visiting. Bury Hill, only half a mile further south-west, is a far more imposing place though the earthworks, owing to a cap of clay on the chalk, are overgrown with hawthorn bushes and Scotch fir. There is a strong circular fort with two ramparts on the crest of the spur and these my husband and I were able to date to the Belgic period. They had, however, been thrown up on the site of a much earlier fort whose single rampart they partly overlie. On the north side this earlier bank, reduced to a scarp by the piling of plough soil against the upper side, runs out from below the Belgic fort and makes a crescentic outer enclosure.

There is little doubt that Bury Hill was refortified as part of the resistance to the Belgic expansionists: the same purpose may explain one phase of the hill-fort of Danebury four miles to the south and mid-way between the Test and those famous English villages, Over, Middle and Nether Wallop. Danebury well repays a leisurely visit; it is a fine fort, finely situated. The earthworks show a fascinating complexity and there are two good examples of long barrow—rare in this region   only six hundred yards to the north-west. The rounded chalk hilltop, including the earthworks themselves, is capped with a plantation of beech and fir. The trees are dying, and sad though this is, it has made it easier to excavate on a large scale. The results have been remarkable.

The first surprise was to discover that some three thousand years ago Bronze Age people had sanctified the hill with a ring of great posts set in ritual pits. The first Iron Age Celts fortified the place in the fifth century

B.C. and appear to have lived up there in the usual kind of round houses. Some change took place in about 400 B.C., and from that time Danebury became an established hill town. The inhabitants now lived in neat rows of small rectangular wooden houses with pathways running between them. Though often rebuilt, these were maintained for three centuries, defended by a single rampart with timber revetments like that at Hollingbury (p. 79).

It was in about 100 B.C. that the defences were strengthened against some threat that may well have been from the Belgae. The most important of the two entrances, the eastern, was provided with most elaborate hornworks and stronger wooden gates. Sling stones were piled along the top of the ramparts. It seems that all efforts were in vain, for the gateway was destroyed soon after it was built and the houses were deserted at about this time. Finally the defences were refurbished in the last century A.D., probably in another unsuccessful attempt to resist a stronger power—that of the Romans.

Danebury never had more than one true rampart: the relatively slight outer earthworks proving to be cattle enclosures. Cattle must have been the basis of a prosperous economy that included trade. More than a score of iron currency bars have been found on the site. The people of this long-lived hill town seem to have had little respect for the dead. In a number of instances bodies seem merely to have been cast out uncovered to rot, or thrown with scant ceremony into pits.

The corresponding camps to the east of the Test Valley, Tidbury, Norsbury and Woolbury (which exactly opposes Danebury across the river) are relatively poor sites and would not be worth naming if they did not help to recall forgotten campaigns and frontier tensions. Only the most southern of them all is in the least spectacular. This is Merdon Castle, and even Merdon owes its impressiveness not so much to the Iron Age Celts as to the Norman builders who raised inside the prehistoric defences a strong keep and bailey. This association of medieval with Iron Age earthworks will be encountered again, most nobly at Old Sarum and the Herefordshire Beacon. To me it seems that the strong point, the massive cone of the motte or mound for the keep, contrasted with the open structure of the prehistoric ramparts, very fittingly symbolizes the concentrated power of the feudal lord as opposed to the tribal society of the Celts.

Having now seen all that is best on the Hampshire chalk, I want only to mention some scattered antiquities lying in the southern part of the county, the sandy filling of my Wessex plate (p. 90), and others on its broken rim, the Isle of Wight, before plunging into the ancient riches of

Wiltshire. The first is a place of quite extraordinary interest for its combination of prehistoric, Roman and Norman architecture. This is Porchester, which is remarkable, too, for a dramatic situation—on a peninsula jutting out into the edge of Portsmouth harbour. The prehistoric contribution, it is true, is not very great; no more than a rampart running across the base of the peninsula and so converting it into a promontory fort. In the fourth century the headland was chosen as the site of the most westerly of all the Forts of the Saxon Shore. Although it is so close to a crowded modern port and its large industrial population, this Roman fort, with the ridge of Portsdown as a wall at its back, has withstood the changes of fifteen hundred years with amazing fortitude. It is a square of 210 yards, its four walls reinforced by the semicircular bastions so characteristic of this late Roman architecture. The masonry of flint and stone is of excellent quality, the blocks being carefully laid even in the core of walls; indeed this great fort rising sometimes above mudflats, sometimes above the water of high tide, is for many of us easily the finest Roman building in the whole of Britain. In the north-west angle of the Roman walls stands the Norman castle, a famous example of an early twelfth-century keep with its inner bailey walls still intact. The Roman fortifications served as the outer bailey, as is shown by the presence of the Norman chapel, an austere piece of Romanesque, in the corner diagonally opposite to the castle. It is a very great pity that many of the foreign visitors who first set foot in England at Southampton should not be able to cover the dozen miles to Porchester to be introduced at once to the long perspectives of our history.

There is, indeed, a site in Southampton itself which deserves attention, not so much for the actual remains of antiquity as for something curious and haunting in the whole atmosphere of the place. This has proved potent enough to induce a young poet to write a sonnet sequence and one of our younger artists with a gift for the macabre to illustrate its strangeness. Bitterne Manor stands on a piece of low flat ground surrounded on three sides by a hairpin bend in the river Itchen; the Portsmouth-Southampton road crosses the grounds immediately after Northam Bridge. Two straight and parallel ditches, slightly embanked, cut off the promontory and these represent the sole visible remains of *Clausentum,* one of the more important Roman ports on the south coast. The old manor, and these relics of a once thriving port where galleys went about the commerce of a lost empire, both folded in an arm of the river, polluted and half drowned by the sprawling suburbs of a modern port, powerfully affect the imagination.

The New Forest is itself an ancient monument, for, replanted, groomed and tended though it has been, this area of beech and oak forest and of sandy heath with its half-wild ponies and its deer, its rare birds and squirrels, does still recall the spirit of a far older England, a country where man was not yet in command. There are a number of small earthworks within the Forest confines, but none worth seeking out except Buckland Rings just outside Lymington on the Brockenhurst road. This is a fort built rather late in the Iron Age and never permanently occupied which, considering that it is built on the sandy gravel characteristic of the New Forest, has exceptionally massive and well-preserved ramparts. The Forest has now, however, so far encroached on Buckland Rings that these fine triple earthworks are thickly grown with oak-trees and fir. This is the last of the Wessex forts to be visited which has special merit in my eyes because I myself shared in its excavation.

One other site in Hampshire certainly merits a visit. During prehistoric times, Christchurch harbour where the estuaries of the Avon and Stour converge was one of the most important points of entry into southern England and particularly into the Wessex uplands. Many finds made all round this inlet of the sea, bear witness to the immigrants who made use of it to pass up the rivers and so on to the hills. A special interest therefore attaches to Hengistbury Head, the gorse-grown promontory whose cliffs divide the southern flats of Christchurch harbour from the sea. A round barrow is the only visible mark left by the Bronze Age peoples, but a double line of ramparts runs across the low, sandy neck of the headland cutting off an area nearly a square mile in extent. Within this protected area there was occupation beginning in a very early phase of the Iron Age and continuing into Belgic times.

Hengistbury Head commands a wide view of the Isle of Wight. This island, a well-known retreat for the comfortably off, the retired, and for escaping writers, and a favourite resort for thousands of holiday-makers who wish to cross the sea without leaving England, is of more interest to geologists than to archaeologists. The Isle of Wight, more than any other part of southern England, felt the impact of the tremendous upheaval which fairly late in geological time formed the Alps and the whole series of mountain chains stretching to the Himalayas. One of the outermost ripples of this storm was responsible for tipping up the chalk which forms the Isle of Purbeck, then re-emerges as the Needles and the ridge of chalk running west and east across the Isle of Wight. Throughout its length this narrow southern rim of the Wessex chalk has been tipped through ninety degrees so that the horizontal strata laid down on the sea-bed in Cretaceous times now stand vertical, their exposed edges making the points of the Needles and the sharp spine of the inland chalk, while the later levels resting on the

I The Long Man of Wilmington, on Windover Hill in Sussex.

II   Aerial view of the
earthworks and Bronze
Age anctuary át
Avebury in Wiltshire.

III   The chambered long barrow of West Kennet, Wiltshire.

IV   The stone circles at Stonehenge, Wiltshire, taken in the late afternoon.

V   The Late Iron Age village of Chysauster in Cornwall.

VI The megalith of Lanyon Quoit in Cornwall. The huge capstone -
nineteen feet long - rests on three stones five feet high.

VII   Part of the Rollright Stones in Oxfordshire: the stone circle of King's Men.

VIII Castlerigg, a circle of thirty-nine stones with the remains of a stone structure in the centre, near Keswick in Cumberland chalk form the vertical stripes of the famous coloured sands of Alum Bay. In addition to this unusual structure the island is full of strange fossil beasts, unique reptiles and amphibia, and also of the fossilized remains of tropical vegetation. The remains of the relatively youthful species, man, are not spectacular, though there are enough to show that this fertile outpost was inhabited throughout prehistoric times. The earliest monuments are two long barrows, both situated towards the western extremity near the Needles. One lies immediately above Freshwater Bay, the other* on the southern, seaward slope of the high ground north of Chilton Chine, about half a mile from Brook House. A remarkable feature of this Brook barrow is the tall upright stone which, with a smaller recumbent beside it, may represent the remains of a megalithic chamber. For the rest, there are a scatter of round barrows on the chalk ridge, a hill-fort on Gatcombe Down, the well-known Roman villa at Brading, and Carisbrook Castle, where there is a good museum and some surviving masonry of the late Roman fort exposed below the earthworks of the Norman castle.

From this island whose southern slope catches all the available warmth of the English sun, I want now to return to the north to approach Wiltshire and the heart of prehistoric Wessex.

B. *The Berkshire and Marlborough Downs*

To approach Wessex from the north, I shall assume that the traveller is making a fresh start from London, perhaps making the journey to Goring and Streatley, those delightful Thames-side resorts where the river has cut a fine curve through the chalk and where, on the steep northern bank, the trees come spilling down to the water's edge giving a great sense of warmth and richness to this spacious valley scenery.

I shall, in fact, start with the Berkshire Downs, an easy route to travel, for the green track of the Ridgeway runs along their crest, along that grey wall which for so many miles shows through the left-hand window of the railway carriage on the journey from Reading to Swindon. Another prehistoric route follows the slopes of the Downs, generally keeping above the spring line, but far below the crest. This is generally recognized as the true line of the Icknield Way, but it should be remembered that even after this route had come into being (at latest by the Iron Age) it probably served only as the summer road and that in winter wayfarers had to take themselves and their animals up on to the more ancient Ridgeway.

From Goring and Streatley it is possible to join the Ridgeway and to

* Some authorities judge it to be a natural formation.

follow it up on to the detached block of Downs immediately above. Up here the way passes Lowbury Camp, a Roman earthwork which may mark the site of a farm, and the conspicuous Saxon barrow from which its excavators took one of those bronze hanging bowls with ornamental medallions that are entirely Celtic in spirit but evidently much sought after, and perhaps imitated, by the Anglo-Saxons.

Crossing the branch line to Newbury the path leads on to the main scarp which from this point curves gently in an unbroken arc for thirty miles to the far end of the Marlborough Downs. Once up there, subjected to the purity of the air, the pallor of the light, the familiar but always satisfying perfection of the chalk contours, the twentieth-century citizen may pause to reflect that he is standing on a prehistoric road and looking down upon Harwell whose many roofs cover the secrets of atomic energy. But perhaps he would rather walk on.

The Bronze Age peoples have left evidence of their presence on these hills by a scatter of round barrows, while their predecessors of the New Stone Age are represented by Churn Knob, a long barrow not far from the Ridgeway in the parish of Blewbury. A few miles further west the way passes the Iron Age fort of Segsbury, or Letcombe Castle, standing on the edge immediately above Wantage. It is delightful walking up here, and delightful to be aware of these relics of many ages without perhaps taking too much notice of them, but it is only after Letcombe that the Ridgeway enters into its own, covering two or three miles which must be regarded as classic ground not only for amateurs of antiquity, but indeed for all Englishmen.

Within this narrow span are the White Horse, Uffington Castle and Wayland's Smithy. Each of these is of interest as an antiquity, but they have been invested with a significance out of all proportion to this everyday interest by the very special place which they hold in the consciousness of our people. They are invested with a power woven from the memories, the veneration and imaginative life of the nation. There is no doubt that the source of this mist of enchantment which has drifted for so long among the Downs is the White Horse, the strange attenuated beast cut in the steep chalk face of the scarp five hundred feet above the Thames Valley. So wide is his rule, so great his spell, that this whole stretch of valley has for as long as recorded memory borne the lovely name of the Vale of the White Horse. Like all great enchanters the Horse can assume various guises and is equally himself through them all. He has been seen as the emblem of Hengist (whose horsiness is unquestioned) and is still recognized by many as the standard cut by King Alfred after his victory at Ashdown, both attributions honouring the historical association of a white horse with the Saxon peoples. Again he has played the part of the dragon slain by St. George, and in this capacity has given the name of Dragon Hill to the flat-topped knoll which stands a little way detached from the Downs not far below his feet. Finally in our own day archaeologists have seen him rather as a figure of the Celtic Iron Age, perhaps the totemic emblem of the Celtic tribe whose stronghold was close at hand in Uffington Castle. This interpretation, although it has been questioned, is likely to be the correct one, particularly as it at once allows the White Horse the magical and religious authority which has enabled him to assume his later guises. These, too, are perfectly to be believed, for if he has been accepted by the people of the country as the White Horse of the Saxons, then that he is— for what else is an emblem?

The truth is the White Horse of Uffington has since Celtic times been the centre of a horse cult and as such has lurked deep in the consciousness of the people, whether he has been attributed to Hengist or Alfred or the remoter gods of the Celts. G. K. Chesterton expressed it well enough in his *Ballad of the White Horse* in which, without having had recourse to archaeology, he ingeniously allowed King Alfred to remake a much older horse:

> Before the gods that made the gods
> Had seen their sunrise pass
> The White Horse of the White Horse Vale
> Was cut out of the grass.

Because through so many centuries the sanctity of the emblem remained alive in the minds of the country people they were ready also to maintain its physical being. It seems hardly credible that for the two thousand years between Augustus and Queen Victoria, the generations of men and women living on the hills or in the Vale kept the image of the horse from the patient, the insidious encroachments of the grass. Yet the mere presence of these curious lines, the long narrow body, the two detached legs, the fantastically beaked head, prove it quite simply to be true.

Although written record of the White Horse goes back to the twelfth century, all accounts of the scourings which kept it in being are much later. By the time they begin to be described in the seventeenth century they are still an 'obligation' on the villagers round, that is to say a religious sanction, but the jollifications that accompanied them were of the secular kind to which religious festivals commonly degenerate when their significance has been forgotten. Only the horse-racing and the 'debauchery' complained of in later days must have grown directly out of the older customs of the festival. The scouring ceremony is first mentioned by Aubrey, but the best early record dates from 1677 when Baskerville wrote:

> 'Some that dwell hereabouts have an obligation upon their hands to repair and cleanse this Land marke, or else in time it may turne green like the rest of the hill and be forgotten.'

It was an obligation which had been faithfully fulfilled while the higher currents of human thought travelled from the Druids to Newton.

The scourings were supposed to take place at the mystical interval of seven years, but in practice their celebration seems to have been irregular. There are eighteenth-century handbills recalling the lively programmes which brought hundreds of country people as well as gypsies, entertainers and thieves on to the sward of Uffington Hill. It is always good to be reminded of these country festivities which did much to lighten a hard life and also gave it local unity and a strongly coloured calendrical pattern. In addition to the horse-races (which included one for unsaddled cart-horses in their harness and bells), there were many other events: a flitch to be run for by asses; smocks to be run for by ladies, the second best in each race to be entitled to a silk hat; cudgel playing for a gold-laced hat and pair of buckskin breeches and wrestling for silver buckles and pumps. There was also the very curious and ancient custom of racing for cheeses rolled down the steep-sided hollow known as White Horse Manger—a custom which we shall find again in the Cotswolds.

During the actual scouring the workers sometimes sang a ballad in the Berkshire dialect, too conscious perhaps to be very ancient; three of the verses run:

> The owl White Horse wants zettin to rights,
> And the Squire hev promised good cheer,
> Zo we'll gee un a scrape to kip un in zhape,
> And a'll last for many a year.

> A was made a lang lang time ago
> Wi a goo dale of labour and pains,
> By King Alfred the Great when he spwiled their consate
> And caddled thay wosbirds the Danes.

> There'll be backsword play, and climmin the powl,
> And a race for a peg, and a cheese,
> And us thenks as hisn's a dummel zowl
> As dwont care for sich sports as theze.

Nowadays the cleaning of the horse is the 'obligation' of the Department of the Environment and we are all, I suppose, dummel zowls. Standing on the bare brow of the Downs where now only the White Horse himself and the empty ramparts of Uffington Castle survive of all this gaiety, the visitor may be pardoned if he thinks of the good things inevitably ignored by economists but surely to be reckoned with in an estimate of the Standard of Living of any age?

Less than a mile of lordly walking along the Ridgeway brings us to Wayland's Smithy, another one out of perhaps a dozen prehistoric monuments so well known as to claim a place in our national chronicles. The Smithy is in truth a megalithic chambered long barrow, probably the work of the most easterly tribes of the New Stone Age people who built so many tombs of this kind in the Cotswolds and on the other side of the Bristol Channel. The chamber has a central passage with a pair of side cells, giving a cruciform plan; originally it must have been completely roofed with stone slabs and hidden below a long mound, but now only one capstone remains in position—still giving, however, a semblance of a little cave—while the covering mound has been reduced to a low bank lying behind it.

Venerable though he is, the legendary blacksmith, Wayland, is of course a very much later creation than this monument, and it must be the influence of the White Horse which has brought the two together. Indeed in Scandinavian mythology Wayland is the owner of a white horse, and it is therefore not surprising to find that his name had already been attached to the long barrow by the middle of the tenth century. Since that time numbers of local legends have grown up to enrich the imaginative appeal of the Smithy. It was said that the Smith worked here to shoe the White Horse; it was said that if a wayfarer's mount cast a shoe, he need only leave a groat on the roof of the Smithy for it to be mysteriously reshod; it was said that if pieces of iron were left there they would be forged into horseshoes. It may be remarked that when the chamber was excavated in the nineteenth century no groats were found, but only a few iron bars perhaps a hundred years old and showing no signs of any transformation.

With the White Horse and Wayland's Smithy, the chief glory of the Berkshire Downs is past, but the Ridgeway goes on invitingly enough, leading to the Wiltshire boundary. Before following it so far it is worth digressing from it to describe a few antiquities lying on the milder slopes of the spurs that run southward towards the Kennet Valley. Of these perhaps the best known is Lambourn Seven Barrows, a group of round barrows, including some of the disk variety, that lies in a hollow about two miles north of Lambourn village. The name seems to represent a magical rather than a mathematical truth for they number more nearly twenty than seven; several of them have been opened and the grave-goods have shown them to cover a wide span of the Bronze Age. There is also a chambered long barrow at Lambourn and more round barrows, good specimens of the bowl kind, on Idstone Down some three miles further west, while in this same area a small but striking Iron Age camp has been given the name of Alfred's Castle. In pushing along the Ridgeway as far as Wayland's Smithy, I have passed several other Iron Age forts on these more southern spurs; there is not much to be said about them individually but I will name them for the guidance of anyone wishing to wander all over the Berkshire Downs; there are Perborough, Oareborough, Borough Hill, Bussocks and Grimbury all within quite a small area to the north of Newbury; then further west, lying right on the Wiltshire county boundary, is Membury, an outstanding large fort perhaps better worth seeing than any of the others.

Returning now to the Ridgeway a mile or so beyond the Smithy, we almost at once cross into Wiltshire, which I shall boldly claim as the richest in antiquities of any county in the British Isles. The whole of prehistoric times from the New Stone Age through the Bronze to the Iron Age is represented with almost equal profusion and unless my narrative is to become no more than a list of names, I shall have to select only the very finest examples. English place-names often have a poetic beauty of their own, nevertheless it would be ludicrous to catalogue the hundred long barrows, the scores of hill-forts, to say nothing of the round barrows where the Bronze Age pastoralists who knew these grazing-grounds so well have been buried in their thousands.

Soon after passing the boundary, the Ridgeway crosses Ermine Street, the Roman road leading from Silchester to Cirencester, and then leaves Liddington Castle, another Iron Age fort, close on the left before cutting across a second Roman road converging on Cirencester from Winchester. Another few miles, and almost exactly half-way between Swindon and Marlborough, the way begins to bend due south round the splendid double-ramparted fort of Barbury, a stronghold said to contain a very large number of huts or pits visible from the air. Pursuing its southerly course along Hackpen Hill, just at the point where the by-road from Wooton Basset to Marlborough climbs the steep western slope, the Ridgeway passes near a monument of a type that provokes some description even if it is not more than two centuries old. This is the Hackpen Horse, one of a considerable stud to be found on the Marlborough Downs, most of them cut in the last quarter of the eighteenth century or the first half of the nineteenth. They are all of them jaunty, naturalistic beasts—except in so far as they may have been distorted here and there in their finer points by the passage of time and growth of turf—generally shown with docked tails trotting towards the left. I suppose that at no time in our history have horses been so much portrayed as during those years, and the chalk cut figures can be seen as no more than a special branch of the art; nevertheless, I believe they had another source of inspiration which justifies their inclusion here. They have a link with antiquity because they were sired by the White Horse of Uffington on the Romantic and antiquarian movement of the eighteenth century. There is no doubt that many of the Wessex landlords who found the labour for this prodigious cutting of turf and fitting of chalk blocks did so because they were affected by this movement, which even for its most peripheral followers went much deeper than a fashion. There were once nine of these Wiltshire horses, some of them in the absence of a sacred obligation have since been allowed to 'Turne green like the rest of the hill and be forgotten'. They represent, I think, a celebration of the past appropriate to the Romantic Age, just as archaeological studies are appropiate to our own scientific century. The single other horse of this stud which we shall find outside the county, that close by Bratton camp at Westbury, was actually superimposed on an older animal and one almost as singular-looking as Uffington himself.

On Hackpen Hill we are already overlooking one of the most famous archaeological resorts in the country. Unlike the White Horse and Wayland's Smithy, and unlike its more immediate rival, Stonehenge, Avebury is not a name which has been woven into our national legends. The great Bronze Age sanctuary which is the most famous of its many antiquities was first discovered to the learned world as late as 1648 when the young John Aubrey came upon it by chance while out fox-hunting. Once it had been made known, the fame of the monument quickly grew; Aubrey himself, with an exaggeration excusable in its discoverer, claimed Avebury to 'exceed Stonehenge as a cathedral does a parish church', while only twenty years later when Pepys went there during one of his rare holidays he made this revealing entry in his diary:

'. . . rode all day with some trouble for fear of being put out of our way over the Downes, where the life of the shepherds is, in fair weather only, pretty. In the afternoon came to Abebury, where, seeing great stones like those of Stonage standing up, I stopped and took a countryman of that town and he carried me and shewed me a place trenched in like Old Sarum almost, with great stones pitched in it, some bigger than those at Stonage in figure, to my great admiration: and he told me that most people of learning coming by do come and view them, and that the King did so: and that the Mount cast hard by is called Selbury, from one King Seall buried there, as tradition says.'

In the seventeenth century, though already, as we shall see, many stones had been broken up for building and others buried, the stone circles were much better preserved than they were forty years ago. During the 'thirties, however, excavation and restoration were carried out with devoted thoroughness and stones long fallen, broken or buried were set up again in their ancient sockets. Socket holes detected in the chalk but with no surviving stones were at that time marked with small concrete pillars, and everywhere in the circles and avenue visitors will come upon these scientific but unsightly substitutes for the huge grey sarsens which once stood in their place. The excavators also established an admirable museum where ancient and modern maps, drawings and paintings of Avebury are on show, as well as all the best finds from the sanctuary and neighbouring sites.

Learned men and kings (see a testimonial in the excellent Red Lion Inn), still go to Avebury, but they are supplemented by thousands of tourists. This flow of visitors to ancestral monuments is curiously reminiscent of that of medieval pilgrims to famous shrines; though without faith or doctrine, their fundamental needs and purposes are, I believe, very much the same. However this may be, there is no doubt that in the summer months (when neither in fair weather nor foul is there any pretty shepherd life to be seen) visitors swarm at Avebury, and the archaeological traveller may prefer to go there in other seasons when the place relapses peacefully into the downland countryside. Let him go in early spring when the winds still blow chilly across the chalk hills but the beeches are grape-coloured with thrusting buds, or in autumn when these same trees are no more than a glowing aftermath of summer in the pale nostalgic air, and he can wander in pursuit of earthworks and stones among cottage gardens heavy with the last dahlias and chrysanthemums. At these seasons he may go where he will meet no one but the inhabitants of Avebury village, or, as Pepys would have it, the *countrymen of that town*. In strong contrast with Stonehenge, which stands on the open Downs, Avebury is made domestic by the charming Wessex village which since Saxon times has fitted itself comfortably round the prehistoric earthworks and stones. Indeed, not only have many of the stones from the sanctuary been broken up and used to build the manor and cottages, but before restoration some of the surviving uprights had been incorporated as they stood in cottages or out-buildings.

Approaching from the north, we shall enter the sanctuary by the Swindon road, an entry which at once gives a striking impression of the remains—though that on the southern, Marlborough, side is even better.

The first thing which the traveller will see is a colossal bank with a deep ditch on the inner side, part of a circular embankment enclosing nearly thirty acres. This great ring-work must have been dug to delimit the sacred area, and it has been hazarded that it may have been used by the tribesmen when they gathered at Avebury for seasonal festivals; standing or sitting on the sloping bank, much like the audience in a Roman ampitheatre or a bull-ring they could have watched the rituals celebrated within.

The gap in the earthwork through which the Swindon road passes has been proved by excavation to be an original entrance, and this is true also of the openings to the south and west. The eastern gap, where the village street leads out to the church and manor house, has never been tested, but there seems little doubt that it too, was an original feature and that Avebury was unique among these embanked sanctuaries in having four entrances in place of the usual one or two.

Immediately inside the ditch on the right-hand side of the Swindon road the traveller will see two enormous standing stones, massive slabs of sarsen, belonging to the great outer circle which follows the inner lip of the ditch. Very many of its stones have disappeared, but from this point it is possible to see an impressive arc of them to the right, where both earthwork and stones show against the trees screening the grey stone manor house.

The whole of this western half of the great circle has been well restored, particularly the sector against the Marlborough road where as many as a dozen of the big sarsens can be seen standing together. On the eastern side few stones are visible, but as this part of the circumference has never been fully excavated it may well be that some are still lying hidden below the turf.

There is no need to offer a detailed description of Avebury, for at each of the little wicket gates giving access to its various parts the visitor will find a frame displaying a plan and history of the whole sanctuary. These show how inside the great circle there are two small stone rings, set side by side. The northern has two huge stones at the centre, the survivors of the 'Cove' of three stones; the southern has a central monolith and a line of much smaller stones. The better preserved of these inner circles is the southern, many stones of which can be seen in the meadow between the Red Lion and the Marlborough entrance. From this southern entrance a double line of standing stones extended for about a mile and a half to the site on Overton Hill known as The Sanctuary. This West Kennet Avenue originally consisted of some two hundred stones set in pairs, but many are now missing and replaced by concrete markers. Confronting pairs seem usually to have been composed of one broad, squat slab and one relatively tall and narrow monolith. These contrasting shapes can be seen also in the main temple, and even the most austere archaeologists are prepared to concede that they may well stand for female and males and represent a fertility cult among the rites celebrated at Avebury.

The Overton Hill Sanctuary has nothing better to show than concentric rings of concrete stumps marking the position of stone and post holes discovered by excavation. It is now thought very probable that these are the remains of a long sequence of religious buildings on the site, beginning with a small sacred hut and ending with a very much larger circular temple, built in wood but with one internal stone circle and a second, linked with the Avenue, ringing it outside.

The earliest known structures at Avebury are the Sanctuary hut and its first enlargement, but people were already living in the area of the main temple and the Avenue at about the same time. This was towards the end of the New Stone Age, perhaps rather before 2000 B.C. and slightly before the foundation of Stonehenge. The tremendous and highly organized effort of digging the bank and ditch and setting up the stones of the great circle and the Avenue seems to have been a single undertaking. It was probably carried out in about 1850 B.C. when Stonehenge had not gone beyond its second, bluestone, phase. Burials of the invaders of the earliest Bronze Age (p. 49) accompanied by beakers and other vessels had been made at the foot of stones in the Sanctuary and Avenue. There seems little doubt that the coming of these vigorous people helped to stimulate the building of Avebury on so vast a scale. After this no major additions were made to the sacred structures, but they were undoubtedly still frequented and retained their sanctity during those later centuries of the Bronze Age when Stonehenge reached its zenith. The length of time separating the heydays of the two greatest fanes of prehistoric Britain was, then, about the same as that between our early Romanesque and late Gothic architecture. The crouched skeletons of two of the Early Bronze Age builders of Avebury were found where they had been buried against monoliths of the Avenue with bowls and drinking-vessels set beside them. Even more dramatic, and a splendid instance of how archaeology can recapture and revive a moment of past time, was a totally unexpected discovery made during work on the great circle. While many of the missing stones of Avebury have been broken up for building, a few of them proved to have been pulled down and buried deeply enough to get them out of the farmer's way. All such buried blocks were, of course, raised and restored to their original positions. When one of the stones in the great circle was being lifted the excavators were astonished to find a skeleton lying beneath it; clearly it did not represent a formal burial, for by their attitude the bones still spoke of a man caught in a moment of movement—in a desperate attempt to run away. Coins of Edward I which he had been carrying in a purse showed that death overtook this man early in the fourteenth century, while the scissors and lancet which he had with him made it as nearly as possible certain that he had practised as a barber-surgeon. (His scissors, now in the Avebury Museum, are the oldest pair known to exist in Britain!) The interpretation put upon these curious facts—and it cannot, I think, be far wrong—is that villagers had been struggling to dislodge the monolith when a zealous passer-by, probably a stranger to the place, had volunteered to help them, and being more skilled at handling a lancet than large stones had been caught by the block as it fell. So it was that the unhappy barber-surgeon found his grave in the hole dug to receive the stone. Evidently the survivors were so terrified by what had occurred that they made no attempt to recover the body and give it Christian burial, but shovelled earth over stone and victim as quickly as they could. Even to-day the villagers are known to resort to the stones for magical cures of one kind or another, and I do not doubt that their medieval ancestors were so nervous when they tampered with them that they instantly assumed the tragedy was no accident but the revenge of the enraged divinities of the temple. In their fear they left the surgeon as an unwitting sacrifice.

Second in order of fame among the antiquities of Avebury, is Silbury Hill, the huge mound which stands on the northern side of the Marlborough –Chippenham road about a mile south of the village. This, of course, is the Selbury mentioned by Pepys. Just as the great circle is always described as the largest of its kind in Europe, so too, and with equal justice, Silbury is claimed as the largest artificial mound. Its appearance suggests a gigantic pudding which is really only to say it is like a bowl barrow of extraordinary proportions. Recent excavation has solved some problems, concerning the date and construction of this monument, but others relating to its purpose remain to be answered. Its construction took place in four stages which were probably continuous. The first phase was the building of a conical mound, one hundred and twenty feet in diameter and eighteen feet high, which Carbon 14 dating has assigned to around 2145 B.C., in the period covering the passing of the Stone Age and the dawn of the Bronze Age. As soon as this first mound was built it was covered by another of chalk rubble some two hundred and forty feet across and this in turn was buried below the larger chalk mound of Silbury III, the material for which was excavated from the surrounding ditch, originally twenty-three feet deep, that is still partially visible. The final stage in the design, Silbury

IV, represents the monument as it now exists, a remarkable tribute to its builders whose work at Avebury and Stonehenge similarly amazes the eye and the imagination.

Silbury Hill does not exhaust the monuments in this unique centre of antiquity. To the south of the same road and distinguished by a jagged coxcomb of trees planted along its crest is the chambered long barrow of West Kennet, another example, remotely comparable to Wayland's Smithy, of a type of tomb we shall find to be far commoner in the Cotswolds. Excavation in 1955–6 revealed that the lofty stone burial chambers were at the eastern end of the barrow and contained the remains of some twenty adults, one youth and at least a dozen children. There is a second long barrow a little to the south-east in the parish of East Kennet. To stray for a moment a few miles away from Avebury, on the Downs between this road and the Vale of Pewsey, there are half a dozen of the unchambered long barrows much more characteristic of the chalk country, while immediately above the Vale at Alton Priors is the Knap Hill enclosure or causewayed camp probably built and used by the same tribes whose dead were buried in the long barrows.

Although excavation may one day change the balance, Knap Hill is at present of little consequence when weighed against the last and oldest of the famous Avebury antiquities, the much larger causewayed camp on Windmill Hill about a mile to the north-west of the temple. This site was excavated during the 1920's and yielded plentiful and important remains of early immigrant farmers of the New Stone Age. As a result their culture is usually known to archaeology as Windmill Hill. No trace was found to suggest that there were ever permanent huts inside the earthwork, although clay hearths were uncovered. Most of the finds came from the ditches which had evidently been used for tipping rubbish and sometimes also as sheltered squatting-places. Many remains were found of the small wide-horned cattle, and of sheep; there was an unusually perfect skeleton of a dog of a breed suggesting a long-legged fox terrier. Looking at the delicate construction of the dog's skeleton so scrupulously assembled in the Avebury museum, it seems a work of art in its own right and it is difficult to add flesh and fur and imagine a lively animal which, rather before the time of Abraham, was running on these hills, its bark sounding far as it rounded up the flocks. Mixed with the bones were plenty of sherds of broken crockery, the plain or very simply ornamented round-bottomed pots always made by these people, flint and stone axes as well as flint scrapers, and antler combs used in the preparation of skin clothes.

After excavation several of the short sections of the causewayed ditches were carefully turfed and kept open, so rendering Windmill Hill by far the most conspicuous and comprehensible of these enclosures which have generally been obliterated by the slow process of time. When I last climbed the hill, however, I found the ditch in a wretched state, the turf rough and broken and the whole made hideous by sagging fences. There are visitors who will feel as they look at these sad holes or at the concrete markers in the temple that it is better to accept the work of time and decay.

Large round barrows lie near the older earthworks on Windmill Hill and there is a splendid line of them, each bearing a clump of beeches, above the turning which leads down to Avebury from the main Marlborough road. These are merely the nearest at hand and most noticeable of large numbers of burial-mounds clustering about Avebury; the same concentration is found at Stonehenge and it is known that the Bronze Age peoples brought their dead, sometimes over long distances, to bury them within sight, and doubtless within the influence, of these potent sanctuaries.

In following the Ridgeway, we turned south to Avebury before reaching the western scarp of the Marlborough Downs where it stands above Chippenham and the headwaters of the Bristol Avon. The most striking site there is the Iron Age fort, Oldbury Castle, whose strong double ramparts crown some fine bare downland. The slopes are embellished by a beech-wood, the slender obelisk of the Landsdowne Monument and on the steep northern side by quite the most spirited and highly bred of the Wiltshire White Horses. This beast is usually called the Cherhill Horse after the village a mile to the north-west; it was cut in 1780 by a 'mad doctor' and for a time was distinguished by a gleaming eye, imparted by filling the turf socket with bottles, buried bottom upper-most, and so resembling the many-faceted eye of an insect. So great is the thirst of some visitors for mere souvenirs, that these bottles, although known to have been empty, had all disappeared within a century.

Four or five miles to the south, another fort, Oliver's Castle, stands on a spur of the Roundway Hill which is better known as a Civil War battleground, an association which has given this Celtic fort its misleading name. I might not have thought Oliver's Castle deserving attention, if it were not that one of the most interesting earthworks in the country passes between it and Oldbury. For anyone following a narrowly geographical itinerary, an earthwork fifty miles long presents a difficult problem; is it better to dismember it, describing the sections whenever they cross one's own route, or to describe it in its entirety and so be led far away from the chosen path? I think that the Wansdyke demands to be surveyed throughout its fifty miles, however sketchily it may be done, and this point where it drops from the Marlborough Downs between Oldbury and Roundway Hill is the one I have selected for the survey. Wansdyke consists of a single bank and ditch running fairly consistently east and west and with the ditch on the northern side—it is planned, that is to say, by a people living to the south of it against an enemy to the north. The eastern tip is thought to lie near Inkpen on the Hampshire border south of Hungerford, from where the dyke runs westward past Chisbury camp to be temporarily lost in Savernake Forest; it begins again due south of Marlborough between the present and the abandoned railway line to Andover, and shows its noblest form in the ten-mile stretch along the southern edge of the Marlborough Downs, until it bends gently northward to our survey point. From here it is only intermittently visible across the Avon Valley but can be traced once more near Lacock Abbey running on top of the Roman road to Bath. Throughout the Bath area it has inevitably been obliterated, but westward it can be seen again at Bathampton (where there is an Iron Age fort) and it passes close to another fort at Stantonbury just north of Stanton Prior; in this section the earthwork again approaches the impressive scale and good preservation found on the Marlborough Downs. Wansdyke can be traced without question from Stantonbury to Dundry Hill but the rest of its obscure course south and west of Bristol to the coast of Portishead has to be left largely to the imagination.

A fifty-mile defensive work which must once have been far more formidable throughout its entire length than it now is even in its most impressive stretches, is no local undertaking; it proclaims unmistakably a broad strategy and wide powers of command. Is it possible to relate this ambitious work to any known historical event? It will have been noticed that near Bath the dyke runs *on* the Roman road and careful excavation long ago carried out by General Pitt-Rivers has proved it to be of late Roman or post-Roman date. Perhaps it is a question which can never be answered with absolute certainty, but arguments as cogent as they are imaginatively pleasing, have been advanced to show that Wansdyke was built at the command of Ambrosius, the great British leader who, together with his lieutenant and probably younger kinsman, Arthur, succeeded in checking the first phases of Anglo-Saxon invasion led by Hengist. According to this interpretation it was completed in about 470 A.D. during a temporary truce between the Roman Britons and the invaders—serving as a boundary between the still British territory of Hampshire, Wiltshire and the south-west and the aggresive Anglo-Saxons in the region of the Upper Thames. It was after this that Ambrosius was able to move forward again and finally, for the Britons under the generalship of Arthur, to win the great victory of Mount Badon which delayed the Teutonic settlement by half a century.

Whether or not the details of this story are correct, there seems little doubt that Wansdyke does represent some part of the bitter struggle between Britons and Anglo-Saxons and that it must mark a check of the invaders. Looking along this embankment, following it as it mounts and sinks again with the crests and hollows of the Downs or westernhills, the traveller can feel that he is seeing the greatest mark left by the impact between the two peoples who together were so largely to create the future history of Britain. The Celts and Teutons were locked in what looked like a death-grip, but in truth it was to lead to a partial fusion, followed by mutual toleration, and so to the strengthening and enlivening stimulus of one upon the other which has gone on ever since. That even in England the Celtic population was able to survive and make a massive contribution to the racial and cultural inheritance of the country was very largely due to the breathing-space won by the courageous and brilliant resistance of Ambrosius and Arthur. The Wansdyke stands as a still not unworthy symbol of that resistance—an episode which was to end in the British King Arthur becoming the most-loved heroic figure of English legend. By the time Arthur had proved himself as a war leader, the dyke may already have begun to look dilapidated, nevertheless he must have been familiar with it, may have appraised it as the best that could be done in time of crisis and collapsing civilization to emulate the Roman conception of a military frontier so splendidly represented by Hadrian's Wall. Thus the spirit of the historic Arthur, one of the last generals to fight for the civilization of Roman Britain, may be allowed to walk Wansdyke, while the legendary King, so fine a creation of Celtic and Teutonic imagination is left to his true haunts at Avalon and Camelot and all the places of Malory's chronicle.

C. *Salisbury Plain*

Wansdyke and the ways of Arthurian legend have led me far from my chosen itinerary. I want now to go back to cross the Vale of Pewsey and enter upon that region which we have seen to lie at the very heart of prehistoric England, the wide, bare chalk uplands of Salisbury Plain. In crossing the Vale the more earnest pursuers of antiquity should certainly visit the chief town, Devizes, where the museum of the Wiltshire Archaeological Society houses many important finds from the county including gold treasures, some in facsimile but some original, from the chieftains' barrows in the Stonehenge region.

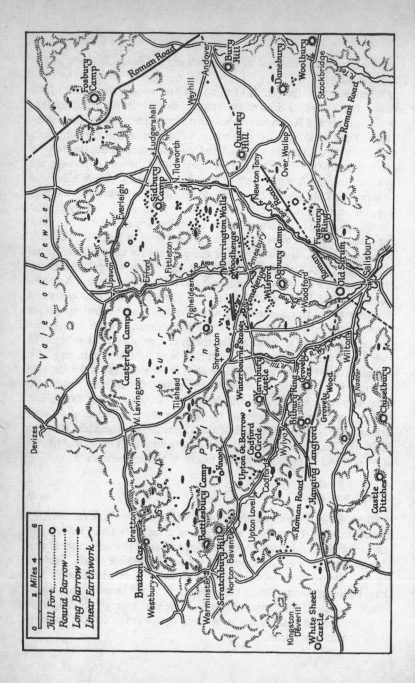

The shift from the uplands which followed the end of prehistoric times left much of the Plain uncultivated and it is this lack of disturbance by the medieval plough which has allowed it to remain so rich in minor remains of antiquity—the patterns of Celtic field systems and the foundations of Iron Age or native Romano-British settlements which show through the turf in many places. This in addition to the great monuments which must in any circumstances have survived to commemorate the days of its prehistoric greatness. Yet this same poorness as agricultural land has in the last hundred years exposed Salisbury Plain to the threat of swords instead of plough-shares. Since it has been one of the chief training centres of the British Army and as the violence of war has intensified, so has the damage caused to the Plain. There are areas closed for poison gas, bombing ranges, humped and pitted like vast expanses of flint-mining, and many other disfigurements and obstructions. There may be a melancholy historic interest in seeing tanks loping over the ramparts built by Celtic warriors but the destruction wrought is considerable. Certainly no modern military works will leave such graceful remains for the future as the hill-forts of the Celts. Concrete and corrugated iron cannot do better than disappear, but commonly do very much worse. Along the northern ridge of the Plain although it is scattered with barrows and bears many marks of ancient cultivation and settlement, there is nothing worth naming except Casterley Camp, a large but weakly entrenched fort which has been dated to the Belgic Iron Age, and nowhere worth lingering before Bratton Castle, a fort of roughly rectangular plan whose double ramparts top the steep face of the Downs five miles from Westbury. Immediately below the camp, indeed with its ears impinging on the outer ramparts, is the Westbury White Horse, a somewhat dejected-looking animal with a hanging, undocked tail. This beast was cut in 1778, and restored in the nineteenth century, but it was so made as to overlie and obliterate an older and smaller horse facing in the opposite direction. This more ancient figure seems to have been grotesque: a long, thin, ill-proportioned brute with a wildly popping eye set at the base of its ear and a thin, upcurved tail with a small fork at the tip which makes one think of the front of an elephant rather than the back of a horse. This freakish predecessor of the present naturalistic Westbury horse has been claimed as prehistoric, but the best evidence suggests that in fact it was cut only early in the eighteenth century, and it may well be that it was deliberately designed to recall the Uffington horse but with a lack of skill and understanding which transmuted strangeness into absurdity.

White Horses ancient and recent have always been cut in places commanding a wide sweep of country and the Westbury example is in this even more fortunate than most of its companions. Anyone who has climbed to Bratton Castle on a clear day can see from the Mendips on the west to the Marlborough Downs as far as Avebury to the east, while below his feet the riches of the Vale of Pewsey are spread out with all the intricate pattern of its fields and orchards.

Turning southward from Bratton but still keeping to the edge of the Plain, we soon come to the upper end of the Wylye Valley, one of the most beautiful of all the valleys tributary to the Avon which dissect and diversify the uplands. The Wylye, now such a modest and sequestered stream as hardly to be visible as it twists, divides, unites again among its meadows, has cut this bold trench through the chalk, where, since they left the uplands, men have come to build a line of mills and of villages. The place-names themselves speak of English history: downstream from Warminster are Norton Bavant, Sutton Veny, Knook, Upton Lovel, Fisherton de la Mere and Wylye—to pick out only those whose names while seeming most English, yet echo furthest among different peoples and tongues—Norman, Saxon and Celt. As a counterpart to this, for one of those pieces of countryside where the monuments of many periods crowd together to remind us of the length and variety of our early history, the traveller need not fare further than the place we have now reached, the edge of the Plain above the Wylye between Warminster and Heytesbury. Boldest and most striking among its antiquities are the two magnificent camps which dominate the valley from the very edge of the scarp—Battlesbury and Scratchbury. They lie not more than a mile apart and each commands a fine view of the other. Battlesbury, with a beech hanger darkening the slope below it, is one of those camps, normally dating from late in the Iron Age, in which several lines of ramparts follow the contours of the hill; Scratchbury in contrast, though quite free from the mechanical regularity of Roman planning, is roughly rectangular in outline—similar to the fort last described, Bratton Castle, which at this point is about ten miles away due north across the Plain. Although it has not been reliably confirmed by digging, it seems almost certain that the powerful strongholds of Battlesbury and Scratchbury must have been in simultaneous use for at least a part of their history. We do not yet know enough to be able to explain why such colossal labours as were demanded by the building of these fortifications should be twice expended; it seems incredible that they could have been raised against one another, yet it is equally hard to imagine any common strategy which they could have served. We shall find one parallel, and it is a close one, in the pair of forts on Hod and Hambledon Hills in Cranborne Chase, otherwise I know of nothing comparable in the whole country.

From these great Iron Age monuments it is possible to see on the one hand remains two thousand years more ancient, and, on the other, a thousand years more recent. There are several long barrows on the undulating plateau, the most striking being the Norton Bavant barrow which from the ramparts of Scratchbury can be seen lying on swelling green down to the north like a porpoise's back among the waves. Then, advancing by several centuries, in the high south-western corner of this camp there is a very large if mutilated round barrow. It makes an excellent lookout point and one may guess that more than a thousand years after it had been raised for a Bronze Age funeral, Celtic warriors must have made use of it for this purpose. Finally when the New Stone and Bronze Ages had sunk deep into the forgotten past and hill-fort warfare was kept in memory only by its surviving earthworks, the ploughs of Anglo-Saxon cultivators on Middle Hill between Battlesbury and Scratchbury cut its slopes into long narrow terraces. These strip fields, so much like gigantic steps mounting the hill, have survived in all their sharpness and are now among the finest examples of their kind.

So, through the Anglo-Saxons, we have joined hands with the villages strung out along the valley bottom, the villages that with their churches, almshouses, inns and mansions can provide some material reminders of almost every century of the last nine. Within a few miles four thousand years have shown their memorials. For myself, if I wanted to enjoy the essential taste of the chalk country, of those parts of England created by the Cretaceous seas, I think I should choose the Wylye Valley where one can pass in space from naked downland with cloud shadows swimming up and down the chalk waves, to succulent waterside meadows and rich boscage, and in time from long barrows to Georgian manors and cottages. As for the last hundred years which no one can claim as beautifiers of the countryside, they have left this valley very much alone. The sound of the tractor I accept; it is already gathering to itself many of the associations of rural hours.

On the segment of Downs between the Wylye and Nadder Valleys there are the usual barrows, round and long, there are interesting earthworks and a good stretch of Roman road in Grovely Wood, and away on the westernmost extremity south of Maiden Bradley, Whitesheet Castle is a fine Iron Age fort with even finer prospects across the Stour to the heavily wooded hills of Shaftesbury. But I do not want to do more than dismiss them with these few words, the main itinerary must keep to the north side of the Wylye, past the much-ploughed circular fort on Codford Hill and so on towards the east and towards Stonehenge. First the road to Amesbury and Andover passes close beside Yarnbury Castle, one of the best-known forts on the Plain. It has no hill summit to add to its strength and dignity, for it stands on a level plateau, its ramparts showing from the road like a level wall—indeed, very much like one of those embanked reservoirs to be seen beside urban waterworks. There are three strong ramparts with two ditches enclosing a space of nearly thirty acres; within this central area is a much smaller ringwork, now almost worn away, the surviving remains of an older Yarnbury built early in the Iron Age, perhaps the third century B.C. The present fort took its place late in the period and continued in use into Roman times. Both Belgic and Roman pottery have been found, and as early as the eighteenth century it was recognized as a good hunting-ground for collectors of Roman coins. There are now several gaps in the defences, but only the one on the eastern side, where the ramparts are noticeably inturned, marks an original entrance. The other openings were probably made to allow shepherds to drive their flocks in to the big sheep fair held at Yarnbury every October for very many years—perhaps for many centuries. The last was in 1916.

The traveller who wishes to approach Stonehenge most fittingly should keep along this road, crossing the little river Till at Winterbourne Stoke. As he reaches the quiet crossroads on the summit, he will be on the edge of one of the greatest, and certainly the richest, congregations of burial-mounds in all Britain. Here was a kind of vast scattered cemetery on ground hallowed by its proximity to the renowned sanctuary. Barrows cluster round Stonehenge on all sides—three hundred of them—but here to the west is the greatest concentration and the area most sequestered from the blighting military activities of Amesbury. Close within the north-eastern angle of the crossroads is a well-preserved long barrow, and its spine acts as a pointer to a line of round barrows starting just beyond the small wood. These in their range of forms make a typologist's heaven. First there are two striking bell barrows and on their left two disks—one of normal type, the other with twin tumps. Just beyond them is perhaps the best-known example of that rare variety, the pond barrow—which consists of a circular depression with a low bank on the lip. Back on the line of the bells are four bowl barrows, and there are many more of this simple type beside the left-hand road as it leads very happily northwards to nowhere.

This completes the enumeration of this famous group, and I will not attempt another. When the ritual and whatever its accompaniment may have been of masks, effigies and offerings have vanished so long ago, when there is no stir left of emotion and the ghosts which emotion keeps alive, when the very people responsible for raising these mounds have been overwhelmed, absorbed and forgotten, then their detailed study can become lifeless enough. Better perhaps to look at them with knowledge but with knowledge unexpressed, these round barrows that are like the floating bubbles of events drowned in time.

Away to the right of the road the bubbles ride the Downs in lines and clusters. First on Normanton Down immediately above Stonehenge where some of the richest burials of the Wessex invaders have been uncovered, then further away the great conglomerations of Wilsford and Lake. So we approach Britian's most famous prehistoric monument through crowding satellites attracted towards it by the magnetism of its own holiness.

There is a disadvantage in this Winterbourne approach to Stonehenge; the first view from the slopes of Normanton Down shows the temple against the army hutments and other military bric-à-brac of Larkhill Camp; they are more than a mile beyond, but it cannot be said that they make a good backcloth. It is a compensation for those who must come by the less interesting Amesbury road that they will first see the stones standing slightly above them against a background of untroubled downland set with beech clumps and burial-mounds.

Seen at a distance, as from Normanton Down, Stonehenge appears small, compact, and unexpectedly rectangular—an architecture in which strong, straight verticals are dominant. Colour plays a great part in the architectural quality of the sanctuary. The huge blocks of sarsen are a pale silvery grey and in many lights they stand out with a strange pallor against the duller tones of the Downs, an effect seen with heightened intensity in Constable's marvellous painting of the stones enveloped in storm-clouds.

By whatever road he comes, the traveller will have to buy his ticket and use the official entrance, reflecting if he will on the course of social evolution which has made entry to a shrine of Bronze Age herdsmen dependent on paying cash to a uniformed attendant. The Department of the Environment has kept the whole apparatus of conservation as unobtrusive as possible and many unsightly concretions of an earlier period have been tidied away. On the other hand, there are the inevitable waste-paper baskets, loss of turf and the crowds.

We may have regretted the tickets, the waste-paper baskets, our fellow visitors; we may feel that publicity has destroyed the spirit of this too-famous building; yet once among the stones all but the most stubbornly resistant moods must surrender to their power. The massive, roughly squared blocks of sarsen seem to possess a forceful presence which asserts itself within the human consciousness. Their silvery grey colour fills the eye but now shows itself to be variegated with dark lichens and with the shadow of grotesque fissures and hollows worn by centuries of rain and frost. One upright has been so deeply and curiously carved by the weather that it looks like one of those huge wooden totem poles made by the Vancouver Island Indians.

The plan of the temple is not hard to distinguish; it has two main elements, an outer ring and an inner horseshoe of stones, but both are double. The outermost circle originally consisted of thirty uprights (about seventeen feet high) supporting a continuous architrave of horizontal slabs, each curved slightly to take its place in the circumference of the circle. These slabs have a hole at each end designed to fit over a knob or tenon on the upright—each upright being furnished with two tenons—and are linked to one another by tongue-and-groove joints. Inside this gigantic sarsen ring is a circle of relatively small and slender stones, originally perhaps as many as fifty in number. These are some of the famous 'bluestones' which until recently it has been accepted were brought from the Presely Hills in Pembrokeshire, the only possible source for their particular variety of blue-grey dolerite. A geologist has now cast doubt on this theory. He suggests, instead, that the stones although certainly originating in Pembrokeshire were moved by glaciers during the Ice Ages rather than by man during the Bronze Age. There is, however, nothing to confirm this opinion.

Within this second component of the outer ring stands the trilithon horseshoe, perhaps the most impressive single architectural feature of the temple. When complete it was formed by five trilithons (pairs of uprights supporting a lintel stone), two at each side and one, the most massive of all, at the toe. Unhappily the north-west side of the horseshoe is much ruined while of the central trilithon only a single upright is in position, the naked tenon on its summit showing clearly against the sky. Just as the bluestone circle is inside the sarsen circle, so there is an inner horseshoe setting of bluestones within the sarsen trilithons. Across the toe of the bluestone horseshoe and therefore immediately in front of the great central trilithon lies a sandstone slab, also of Welsh origin. Ever since Inigo Jones made the first plan of Stonehenge for James I, this slab has popularly been identified as the Altar Stone, but is far more likely once to have stood as a monolith. Certainly this central enclosure where the Altar Stone now lies must have have been the most holy, the most charged with *mana* in the whole sanctuary. One may suppose that for medieval Englishmen a whole realm of religious emotion and faith was focused like the light in a burning-glass on the masses celebrated before the high altar of Canterbury Cathedral, while the whole of Christendom was similarly drawn towards St. Peter's. It is not, I believe, unwarranted to imagine that the Bronze Age tribesmen throughout the southern English uplands were aware of some such concentration of their religious feelings in what is now this oval patch of turf in the midst of Stonehenge.

The architecture of Stonehenge is unique in its elaboration and advanced technique. Nowhere else in prehistoric Britain do we find anything so near a great 'building' in our own sense of the word, nor anything to equal the masons' work represented by the accurate shaping and jointing of huge blocks. There are even such refinements as curving the lintel stones as arcs of the circle and their widening towards the top to counteract fore-shortening. Stonehenge had as long a history as one expects for a great cathedral. It seems to have been first founded at the end of New Stone Age times, early in the second millennium B.C. when, as we have seen, it consisted of the bank and ditch and ritual pits within. There may have been a wooden building at the centre of the circle and the Heel Stone was set up at this time. The second phase begins in about 1700 B.C., by which time the beaker-using invaders of the earliest Bronze Age were playing their part in developing the sanctuary. It was at this time that the blue-stones were first used, set in two circles, while the Avenue (p. 124), probably a processional way, was added. So far Stonehenge was a modest enough monument, though undoubtedly the centre of a sacred area. It was with the rise of the Wessex culture that it was raised to its unique grandeur. The great sarsens were brought from near Marlborough and raised on the present plan and the bluestones, after various vicissitudes, reshaped and set up to echo the circle and horseshoe of sarsens. The date of the Wessex culture has been much in dispute, but it is now possible to bring it down to the centuries after 1500 B.C. and so once again to believe that its wealthy chieftains could have had trading contacts with Mycenae, and even have employed a Mycenaean architect for their great temple. Carvings of a dagger of a kind known from the famous Shaft Graves of Mycenae have been identified on a sarsen (there are also a number of portrayals of metal axeheads).

No later additions of importance were made after about 1400 B.C. and there is no evidence to connect Stonehenge with the Celtic priesthood of the Druids. Those modern Druids who travel there to celebrate the sun rising over the Heel Stone on Midsummer's morning are following what was an antiquary's fancy and no more. On the other hand it is as certain as such things can be that the axis of the temple was sited on this sunrise. It is also very probable that rites and worship conducted there, at any rate after the first phase, were directed towards the heavenly bodies and may have involved observation of their movement.

Visitors may or may not have noticed the Heel Stone; a useful signpost for the outlying earthworks associated with Stonehenge. The Heel Stone marks the beginning of the Avenue which is a modest affair, not comparable with its counterpart at Avebury, consisting only of two low banks with flanking ditches cut about seventy feet apart. From the Heel Stone it is just visible heading towards the east side of Larkhill Camp, but for the greater part of its course it can only be detected from the air. About five hundred yards from the temple it begins to curve east and then south to join the Avon on the near side of Amesbury. The Avenue was laid out in the second phase of Stonehenge, and so probably was the earthwork known as the Cursus that lies just to the north. It is an embanked strip nearly two miles long by about one hundred yards wide; it owes its odd name to Stukeley who thought it might have been intended for the celebration of funeral games. To the west it ends in Fargo Plantation, the belt of trees on the skyline of the Bath road; the east end has been found to abut on to a long barrow. Digging and field study have also quite unexpectedly suggested that when first the bluestones were brought to Salisbury Plain they may have been used for a circle or other construction related to the Cursus and not to Stonehenge. If this is the true history, then they may not have been moved to the present site until the 'Wessex' period. The Cursus is the best preserved of three or four monuments of its kind known in southern England, but what the function of these narrow earthworks can have been is as much a matter for guessing as it was in Stukeley's day.

Enough has been said to show that the Stonehenge complex (and how complicated it is) has a long, fluctuating history which is only now beginning to be understood, but, whatever intellectual storms may rage, they will not disturb the venerable stones themselves, and visitors will continue to go to them and to marvel—as visitors have marvelled already for eight hundred years.

Although Stonehenge must by comparison render any other site something of an anti-climax, before leaving the Plain the traveller should push northward, following the Amesbury–Marlborough road until about a mile and a half north of Amesbury, it passes a circular maze of concrete stumps, recalling those seen at the Overton Sanctuary (p. 110). This remarkable site was discovered by air photography, and subsequent excavation proved it to have been another sacred enclosure of the henge type monoliths with no less than six oval settings of posts, their long axes apparently orientated on the Midsummer sunrise. Looking at the concrete markers set in the former post-holes, one would hardly suspect, what was in fact the truth, that the excavators found near the centre of the sanctuary the skeleton of an infant with its skull cleft open—probably a dedication sacrifice. The post-holes probably represent a circular, roofed wooden temple, comparable to the sanctuary.

A short distance beyond this temple (i.e. Woodhenge) lies the now almost obliterated Durrington Walls, an earthwork which would hardly claim attention were it not that it constitutes the remains of another henge monument that was once of considerable size and importance. When excavated in the 'fifties and 'sixties it was found to date to the late New Stone Age and was thus roughly contemporary with the neighbouring sanctuary of Woodhenge. Indeed the surrounding area was a focal centre for early human occupation. Just a quarter of a mile to the north-east, close to the Stonehenge Inn, is a flint-mine, and there are many early round barrows. Inside the bank and ditch, which were more extensive though much less massive than those of Avebury, there had stood two circular wooden buildings, the larger having features in common with Woodhenge.

In the strip of country between the Avon and the Hampshire border dominated by the big military camps of Bulford and Tidworth, there are barrows both round and long, as well as innumerable tracks and minor earthworks, but nothing worth special recommendation except perhaps the fort of Sidbury to the north of Tidworth, which occupies an exceptionally strong position on a seven-hundred-foot isolated summit. If, however, we move southward from Amesbury we come to Ogbury close beside the Avon at Durnford, a large but weakly entrenched camp probably constructed early in the Iron Age and subsequently abandoned and turned over to agriculture—for the banks of Celtic fields can be seen inside the defences. Four miles to the south-west on the other side of the Bourne and in the parish of Winterbourne Dauntsey is the smaller but stronger and far more interesting fort of Figsbury Rings. This fort, too, has a commanding natural position on a promontory of the chalk; the roughly circular outer rampart and ditch enclose an area of fifteen acres. This is ordinary enough; what is freakish about Figsbury is the presence a long way inside the main defences of a second circular ditch with no trace of a corresponding bank; the orthodox view is that the ditch served as a quarry for the outer rampart, but why the builders should have troubled to dig so deep for material or to carry it so far seems to me to defy any reasonable explanation.

The Roman road from Winchester to Old Sarum runs about half a mile to the south of Figsbury and there is a good stretch of it to be seen there, on the far side of the modern highway. After crossing the present road its line is followed by a lane, and this provides a very pleasant way to approach Old Sarum by the original ford across the Bourne. The site of a Roman Town, *Soriodunum*, has long been thought to lie in this area, which was an important road junction in Roman times. Excavations have now uncovered the foundations of buildings which may yet prove to belong to this elusive site. It is my opinion that Old Sarum is not nearly so well known as it deserves to be, for, as the air photograph shows, it is a most spectacular site and certainly has an unusually interesting history. The outer line of the powerful circular earthwork dates from the Iron Age and Old Sarum, on its hill just to the north of Salisbury, might be expected to be the prehistoric upland forerunner of the present city, just as St. Catharine's Hill is of modern Winchester and the Trundle of Chichester. Here, however, the upland site survived far longer before the shift was made down to the valley; the earthworks of Old Sarum are in part early medieval and they enclose the foundations of a Norman cathedral and other remains of a town flourishing until the twelfth century. Looking from the hill-top to the city lying round its famous spire at the confluence of many rivers, the reality of this step down from the uplands is easy to grasp; one can imagine the citizens and countryfolk standing up here to see the foundations of the present cathedral being laid, and then week after week watching the top of the great building mount up towards them.

D. *Cranborne Chase*

Salisbury is of course the most convenient as well as the most beautiful centre for all the western parts of Wessex. Those who are going to concern themselves with the antiquities of the region should certainly go to the museum in St. Ann Street where there is an excellent prehistoric collection and many exhibits helpful for the understanding of Stonehenge.

We can leave the city by the south-west where the Gothic lyricism of the cathedral finds so natural a setting in the classical and domestic good sense of the Close, pass the water meadows where Constable painted, and make for the northern edge of Cranborne Chase. This is an itinerary where walkers are the best served, the old Shaftesbury coach road is now an agreeable track following the steep scarp above the Nadder Valley for mile after mile, always with the bare chalk Downs on the left and the valley on the right broken by warmly wooded hills which have been formed here as in the Sussex Weald by the exposure of underlying Greensand. The names of the villages along this valley offer the same unstudied historical poetry which we found a few miles away beside the Wylye. I cannot resist another recitation: Compton Chamberlayne, Teffont Magna and Teffont Evias, Sutton Mandeville, Swallowcliffe and Ansty. The path up from Harnham, crossing the Roman road from Old Sarum to Dorchester just against the race-course, passes many *tumuli* but nothing of great note before Chiselbury Camp, an almost perfectly round fort lying on a level headland above Compton Chamberlayne and Fovant. The single rampart and ditch enclose about ten acres and the original entrance is on the south-east, on the side nearest the track, where two separate openings through the rampart are protected by a semicircular outwork. On the northern side a hollow track between two banks runs for about three hundred feet from the outer ditch and then ends abruptly on the edge of the steepest part of the scarp. Covered ways of this kind are thought to have been designed for driving cattle but it is hard to see how such a purpose could have been served in this precipitous place.

Once I was standing there by the track, where the scarp drops almost as sheer as a sea-cliff, allowing my eyes to enjoy the pygmy life of the valley bottom, when I caught a flash of white near at hand and drawing in the focus of my gaze I saw that the slope at the top of the scarp was sewn with little rounds of white, mushrooms pitched there in scores like the tents of a military encampment. Dreamy and diffuse a moment before, now I was concentrated avarice. There is nothing in nature which so perfectly satisfies the collector's passion as these silky, tender-coloured thornless fungi—which make, besides, such succulent eating. I wound my Ordnance map into a cone and began to fill it with mushrooms, one foot far below the other on the steep slope. I thought of the samphire gatherer, but there was nothing dreadful in my occupation except its greediness. Afterwards as I walked back along the rampart top, I wondered for how many centuries the spores had been renewing themselves there, whether in some Iron Age autumn a Celtic picket (the camp was never permanently occupied) had been tempted as I had been and had dropped down from the wall to gather the remote ancestors of these fungi. My map of Cranborne Chase is still covered with brown stains and the paper is raised in blisters above the canvas backing.

Another three miles along the track one can stop at the site of the Iron Age settlement on Swallowcliffe Down and look due north across Swallowcliffe village to the Greensand hill, thick with trees, which is crowned by the strong earthwork of Castle Ditches. No one would make the descent and climb from this place, but it is easily reached from the valley road, as also is the overgrown fort of Castle Rings some miles further on at the eastern end of the Shaftesbury ridge.

From Swallowcliffe Down the walker can turn southward skirting the head of the little Ebble Valley until he comes to the great fort of Winkelbury, a place fortified by the Belgae on a commanding promontory already occupied early in the Iron Age. Winkelbury was one of the first sites in the Chase to be excavated by General Pitt-Rivers, and the mention of his name together with the near approach that we have now made to the main scenes of his later life and work as an archaeologist make it necessary to break my itinerary for a fresh beginning.

There are many regions of Britain where much of our knowledge of its prehistory is due to one man, but I do not know of any other in which the individual seems to dominate the countryside and its ancient history, to be of even greater significance than his own discoveries. In this I think that General Pitt-Rivers comes nearer to the artists and poets; as we associate Wordsworth with the Lake District, Constable with Suffolk, Crome with Norfolk and Hardy with Wessex, so Pitt-Rivers has been able to permeate and enrich the country of Cranborne Chase. He drew this power from a combination of personality, ability, rank and possessions. When after his army career he inherited Rushmore near Tollard Royal and its vast family estates he began the excavation and field survey which resulted in the publication between 1887 and 1898 of the four huge blue-and-gold volumes of *Excavations on Cranborne Chase*. They also resulted in the establishment of the private museum at Farnham—which can most easily be reached by turning to the right off the Salisbury-to-Blandford road—perhaps our only wholly rural museum and one which compares the material culture of modern primitives with that of the early inhabitants of Cranborne Chase. It is altogether in keeping with the General's personality that we should now be able to run off a lane on bare Wessex Downs and see some first-class Benin bronzes.

Pitt-Rivers's excavation, recording and publication were so good, so far in advance of his time, that he is generally accepted as the chief founder of scientific field work. Undoubtedly we remember and honour him for this, yet I do not believe he would still live in the Chase if he had not been an extraordinary character, if he had not cultivated strange plants and animals, exercized an eccentric personal tyranny over his tenants and assistants, and conducted his whole life with the unquestioned self-assurance possible to the lord of thousands of acres. Had he lived in the Middle Ages he would perhaps have become a legendary figure, the hero of many stories and with his name attached to antiquities or natural features of his countryside. Men no longer have the imagination which creates myths and legends, but somehow the old man has got under the skin of Cranborne Chase.

Although at Winkelbury we were already near Tollard and Farnham and many of the sites made famous by the General's excavations, it will, I think, be more practical to retreat and approach the area anew by the route most commonly used by visitors—the road running across the Chase from Salisbury to Blandford. This highway enters into a stretch of country charged with archaeological significance at the point where it crosses the Wiltshire-Dorset boundary and where it is for the first time joined by the Roman road to Dorchester. Near this place both ancient and modern highways first pass the spot where Pitt-Rivers excavated a Roman settlement, and then cut across the three-mile line of bank and ditch known as Bokerly Dyke. This dyke, though a modest affair when compared with Wansdyke, makes quite an impressive show where, on the left of the roads, it can be seen swinging uphill towards Pentridge and Tidpit Down. Pitt-Rivers was himself able to show that Bokerly Dyke is late Roman and subsequent work has proved that one section of it (roughly, that to the east of the roads) was built during the first half of the fourth century, that it was extended and even made to block the Roman road at a time of crisis, probably the great Pictish raids of 367 A.D., finally again strengthened and thrown across the road in the first years of the fifth century to defend the Province from barbarian attack. Although it now ends apparently inconclusively, there is no doubt that in the days before the Saxons, each terminal rested on forest and that it served as a barrier across this broad downland saddle. What was its purpose? Partly because of the large number of native Romano-British settlements and the extreme rarity of Roman villas on Salisbury Plain and Cranborne Chase it has been suggested that these were Imperial estates of a kind known elsewhere in the Empire, domains where the peasantry worked directly to produce grain, cattle, hides and other goods for the benefit of the central exchequer. If this is correct, it may be that Bokerly was intended to protect a particularly important part of the estate, while Woodyates, where quite exceptionally large numbers of coins were found, was a station for auxiliary troops looking after the Imperial domain. This is a bold interpretation of the evidence, but it is satisfying to relate these undistinguished banks and ditches, these small disturbances of the soil, with events which had their part in the decline and fall of the Roman Empire.

An even more impressive earthwork in this area, and one that belongs to an earlier period, is the Dorset Cursus, one of the largest and least known of the late Stone Age, early Bronze Age monuments in Britain. This Cursus, which is six miles in length and contains an area of two hundred and twenty acres, runs almost parallel to, and about half a mile to the south-east of, the A354 Salisbury–Blandford Forum road. The Cursus is a long narrow enclosure only some three hundred feet wide bounded on each side by a bank and an external ditch. It is associated with four long barrows and it has been suggested that the monument must have been connected with the cult of the dead. (At Stonehenge, also, the Cursus was associated with a long barrow). Certainly it served some ceremonial purpose and its sheer size, with all the effort involved in the moving of some six and a half million cubic feet of earth indicates the importance of this Cursus for the people who built it.

Continuing now along the Blandford road the traveller is reminded in the most dramatic fashion that from the crossing of Bokerly Dyke the modern road has been built on the very bank of the Roman one. Just after the side turning to Pentridge, even a motorist must notice how, as the tarmac he is following bends to the right, the Roman road shoots out from beneath it, running dead straight ahead, its central causeway and side ditches showing like a strong line ruled across the plateau.

Close behind Bokerly Dyke there were three long barrows, and here, between the emergent Roman road, the modern highway and the left-hand lane leading to Cranborne, there is a large and varied group of burial-mounds, including two further long barrows as well as examples of the bowl, bell and disk varieties. There are many long barrows near the line of the road, most on the south side, though the famous Wor Barrow is on Handley Down to the north. Among the rest, one of the two Thickthorn mounds lying between the Gussage and Crichel brooks has been duly dated to the New Stone Age. In spite of the danger of a surfeit of barrows in the diet provided by the Salisbury–Blandford road, I must mention one more for it is quite the finest of all—and indeed perhaps the finest earthen long barrow in the whole country. This is the Pimperne barrow which is reached by a green road turning off to the right soon after the village of Tarrant Hinton. At first sight the great length of its narrow grassy spine looks like a section of a dyke, but inspection shows the true long barrow plan, the eastern end being broader and higher than the other and the sides enclosed by flanking ditches. An excavation worthy of such a monument would be very costly, but it must some day be undertaken for it seems likely that this mound, so little disturbed, may still cover intact burials and other remains which would tell us much that is new concerning the way the New Stone Age peoples constructed their tombs and performed their funerary rituals.

From Pimperne there are only a few downhill miles to Blandford Forum, a town which the happy synchronization during the eighteenth century of flowering genius in two local architects (the brothers Bastard) with the opportunity offered by a catastrophic fire, has made one of the most graceful country towns in England. I do not, however, propose immediately to descend upon Blandford, but to make another of the retreats, the zigzags in my itinerary, which are so irritating but absolutely necessary if I am to do what certain academic persons call 'covering the ground'.

This retreat is upon Salisbury, in order to advance again down the more southerly part of the Chase and the adjoining countryside west of the Avon. Close by Salisbury there is nothing of great note; Little Woodbury, famous among archaeologists as the site of an already classic excavation of an Early Iron Age farmstead, is visible only from the air, while just on the other side of the Ebble, Clearbury Ring is not a very impressive fort in spite of its fine natural position on a hill filling the angle between Ebble and Avon. Four miles south of Clearbury is the much larger Whitsbury Castle Ditches, an oval camp with three lines of ramparts. Though only enthusiasts will wish to follow its course, it is worth mentioning the meandering dyke known as Grims Ditch, one portion of which runs from Clearbury to Whitsbury while the longer section runs due westward crossing the Blandford road where we might have noticed it just to the north of Bokerly Dyke. It is more ancient than Bokerly, probably having been constructed by immigrant farmers in the Late Bronze Age. On the barren stretches of Rockbourne Down in the angle of Grims Ditch there are an extensive Romano–British enclosure, an Iron Age farm site and several round barrows. South of Rockbourne there is a rather feeble fort, with ramparts lacking any special features, on Damerham Knoll and another beyond it on Pentridge or Pembury Knoll. South-west again is Soldier's Ring, a site most perversely named for it is a kite-shaped enclosure whose straight, deftly-cut sides and sharp angles help to betray its Roman date. It is comparable with the enclosure already mentioned on Rockbourne Down, and both are believed to be Roman pastoral compounds, probably connected with the farming of the Imperial estate (p. 129).

All these places are of minor importance and to be visited only by those with time to spare, but now at Knowlton on the country road from Wimborne St. Giles to Wimborne we are approaching a most remarkable group of monuments and one of which I, personally, have haunted memories. The Knowlton Circles include typical henges, and might indeed be recognized as representing the Avebury or Stonehenge of Cranborne Chase. Only one of the four sanctuaries is sufficiently well preserved to make an impressive spectacle, yet there is, or so it seemed to to me at my first visit, some peculiar influence in the air of the place, an influence which, as it is certainly not altogether agreeable, might truly be called a taint. Perhaps places where men have felt intensely or acted violently never quite rid themselves of the effects; perhaps such feelings are created only in the imagination of later beholders—yet even so their survival is real. The one circle (and it was not originally by any means the largest) which has not been flattened by ploughing, has high banks and two entrances recalling a small Roman amphitheatre—and indeed we shall find at Maumbury Rings near Dorchester a henge sanctuary actually adapted as an amphitheatre in Roman times. Yet at Knowlton the historical drama enacted in the central arena has been a very different one. This circular space where there must once have been a setting of posts or, more probably, of standing stones, is now occupied by the ruined shell of a Gothic church, a small church with square tower and nave built in a simple country fashion. The nave is partly choked with bushes and the tower embraced by heavy masses of ivy; when I was first there, standing within the roofless nave on a brooding, oppressive late afternoon, a white barn owl suddenly dropped from the ivy with that creaking sound, made, I believe, vocally and not, as it appears, by the wings, which seems to enhance the soft, quilted silence in which the bird will then drift away. No scene could come nearer to the romantic ideal than this where the ruins of two religions guard the bird of ill-omen in an ivy-covered tower, and where, moreover, there lingers in the air some flavour of the sinister and macabre. I know nothing of the history of this lonely church, but when in the twelfth century a Christian cleric saw fit to have it built and consecrated, it must surely have been because the country people still gave to the sanctuary some of the *mana* with which it had originally been invested, and still went there for purposes which the Church could not countenance.

In this enchanted neighbourhood even round barrows are not simple round barrows. The very large one, thickly furred with trees, standing to the east of the Circle, has been shown by aerial photography once to have stood within a wide precinct enclosed by a ring-ditch.

From Knowlton I want to move quickly southward to survey the forts along the Stour Valley which marks the south-western limits of Cranborne Chase. Those who wish to go on foot should bear to the west until they join the Roman road to Dorchester—the same road which we last saw leaving the Salisbury–Blandford road near Pentridge—and follow it to the very walls of the lovely and imposing fort of Badbury Rings. The Roman road is wonderfully preserved in this area, the central causeway is thirteen yards wide, but with its side banks and ditches the overall width is as much as forty yards. There is no doubt that although not a town, Badbury was inhabited in Roman times and served as a port of call for travellers. Because of its Roman associations it was long thought that the three barrows which stand by the Roman roadside just west of the fort were Roman too. Recent excavation of one of these barrows, however, showed it to belong to the Bronze Age and it thus seems likely that the neighbouring barrows are of the same period. However, at Knob's Crook, at the southern edge of Cranborne Chase, six miles north-west of Ringwood and close to the village of Woodlands, a Roman barrow of unusual interest has been excavated. Not only was the barrow of early date in the Roman period between 70 and 85 A.D. but the occupant's skull had been neatly trepanned. Although it could not be conclusively proved, it is likely that in this instance death had resulted from this primitive form of head surgery.

Badbury itself is a strongly fortified Iron Age camp, oval in plan with two massive inner ramparts and a third, considerably weaker, enclosing them at a little distance. It is made a conspicuous landmark for miles around by a neat circular clump of trees on the summit, while a capping of loam has encouraged the growth of brushwood over most of the interior. One original entrance is to the east, but what appears to be a more important one lies on the broader, western side where a detached length of rampart protects the opening.

Advancing up the Stour Valley towards Blandford we come to Buzbury Rings on a hill above the small tributary stream, the Tarrant. It is a double enclosure rather weakly defended but with the marks of hut floors showing very clearly in the small inner compound. From the Tarrant it is about three miles to Blandford where we shall find all the graces of the eighteenth century but no antiquities. On the other side of the town, however, a few miles further up the Stour, we come to two camps delightful to visit and most noble specimens of Iron Age military architecture. They will form a fitting place from which to leave the rich and hallowed archaeological territories of Cranborne Chase.

Even the names of Hod and Hambledon hill-forts seem designed to make them as inseparable a pair as Castor and Pollux—in contrast with those other twin forts, Battlesbury and Scratchbury whose names are both harsh and incompatible! Certainly geographical history has conspired to unite them, for they occupy closely adjacent hills together isolated from the main massif of the Chase by the little Iwerne, a tributary stream which joins the Stour immediately to the south of Hod Hill. Thus both camps may be said to guard the entry of the Stour into the broad belt of the Dorset chalk. Anyone who has the habit of identifying forms in chance configurations, whether these are the features of nature or stains on the ceiling, will find good material in the relief map of these hills. With the north duly set to the top, to me it seems obvious that Hod Hill represents the powerful square head of a beast snapping at Hambledon which is a turtle-dove rising in alarm with its big tail outspread just beyond the reach of the open jaws of its pursuer. Whether or no others will follow me in this identification, I believe it would be hard to find anyone who would not be moved by the beauty and historical harmonies of this fragment of Dorset. The valleys of the Iwerne and Stour are cheerful with villages and vegetation; straight out of their charming prettiness rise the heroic masses of the two hills, each fringed with woodland along its lower slopes but mounting to bare rounded crests above.

Approaching from the south, it is Hod Hill that we reach first. This, as we have seen, is a squarish hill with a level top, and the ramparts, following the contours, also assume a roughly rectangular plan. On three sides there are triple banks, but to the west where the Stour and the steep scarp above it make an almost impregnable natural barrier, the builders felt able to save labour by reducing their number to two. The finest of the original entrances is near the western end of the south side where a track must have led up from the valley; the ramparts are inturned and the inner one, prodigiously steep, even to-day still stands over forty feet above the bottom of the ditch. Modern excavation has yielded a fascinating, if somewhat grim, glimpse of the end of this fort. Like Maiden Castle (p. 138) it was one of the strongholds which the Roman general Vespasian took by storm during his march westwards following the initial invasion of 43 A.D. Such hill-forts, so impregnable to native forces and resources, were terribly vulnerable to the Roman artillery of ballistae and catapults. An examination of the spread of Roman missiles found at the site made it possible for the excavators not only to estimate the positions on which the Romans had set up their artillery but also what had constituted their main targets. In comparison slingstones piled beside the huts within the fort, represent the weakness of the British 'artillery', which was one of the reasons why the Roman legions could defeat numerically superior native forces. The immediate sequel to the capitulation of the defenders can be seen in the north-west corner of the site where a rectangular earthwork was laid out with all the precision of a military textbook converting this section of the native British stronghold into a Roman fort. Here the garrison was a mixed force of legionary troops (infantry) and cavalry. It was maintained only for some seven or eight years until this mild southern country had been pacified and the armies were pressing on against the stubborn resistance of the west and north.

Hambledon Hill is a far more complex site and its history a longer one. From Hod Hill it is reached by dropping down to the pretty lane which runs from Steepleton Iwerne to Child Okeford and climbing up the eastern outer tail-feather of the dove. On its body, that is to say at the junction of the four promontories making Hambledon Hill, there are traces, so faint as to be hard to distinguish, of a simple ringwork, which is the earliest earthwork on either of the two hills. Recent excavations have dated it to the New Stone Age; as a Neolithic enclosure on the site of a great Iron Age fort it can be compared with those at Hembury and Maiden Castle. Immediately beyond it, on the long northern spur occupying what corresponds to the upper breast, outstretched neck and head of my bird, we find the fort of Hambledon proper, a magnificent stronghold with three tiers of ramparts defending an area of about twenty-five acres. Crossing a strong outlying barrier which gives additional protection against enemies advancing along this level neck, we can go through the south-eastern entrance and find a convenient vantage-point on the round barrow which stands a little way inside. This southern part of the fort is probably the area most recently enclosed, for it appears that in an earlier phase the defences ended with the more southerly of the two cross-banks that can still be seen traversing the narrow strip of the fort and dividing it into three segments. Crossing this southern transverse bank (it has been partially levelled, probably when the southern extension was made) we come upon a long barrow lying along the central ridge, a position which makes it a conspicuous landmark for many miles. After the northern transverse bank, even fainter than the other, the ridge swells again into a wider headland with splendid prospects up the Stour Valley and westward as far as the Mendips. So we have walked the length of Hambledon fort, all the way within the protection of its massive three-fold defences. In half a mile we have passed monuments from the Stone Age, the Bronze Age and at least three phases of the Iron Age; looking back to Hod Hill we can see the neat mechanical handiwork of the Roman legionaries who, by force of arms, brought an end to prehistoric Britain.

E. *Dorset* (*Outside Cranborne Chase*)

The great expanse of brick and respectability which sterilizes the Bournemouth region encourages us to renew our journey from the Isle of Purbeck. The ridge of chalk which runs along it is the direct continuation of that of the Isle of Wight, and one cannot but see its slender termination at Studland as a hand held longingly out to grasp that of the Needles which however, remains out of reach as if the island has voyaged away, carried by its white sails. The alternative name for this promontory is, I see from the map, Handfast Point.

The Isle of Purbeck with its well-known picturesque setting for Corfe Castle is, in truth, of far greater interest for those who seek the remains of later history. Nevertheless this stretch of Nine Barrows Down has an exceptionally fine group of round barrows, the largest of them affording a last view of the pale wedge of the Isle of Wight floating on the blue boundary of sea and sky. About a mile east of Corfe there is a single long barrow and a stone circle. Nor, after passing Corfe, can I ignore Kimmeridge whose native black shale was exploited in the Iron Age and later for a highly specialized manufacture—that of bracelets. These ornaments, widely exported, were turned on a simple pole lathe, and even to-day the shale disks which fell from the centre of the bracelets turn up in the soil. The villagers who found them naturally did not at first suspect them of being the wasters of prehistoric industry, and gave them the name of Kimmeridge coal money, thinking them to be the currency of some fairy population.

Indeed, in this immediate neighbourhood there have been several of the close and particular relationships which make such a fascinating part of the interplay between a people and its land. Of these the use of Kimmeridge shale is the earliest, then follows that of Purbeck marble, a limestone built up of the shells of millions of freshwater snails which lived and died in a shallow Jurassic lake. This dark marble, with the shapes of its unwitting creators showing as clearly within it as they can ever have shown beneath the waters of the lake, was greatly sought after by early medieval builders and appears in a hundred places, including the slender shafts of the Salisbury Cathedral lancets. Then, just across Weymouth Bay is Portland, the island which in the late seventeenth and eighteenth centuries became a huge quarry as its fine, pale oolitic stone was taken for building after building—on the greatest scale for St. Paul's Cathedral which for a time enjoyed a monopoly of its resources. It offered the perfect medium for the expression of the severely restrained magnificence of English classical architecture.

By following the coastline westwards we come upon an unusual site in a particularly striking setting. The earthworks on Binton Hill consist of a bank and ditch extending for nearly two miles to enclose Lulworth, the only natural all-weather harbour for miles around. Their interest lies in the fact that they appear to protect the harbour against attack from inland. It has been suggested that these earthworks are the remains of a transit camp or beach-head probably established by some groups of Early Iron Age settlers coming into Britain.

Returning to the Downs and following them until the chalk edges right up to the sea, a strenuous pull up the cliff path will bring the traveller to Flower Barrow Camp. Its strange double ramparts form a bow with its ends resting on the cliff edge above Worbarrow Bay. The earthworks are perfect and lofty enough to make this an example of Iron Age architecture worthy of its magnificent natural setting. Just north of Osmington is the last and largest of our chalk-cut white horses—a beast unique also in the possession of a rider and in being so placed as to be best viewed from the sea. This equestrian effigy in the flat is certainly to be connected with a royal patron of Weymouth, George III, whom the municipality also honoured by a fantastic statue on the promenade and by providing the bathing women of the town with belts on which *God Save the King* was embroidered in gold. Hardy was probably right, however, when in *The Trumpet Major* he implied that its cutting was more immediately inspired as a commemoration of the battle of Trafalgar. I confess to a great fondness for these chalk figures, otherwise there is nothing but the tenuous connection with their famous sire at Uffington to excuse their inclusion in this book.

After following the ridgeway on White Horse Hill past a cluster of round barrows to the north of Sutton Poyntz, it is very well worth while to leave it and walk south for a mile to visit the camp of Chalbury with its splendid view across Weymouth Bay to Portland and along the sweep of Chesil Bank. In so doing it is impossible not to notice the dramatic geological change as one crosses the fault between the chalk and the limestone. Chalbury itself is stone-built; its single rampart was originally faced with large slabs set on edge and reinforced with masonry. Even now the tops of many of these blocks can be seen projecting through the turf. some of the larger circular depressions inside the fort have been proved to mark the sites of substantial round huts with stone wall foundations and roughly paved floor. There was a good deal of evidence in the rubbish found among them to suggest that even as late as the Iron Age some form of cannibalism was practised in Britain. The inhabitants were certainly akin to the earliest builders of Maiden Castle, but Chalbury was abandoned much earlier in the Iron Age and so shows no sign of the extraordinary elaboration of the defences carried out by the later conquerors of Maiden Castle.

That astonishing fortress must be our next main objective, but first on returning to the ridgeway the clusters of barrows east of Came Wood should be noticed as well as the Culliford long barrow which lies north of a conspicuous tree-set round barrow known as Culliford Tree. The ridgeway soon strikes the Dorchester–Weymouth road and on the far side of this highway about a mile towards Dorchester the colossal ramparts of Maiden Castle can be seen enclosing a hill which lies a little to the north of the main crest of the Downs. To say that Maiden Castle is the greatest of our hill-forts is quite insufficient. To me it seems to differ in kind from all its rivals except perhaps, Hambledon Hill. The colossal scale of the quadruple ramparts, the flexibility with which in spite of this bulk they follow the contours of a shapely hill, the fantastical and decorative elaboration of the two entrances, make Maiden Castle at least as much a work of art as the finest medieval fortifications. Indeed, when seen from the air it has the quality of sculpture or of moulding, a creation very appropriate to the Celtic peoples who were capable of superb curvilinear abstract design and of the powerful moulded forms shown in their armour, horse trappings and other bronzes. Here they were carving in the noble medium of the English chalk.

Maiden Castle carries a long history behind the present visible structure. Completely obliterated by the Iron Age fortifications are the ditches of a New Stone Age enclosure of the 'causewayed' kind which yielded among the usual litter of flint, pottery and bones a very rough image of the Mother Goddess. This compound was already abandoned when later Stone Age peoples raised above it a ritual structure probably comparable to the 'Cursus' near Stonehenge, a pair of parallel ditches running just along the hill-top but now, like the compound, quite invisible on the ground. At one end of it a corpse had been buried apparently after a religious feast; the limbs had been dismembered and, after several unsuccessful attempts, the skull broken open for the extraction of the brain. Although from many places and different ages we have evidence suggesting that our ancestors ate human flesh, this solemn interment at Maiden Castle is our only certain record of its practice as a ritual act.

For perhaps some sixteen or seventeen hundred years the hill-top seems to have been unoccupied. It was not, however, unused. There are several round barrows near the fort, including the Clandon barrow on the north-west side where it must surely have been a chieftain who was buried with an amber cup and ornaments of gold. No doubt, too, the Bronze Age herdsmen allowed their cattle and sheep to crop over the banks and hollows of the long-derelict Stone Age earthworks. Then, quite early in the Iron Age, in the third or fourth century B.C., Celtic tribesmen established a small stronghold there, enclosing the eastern summit in a single bank and ditch. These ramparts were of the kind we have found to be characteristic of the earlier Iron Age; banks of chalk supported on a wooden framework and held almost vertical between revetment walls. Later, as numbers and wealth increased, the single defences were enlarged to enclose the whole of the long, slightly waisted outline of the hill. Still there was nothing exceptional about Maiden Castle; it was one of very many defended hill-tops of the day. In the last century B.C. an invading Celtic people who may have been Venetic refugees from Caesar's campaigns in Brittany (p. 56), took possession of the fort, and, with the Belgae perhaps already threatening from the east, undertook the stupendous multiplication of the defences whose results we have inherited. The great depth of protection secured here by several lines of rampart, and found at this time on a smaller scale at so many other Wessex forts, is believed to have been designed to meet a new weapon—the sling. Simple though these leather slings were, their range of up to a hundred yards was vastly greater than that of the spears which hitherto had been the chief offensive weapon. Once adopted, they were used for defence as well as offence. At Maiden Castle pebbles from Chesil Bank served as sling-stones, and dumps of over twenty thousand were found buried behind the ramparts—ammunition never used by defenders already defeated. For, as is well known, this fortress, the strong-est of its kind in Europe and a perpetual monument to the military engineering of the Celts, did not prove impregnable. It did not prevent the whole territory from falling under Belgic domination, nor, finally, could it be held against the Romans. It was stormed, probably in 45 A.D., by that Second Legion whose triumphant campaign across southern England was led by a general later to become the Emperor Vespasian. The dramatic events of that storming have recently been recalled to mind after nearly two thousand years of oblivion. In the level space within the maze of earthworks protecting the eastern gateways, the excavators stumbled upon a war cemetery—a huddle of graves where women as well as men had been buried with their death-wounds upon them—hurriedly, perhaps by night. That these bodies were in truth those of slaughtered

Britons was proved by the vessels containing food and drink, which in spite of the haste had been buried beside them. That their conquerors had been Romans was confirmed by what to me is one of the most dramatic, the most moving discoveries ever to have been made in this country. In one of the skeletons the iron head of a Roman dart was found embedded in the spine. Here is the point of history striking suddenly, brutally, into the prehistoric life of our island.

Although after the sack the Roman authorities saw to it that the new tribal capital was established at Dorchester, two miles to the north-east on the banks of the Frome, one later event has left its traces at Maiden Castle. For some reason never to be known, a Late Roman temple was built inside the ramparts, its foundations resting on the grass-grown floors and storage pits of the prehistoric settlement.

Just to the right of the road between Maiden Castle and Dorchester is a monument very much less conspicuous than the fort but with an even longer history. This is Maumbury Rings, a substantial, circular bank with a pair of opposing entrances. The main bulk of these banks was piled up nearly four thousand years ago at the end of the New Stone Age or early in the Bronze Age, to enclose a sanctuary which must have resembled a much smaller Avebury. When the Roman town was established at Dorchester the town council would have been expected to follow custom and provide an amphitheatre where the citizens could enjoy such spectacles as the fighting of men and animals, interspersed, perhaps, by an occasional drama. There, less than a mile from the town and on an existing road, were the banks of the forgotten sanctuary — circular, it is true, where amphitheatres should be oval, but representing a considerable saving of labour and expense. So they were adapted for the new purpose by a people who had no notion that remote ancestors had met there for religious observances that may have been dark and barbarous but were certainly more significant than anything which they themselves could stage. As though they were to serve in turn all the main purposes of man, these banks which had played their part for religion and for pleasure were now to be given over to war. In 1643, only a slightly shorter period of time than had divided their secular from their religious use, the Parliamentary forces besieging Dorchester used Maumbury Rings to mount their heavy artillery. The platforms flattened out for the reception of the guns are still plainly visible. In another three centuries we of this generation were again to employ them for military ends. When I was last there they were still serving as an abutment to the already slightly decrepit concrete blocks which had been made so hastily in 1940 in our gallant but often amateurish efforts to defend ourselves against invasion. It is, I think, as well that the banks raised with deer-horn picks and bone shovels (still to be seen in Dorchester Museum) never had to withstand the impact of charging German tanks.

At Dorchester very little of the Roman town is still visible although one interesting sidelight on the activities carried out in *Durnovaria* is known. In the third and fourth centuries a 'school' of mosaicists established itself here and examples of their work, recognizable on stylistic grounds, have been uncovered in the villas of the surrounding countryside, such as Frampton, Hinton St. Mary, Low Ham and Lufton. But if the modern town of Dorchester is lacking in visible remains of its earliest origins these can be seen in the museum which is a model of its kind, containing quantities of prehistoric material, including gold and amber from the Clandon barrow, all admirably shown, as well as collections illustrating the history of Roman *Durnovaria*.

It is worth going just outside the town to Poundbury not only to see the Early Iron Age fort which may have been established before even the first Celtic fortification of Maiden Castle, but also in the hope of finding a monument rare in this well-watered country—the embankment of an aqueduct which once supplied *Durnovaria*. This aqueduct which probably had its intake some miles up the Frome at Notton can best be seen by looking up the valley from the north-west corner of Poundbury where it shows like an embanked shelf running round the adjacent slope of the hill. It represents a remarkable piece of engineering, the twelve-mile long aqueduct channel following a circuitous route to maintain a steady downhill gradient with a measured fall of two feet per mile from source to delivery point. After the Romans left it was to be many centuries before such regular water supplies were again to be provided in Britain's towns.

The downland stretching away from Dorchester as far as Cranborne Chase is not rich in antiquity; there are round barrows, of course, and a long barrow on Smacam Down east of Sydling St. Nicholas, otherwise the finest treasures are the names of its villages—Piddletrenthide, Puddletown, Affpuddle and the famous Tolpuddle itself. There is, however, one unique monument as interesting in its implication of the continuity and conservatism of rural life as anything in the country. This is the famous, the notorious, Cerne Abbas Giant, a hill figure cut on a westward-facing slope of the Downs only a quarter of a mile from the village on the north-west side. The Giant is roughly naturalistic in style and appears to be stepping towards the right while brandishing a huge, heavily-knobbed club in his right hand. Like the Long Man of Wilmington, but unlike most other hill figures, the Cerne Giant is drawn in outline, an outline formed by a chalk-filled trench about two feet wide and two feet deep. This technique has allowed the representation of internal features, including facial features (with the nose modelled in relief), nipples, ribs shown with a Rouault-like emphasis, and the erect phallus and testicles which are the source of so much interest and so little open comment. The proportions are truly gigantic; the height of the figure is 180 feet, the club is 120 feet long and the phallus measures thirty feet. In the drawing reproduced in the *Gentleman's Magazine* of 1764, the earliest known portrait, the navel is strongly marked; this has now become overgrown but can still be faintly distinguished in air photographs. Near the top of the hill and immediately above the Giant's raised left arm is an unusual enclosure known locally as the Frying Pan; it has a double bank and ditch, very roughly rectangular in plan and measuring a hundred feet by seventy-five feet. What is highly interesting and significant about the Frying Pan is that until quite recent years it was used annually for maypole dancing on May Day, a celebration which throughout Europe is frankly concerned with fertility, the pole symbolizing at once the phallus and the tree.

There are no very early references to the Giant, but there are legends which suggest that its existence was known but deliberately held secret. William of Malmesbury recounts a legend concerning the foundation of Cerne Abbey which can hardly be irrelevant. It tells how when St. Augustine arrived with other missionaries to convert the Dorset heathen, they were violently received, tails were tied to their garments and they were driven ignominiously away. The saint called God to his help to provide all children born in the village with tails until such time as the parents should repent of their paganism. This, the legend says, they soon did, St. Augustine returning by invitation and founding an abbey which he called Cernal because he had there seen God (Latin, *cerno,* I see, and Hebrew *El,* God)! This tale, already highly suggestive, is brought closer to the Giant by Walter of Coventry, writing in the thirteenth century. He describes the same extraordinary events, but after mentioning Cerne and saying that it is in Dorset he adds, 'In which district the god Helith was once worshipped'. Next Camden states that Augustine founded Cerne Abbey to celebrate having 'broken in pieces Heil the idol of the heathen English Saxons', while Gibson, Camden's seventeenth-century editor, was the first to identify Heil with the Cerne Giant. In 1764 Stukeley declared that the Giant was known locally as Helis. These legends, records, local names, all harmonize admirably with the history and interpretation suggested by the figure itself. The Giant with his knobbed club suggests Hercules;

the undistinguished naturalism of the work would be appropriate to provincial Roman British art; there are Roman bronze representations of a club-bearing Hercules remarkably like the Cerne figure; it is possible to link the name Helith by way of the 'wild hunter' Helethkin or Herle with Hercules (curiously enough another line of derivations connects the Roman god with Harlequin). Thus there is a very good case indeed for believing that this outline was cut on its Dorset hillside during the Roman occupation, possibly towards the end of the second century when the Emperor Commodus was deliberately reviving the cult of Hercules. Yet from the beginning the fertility element was strong, and the Roman god must have been partly identified, as so often happened, with some local cult or notion, let us say with a British Priapus, whose symbol was added unto Hercules, and whose power and significance were, inevitably, to prove the most enduring among a peasant population.

Here at Cerne, as at Uffington, what strikes most deeply into the imagination is the realization that for more than a millennium and a half, country people have kept this figure in being, defending it against the steady encroachment of grass and weeds. Indeed, the survival of the Giant is more astonishing than that of the White Horse, partly because of the more delicate and tenuous form, a mere line on the turf, but still more for his unashamed paganism, the frank assertion of a symbol which for at least thirteen centuries of his existence must have given violent offence to the supposed faith of those who tended it. It is an added triumph that it is not only the parish priest he has had to overrule; for nearly a thousand years he was the near neighbour of Cerne Abbey. Now he is no longer served by true followers, for his maintenance has become the responsibility of the National Trust. Nothing could be more fitting to the age, yet perhaps even reason and officialdom will not altogether succeed where Christianity failed; it is said that young girls are still not beyond seeking the Giant's aid by an occasional visit, or even by a night spent on the hillside.

Cerne Abbas has certainly saved the country to the north of Dorchester from sterility, but it is the upland area to the west of the Down, between the Maiden Newton road and the sea, which is far richer in antiquities— although of a less unusual kind. There are in fact three circles of standing stones in this small area, and among the eleven long barrows several have megalithic burial-chambers. It would, in fact, be an excellent place in which to study the relationship between the earthern long barrow of the Wessex and Sussex kind and the chambered long barrow of the west, a relationship which still baffles archaeology.

By far the most enjoyable part of this area is the stretch of Down which runs from the south of Maiden Castle (where we left the ridgeway on the Weymouth road) to the sea near Swyre. It is a ridge with wonderful prospects along the coast and where, with a telescope, one might watch the wild elegance of life in the famous swannery at Abbotsbury and where, too, at the Hardy Monument on Blackdown one can do honour to Thomas Masterman Hardy, Nelson's friend, who is commemorated here because his family home was at Portisham. Among innumerable round and a few long barrows, the most interesting antiquities on these Downs are the Hell Stone, a chambered long barrow north-east of Portisham whose fine megaliths have been rebuilt in a picturesque if incorrect fashion, the remains of a stone circle on Hampton Down a little further west, and a second chambered long barrow, more gently named—the Grey Mare and her Colts—which occupies a most lovely position on the hill overlooking Abbotsbury. Finally, turning a mile inland, there is a larger and better-preserved ring of standing stones on a spur above the village of Little Bredy.

Although its pleasures cannot be compared with those of the marine ridgeway, the Dorchester-to-Bridport high road passes quite a throng of prehistoric remains. Near Winterborne Abbas (where the Roman road leaves the modern one and heads for Eggardon Hill), there is the Pound long barrow on the right and two others, those of Longlands and Winterborne Steepleton, on the left; just between them and close beside the high road stands the Nine Stones, the last of this group of West Dorset stone circles.

Further on, round and beyond Kingston Russell, the Ordnance map is enough to show the concentration of minor sites; particular mention might be made of the long barrow and other interesting earthworks on Martin's Down and the earthen circle, probably a sacred enclosure, opposite the turning to Litton Cheyney.

I should be reluctant to leave the chalk of southern England, the downland whose ample plains, whose nobly rounded hills and combes, have been found to carry so many of the marks of prehistoric life and so many, too, of its most famous monuments, with this poor catalogue of wayside relics. One ancient site still remains which does in fact stand on the last bastion of the chalk, and offers a worthy parting place. Fortunately no motor road approaches closely to Eggardon Hill; the nearest is at Askerswell, but any unhurried traveller will do far better to use the Roman road, either following it from its first parting from the main road before Winterbourne Abbas or joining it north of Kingston Russel. This road keeps along high ground for mile after mile, rarely dropping below the six-hundred-foot contour line. As it approaches Eggardon it passes standing stones on its right and then enters the high narrow crest on which five promontories converge. It is impressive here, and in many lights sombre enough for some fatal Hardy backcloth. It seems ancient and remote. The tracks leading in from their five spurs run together among a scatter of round barrows. Standing on the crest there is no difficulty in picturing an England without railways or metalled roads where all thoroughfares were as simple, as lonely, as those at this lofty cross-roads. Straight ahead rise the tiered ramparts of Eggardon, a magnificent Iron Age fort on the westernmost of all the spurs, a promontory which passes eight hundred feet at its highest point. From this summit there is a superb outlook towards the west country, the chalk drops sheer away from the western ramparts and there is no more of it; this pure deposit of the Cretaceous seas which has carried us all the way from the white cliffs of Dover has come to an end; there is no more chalk between us and America. Instead we are looking down upon a charmingly diversified landscape of limestone mingled with Greensand; some of the abrupt, perky little hills, so unlike the slow curve of the chalk, are crowned with woodland or tufts of trees and recall those miniature blue-green worlds which show over the shoulder of the Virgin Mary or in other background crannies of Italian paintings. For me Wessex ends with the chalk, and at Eggardon the West Country begins.

Chapter Five

THE SOUTH-WEST

A. WEST DORSET AND EAST DEVON
B. BATH, BRISTOL AND THE MENDIPS
C. THE QUANTOCKS, EXMOOR AND DARTMOOR
D. CORNWALL

MANY people, I know, would include West Dorset and even East Devon and parts of Somerset in Wessex, but to me they belong wholly to the south-west, while Wessex must always remain the white land of the southern chalk.

On the other hand, it cannot be denied that the South-West, when so widely defined, does fall into two parts. First all that country which is geologically middle-aged; the Gault and Greensand of west Dorset with the mysterious smoky Blue Lias which is exposed at Lyme Regis in a crumbling cliff full of ammonites, belemnites and many of the grotesque reptiles of the Jurassic world in which it was formed. Here already one finds country characteristic of the west, bare uplands with small valleys, intensely fertile valleys, which in the spring seem like panniers lined with moss and fern, and spilling over with kingcups, bluebells, primroses, anemones, daffodils, all those flowers of the stream, the sheltered copse and meadow which have been so often praised by our poets that their very names can be heard singing. To this division also belongs all Somerset between the Mendips and the Quantocks, much of it young alluvial land, and that part of east Devon which is as red as a cow, a redness left in its sandstones and marls by the desert sun of Permian times.

For the rest the main body of the South-West is made up of ancient rocks which relate it to the highland country of Wales and the North; there is, however, one influential distinction between them, the rocky plateaux and valleys of this peninsula have never been carved or ground by ice, for throughout the Ice Age they lay clear of it, well beyond the edge of the glaciers. Their structure, with ridge and valley running east and west, is due to folding during the second great age of mountain-building, that so-called Armorican upheaval which immediately followed the formation of our coal measures. It is good exercize for the imagination while walking along some deep Devon lane with a flowery stream flowing down through the hazels, to think how this delicious, this paradisical crevice between hills was created by grim upheaval at a time when fishes were still the dominant population and the highest form which life had achieved. The upheaval pressed the rocks against the resistant mass of the Welsh mountains and the result was the sharp folding of the strata often so conspicuous on the coasts, for example in the extraordinary zig-zag pleating visible in the cliff and foreshore at Bude in Cornwall. The main upland areas, areas where we shall find the remains of prehistoric activity to be greatest, are the Mendips, composed of an ancient and very hard variety of limestone, the Quantock Hills and Exmoor of a yet older dark-coloured sandstone, and Dartmoor, Bodmin Moor, St. Austell and other moorland, all of them granite masses which are in fact no more than the denuded roots of the lofty mountains built at that remote time. Perhaps the most interesting region of all, and the most ancient, is round the Lizard headland of Cornwall where rocks laid down long before the first faint shapings of life have been tossed about in confusion and mingled with such volcanic outpourings as the famous Lizard serpentine, now cut and polished into a litter of useless ash-trays, bowls and candlesticks.

Approaching the South-West, as we have, from Wessex, we enter first into the lowland country of mild yet sudden hills and wide, wooded vales which we looked down upon from that last crest of the chalk, the fortified mass of Eggardon Hill.

In this part of Dorset and Devon there are, indeed, very few antiquities for its Greensand and Lias were heavily forested in early times. There are, however, some marks of Iron Age settlement. The road from Beaminster to Axminster follows high ground and soon after Broadwindsor it climbs towards its highest point where it runs below the steep brow of Pilsdon Pen, a hill which passes nine hundred feet and whose heather-and-bracken-covered ridge in many lights makes it a forbidding presence in this pre-dominantly green and tender countryside. The southern end of the Pen immediately above the road is defended by the ramparts of a strong Iron Age camp with its main entrance on the north, this being elaborately fortified as a protection against attack along the level ridge. The outlook from the ramparts is extraordinarily fine; westward one can turn back to the chalk scarp, to the north the Axe winds through its prosperous valley, while to the south one commands the wide trough of Marshwood Vale whose little woods and tree-filled hedges still give it something of the forested look which must have been familiar to the Celts who built and held these ramparts. Beyond the pretty irregularities of the coastline between Bridport and Lyme Regis (a pretty English coast that one could hardly suspect of sheltering so many savage monsters, the ichthyosaurs and other reptiles of the Lias), the sea is clearly visible whether it shows as a shining blade lighter than the sky or as a dark blue rod laid against it. At the western end of the Vale, it is possible to distinguish another fort, Lambert's Castle, close by the village of Marshwood, while beyond again Musbury overlooks the mouth of the Axe.

After Pilsdon Pen there is little that is worth a visit on the near side of Honiton, although for those who may have time to while away in this most agreeable country, I will name Membury and Stockland Great Camp to the north of the road, and to the south the round barrows on Gittisham and Farway hills and on Broad Down, Blackbury Castle, and Sidbury Castle which occupies one of the line of headlands, regular as buttresses which tributary streams have cut along the western bank of the Sid. Four miles beyond Honiton on the Cullompton road, is a site pleasant to visit, spectacular, and of very great interest in our prehistory. This is the fort of Hembury which tops a hill immediately above the road rather like a milder and more wooded Pilsdon. The two are, indeed, very similar, both of them long oval forts occupying the southern extremity of yet longer ridges—but Hembury is the more interesting because it has been excavated. An easy path leads up through trees and the far side of the hill is also extensively wooded; the interior of the fort, and in some places the ramparts themselves, are covered with bracken which in summer and autumn makes a breast-high sea of green or tawny orange all but swamping the fortifications. Particularly is this true at the far, northern end where a particularly fine inturned entrance leads in through a slight hollow down which the bracken seems to swirl like a whirlpool. Excavation proved, quite unexpectedly, that like the Trundle and (as was later discovered) Maiden Castle, the Iron Age ramparts overlie a New Stone Age enclosure with a causewayed plan; such an association immediately links this flat-topped, heathy, Greensand hill with the smooth rounded contour of the Wessex chalk. Unlike its Wessex counterparts, however, this Devon camp has been shown to possess at least one hut site, the remains of a fairly substantial building. Although Hembury, the most westerly of all known causewayed camps, is only thirty miles beyond Maiden Castle, its occupants must have had to contend with widely different agricultural and pastoral conditions, and when they lent over their fences to scan their territory their eyes certainly rested on a very different landscape.

As is usual with our hill-top sites in the south, there seems to have been no occupation during the fifteen hundred years of the Bronze Age, but very early in the Iron Age Hembury was again tenanted. This settlement which may have begun in the fourth or even the late fifth century B.C., was unfortified, the first Iron Age ramparts going up in the third century. These were multiplied and strengthened in the last century B.C.; finally a rather weak rampart was thrown across the middle of the fort in Belgic times.

After Hembury there are no antiquities of note in all the low-lying country between the Blackdown Hills and the river Exe and I will therefore take the opportunity to break off and approach the ancient, rocky part of the peninsula afresh from the north—a step which demands a preliminary retreat towards the north-east as far as the isolated limestone wall of the Mendips and a little beyond.

B. *Bath, Bristol and the Mendips*

I will, in fact, retreat to Bath, a city created by a society perhaps more remote from the life of prehistoric times than is our own. Perhaps, indeed, this gracious eighteenth-century city full of the confident perfection of its terraces and crescents has most in common with the Roman spa, *Aquae Sulis,* whose remains it incorporates. The large Roman hot bath is well worth seeing, its special appeal lying not in the stimulating strangeness of many prehistoric sites, the feeling of contact with a world very unlike our own, but the converse of that emotion, equally a pleasure, in the recognition of a cosy similarity. One looks at the bath, so like a small but dignified school swimming-bath; one bends down and examines the length of lead piping which the Romans laid to bring in the water from the hot spring. 'Good gracious,' one says, 'so they had plumbers too!'

There is, however, one work of art in the collection of the associated museum which does hark back to the strange and darker world. This is the pediment surviving from the temple of Sul, the goddess of the hot spring from which the town has drawn its prosperity and its name. On a shield which forms the centrepiece of what is otherwise a conventional Roman arrangement of trophies, is a haunting face, with fierce yet tormented eyes, entirely encircled by the writhing locks of its own hair and beard—locks which might equally well be flames and which conceal behind them a pair of wings. Although the essentially Celtic and unclassical spirit of this piece of sculpture has always been recognized, it has, from some preconception, been identified as a Gorgon's head. It seems far more likely that it is in fact a rendering of the Celtic sun-god, perhaps indeed, in spite of the difficulty of the sex, of some aspect of Sul, the presiding deity of the place. However this may be, in looking at what is certainly the finest example of the monumental sculpture of the romanized Britons, we are seeing a creation which expresses something of the spirit, of the imaginative vision of the ancestral Celts, of the prehistoric Britain which could not in its own day achieve so enduring an expression.

There are a number of minor earthworks, Celtic field lynchets, barrows and undistinguished fortified enclosures, on the hills round Bath, particularly on Lansdown and Bathampton Downs. On these last hills we again encounter Wansdyke which from here runs south-west to Englishcombe, then on to be seen at its best where it adjoins Stantonbury fort near Stanton Prior; it mounts towards Dundry past Maesknoll fort and the large round mound of Maesknoll Tump before dropping over the steep shoulder of Dundry. From that point it becomes so faint as to be very hard to trace as it follows its westward line across the coastal plain to end near Portishead in the marshy borders of the Severn Sea. Not far to the south of the line of Wansdyke is one of the most unusual monuments in this part of the country, the complex group of stone circles and avenues which lie between the parish church of Stanton Drew and the banks of the little river Chew. The largest circle, with a diameter of over three hundred and fifty feet, stands in the meadow near the stream; it is badly mutilated but there are still two dozen stones standing—blocks of conglomerate and limestone averaging about six feet in height. Another much smaller ring of eight stones adjoins it on the north-east side, and both circles, large and small, have short and straggly alignments of stones leading in an easterly direction. A third circle, intermediate in size and with a dozen standing stones, occupies higher ground some seven hundred feet south-west of the great circle; to the west again and close beside Stanton Drew church is the Cove, a group of three long blocks of stone, two upright and one now recumbent. They are interesting, these scattered groups of megalithic architecture, yet, partly perhaps because of their simple rural surroundings, they are not impressive and fail to rouse the imagination. They lack both the tremendous impact of Avebury or Stonehenge and the wistfulness, melancholy, the sense of *les temps perdus* of all the monuments which stand in lonely places, utterly deserted on moors and fells. Here in the sleepy atmosphere of a Somerset village one can only look at these blocks still marking out the form of long-forgotten rituals and wonder vainly what was enacted here three or four thousand years ago   what were the movements, the ritual accoutrements of the participants; what the imaginative obsession which informed them.

Due west of Stanton Drew, beyond Dundry Hill on the high ground crossed by the Bristol–Axbridge road, there is a small group of long barrows. The most attractively named is Fairy's Toot near Nempnett Thrubwell, once a fine chambered tomb. Its ruin at the hands of road-menders is described in a *Gentleman's Magazine* of the late eighteenth century with a zest which must cause pain to the archaeologist who would dearly like to recover the skeletons together with the 'catacombs' in which they lay. Now there is no more than an untidy mound from which a few stones protrude. A mile or so further north there are the long barrows of Redhill and Felton, and between them the remains of a chambered example known as the Waterstone for the reason that the huge roofing slab, now fallen, has a hollow face in which rain collects in a small pool.

One other site in the neighbourhood of Bristol demands a visit both for its own sake and for the dramatic beauty of its position. This is Cadbury Camp (to be distinguished from the famous Cadbury Castle, p. 159) which lies towards the narrow extremity of the tongue of high ground running from Bristol to meet the coast at Clevedon. It is a strong and perfectly preserved Iron Age hill-fort with double ramparts strength-ened to three at the point where approach along the ridge is easy. Standing on the walls at the western, seaward end one commands a scene exquisitely composed of land and water. Straight ahead the woody spine of the ridge hides Clevedon and one looks over the glimmering wedge of water which is the Bristol Channel and the Severn Sea straight to the Welsh coast, where Cardiff is reduced to an innocent blur at the foot of the wall of the South Welsh mountains. It is a wall softly coloured and insub-stantial yet proclaiming in some mysterious way its lofty mass and moun-tain dignity. Immediately below to the north lies the lush green strip of the curiously-named Gordano valley leading to Portishead and Avon-mouth, while in the opposite direction the prospect as far as the Mendips is across a low coastal plain, cut up into innumerable jigsaw pieces with the fine bright lines of dykes and streams. Finally, due east, at the base of the ridge on which Cadbury stands, the city of Bristol climbs up from its river to its hills, with the strong rectangular shapes of warehouses and factories asserting their logic against this otherwise fairy landscape.

Although Bristol itself was not a Roman town the nearby site of Sea Mills, Roman *Abonae*, was, and may have been used as a base port for the *Classis Britannica* during the early part of the Roman period. At a later stage the site developed into a civilian port and town connected by road with Bath and by ferry with South Wales. Part of the foundations of a Roman house are still visible at Sea Mills together with walls and stone guttering belonging to other structures of the ancient port of *Abonae*.

It is now time to approach the Mendips themselves, but I propose to do so not by the watery plain across which we have been surveying them but from the eastern end, a move which necessitates a return to the country south of Bath. Here, before mounting on to the main ridge, it will be well to mention a group of long barrows scattered round the headwaters of the Avon to the south of Bradford-on-Avon, a small town that possesses the best Saxon church in the country. By far the most important is the northernmost of the group, the chambered long barrow of Stoney Littleton which lies on a hill slope three-quarters of a mile south-west of Wellow church. Like Fairy Toot, this is an outlier of the finest and supposedly earliest type of the Cotswold megalithic barrow; like them the imposing entrance portal is approached through a forecourt, or recess, in the large end of the mound, and itself leads into a passage with cells opening off it on either side. Here at Stoney Littleton there were six side cells in all, skilfully built of megalithic uprights packed with drystone walling and with a roughly but effectively corbelled roof. Although it was plundered of its skeletons and grave-goods in the eighteenth and early nineteenth centuries, the architecture is itself unusually complete, and other than the Cotswold Hetty Pegler's Tump there is nowhere in England or Wales where one can better experience the ancient character of these earth-fast sepulchres, where the bodies of the Stone Age dead were returned to the Great Goddess.

Of the more southerly members of the group, I will mention the Devil's Bed and Bolster near Rode only for the sake of its name; the other three are immediately north and west of Frome.

In mounting on to Mendip, that isolated ridge of Carboniferous limestone whose substance had been laid down before the coal-measure forests were flourishing, we are again in country where a continuous route is possible, and where, on thousand-foot uplands, the enduring handiwork of prehistoric man is conspicuous among that of his descendants. At this eastern end by which our approach is made the ridge is much broken, and having in part been thickly forested has far less of antiquity to show than the western parts. The traveller may like to climb up by the Roman road from Bath to Ilchester, the Fosse Way, and find himself at a Roman crossroads near Oakhill where this road encounters another coming from the east and running along the summit of Mendip. No doubt it served the lead-mines which were of such importance in the economics of the Roman province. On the way he should turn aside to see the exceptionally fine specimen of a promontory fort on Blacker's Hill near Chilcompton and Downside; the sides of the headland fall away into steep ravines, and running between them is a massive rampart which still stands forty feet above its ditch. Passing over to the southern side there is the strongly defended fort of Maesbury with its multiple walls and also a little-known stone circle at Cracknell above Croscombe, about two miles west of Wells. Immediately to the north of that most enchanting small cathedral city there is a long barrow as well as round barrows on Pen Hill, and then, two miles further towards the sea, is one of the most famous sites of Mendip and one of the most romantic in our prehistory. This is the Wookey Hole ravine. Suddenly, at a step, we are back at a far earlier time, at a place inhabited long before any man had cultivated the soil of Britain or led animals to its pastures.

The ravine cuts into the southern face of the Mendips, ending in a precipitous rock face below which the river Axe flows out from tunnels and vaults it has dissolved for itself in the limestone mass. It glides out silently and darkly as though it had gained a profundity of feeling in its subterranean journey. We are concerned with three caves in the ravine, all of them occupied by troglodytes though at very different periods. The first is the Hyaena Den, a small cave in the right-hand side of the ravine approached across a rustic bridge. The Hyaena Den was first discovered in the middle of the nineteenth century and digging was begun there, almost in the year of the publication of the *Origin of Species,* under the direction of Sir William Boyd Dawkins, who was himself so much concerned in the struggle which led to the recognition of the hitherto undreamt-of antiquity of man. It proved to contain vast masses of animal bones which had been lying there between twenty and a hundred thousand years. There in the heart of Somerset, Victorian gentlemen unearthed the remains of cave lion, cave and grizzly bears, mammoth, woolly rhinoceros, bison, Irish elk, and many other species including great numbers of hyaenas. These last unpleasant beasts had been responsible for dragging in many of the other species, either as prey or carrion: but not all of them, for the ashes of camp fires, burnt bones and implements of flint and chert told of the use of the cave by Old Stone Age hunters. Whether the human families had actually to expel the hyaenas before they could claim the shelter of the cave who shall say, but the place must have been foul and fetid enough with the rank smell of the dogs and their putrifying middens. On the other hand, any cave was welcome in glacial winters and at Wookey the water supply was excellent. Certainly hunting parties returned to the place from time to time over a great span of years, though all within the last phase of the Old Stone Age when the glaciers having ground their way southward for the last time, alternately melted back during a slightly warmer spell or advanced again with the intensifying cold—the minor oscillations which preceded the end of the Ice Age. High above the Hyaena Den opens the Badger Hole, another small cave which has been explored in recent years. The last occupants were, indeed, badgers; they were preceded by Roman Britons, while the first human inhabitants were again Stone Age hunters.

Wookey Hole itself has a high, narrow entrance just above the spot at which the Axe glides out from under the precipice at the head of the ravine. It is far more spacious than the other caves, with three open chambers hung with stalactites through which the Axe flows and widens to a lake. It is now flood-lit and makes a pretty spectacle for those who like such places. More caves stretch deep into the rock below the water, and divers have already discovered seven of them—dangerous exploration which has had its fatalities. Here in Wookey there was no Stone Age occupation, but the chambers made a home for Celtic Britons of the Late Iron Age, poor cousins of the villagers of Glastonbury and Meare (p. 158). It remained the home of their descendants long after the Roman conquest. There is a tradition that in the Middle Ages, Wookey Hole was the lair of a troublesome witch, and her body, turned to stone by an exorcizing monk, now stands in the cave as a large stalagmite. It seems not altogether impossible that this represents the vague memory of a tragedy which in fact overtook its British occupants. Excavators found that the outer part of the cave had been used as a stable for goats—it contained their dung, the charred stump of a tethering-post, a pot probably used for milking, and the bones of two goats. In a rock fissure close at hand was a human skeleton, body of some troglodyte who had died fully clothed and equipped—carrying knife, dagger, bill-hook and a stalagmite ball which must I think, have been an unavailing lucky charm. Whatever the cause, and one suspects suffocation by smoke, this tableau of death waited two thousand years for the curtain to rise upon it.

Not far west of Wookey is the far larger and more spectacular Ebbor Gorge, worth visiting for its own sake, and with caves where other Old Stone Age remains have been found. This, however, is the point at which one should again mount on to the summit of the ridge to see the sights of Priddy which are both many and varied. First, well to the south of the village, there is a long barrow of no very distinguished presence and of less interest than the remarkable scatter of over a hundred round barrows on the hills round about, many of which have yielded important funerary vessels and bronze implements. The most striking are Priddy Nine Barrows not far from the Miners' Arms, and the Ashen Hill group of eight bowl barrows forming a line a little way to the north of them. Finally, at the Castle of Comfort Inn, are the well-known Priddy Circles, a row of no less than four earthen rings each with an inside diameter of about five hundred and fifty feet. They may be sanctuaries related to the familiar Bronze Age form, but they are without any entrances and the ditches lie outside the banks.

There is no need to doubt that the next site is indeed one of these sanctuaries. Gorsey Bigbury, near Longwood Farm in the parish of Charterhouse, is a circular enclosure one hundred and sixty feet across and with a ditch duly lying inside the bank. The single entrance is on the north side. Excavation has dated it to the Early Bronze Age and it is very probable that there was once a horseshoe setting of wooden posts inside the earthwork.

This parish of Charterhouse holds within its boundaries the centre of the Roman lead-mining industry, the most intensive workings having been made within the area known as the Town Field. Lead, with the silver it contained, was one of the most important mineral resources of Britain and one of the minor attractions which helped to draw the Romans across the Channel. They were up on Mendip exploiting the mines with extraordinary speed, for the first known 'pig' of lead shows it to have been poured into its mould in 49 A.D., only half a dozen years after the first landings in Kent. What the Roman engineers found when they arrived is not exactly known, but the Britons were already mining on a small scale, for net-sinkers of Mendip lead were used in the Glastonbury lake village, and it seems that it was being used as a source of silver already in the time of Augustus. The Romans, however, soon enormously increased the capacity of the mines, working them at first under military control, an arrangement which was probably relaxed when the region was entirely pacified and the military frontiers had been advanced to Wales.

The miners had a small town here at Charterhouse, presumably a rough, tough place rather like an American frontier town in pioneering days, but with a certain authority provided by the soldiers and by the fact that all the proceeds of the mines were Imperial property—the very 'pigs' being marked with the Emperor's name. Odds and ends of the miners' possessions are found from time to time, including coins and brooches so numerous that one feels they were regarded much as we regard safety-pins. The only conspicuous relic of the town is a small oval amphitheatre at

Charterhouse, where we can suppose that the tastes of the community were satisfied with bull and bear fighting and other sports of the kind that were still enjoyed on Thames-side in Shakespeare's day.

On Mendip the traveller can make within a little space vast excursions in time. From this small mining town which we imagine so well from our own experience, with its regular work and pay-days, its officials and soldiers, its regulations, gambling and sport at the stadium, we make our way deep into the rock, deep into time and into the depths of human consciousness. Cheddar Gorge, in spite of its tourism, in spite of its association with one of the least subtle of cheeses, is yet one of the very few places in this island where it is possible to imagine the hunting communities of the Old Stone Age experiencing life in forms utterly unlike our own. One branch of the gorge begins not far from Charterhouse, but the highway follows a more southerly branch. By path or road the traveller can wind downwards between mounting walls of limestone, grey and buff, dissolved by water into ledges, flutings, columns and bastions with surfaces like wrinkled peasant-skin. These rocks are hung with ivy and lodge thousands of jackdaws which may leave their crevices to swirl against the sky, spattering the ear with their quick, discontented cries.

Towards the bottom of the ravine where the cliffs stand so high overhead that one feels as deeply imprisoned as in Manhattan, the dark eyes of caves look out on to the gorge and among them are several which gave shelter to the Palaeolithic hunters. Here the families lived near the cave mouth where daylight could reach them, perhaps building a screen against the wind and sleeping with the fire between them and the arctic night. In winter the cave was for each family group its centre of existence. There flint implements were flaked and bone ones carved and ground, skins were prepared and turned into clothes, thongs and foot coverings. There, if chance decreed it in these hasty lives, infants were born and the dead buried. There the successful hunters bore back their bag of reindeer, horse, bear, and boar, and devoured the meat by the camp fire. How often returning hunting parties must have crossed the lip of the gorge in early winter twilight and seen the cave, not now like a dark eye, but a red one, glowing with firelight. The men went down the tinkling, icy tracks, familiar to their feet, aware without thought that there, with warmth and food and rest, the women were awaiting them inside the cave.

In the chief Cheddar show place, Gough's Cave, the visitor can see hunting knives, spear and dart heads, scrapers for skins, made on slender flint flakes; there are also those rare perforated antler tools which were probably used for the softening of leather thongs. There, too, like the relics of a saint, the skeleton of Cheddar Man is exposed under a glass case. This man, together with his predecessors and descendants, lived in the gorge towards the very end of the Ice Age, when reindeer and horse were the most abundant game. Another small opening, known as Soldier's Hole, which can be reached by scrambling some two hundred yards above Gough's may have been inhabited rather earlier; two of the thin laurel-leaf shaped spearheads, most delicately chipped, that were a characteristic of this earlier phase, were found in Soldier's Hole and are now exhibited in Gough's Cave.

Almost exactly opposite Cheddar Gorge on the north face of the Mendips is Burrington Combe, smaller and rather more gentle than Cheddar, but yet wild and impressive enough. Here the centre of interest is Aveline's Hole, a cavern roughly torn in the foot of the cliff on the east side, just opposite to the cleft which is supposed to have inspired Toplady to write *Rock of Ages Cleft for Me*. Since the eighteenth century, vast quantities of skeletons and other finds are recorded as coming from this cave, but most have been lost. There still remain, however, skulls and various relics of Stone Age men very similar in general type to the inhabitants of Cheddar. Flint and bone implements suggest that Aveline's Hole was occupied even later than Gough's Cave, let us say about ten thousand years B.C. Unhappily there is none of the magnificent art of the French and Spanish cave-dwellings of this period, but here in Burrington Combe carefully gathered fossils and pretty sea-shells pierced for a necklace show an aesthetic and decorative urge even in these bitterly cold outposts of nascent human culture. The large oblong fort of Dolbury can be reached from the Combe.

The two remaining sites on this route are on the coast, where the Mendips tail away towards Weston-super-Mare. One is to the south of this resort, the promontory fort on the narrow headland of Brean Down; the other, far more imposing, is to the north of Weston—the great stone-built fort of Worlebury which seems to have been occupied by an Iron Age people akin to those of the lake villages (p. 158) and to have ended in destruction and massacre. Though now overgrown by woodland, nearly a hundred circular pits were found inside the defences; they were cut as much as five feet deep in the limestone and had many of them been used for grain storage. Charred wheat, barley and pulse remained in some.

South of the Mendip wall is the wide expanse of western Somerset, low-lying, much of it hardly reclaimed from marsh like the sombre reaches of Sedgemoor. From it there project here and there isolated hills such as Brent Knoll and Glastonbury Tor and the low ridge of the Polden Hills all of Jurassic limestone, younger than that of the Mendips and far less ancient than the Devonian rocks of the Quantocks which delimit the area on the west. As the traveller will by now have come to expect, it is mainly on these small patches of upland that antiquities will be found, but west Somerset can offer, as we shall see, one important exception to this upland pattern.

The isolated mass of Brent Knoll about six miles south of Weston was an irresistibly attractive natural site for a fort and the Celtic tribesmen did not fail to make use of it—throwing a single rampart and ditch round the summit and adding to the defences by the artificial scarping of the hillside. It is when we move eastwards from the Knoll that we come upon prehistoric sites which are not only low-lying but were deliberately chosen for the protection not of steep slopes but of marsh. These are of course the famous lake villages of Meare and Glastonbury. If I am to remain true to my intention never to lead those who follow me to any of the faint and unconvincing marks of prehistoric life where either faith or expert knowledge are needed to find any significance in a few banks and hollows, I must not stay long at the lake villages. Nevertheless, just because they were set among meres and not on hill-tops, these two villages have been able to show in unique detail the material background of the life of the Celtic Britons of the Iron Age, of a people related in varying degrees with the builders of the hill-forts which everywhere attract us with their striking architecture and fine positions. The reason for this is simply that the moisture and peat which formed over the deserted villages has preserved many of the possessions which elsewhere have perished. The excavators of Glastonbury (which lies about a mile north of the present town) found the logs and faggots which had formed the artificial island on which the huts were built, they found the stakes of the enclosing palisade, the floors of the round huts, some sixty in number, which had often been remade again and again as the foundation sank slowly in the underlying mire. They found complete hurdles, indistinguishable from those of to-day, fragments of well-built carts, dug-out canoes which the villagers used to come and go from their hand-made island. Where normally we recover only potsherds, Glastonbury and Meare yielded baskets and beautifully turned wooden bowls; where at best we expect of find only the metal parts of iron knives, saws, bill-hooks, these villages put them into our hands complete with their wooden hafts, gracefully shaped and serviceable. Those who know how to let sentiment take command over reason may like to visit the uneven fields which to-day mark the sites of Glastonbury and Meare, but let everyone go to the Castle Museum at Taunton where all the finds are admirably displayed. Here they will see not only the perishable things which I have described, but the famous decorated pottery, and objects which prove the wide trading activities of the villagers —tin from Cornwall, lead from the Mendips, Dorset shale, glass beads and amber, and quantities of iron, thought to have been imported from the Forest of Dean. This iron was used not only for a great range of tools, but also for the clumsy iron currency bars which were the medium of exchange throughout south-western England before true coins came to displace them. Undoubtedly these villages were prosperous, but there is no reason to suppose that they were very exceptionally so; looking in the cases at Taunton may give a new idea of the very tolerable standard of living which had been achieved by the Britons at the end of prehistoric times. Glastonbury and Meare were probably established by about 150 B.C., and were still inhabited until just before the Roman conquest.

Rather more than a dozen miles south-east of Glastonbury (after crossing the Roman Fosse Way on its straight course to Ilchester) is one of the most magnificent hill-forts in the West Country, the fort of Cadbury Castle whose four lines of powerful ramparts enclose a domed hill-top which rises high above them, seeming to rest on the stepped plinth which they provide. These ramparts are cut from the rock and in places have dry-stone masonry still intact on their inner face; sometimes the crest of a wall, even in its present tumbled state, stands more than forty feet above the bottom of its ditch. From 1967 the site has been systematically excavated revealing, in the words of the excavator, 'a palimpsest of four millennia of human activity'. A New Stone Age settlement of some twenty acres in extent was apparently the first occupation on the hill and there was also some Bronze Age settlement before the building of the striking Iron Age fortifications. Inevitably the fort fell to the Romans, and military equipment and buildings have been discovered within the hill-fort marking a brief occupation of the site by some Roman garrison. It was, however, the next chapter in its long history that drew big crowds to the Cadbury excavations. The pioneer antiquary, Leland, had found a belief among local folk that Arthur had been at the Castle, and he himself added the speculation that here was Camelot. It proved that the hill had indeed been refortified and a 'feasting hall' built on the summit at just the right date for the historic Arthur—round about 500 A.D. Though not Camelot (surely a place of fantasy) it is justifiable to believe that Cadbury was an Arthurian base during the period when his famous victory of Mount Badon checked the Saxon conquest of the West Country. Even then its role in national history was not over, for digging confirmed the written record that Cadbury became an important *burh* and mint at the time of Ethelred's losing struggle against the Danes.

The fort has one rival in Somerset, that on Ham Hill which dominates the country about twelve miles to the south-west in the parish of Stoke-sub-Hamdon. Here again are stone-cut defences crowning a magnificent natural site, the outcrop of oolitic limestone which is the source of the famous Ham Hill building stone—a stone still much used, which provided the material for many medieval churches and which was probably already quarried in Roman times. The British camp is known to have been refortified by the Romans (Ilchester is only a few miles away) and the abundant finds which have been made as a result of quarrying include many Roman as well as Celtic objects. Among these finds, now to be seen in the Taunton Museum, is a Roman soldier's *lorica* or small bronze scales, and a chariot wheel, also Roman.

Both Cadbury and Ham Hill are exceptionally fine examples of British military architecture in which the builders have taken advantage of bold limestone hills. The chalk could never offer such sites, and it is interesting when looking at the rough grandeur of this stone architecture to contrast it in memory with the forceful yet milder plastic forms characteristic of the chalk.

In moving so far westward to reach Ham Hill we have passed by the long, low ridge of the Polden Hills, but in truth, though finds make it certain that they were well-populated in the Iron Age, there are no monuments deserving mention. One of the chance finds, is, however, too well known to be ignored: in the year 1800, a ploughshare struck and exposed a hoard of Celtic bronzes—horse ornaments and bits, shield boss, brooches and other pieces—many of them finely ornamented and enlivened with red enamel. The Polden Hill hoard had been buried—probably at about the time of the Roman conquest and offers some of the best examples of the last phase of the native British art.

C. *The Quantocks, Exmoor and Dartmoor*

Almost parallel with the Poldens on the western side of Bridgwater and the Parrett rises the far larger ridge of the Quantocks; these ridges together with the Mendips are, of course, three of the wrinkles formed during the Armorican earth folding some two hundred and fifty million years ago. The Quantocks are formed of an ancient sandstone which supports heather moors and which has been worn into deep combes often densely

9. The burial chamber at Pentre-ifan, Pembrokeshire.

10. The passage grave of
Bryn-Celli-Ddu, on
Anglesey, with, to the right
of the picture, the slab
covered with incised
patterns, originally found
prone above the ritual pit.

11. Shafts in the New Stone Age and Bronze Age flint-mines of Grimes Graves, Norfolk.

12. The menhir of Long Meg, which is surrounded by a circle of fifty-nine stones, known as 'her daughters', above Penrith, Cumberland.

13. The Roman temple of Mithras, which lay on the west bank of Walbrook in London (*Londinium*).

14. Remains of a Roman bath in the City of London.

15. Mosaic depicting Europa and the Bull, from the dining room of the Roman villa at Lullingstone, in Kent.

16. The Roman lighthouse tower which stands inside the castle at Dover.

wooded. Such rough country has helped to keep the range sequestered and even now red deer linger in its valleys, remote collateral descendants of the 'poor dappled fools' which disappeared three centuries ago together with the Forest of Arden. These hills are not rich in antiquity, yet there are a number of round barrows and several earthworks; few if any of which have been explored. The most impressive of them is the roughly circular fort with double ramparts on the north side of the hills above Dodington. Its name of Dowsborough, originally written Dawsboro, links it with Dawse Castle, a coastal site near Watchet—both names implying the use of the sites as beacon hills.

The Quantocks are little more than the doorstep to Exmoor. The moor, like the smaller hills, is of Devonian sandstone, and like them it is dissected by the valleys often wooded, and fertile when compared with the expanses of heather above. These moors are of far greater extent than on the Quantocks—a slow rise and fall of a 'wine-dark sea'—one of the largest stretches of uncultivated land in southern England. The higher country is to the north where Dunkery Beacon passes seventeen hundred feet; this area is cut by the Exe and its tributary the Barle, and by many short rivers running northward into the Bristol Channel. A lower southern portion of the moor is divided from the rest by the valley of the Yeo, while that lying east of the Exe is commonly distinguished under the name of the Brendon Hills.

Exmoor is far less rich in antiquities than Dartmoor, although it is fair to say that it has also been less studied, having failed to inspire anyone with the madness, the infatual love, necessary to secure years of survey, discovery and excavation. It has few of the 'hut circles' and stone alignments which we shall encounter in such numbers on Dartmoor, but it can show a few circles of standing stones. In its prehistoric remains as in its geology, Exmoor rather resembles the Quantocks: that is to say there are many minor remains, particularly round cairns (stone-built barrows) and small defensive enclosures and other earthworks   enough to show that the region was not neglected in the Bronze and Iron Ages— but none of them in the least spectacular. On the other hand on Exmoor almost as much as on Dartmoor, among the curlew, the little hill sheep and the herds of half-wild ponies, one is in a primitive countryside where past history seems very close. Each of these uplands can in that sense be accepted in their entirety as monuments of antiquity and that is how I wish to present them. Having done so, I shall merely add one of those scrappy catalogues of particular sites which do so much to make *Guides* an intolerable form of literature.

Approaching from the Quantocks, we first strike the Brendon Hills where there is a good crop of round barrows and two earthworks just conspicuous enough to demand attention—Clatworthy Castle, a triangular enclosure, and two miles north-west Elworthy Barrows camp, built on an open common, with gaps in both wall and ditches which suggest it was never finished. On the broken and prettily-wooded coastal region north of the Brendons, there is a small but quite strong fort known as Bats Castle in the historic setting of Dunster deer park; as befits its name, it is dark, overgrown, inaccessible and a goal only for the most determined. There is a second, larger but weaker fort reached by the same path and no more than a quarter of a mile away. On Minehead North Hill lies the small circular enclosure of East Mynne while following the coast along the high ground between Minehead and Porlock, we find Bury Castle at Selworthy, a sub-rectangular fort with an unusually wide berm between ditch and rampart. Here, just south of Porlock church near a path leading up to Dunkery Beacon, is the first of the Exmoor stone circles, not a very striking specimen: small—only eighty feet across—and with eleven of its twenty-one stones fallen and some of them thrown outside the ring. A better example is to be found nearer to the heart of the moor, just to the south-west of the Barle bridge at Withypool; this has as many as thirty-seven standing stones and a diameter of a hundred and twenty feet.

Pushing to the southern dividing line of the Yeo valley, there are several small camps in the neighbourhood of Dulverton: Old Berry Castle, and Brewer's and Mounsey Castles both of which overlook the Barle. Passing Withypool once more and striking back towards the coast, it is worth mentioning Staddon Hill, a circular fort visible from Dunkery Beacon, Cow Castle at Simonsbath and a fort on Shoulsbury Common. Crossing the Devon boundary we next reach the well-known landmark of the Chapman Barrows east of the Blackmore Gate entrance to the moor, and near them the three standing stones and other barrows on Homer Down; west of Blackmoor is Kentisbury Barrow. Returning to the coast after this breathless round of northern Exmoor there is an interesting site at Glenthorne, just inside Devonshire. This is Old Burrow Walls adding to the baffling confusion of Barrows, Burrows, Berrys and Burys in this part of the world—a circular enclosure one hundred yards across and with a substantial mound at the centre. This is now known to be a Roman signal station built in the early conquest period and commanding an extensive view of the Bristol Channel across to the south coast of Wales some seventeen to twenty miles away. There was a sister fort of almost identical construction at Martinhoe just on the other side of the seaside town of Lynmouth. The reason behind the building of these signal stations at an early date was almost certainly the hostility of the tribe inhabiting South Wales, the Silures, who fought a long and bitter guerilla campaign against the Roman troops until subdued by the general, Julius Frontinus, during his governorship of Britain in 74–78 A.D. Presumably both fortlets were intended to act as look-out posts as well as signal stations working in liaison with the Roman fleet in Britain, the *Classis Britannica*, which would have provided sea patrols along the Bristol Channel, perhaps operating from a port such as Sea Mills, *Abonae*, near Avonmouth. (see p. 151).

Going a little further into Devon there is the fort of Countisbury overlooking Lynmouth Bay, while in the Valley of the Rocks near Lynton, a place where tumbled boulders and precipitous faces of naked rock make a natural chaos that has proved attractive to tourists, there is a group of hut circles with an enclosing wall or 'pound' of a kind we shall find in numbers on Dartmoor. Visitors to the Rocks usually also seek out the standing stone, presumably an ordinary Bronze Age menhir, which has been given the name of Cewydd's Stone. From the end of the Valley of the Rocks, a delightful cliff road leads on to Martinhoe where there is a small fort, worth looking at as a part of the coastal scene.

In all that part of north Devon beyond the Exmoor sandstone and north of Dartmoor, the soft, mild countryside bears hardly a mark of prehistoric man, the reason being the usual one—that he found it too thickly forested. I shall therefore retreat to south Devon, left at the approaches to Exeter, in order to advance on Dartmoor from the eastern side. Exeter itself has a museum housed in a ponderous Gothic building suited to the nineteenth-century architecture of a cathedral city. The collections should be seen particularly for the guidance which they give to the antiquities of Dartmoor. Of the Roman city of *Isca Dumnoniorum* there are no remains above ground, but here and there it is possible to crawl below recent buildings to see pavements and other traces of the most westerly centre of Roman civic life in England. The hideous destruction worked by air raids made it possible to excavate other parts of *Isca,* but although the results were historically interesting, nothing was uncovered that was suitable for preservation. To the north, at Stoke Hill, which is some one and a half miles from Exeter, there is a Roman signal station about five hundred yards north-east of an Iron Age hill fort.

South of Exeter there is little visible on the Haldon Hills. A reconstruction of a rectangular hut excavated up there some years ago has become the stock illustration of New Stone Age housing, but in spite of this fame there is nothing to be seen on the ground. The real interest of this coastal region returns us to the Old Stone Age, for here again we are in a country of limestone caves offering suitable shelter to the hunters, and where their precious rubbish of discarded tools, food bones and the rest could survive for our interpretation. This limestone is of great geological interest for it was laid down in clear seas in the Devonian Age when elsewhere the Old Red Sandstone was being formed—a history which makes it one of the most ancient true limestones in Britain. The caves themselves, particularly Kent's Cavern, Torquay, and the Windmill Hill Cave, Brixham, are of significance not only for the important Palaeolithic material which they yielded but for their place in the history of science. Careful excavation was begun at Kent's Cavern as early as 1825, when the Roman Catholic priest, Father MacEnery, was able to satisfy himself that humanly-worked flints were contemporary with the bones of an extinct species of rhinoceros and other long-vanished beasts. But society and the intellectual climate were not yet ready for this discovery: it was still almost universally accepted that man had enjoyed a special creation some six thousand years before. These new horizons were too wide for the human eyes of their day. Excavation under various hands went on at Kent's Cavern during the second quarter of the century, but its evidence was steadily denied; it was declared that the deposits had been disturbed and that the implements were not of the same age as the extinct animals. Then in 1858 quarrymen working above Brixham Harbour discovered new caves, and a powerful committee including the geologists Ramsay, Prestwich and Lyell was set up to direct their excavation. Here, in the Windmill Hill Cave, the close association of tools and bones under a sealing layer of stalagmite could not reasonably be contradicted. Nevertheless, the evidence was not really much better than it had been at Kent's Cavern, its acceptance was due to the development of scientific thought in the intervening years. Lyell and Prestwich were declaring their belief in the Brixham discoveries in 1859, the very year of the publication of the *Origin of Species*. In 1858, the Neanderthal skull had been found. So knowledge and discovery gathered to a point in the strange way that they will when the moment for their comprehension has arrived. From that time, for better or for worse, thinking men were bound to accept the immense antiquity of their species and to accept in some form or other the doctrines of evolution.

At Brixham the flint implements and other remains of the human inhabitants of the caves were few and poor, but at Kent's Cavern there is one of the best series of Old Stone Age finds in the country. Human occupation of the caves began much earlier than in any of those on Mendip; it began in that part of the Old Stone Age once known as the Middle Palaeolithic, when the Neanderthal type of man was dominant in Europe. In other layers and other parts of the cavern flints dating from at least two periods of the succeeding Upper Palaeolithic were recovered—enough to show that hunters were living here on the Devon shore at roughly the time when related tribes hunted on the Mendip Hills.

Visitors to Brixham, to Torquay, this old fishing town and this modern seaside resort, may like to let their minds wander round the caverns thinking alike of the revolutions in human thought which they helped to bring about, and of the ancient hunters who left the materials for such a revolution in the squalid litter of their cave dwellings.

Here in this coastal region which has Newton Abbot as its centre, one is always aware of the presence of Dartmoor filling the western horizon. Dartmoor, like Bodmin Moor and most of the lesser moors between it and Land's End, is a granite mass, the denuded core of far more lofty mountains piled up during the Armorican folding. When these upheavals in the earth's crust occur, half-liquid magma pushes up into the cavities at the base of the mountainous folds of rock and solidifies, then, as millions of years go by with their millions of seasons of rain and frost, first the lofty peaks are denuded away, then the lower and larger masses, until a time may be reached when the granite core, the solidified magma so much harder than the overlying rocks, is all that remains. While in Exmoor and the Quantocks the sandstone has proved enduring, in all these more westerly areas, the granite stands exposed with little more than a covering of peat or the thin soils made by its own decomposition.

Dartmoor is formed by two main granite highlands divided by a rather lower belt between Ashburton and Tavistock; the nothern block is both larger and more lofty—passing two thousand feet at High Willhays and Yes Tor. Because of its height and exposure to Atlantic winds this part of the moor has always been much wetter and hence more prone to bog formation and the growth of peat—conditions which tended to discourage prehistoric settlement. Even more than Exmoor, the compact granite upland area of Dartmoor asks to be accepted as a single monument of antiquity—indeed far more, for here vast numbers of huts and villages with the outlines of their plots and fields are still visible. So extensive are they, that when the light is favourable, one can almost restore the prehistoric landscape. For this reason I shall not try to describe them separately, to lead the traveller from one to another, but to give a more general

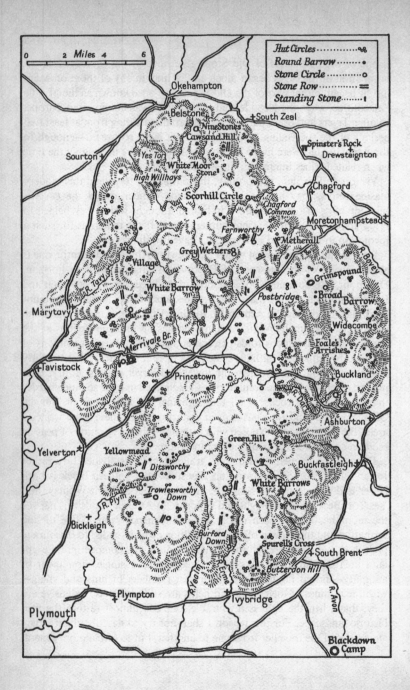

Hut Circles..............🏵
Round Barrow........•
Stone Circle...........○
Stone Row............═
Standing Stone........ı

0   2 Miles 4   6

Okehampton

Belstone
Nine Stones
Cawsand Hill
South Zeal
Spinster's Rock
Drewsteignton
Sourton
Yes Tor
White Moor
Stone
High Willhays
Chagford
Scorhill Circle
Chagford
Common
Moretonhampstead
Fernworthy
Metherall
Grey Wethers
R. Bovey
Village
Grimspound
White Barrow
Broad
Postbridge
Barrow
R. Tavy
Widecombe
Marytavy
Merrivale Br.
Foales
Arrishes
Tavistock
Princetown
Buckland

Yelverton
Green Hill
Ashburton
Yellowmead
Buckfastleigh
Ditsworthy
White Barrows
Trowlesworthy
Down
R. Plym
Bickleigh
Burford
Down
Spurell's Cross
South Brent
Butterdon Hill
R. Yealm
R. Erme
Plympton
Ivybridge
R. Avon
Plymouth
Blackdown
Camp

account of these settlements and then name individually some of the best of the stone circles, standing stones and stone rows or alignments for which the moor is equally famous. The Ordnance Survey map will do the rest.

Numbers alone would make any other course impossible. There are still thirteen hundred and fifty hut sites on Dartmoor out of an estimated total of fifteen hundred. All are round in plan, the name 'hut circle' invariably given to them on our maps referring to the stone-built walls which once were covered with a dome-like or conical roof of turf or heather thatching. They have a single entrance marked by a pair of upright stones or jambs considerably taller than the walls, and it is a tribute to the long persistence of the north-west gales that nearly all the doors face south or south-west. The roofs were supported by a central post with a ring of smaller ones between it and the walls. The most usual form is not larger than twenty feet across and may be as small as eight feet, while the walls show a revetment either of masonry or standing stones on the inside, but outside smaller stones are simply sloped up against it. The second kind of hut is larger, occasionally more than thirty feet in diameter, and has walls four or five feet thick lined with standing slabs both inside and out. These were originally packed with small stones but have often been denuded and left exposed as a double ring of upright slabs. Rarely, inner sleeping quarters were walled off from the living room.

It seems that while all the Dartmoor people were akin, weather conditions divided them into pastoralists and cultivators. In the south-western valleys from the Meavy to the Avon, where there was high rainfall and good pasture, most of the settlements, whether single farmsteads, hamlets or villages of up to thirty houses, were predominantly pastoral, enclosed by substantial stone walls or 'pounds'. Some, as at Rider's Ridge, might include stock pens. In contrast, throughout the eastern parts of the moor, rainfall was light enough to allow the cultivation of barley in little squarish fields of up to half an acre. Here family groups typically lived at the edge of their fields in clusters of from two to four huts, generally rather larger than those of the pastoralists.

Nearly all the Dartmoor settlements of whichever kind date from the middle to later Bronze Age, between about 1400–900 B.C. The same type of dwellings, however, continued to be built until Roman times.

The greatest concentration of hut circles is in the south-east, particularly round the upper waters of the Yealm and to a lesser degree in the Plym Valley, but they are common enough on the west and south flanks of the northern plateau—including a well-known group beside the river Tavy.

Hut circles are certainly by far the most abundant of the Dartmoor antiquities, but more distinctive are the alignments and avenues of standing stones often linked with stone circles which recall, though on a much smaller scale, the stone rows of Brittany. In this country they can be compared with the Stanton Drew circles (p. 150) and even, more remotely, with Avebury itself. There is no doubt that the stone rows and circles are normally of the Bronze Age; in many places they are related to round cairns and to small stone burial-chambers or 'cists'. There is indeed no evidence of New Stone Age peoples on Dartmoor; even megalithic tombs of the kind we shall soon be seeing in Cornwall are lacking on Dartmoor— so far as I know the only exception is the Spinster's Rock on the extreme edge of the moor at Drewsteignton, between Exeter and Chagford. The earliest settlement on Dartmoor seems to be marked by some of the round cairns and cists which date from an early phase of the Bronze Age—older than any of the hut groups at present known.

Dartmoor, as I have insisted, should be enjoyed as a whole, a region which geology and climate have held remote. It is best learnt and enjoyed in this spirit, by those who want to walk and ride there or fish its many streams and young rivers. They will come upon the granite remains of dwellings, tombs, religious buildings, as an integral part of this ancient realm where nature and the remains of prehistoric man seem hand in glove. Before leaving it, I will, however, name some of the best places to see stone rows, circles, cairns and the rest, though with a feeling that such a catalogue only profanes the spirit of the moor. In the north (where much of the highest ground is sterilized by an artillery range) there is the Nine Stones circle at Belstone not far to the east of Okehampton. The region south and south-east of Chagford is relatively rich in antiquity; south-east of this pleasant small town, but still on the north side of the Moreton-hampstead-to-Tavistock road there is a stone row at Metherall. Between Shapley and Widdicombe, Grimspound is an exceptionally fine example of a walled enclosure with huts, while at Foales Arrishes on the Widdicombe-to-Haytor road the huts are very well preserved and easily accessible. Further west there is a stone circle at Fernworthy and a better-known example, with the familiar Wessex name of the Grey Wethers is, westward again, three miles to the north of Postbridge. Most people who know the moor know the picturesque bridge at Postbridge with its span of huge stone slabs resting on rude piers of unmasoned stone. No one seems to know its age but it is probably not very great—one of our latest pieces of megalithic architecture—it has outlasted its usefulness and now stands beside the motor-road, a place for picnics and paddling. Following this road there are some exceptionally fine Bronze Age burial-cists before Two Bridges, and others on Royal Hill to the south. About five miles further along the Two Bridges–Tavistock turning a most varied group of monuments lies on both sides of the road where it mounts from Merivale Bridge. Here, indeed, the traveller can see an assortment of all the most characteristic Dartmoor monuments in one place. There is a number of good hut circles and enclosures on the south side of the road, and on the north more huts, two double stone rows with a cist and cairn on their line and finally, furthest from the road, a stone circle and pair of standing stones.

The other area rich in monuments of this kind is along the southern side of the moor above Plymouth—the same area round the valleys of the Plym, Yealm and Erme where hut circles are at their thickest. A good round of them can be made by taking the moorland path up from Sheepstor across the head of the Plym and coming down again by the Erme Valley to Harford. Round the source of the Plym there are stone rows and circles on Trowlesworthy Down, four concentric circles at Yellowmead, and a mixed bag at Ditsworthy Warren—hut circles, a cist and stone rows which include one gigantic monolith nearly eighteen feet high. Towards the upper Erme it is the same story: on Stall Moor a row of small but close-set stones starts from a circle and crosses the Erme to end over two miles away on Green Hill. West of Hillson's House there is an exceptionally fine stone row again associated with cairns and circles, and another on Burford Down. East of the Erme on Butterdon Hill, last outpost of the moor above Ivybridge, there is a long row running to Spurrell's Cross. This is the place to mention Blackdown Camp—if only to make some break in the geometrical procession of lines and circles. It is about half a dozen miles south-east of Butterdon on an outlying hill on the Dartmouth–Plymouth road not far from the branch line to Kingsbridge. No one but a man possessed by the most virulent form of archaeological enthusiasm would wish to visit all Dartmoor antiquities, so monotonous in their similarity and so remote from the currents of history. They are, as I have said, a part of the furnishing of this granite island, delightful to come upon and appreciate as giving a deep perspective in time to their setting of heather, bog, field wall and stream.

D. *Cornwall*

Down from the moors and across the Tamar, the coasts have converged rapidly north and south of us and we are in the Cornish peninsula, a county which has recently lost its own language but which is still not quite a part of England. It is a peninsula with blocks of moorland formed of granite and here and there of other igneous rocks, surrounded by rather lower-lying land. These lowlands were below the sea quite late in geological time—just before the Ice Age—an experience largely responsible for their slightly rolling but generally rather featureless appearance. The olive-green, monotonous, yet always rather strange countryside of inland Cornwall: in its colour and effects of light, in the way in which its low whitewashed houses gleam among the dull green slopes, it is far more like Brittany than it is like the rest of England. The Celtic tongue which used to unite the two peoples represents the natural kinship of their lands.

For the remains left upon it by prehistoric man those which most conspicuously distinguish the peninsula are the megalithic tombs. We have already seen a number of examples of megalithic architecture but almost all of them have been outliers of the chambered long barrows, a special variety of tomb building which, as we have seen, was introduced by immigrants who settled both sides of the Bristol Channel. Here in Cornwall for the first time we find numbers of the type of tomb conveniently termed a dolmen, with a chamber small in area but built of massive blocks and often roofed with a single colossal capstone. Nearly all of them are crowded in the western extremity of the country against Land's End; we shall find others very much like them in the Pembroke and Caernarvon peninsulas and in Anglesey and they seem to mark as clearly as the streamers of a paper chase the route followed by their seafaring architects.

The second great distinction of prehistoric Cornwall was due to its possession of tin. This certainly increased its importance and prosperity in the Bronze Age, but so far as field monuments are concerned, left its mark most strongly in the Iron Age when the trade seems to have been seized by invading Celtic tribes who secured their valuable territory by building the circular forts of a kind peculiar to Cornwall.

As for the distribution of ancient sites, we shall find that as usual most are on the upland areas—the moors of Bodmin, St. Austell and St. Breock, of Redruth and Land's End—there are, however, numbers of Iron Age forts on the lower ground.

Certainly there is nothing to keep us in the Tamar Valley and we can mount at once on to Bodmin Moor at the south-east corner which lies nearest to Dartmoor. This is an encouraging place to begin—and some encouragement may be needed as Bodmin Moor, much less bold and varied than Dartmoor, can be one of the most sombre and melancholy places imaginable; its naturally bare and lifeless plateau is scarred and faintly degraded by ancient tin-workings. At this point however, if we climb up from Liskeard through the village of St. Clear, we shall at once encounter one of the most interesting and impressive groups of monuments in the whole peninsula. The first and most southerly is the dolmen of Trethevy, one of the very few in the eastern part of the county and a magnificent example of this form of megalithic architecture. Indeed, any architect might be satisfied to have raised a building that would stand almost unshaken for four thousand years. It was probably late in the New Stone Age that men equipped with wooden rollers and levers and some tough thongs, heaved eight massive uprights into place and dragged up a cover slab four yards long; their energy generated by some great imaginative ideal, an inherited ideal that was pursued exultingly and without question. After the first burials were made no doubt the chamber was hidden under a mound; rain and wind, helped perhaps by men looking for building-stone, have reduced the covering to no more than a faint swelling in the ground, leaving the chamber stark and bare again. There it has stood through all our history and into the atomic age, its stones still balanced with the same weights, strains and stresses imparted to them in the Stone Age. Trethevy has a U-shaped chamber divided into a shallow antechamber and a much larger chamber by a huge rectangular block of granite reaching right up to the capstone. It is, however, possible to pass from one into the other, for this block has a roughly rectangular opening at its bottom right-hand corner: small, but yet large enough to allow the passage of a human body, alive or dead. There is also a small round perforation through the capstone where it overhangs the antechamber; it is probably natural but a seventeenth-century antiquary believed that it was intended 'to put out a staff whereof the house itself is not capable'! One of the front uprights of the antechamber is missing and the back slab of the main chamber has fallen, otherwise Trethevy Quoit appears to be in perfect condition. No finds of any kind are recorded from it, but comparable tombs elsewhere, for example in north Wales, have sometimes yielded fragments of large numbers of skeletons.

About two miles to the north-east are three of the finest circles of standing stones in Cornwall, the Hurlers in the parish of Linkinhorne. The three rings are almost contiguous and in line; the central one with a diameter of about one hundred and thirty-five feet is the largest; the other two measuring just over a hundred feet across. They owe their name to a legend which with variations is attached to standing stones all over the country. Camden recorded: 'The neighbouring Inhabitants terme them *Hurlers,* as being by devout and godly error perswaded that they had been men sometime transformed into stones, for profaning the Lord's Day with hurling the ball.' Stories of this kind, frankly recognized by Camden as the Golden Lie, no doubt embody the long struggle of the Church to defeat the ancient power of the holy stones over the country people; they most readily became attached to stone circles because these recall the round games and dances which were so much a part of Merry England.

Less than a mile away from the Hurlers, Stowe's Hill supports a natural oddity, the fantastically formed outcrop known as the Cheesewring; far less conspicuous is the stone rampart of a fort which encloses the summit. It is very possible that several of these stone forts in Cornwall may be dated to the Bronze Age and not, as we have come to assume elsewhere to the succeeding period.

On the summit of the hill on whose slopes the Hurlers stand and between the rings and Stowe's Hill is a gigantic round barrow which has contributed to a curious history. A large cist covered by a correspondingly large capstone can still be seen near the edge of the cairn—evidently added after the building of the mound. When the cist was discovered during the nineteenth century, it was found to contain rich Early Bronze Age grave-furniture, including a unique little cup of gold, ribbed, and with a finely chased handle. These finds were published and then fell into oblivion. Forty years ago, they were being lamented as lost, but in truth they were only forgotten. The gold cup ranked legally as treasure trove, and so by associations probably at least as ancient as the cup itself, was the property of the reigning monarch. It seems that all the contents of the cist were sent to Queen Victoria, and one piece, a bronze dagger-blade, was duly included in the royal collection of curios at Osborne, where, however, in 1936 a visiting British Museum official could find nothing else. Slow, tactful inquiries for the cup itself had already been made, and at last Queen Mary was approached through the librarian at Windsor. Queen Mary, with her highly trained collector's memory, recalled it; she believed her husband had had just such a ribbed gold cup in his dressing-room, which before his accession had been kept at Marlborough House. So it came about that the little ritual vessel which had once been taken from this remote stone-lined grave on Bodmin Moor was now taken from Buckingham Palace and deposited in the British Museum during the short reign of Edward VIII.

The number of stone circles on Bodmin Moor makes one wonder how they were divided. Did each community possess one, like a parish church, or were they attached more loosely to tribal territories? When all memory of their use has gone, leaving nothing but a hazy veneration and a few magical practices among the people living near them, we cannot hope to understand their social background. At least here in Cornwall we can see them side by side with settlements—for it is reasonably likely that some at least of the huts and forts are of the same age. As well as the Hurlers there are half a dozen stone circles on this moor. There is a small one, the first of the Nine Maidens whom we shall meet several times in the county, only three miles north of Stowe's Hill, and another of greater interest on the slopes of Hawks Tor five miles to the west of the Maidens. This is the Stripple Stones, a ring nearly one hundred and fifty feet in diameter which differs from all the rest in being enclosed by a bank with inner ditch— a feature which allies it to the other embanked sanctuaries many of which we have already seen in Wessex (p. 52). The Stripple Stones is, I believe, the most westerly example. The embankment has a single entrance through bank and ditch, and this entrance faces westward towards a point where, rather less than a mile distant, there stands the smaller circle of the Trippet Stones. The next ring is both small and nameless—a great imaginative impoverishment, for in our ears 'The Hurlers' and the 'Nine Maidens' and even the slightly absurd sound of the 'Stripple' and 'Trippet Stones' gives these monuments a character, an individuality far beyond that of a few unremarkable blocks of granite standing, leaning or fallen on the diameter of a circle. This anonymous circle, near the farm of Leaze, brings us to the southern edge of a region very rich in antiquities which is centred on Roughtor and the highest part of the moor. The tor itself has two granite outcrops weathered into the likeness of stacks of gigantic stone buns, and these have been brought into commission as part of a stone fort. This is now so much ruined as to be hard to trace; the outcrops which evidently formed the narrow ends of a long, narrow fort, are joined by a double line of walls on the west side, but on the east, where precipitous slopes offered good natural protection, few remains of walling can be seen.

The Roughtor fort gains interest from its association with hut circles; there are a few, as well as three springs, within the defended area, while many more clusters with their small enclosures round them can be found on the slopes of the ridge below the tor. Others, still in village clusters, lie down the valley of the De Lank river. In the same region, immediately to the south and south west of Roughtor, are two circles of an unusual kind, both associated with hut circles. These are Stannon and Fernacre, large rings composed not of the normal regularly spaced and substantial blocks, but of large numbers of smaller stones arranged without any order. It seems likely enough that they were once packed with earth and still smaller stone to make enclosures comparable to the rings of Priddy and not true stone circles at all. Whatever they may be, it is very probable that all the remains in the neighbourhood of Roughtor should be seen together, the fort on the hill-top protecting the huts and sanctuaries which cluster round it as a medieval castle protected its village. If, as has been supposed, all may be dated to the Bronze Age, it would be an association of unique interest. Though some have been dug, none of these Bodmin sites has been dated and there is nothing to prove that they are earlier than the Iron Age.

Leaving Bodmin Moor, which is far the largest of the Cornish highlands and the richest in antiquity of any except Land's End, we can quickly reach one of the round forts already recognized as a Cornish speciality. This is Tregear Rounds north of Wadebridge in the parish of St. Kew. Its double ring of banks stands on the slope and not the crest of the hill, and a hollow track leading down to the stream has been protected by a third rampart. A small amount of digging has dated Tregear Rounds to the Iron Age and probably to the first century B.C.

Across the Camel, which, with its southern counterpart the Fowey, so nearly cuts Cornwall in two parts, there are two monuments worth visiting on the St. Breoke (or Breock) Downs. One is a dolmen on the slope of a ridge above Pawton; the chamber is without any entrance or antechamber such as we saw at Trethevy and is roofed with one of the largest capstones in the peninsula—over sixteen feet long and two feet in thickness. As a considerable mound, apparently oval in plan, is still visible, the Pawton tomb might reward excavation and tell us something of these Cornish megaliths of which at present we are exceptionally ignorant.

A little further west, near the road from Wadebridge to St. Columb Major, on a high piece of downland among many round barrows, we find another company of Nine Maidens. It is not a circle but a stone row, the sole example of its kind in Cornwall. Its nine stones, from five to six feet high where they are still upright, are irregularly spaced along a line of three hundred and fifty feet running north-east and south-west, parallel with the modern road.

In this same parish of St. Columb Major, but nearly three miles to the south-east of the village, is the finest of all the round forts of Cornwall. This is one of the two sites which share the name of Castle-an-Dinas. It has three rings of huge earthen ramparts with a fourth, much fainter, outside them; the overall measurement is eight hundred and fifty feet. Castle-an-Dinas would make an excellent stronghold for overlords concerned to guard and control the tin-trade. It stands close to some ancient tin-workings and between the rich deposits of the St. Austell moors and the old port of Harlyn Bay (behind Trevose Head); it commands what is now the main road down the peninsula. It is not hard to think of it as the fortress of primitive merchant adventurers, magnates of the earliest metallurgical business in the world.

A fortress of a very different kind can be seen at no great distance to the west; the promontory fort on Trevelgue Head near Newquay is perhaps the best example of a type of fortification very common round the Cornish coasts. The extremity of the fortified area is virtually an island, cut off from the rest by a rocky chasm which serves as a ditch to one of six lines of rampart defending the place against attack on the landward side. Either, then, there was a bridge across the gap in prehistoric times, thrown up by who knows what feats of primitive engineering, or the sea has increased the fissure during the last two thousand years. Excavation has shown that this exposed headland was occupied for some eight centuries, perhaps because it was used for metal-working. Iron-mines have been found under the cliffs, rock-cut furnaces are known and traces also of bronze-smelting. The first occupation was relatively early in the Iron Age, probably as early as the third century B.C. when, it is claimed, wretched inhabitants lived in wattle huts behind a single palisaded bank and ate nothing but limpets and mussels—particularly 'mussel broth' a combination of mussels and mussel shells, pounded together and stewed. Perhaps it should be called mousse . . . or perhaps the excavators got the recipe wrong? Later much stronger huts were built with wooden framework and stone walls. The headland seems then to have been occupied at least intermittently through the Roman period and on into the Dark Ages.

There are two mounds, apparently round barrows, inside the fort, but nothing was found when they were opened; on the other hand, a very conspicuous pair of barrows joined by an earth bank which stands on the cliff edge about half a mile to the east of Trevelgue were both found to have been raised over crouched bodies, one of them holding a shapely and well-polished granite battle-axe.

If we went due east instead of west from Castle-an-Dinas we could reach a third fort, Castle Dore on the approaches to Fowey, a double-walled round fort which has been most carefully excavated. It showed the marks of about a dozen round wooden huts with stout timber uprights and a conical roof resting on a low outer wall. The fort appears to have been continuously occupied from the second century B.C. until well after the Roman conquest. Evidence was found of a Dark Age occupation that might justify the traditional identification of Castle Dore with King Mark and the immortal legend of Tristan and Iseult.

Ignoring a few scattered forts I will pass directly to the next upland area —the moors lying south of Redruth. The most remarkable site of these moors is Carn Brea which lies towards their northern limit between Redruth and Camborne. This hill cannot be missed for on one of its three summits there is the ruin of a medieval castle and on another a modern monument. The hill indeed has experienced human activities over a long range of time, for its prehistoric settlement seems to date back to the New Stone Age. The same two peaks which support castle and monument are enclosed by straggling and irregular stone walls, originally in coursed dry masonry, now ruinous and incomplete. These walls, which protect an area over a thousand feet long, were probably built in the Iron Age, but the first occupation seems to be about two thousand years earlier. When the interior was explored the diggers were able to find some hundred little round stone-built huts, and rock-shelters of a still more primitive kind, but they were unable to distinguish any order in the rubbish within them. This presented a jumble of all periods from the Stone Age to the present. Pottery and elegant leaf-shaped arrowheads, however, make it fairly certain that the hill-top was already inhabited by the end of the New Stone Age, though most of the surviving huts were probably very much later. Carn Brea has been extraordinarily prolific; a small hoard of Bronze Age socketed axes was found on the slopes of the hill, and in the middle of the eighteenth century two hoards of British gold coins of the usual Celtic type were discovered, apparently within the fortified area. These last must surely represent some of the profits of the tin-trade buried by capitalists who had not yet advanced far enough in their iniquity to command a strong room. Stray coin finds prolong the history of Carn Brea right through Roman times.

One powerful attraction accounts for man's fondness for these harsh granite slopes, for all the relics of trade and industry which they have been found to hold. It is the same attraction which accounts for the ruins of pithead buildings and gear which still give the neighbouring countryside that air of unending melancholy which goes with a dead industry: the tinstone infused among the rocks in times too remote for comprehension when the granite itself was a molten mass roasting and transforming the surrounding rocks.

The other monument on these moors deserving a visit is the dolmen known as Giant's Quoit which stands at Caerwynen four miles to the south-west. The capstone fell during the nineteenth century, but although split, it has been replaced on its three uprights with reasonable accuracy. As the peninsula narrows towards its famous End, distances grow appropriately smaller. From this dolmen on Redruth Moor it is not more than eight miles to the base of the Lizard promontory. There along the southern side of the Helford River, there is a line of three forts, and one of them at Halligye near Trelowarren in the parish of Mawgan in Meneage should certainly be visited, not for its own sake but to see the finest example of a fogou in all Cornwall. These subterranean refuges, a Cornish speciality, are usually found in or near an Iron Age village, or, as at the present site, opening on to the ramparts of a fort. They were constructed in very much the same way as a tunnel air-raid shelter. Wide and deep trenches were dug, then lined with drystone walling, slightly corbelled and then roofed with large transverse slabs; finally earth was piled back over them. All entrances and internal doorways were made small and solid by the use of heavy monolithic jambs and lintels—doubtless because they made good defence points, places where a foe could conveniently be dispatched while still bent double. Although they must often have been used peacefully enough as retreats from the enmity of winter, no effort of the imagination is likely to exceed the reality of the wild scenes which some of the fogous must have known. Their value depended on their familiarity to their owners and their strangeness to the enemy. The owner had as many boltholes as a rabbit which would enable him to escape, or perhaps to return and take his opponents, groping in hostile darkness, brutally from behind. Crouch in a fogou in this unbroken prehistoric darkness and fill it, if you will, with scuffles, blows, gurgles, shrieks and thuds. It will probably have heard them all in its day.

The Halligye fogou is still complete, so complete as to be pitch-dark, and the explorer must carry a light. The main passage is as much as fifty-four feet long; there is another, very massive, at right-angles to it at the east end and a much smaller one at the west. Near the junction of this small gallery a ridge of rock two feet high has been left projecting from the floor; it has been recognized as a true stumbling-block, a trap intended to bring down an enemy pursuing one through the darkness.

After this it is perhaps something of an anticlimax to recommend the inspection of a large cist which lies several miles further south in the parish of St. Keverne. It has the unusual name of the Three Brothers of Grogith and its large cover-stone is pitted with the little circular hollows which archaeologists call cup-marks without having the slightest notion of their purpose.

The Penwith peninsula which at Land's End reaches furthest west of any part of England is still heavily marked by the enterprise of its earliest inhabitants, many of them drawn there by its native tin. Penwith is a quintessence of all Cornish scenery; the flattened inland landscape, worn by the wind and rain, worn on the sea-bed, dull green turf and darker spreads of heather; in contrast the brilliant quality of the light, alien to England, rays refracted and intensified by the surrounding mirror of the sea. In this light all the furnishings of the sea coast, the appliances of fishermen, lighthouse-keepers, and coastguards, seem cut in agate; hard outlines, colours and shapes clear and formal, red, black and white like a game of chess disposed on its board. Yet all these brilliant objects and their sombre background are alike often veiled in mist, a white mist in which every minute particle of water reflects the light of the hidden Cornish sun. When at last the veils begin to thin, the wind seems to cut them to ribbons on the sharp forms of the landscape, but over the moors it rolls them up more gently. These, perhaps, are the best moments of all to see the great stone tombs, to see them emerge from the mist—is it of time or place?

Crossing the narrow neck of the Penwith peninsula the first arresting monument stands right in the centre—the second Castle-an-Dinas which secures an isolated summit on Gulval Downs three or four miles north of Penzance. It is very much like its namesake (p. 174), with its three circular ramparts and intervening ditches, but here the walls are stone built—though damaged by the erection of a modern tower. Castle-an-Dinas draws its greatest distinction from the village of tin-workers which it was probably built to defend. About a mile away on the west slopes of the hill is the Late Iron Age and Roman village of Chysauster, meticulously excavated and now carefully maintained. It is laid out in an orderly way with nine houses opening on a slightly curved lane in opposing pairs. The houses are of an unusual kind, known in Wales and further north but believed to be of Mediterranean origin. The principle of this domestic architecture is so utterly unlike our own that it is not easy to describe.

The external outline is a rough oval, but the oval wall is immensely thick and contains within itself all the rooms, their doorways opening on to a central courtyard. In nearly all the houses the 'best room', oval or round in shape, is exactly opposite the narrow, roofed passage that leads into the courtyard from the lane. This larger room appears to have been thatched or turfed, but a few of the smaller cells were corbelled. Most of the floors were paved, and the larger rooms were usually furnished with hollow granite basins, presumably used as mortars; fragments of rotary querns or handmills were also found. There were serviceable drains, usually laid below the paving stones.

Behind each house was a private garden, skilfully terraced and secured by an outer retaining wall of large blocks. A much-worn road led down from the village to the tin-deposits in the valley below as well as to the nearest stream. Where so much is preserved one longs to see it peopled; to know how many of them worked in the mines and how regularly; how much time they gave to their gardens: how far they were their own masters and how they marketed their produce, getting the ore to the merchants who, as we are now fairly confident, shipped it from St. Michael's Mount as the first step on the long route across France to their Mediterranean customers. At least it is not difficult on going into one of the Chysauster houses to see it in an Iron Age summer, the sun glaring in the courtyard where the dogs lie on the paving, the rooms dark as caves, a woman sweating as she pounds away with the heavy grindstone, small children kept safely in sight by the closed door of the passageway. All a little smelly and untidy, but not too uncomfortable and wonderfully companionable, with the eight neighbouring families, every detail known of their affairs—of expected births, betrothals, deaths; scandals, failures and achievements.

Penwith is so thick with remains that it is difficult to steer a route among them; the traveller consulting the one-inch Ordnance Survey map will see that the whole region is grey with Gothic type. Perhaps it will be best to follow footpaths towards the north-west where in less than three miles we can reach the famous Zennor Quoit, a striking piece of megalithic architecture well set on a ridge. It nearly resembles Trethevy, at the other end of the county, possessing the same antechamber and chamber, but with no opening between them. Although the great capstone has slipped backwards and no longer rests upon them, the two slabs which stand before the antechamber still make an impressive portal; one would like to understand what ritual meaning, or what blindly followed tradition, gave rise to this idea of a portal giving on to a blank wall. It is evidently akin to that of the 'dummy portals' we shall find in long barrows in the Cotswolds and Wales, but is not, I think, identical.

If we follow the winding coastal road westward from Zennor, there are many ancient sites scattered over the country on the left-hand side—villages, barrows, standing stones. Among them it is certainly worth turning off at Kerrowe to see the megalithic gallery at Pennance, where the chamber still retains more of the mound and its enclosing wall than is commonly found in this part of the world. A lane can then be followed southward until it meets the Newmill road at the head of the little Try Valley. Here on the slopes of Mulfra Hill is another dolmen, a much smaller version of Zennor and again with a leaning capstone. On the western slopes of the same hill, at Bodrifty, an Iron Age hut settlement has been excavated, it covers some four acres, where traces of the hut platforms, lyncheted fields and the enclosing ring wall are still visible. Antiquities now crowd thick and fast. If we follow the Newmill road back to the coast it passes a stone circle and comes out on the coastal road just opposite the long promontory of Gurnard's Head where there is a fort and three or four chambered round cairns (one like that at Pennance) on the track between the Head and Bosporthennis.

Better game, however, is to be found if, instead of returning to the coast, we make a zig-zag way, across the rough country south-west of Mulfra Quoit. Here we can pass another Nine Maidens circle and find the curious, and indeed unique, ruins of Men-an-Tol. There are now other stones standing near it, but these are known to have been moved in recent times; the one extraordinary feature of Men-an-Tol is a large, thin polygonal slab with a perfectly round hole through its centre. It is certainly the surviving relic of a tomb, probably it served as a partition in a gallery grave. We shall find 'port-hole' entrances elsewhere in megalithic architecture, but few so perfect as this one. Until quite recently it kept magic properties; sick people crawled through it to be rid of their pains and children were passed through as a cure for rickets. Others, less stricken, consulted it 'to be informed of some material incident of Love or Fortune which they could not know soon enough in a natural way'. This perhaps was wiser than the pseudo-scientific Lockyer, who tried to turn Men-an-Tol into an astronomical instrument for observing sunrises and sunsets at certain 'critical' times of the year.

It is now a short walk across Green Burrow to the place where Lanyon Quoit stands beside the road between Penzance and Morvah. It is such a fine upstanding megalith so conveniently set near the road and at such a short distance from Penzance where, seasonally, there are many people with not enough to do, that it is one of the most visited monuments in the West Country. A flat capstone, nineteen feet long, rests like a table-top on three legs. The height of this tripod is still five feet, and it is reliably recorded that in the eighteenth century 'it was so high that a man could sit on horseback beneath it'. It fell in Waterloo year, and although carefully re-erected, some of the stones were broken and the total size had to be reduced. The remains of the mound are slight, but enough to suggest a long plan with the chamber at the northern end. Lanyon Quoit has, indeed, been recognized as the only long barrow in Cornwall, but this is a questionable claim.

If we take the road back towards Morvah, it leads us close to Chun Castle, a fine round fort on a hill which commands all the country behind Land's End. Its defences are of quite extraordinary strength; a double rampart of drystone walling faced with massive granite blocks; within recorded memory the inner one still stood twelve feet high. The entrance on the west side, is most skilfully designed to put any attacker helpless at the mercy of the defence—Chun Castle must have been almost impregnable unless surprised in a Penwith mist. Like all the rest of these round forts, it should be connected with the tin trade, and here tangible evidence has been found—a large cake of tin slag found in the interior, together with iron slag and an elaborate smelting-furnace. We have now come to expect villages lying close beside these forts for their protection; at Chun there are three of them, all probably very much like Chysauster, small groups of courtyard houses. A short way below the Castle on the west side of the hill, is Chun Quoit, a closed dolmen with its capstone still firmly in place.

From this point the traveller may visit the stone circles east of St. Just or the large multiple-chambered round cairn of Carn Gluze and the smaller one at Brane. I will lead him on past the fort of Caer Bran, past Carn Euny with its village and fine fogou, past even the Nine Maidens of Boscawen (one of the best of its kind, but we are tired of its kind by now), and so up on to Chapel Carn Brea, a solid, rounded hill overlooking the last few miles to Land's End. The huge round cairn up here, once crowned by a chapel, was long ago found to cover a megalithic gallery, but I have climbed up here only for a parting prospect. There is the final promontory with the cliff-fort of Maen Castle and the tomb of Table Men as our last, westernmost, antiquities. On three sides of us is sea; we could not, if we would, advance beyond Dr. Syntax's Head for it is more advanced than Dr. Johnson's. All round us in these rugged cliffs the granite holds out against the sea, against the long ridges, which, towering or mild, roll in perpetually from the Atlantic. They have had their turn under the sea, these colossal boulders, but now they seem well established, bulwarks that should outlast all human interests.

Chapter Six

OXFORDSHIRE TO THE FOREST OF DEAN

A. Oxfordshire and the Cotswolds
B. The Malverns and the Forest of Dean

A. *Oxfordshire and the Cotswolds*

THIS region is given a very real unity by its geological history. Almost the whole of it is limestone country, the Jurassic limestone which in the south is represented by the famous Bath and Portland stones. Northward, as I have said (p. 39), it extends right up the country through Northamptonshire and Lincolnshire to northern Yorkshire, forming a belt of well-drained upland country which in prehistoric times was the chief inland link between southern and northern England—between the Wessex chalk and the north-country wolds and moorland.

Although it has no building stone which can quite equal Bath and Portland, it is essentially a region of stone architecture. The Cotswolds are, of course, famous for their ancient towns and villages where everything from the splendid churches to the humblest cottages and barns are built of the limestone on which they stand. The fields are stone-walled, and even the roofs were until recently made of special varieties of limestone which could be split into tiles.

The Oxfordshire stone is much of it poor; indeed the Headington quarries just outside the town have proved most treacherous, yielding a stone which in a hundred years or so flakes and scales away into a dismal ruin. Oxford colleges have had to spend hundreds of thousands of pounds on refacing their buildings. Nevertheless Oxfordshire can show delightful stone-built villages, though neither in the landscape nor in the architecture is the limestone as conspicuous as it is in the Cotswolds.

We had the southern edge of the present region in sight when we were on the Berkshire and Marlborough Downs and were able to look straight on to it across the Thames Valley. Indeed, the first place I wish to mention is actually on the south of the Thames and in full view from the east end of the Berkshire Hills where we first mounted them from Goring and Streatley. This is the hill-fort on one of the two plump round hills known as Wittenham Clumps to the north of Wallingford; it consists of a single rather feeble bank and ditch, but the natural situation is a fine one and the fort lies close to the interesting ancient track known as the Paynim Way. Nearby is the second Dorchester, now a large village with a magnificent abbey church, and in Roman times a small market town. Very little of this survives, although as so commonly happens some of the Roman material has gone into the fabric of the abbey church; the most attractive thing at Dorchester is a gleaming watery site where the Dyke Hills earthwork seems to have been designed to defend the headland between the Thames and the tributary Thame. It is also worth lamenting the ring-works dating from the end of the New Stone Age which were excavated on the north side of Dorchester but have now been devoured by gravel quarries—whose endless rapacity is destroying great stretches of the Thames Valley.

Southern Oxfordshire is not rich in monuments, and the only other which I wish to name is the Devil's Quoits, three stones which stood, widely spaced, on the south-west side of the village of Stanton Harcourt. It had long been suggested that they might be the survivors from a stone circle, but few people believed it and there was surprise when excavation made necessary by the construction of an aerodrome showed that the stones were in fact part of an embanked sanctuary of the Bronze Age. The Quoits were buried close by where they had stood.

Stanton Harcourt is in relatively low-lying country; it is now time to advance into the northern part of the country where the limestone rises to form hills that are already virtually a part of the Cotswolds. Here, about three miles north of Chipping Norton and exactly on the boundary between Oxfordshire and Warwickshire, we shall find a famous group of monuments. I do not claim that the Rollright Stones are a beautiful or stirring sight, the limestone has weathered badly; pocked and flaking, it has no quality of either form or colour, and all the monuments are aesthetically ruined by their enclosure within mean iron railings. They owe much of their significance and value to what has been added to them by the imagination of the country people who have inherited them from the past. As Sir Arthur Evans wrote: 'The folklore of which the Rollright Stones have become the centre is of the highest interest, and it would be difficult to find any English site in which it is more living at the present day. I have myself taken down from the lips of the country people in the immediate neighbourhood, but especially about Little Rollright, a quantity of tales relating to the stones.' This imaginative marinade in which they have been steeped reveals itself in names which give character and romance to these physically undistinguished stones. The King Stone is an isolated stone with a bite out of one side—possibly it once formed half a 'port-hole' entry to a chamber: it stands by a slight rise, once thought to be a barrow but in fact natural. The King Stone is on the northern, Warwickshire, side of the road; on the opposite side, in Oxfordshire, is a stone circle known as the King's Men, while across a field to the east is a group of stones, undoubtedly the remains of a megalithic burial-chamber, which has evoked the best name of all—the Whispering Knights. The story which unites them is as follows:

A King was setting out to conquer all England, but as he led his army up the hill at Rollright he met the witch to whom the land belonged. A few steps further and he would be on the crest with Long Compton visible in the valley on the other side; he was therefore delighted when the witch said:

> Seven long strides shalt thou take
> If Long Compton thou canst see
> King of England thou shalt be.

And he himself cried out:

> Stick, stock, stone,
> As King of England I shall be known.

He took the seven strides, but he did not know of the existence of the long barrow and its extra height prevented him from seeing Long Compton. The witch, with the unfair triumph of supernatural powers, pronounced:

> As Long Compton thou canst not see,
> King of England thou shalt not be,
> Rise up, stick, and stand still, stone,
> For King of England thou shalt be none;
> Thou and thy men hoar stones shall be
> And I myself an eldern tree.

Immediately the King and his men were turned to stone, as so also were some treacherous followers who had been whispering plots together in the background; the witch obeyed her own prophecy and became an elder-tree.

That this story, unexpected enough in the English countryside a few miles from Oxford University, is itself a rationalization of far more ancient beliefs is suggested by other Rollright tales and customs. For example, that the King really was the chief for whom the long barrow was built might be implied by a practice recorded by Stukeley; he describes a square plot near the King Stone, 'Hither on a certain day of the year the young men and maidens customarily meet and make merry with cakes and ale.' Again, that the witch was a tree-spirit, an Oxfordshire dryad, hardly needs the corroboration of a practice described to Sir Arthur Evans by an old lady who had it from her husband's mother: 'On Midsummer Eve when the "eldern tree" was in blossom, it was the custom for people to come up to the King Stone and stand in a circle. Then the eldern was cut, and as it bled the King moved his head.' The Whispering Knights, too, became more interesting as oracles. An old woman, one Betsy Hughes, whose mother had been murdered as a witch, confessed to Sir Arthur that when she was a girl she and her friends would slip off to the stones at the time of the barley harvest, when they were working until dusk. There, with a good deal of giggling, they would take it in turns to lay their ears to a crevice and listen for the whispering; another old crone completed the picture by recalling that the Whispering Knights were used to tell the future. 'Time after time I have heard them whisper—but perhaps after all it was only the wind.'

With these notions go others which are of interest not because they are peculiar to Rollright but, on the contrary, because they are so widespread in Western Europe. The stones in the circle cannot be correctly counted; all the stones go down at midnight (some say only on special festivals) to drink at the spring in Little Rollright Spinney; when the capstone of the Whispering Knights was taken for a bridge at Little Rollright it needed six horses to drag it downhill and then every night it threw itself back on to the grass; when the desecrators gave up their attempt in despair it proved that one horse could draw the slab back up the hill without effort.

All these legends, and still more the memories of customs carried on almost within living memory, show that we do not have to follow the setting sun into the lands of Celtic twilight to find remains of the prehistoric past which still have life in them. They are here in the heavy summer light of the English midlands. Let the traveller, the seeker after antiquities, accept this lesson from Rollright: the past has left marks deep in the human mind as real as the tangible marks which we search out among our fields and hills.

Two sites to the south of Chipping Norton should be named before we cross the Evenlode, the county boundary and the straight line of the Fosse Way to reach the greatest of the limestone uplands the Gloucestershire Cotswolds. These are first the Hoar Stone (one of at least three in the county with this generic name) just south of Enstone village, the remains of a long

barrow much overgrown but with a considerable part of the barrow surviving, and second the Lyneham long barrow between Shipton-under-
Wychwood and Chipping Norton, a mile south of Sarsden. The Lyneham
mound is about one hundred and seventy feet long and can best be recognized by a single large slab standing at the north-east end. It was dug late
in the last century in a rough and reàdy fashion and the tops of the uprights of two chambers found at that time are still visible. The excavators
found 'skulls and human and animal bones and hearths' as well as two
Saxon burials.

Returning to Chipping Norton for the approach to the Cotswolds we
must pass the fort known as Chastleton Camp, cr Chastleton Burrow,
which stands above the Evenlode at the junction of the three counties of
Oxfordshire, Warwickshire and Gloucestershire. It reminds us at once that
we are now in stone country, for the roughly circular ramparts are true
walls and not revetted banks. Standing as much as four feet high, some
stretches are built of large limestone blocks, others of finer-quality masonry, with fitted polygonal stones. Chastleton has been dated to a fairly
early phase of the Iron Age, perhaps to the second half of the third century
B.C. It commands a splendid view across the valley to our next objective,
the north-eastern scarp of the Cotswolds.

The Cotswolds represent one of the fairest relationships between man
and nature which survives for us to experience. The whole region is a
monument to the wool industry, which brought wealth without industrial
squalor, and to the devout faith of the men who created it. Visitors must
always go to these uplands to enjoy the unspoiled villages with their big
churches; the little wool towns often hardly changed architecturally since
the seventeenth or eighteenth century, and with churches large enough for
modest cathedrals; the comfortable farms and manor-houses all set
among fields of soft, cigar-box brown, divided by grey walls and given
greater strength and shapeliness by beech-woods and hangers. I hope,
however, that it will only add to this enjoyment to look also a little deeper
into time, to see the obscure handiwork of the earlier owners of this upland
territory, men and women who must, after all, have contributed much to
the ancestry of Cotswold farmers and woolmen and their modern descendants, who still keep the countryside both fair and profitable. There will
be a certain monotony in accounts of the chambered long barrows left by
the farming population of the New Stone Age.

In most of these very interesting monuments the long mound was
originally enclosed within drystone walls that gave it a formal, trapezoidal
plan. At the wider end the mound projects to form a court-like entry to

the megalithic chamber behind. This may be an elaborate affair with a gallery and side cells, or a simple rectangular chamber. In a third variety the portal at the centre of the forecourt is a sham, the actual burial chambers opening inconspicuously on to the sides of the mound. It has long been assumed that the gallery type was built by the first-comers, the others being later degenerations. It has now been suggested that all may be roughly contemporary and owe their differences to outside sources rather than to local evolution.

Perhaps excavation may settle the question in time. It still remains very probable indeed that although the idea of the covering mound may owe something to the long barrows of southern and eastern England, the megalithic architecture of the Cotswolds was inspired by immigrants who came from France by way of the Bristol Channel and settled on both sides of the Severn. There are similar tombs across the water in South Wales (p. 207).

The north-eastern corner of the Cotswolds with which we begin, a corner which seems to contain a large number of the most famous Cotswold names—Stow-on-the-Wold, Bourton-on-the-Water, the two Swells, Upper and Lower, together with Upper and Lower Slaughter—also contains the greatest concentration of long barrows. No less than seven of these lie near Upper and Lower Swell. Yet numbers are misleading; unfortunately this group has been too much damaged during the last four thousand years, and particularly the last hundred, to be rewarding to the visitor. They are only worth looking at as a small ingredient in a most charming piece of country. Three of the Swell barrows are in or near Poles Wood Plantation, but they have been roughly dug, and only one, Poles Wood South, has a visible megalithic chamber—a small affair opening on to the north-west corner. Among others in the neighbourhood is the Eyford barrow on the road to Guiting Power; it is an example of the type with several small chambers towards the west end, one of which proved to contain parts of the skeletons of a man and a woman, four children and a dog; there were eleven bodies in the barrow altogether, all of them very short, possibly members of the same family. Eyford is now as battered, shapeless and overgrown as the rest of this north-eastern group, none of which is a good advertisement for the work of Victorian excavators. The truth is that in the whole of the northern part of the Cotswolds, only two long barrows are worth a visit, and one even of these is no more than the skeleton of its ancient form. This is the Notgrove barrow which lies between that village and Salperton to the north-west of Northleach. The mound itself has almost disappeared leaving the slabs of the burial chamber standing free;

these, however, are of considerable interest for they represent the more elaborate type of Cotswold tomb. Two opposing pairs of side cells open off the central passage. Though the monument has recently been re-excavated and put in good order, the bare stone slabs, like all Cotswold stones not large enough to be impressive in their own right, are a poor substitute for the dark, earth-fast sepulchre of which they once formed part; we must wait until we get to Hetty Pegler's Tump before we can understand the real power of this architecture, and imagine the awe which it could inspire among the initiates of the cults which must have centred on the great tombs.

The second notable long barrow is called Belas Knap (it is worth noting that not very many of the Cotswold barrows have folk names attached to them) and it lies far to the west of the rest, about two miles south of Winchcomb and not more than half a dozen miles from the centre of Cheltenham. Luckily the mound is well preserved and judicious restoration has made a monument which gives at least some idea of what these tombs and holy places looked like four thousand years ago. It shows well the oblong form of the mound held within a low retaining wall of fine drystone masonry and it possesses the characteristic 'horns' or recessed forecourt at the larger end. This court makes the approach to a dignified megalithic portal with a pair of large jambs, transverse slab or door stone between them, and a large lintel across the top. But whereas at Notgrove an entrance in just this position must have led into the gallery and its cells, this construction at Belas Knap is a sham, it is built against the solid mass of the barrow and has never at any time given access to anything. It is, in fact, a classic example of the 'false entrance' for which we have already seen fairly close parallels in the south-west and in Kent (p. 70). The true burial-chambers open from the long sides of the mound and are infinitely smaller and meaner than the central chambers of the Notgrove, Hetty Pegler and Nympsfield kind (p. 198). Some have compared these dummies to the false entrances to Egyptian pyramids, claiming that they, too, were made in an attempt to mislead tomb-robbers and keep the burial inviolate; others have attributed the device to human laziness, seeing them as a degenerate form which kept the portal, essential for ritual purposes, but shirked the construction of a large and complex megalithic chamber. For myself I do not find either explanation satisfactory; primitive peoples do not violate their own sanctuaries and here in the Cotswolds there is no evidence to suggest the presence of alien invaders in any force at a time while long barrows were still being built; nor were these New Stone Age peoples in the habit of burying precious grave-goods with the dead which could provoke cupidity. On the other hand if the builders were still willing to raise tons of stone and earth to make the mounds. I cannot think that the small amount of extra labour needed to make the dignified central chamber would have been found burdensome enough to promote such a radical change of plan. I believe that the false entrance was intended to mislead not human beings but supernatural creatures—spirits—but more than that I will not attempt to guess.

From Belas Knap it is a pleasant walk over Postlip Warren to Cleeve Cloud and Cleeve Hill, the well-known hills overlooking Cheltenham. On Cleeve Hill there is a semicircular fort, the ends of its double ramparts resting on a natural cliff—though now perhaps reduced by quarrying. Another fort certainly worth seeing is nearby on Nottingham Hill. The fine scarp which runs north-eastward to the justly famous Cotswold towns of Broadway and Chipping Campden has a number of small earthworks and a moderately strong promontory fort in Beckbury, on a spur above Hailes Abbey. There is a fort, too, on Meon Hill whose isolated summit rises from the rich lands of the Vale of Evesham ten miles south of Stratford-on-Avon. No one has as yet tried to identify it with any Shakespearean landmark, and for a hill made famous by literary associations we must look right down to the southern end of the Vale where the bulk of Bredon Hill, a massive outlier from the Cotswolds, rises near the junction of Warwickshire, Worcestershire and Gloucestershire. The north-western angle of Bredon where it reaches a thousand feet and carries a small stone look-out tower, has been cut off by two lines of ramparts on the south and east. With the steep natural fall of the ground on the other sides these defences with an entrance way through their centre make a sufficiently strong fort. Excavation dated it relatively late in the Iron Age, perhaps to the second century B.C., and it seems to have met a violent end probably at the hands of Belgic forces and not long before the Roman conquest. The excavators found that the wooden gates of the entrance had crashed in flames carrying with them a number of heads most of which bore the marks of violent deaths. Some have interpreted this grisly find as a massacre of the defenders, but it seems far more likely that it had been the custom of the tribe holding the fort to display the heads of enemies or traitors, as was the custom with us until a few centuries ago, and that it was a collection of such trophies which fell when the fort was stormed.

The outlook from Bredon is superb; westward across Avon and Severn to the sudden spine of the Malverns and the more gradual slopes of the Forest of Dean, north and east over the fields and orchards of Pershore and

Evesham, southward to where the massive scarp of the Cotswolds fills the horizon. It is still a place to be on a summer day, letting eyes and mind wander together. Looking at the field shapes and the lines of rivers and hills it is easy, infected by Housman's words, to allow, as he must have done, coloured memories of one's school atlas to impose themselves on this real map, and then, infected by his sense of transience, to think of the Celts gone from this stronghold, the Romans from distant Gloucester, the monks from nearby Tewkesbury. Yet beyond transience, continuity; the slow clearing, grooming, making fertile of all these fields, the building of farms, villages, towns, cathedral cities—all the slowly accumulating activity which has gone on since the builders of the long barrows first brought their boats up the Severn and made their way on to the limestone hills.

Returning to the Cotswolds, I do not propose to seek out the ruins of further long barrows—ploughed, plundered for stone, hogged by long-dead antiquaries—they make a sad sight at Hazleton, Dowdeswell and Withington. Instead I will lead the visitor directly to the Roman villa of Chedworth, for of all Roman villas in Britain it is, I think, the most likely to please and reward him. In the first and second centuries, at the height of its prosperity as a private estate, it was a large country house, probably better appointed and more comfortable than anything to be known in England again before the sixteenth century. Evidently Christianity had been accepted by the later owners of the villa, for the sacred monogram appears on one of the floors—a very rare instance—especially in a place which implies a wealthy, upper-class, convert. Apart from the fact that it is large and well preserved and has had a very interesting history, well illustrated by its museum, Chedworth is particularly worth seeing for the sake of its position. On the slope of a pleasantly sheltered valley deeply buried in woods, it can still suggest with convincing realism what conditions were like in these country houses of the Roman Province. The estates of many of them were, like Chedworth, carved out from valleys which had hitherto been left to the trees and their wild inhabitants. Many of the families of wealthy romanized Britons or foreign officials who owned them must have known what it was like to live thus folded among trees, little oases of civilization in a land still only half-civilized.

Among ruined long barrows in the Coln Valley within a few miles of Chedworth, I will name only two; there is an unusually enormous specimen in the parish of Coln Rogers; this Colnpen mound is three hundred feet long, and although it lacks any architectural features, when seen against the sky-line the immense spine is very clear and shows the characteristic profile of these long barrows, always higher as well as wider at the 'horned' end. There is a round barrow close to the east end of Colnpen and a row of three others, apparently unopened, on the edge of the valley three hundred yards to the north. The second Coln Valley barrow is at Lamborough Banks north-west of the village of Ablington. It seems to have been exceptionally well preserved until about the middle of the last century when it suffered one of the rough excavations of the period. The results suggest that it must have had a horned court with dummy entrance. It is now a good deal overgrown, but would probably richly reward a complete and careful excavation.

The barrow in this region which is most worth visiting is a little to the north between Eastington and Aldsworth near the source of the small river Leach. This monument stands just behind Lodge Park, the beautiful seventeenth-century dower-house of Sherborne. Such a setting in open parkland beside an architectural treasure of the greatest charm and distinction, is greatly to be preferred to the usual barrow site in a ploughed field, rough pasture, or a nettle-filled copse. Nevertheless that is not the only reason why it should be seen; it is quite exceptionally unspoiled. Indeed a well-known and outspoken archaeologist has written of it: 'This is the finest Long Barrow I have ever seen; it is certainly the most perfect specimen in Gloucestershire, and should be left exactly as it is and never excavated, in order that posterity may be able to see at least one unmutilated Long Barrow.' The mound is one hundred and fifty feet long, covered with turf, and still rises to a very considerable height towards the southeast end where two uprights and a lintel stone show through the grass. The tips of other uprights can be seen behind the lintel and the whole suggests a complete chamber of the gallery type; I confess that when I first saw it, thoughts far less noble and distinterested than those just quoted came into my head. I longed to excavate without delay.

About two miles to the east on the Northleach–Burford road a track opposite the turning to Windrush leads to a neat, circular fort with a single well-preserved rampart, built on level ground in open farmland.

Having named the best of the sites on the south-eastern slopes of the Cotswolds I want to return to the north-western scarp which I left at Cleeve Cloud above Cheltenham. All along this face the limestone rises sheer above the expanse of the Severn Valley, itself flat, green and laced with streams and dykes. It is always lovely here on these natural ramparts, perhaps loveliest twice in the year—once in the spring when the white pearblossom of the perry orchards shows like breaking foam on the lower slopes of the escarpment; once in the autumn when the beech hangers of the upper slopes burn between earth and sky. The scarp was evidently well populated in the New Stone Age, for the communities of that time chose to build a line of their tombs close to its edge in positions which commanded the finest views over the Severn and on to the Welsh mountains where, as we shall find, kinsfolk of theirs had their territories.

There is an interesting fort on Leckhampton Hill only two miles south of Cheltenham, but more attractive to visit is Crickley Hill on the Cheltenham – Birdlip road, a headland with precipitous sides where there are small caves and rock-shelters. These look as though they should have attracted prehistoric man, but they have been quarried and their principal tenants have always been—as they are to-day—jackdaws. The headland is approached through a beech-wood and it is not difficult to distinguish the double lines of rampart which run across the neck; with its sheer, lofty sides Crickley fort must have been almost impregnable. There are long barrows on either side of Crickley at Shurdington and Coberley, but these are hardly so well worth looking for as the round barrows concealed by the wood just across the road from the 'Air Balloon', a popular inn near the base of the Crickley headland. One of these is so high and so steep-sided that it may well be Roman.

On fine week-ends scores of cars draw up along the edge of the escarpment between the 'Air Balloon' and Birdlip, and there the owners eat exhausting picnic teas and try to restrain their children from danger while gazing out over Severn in a vacantly enthusiastic way which their prehistoric ancestors would certainly have found hard to understand.

Birdlip is a name well known in archaeology because one of our finest engraved bronze mirrors was found there, a true masterpiece of Celtic art of the Late Iron Age; nothing however, remains to be seen of the slab-lined grave in which it was found, lying beside the skeleton of the woman whose living features it must so often have reflected. The long miles of Ermine Street between Birdlip and Cirencester are a fine example of the modernized Roman road.

Following the pretty road running westward through the beech-woods which here line the scarp, the traveller should look out for the long barrow of West Tump, now thickly screened with trees and undergrowth on the left-hand side of the road, but once commanding a prospect over the valley. It was excavated in the nineteenth century and revealed the characteristic tapering rectangular outline marked by a drystone wall. Between the horns, as the excavator observed, were 'two upright stones forming as it were a doorway; but this proved to be a deception. . .'. He had in fact found a false entrance of the kind with which we are now so familiar. The principal burial-chamber discovered was on the south side towards the tail of the mound. It proved to be as much as twenty-four feet long (including the entrance passage) and to contain the bones of at least a score of bodies. Most of the remains seem to have been in confusion, but at the innermost end of the chamber and resting on a semicircular paving of slabs 'was deposited in a contracted form, the skeleton of, probably, a young female, with the remains of a baby in close proximity'. The diggers were of the opinion that 'the barrow was erected in honour of this Cotteswold chieftainess'; it is equally likely that the probable young female was merely the last, and therefore the least disturbed, of the burials in the chamber.

Within a short distance we come to Cooper's Hill which lifts an immensely steep headland above the road. There was once a hill-fort on the head, but quarrying has lost it among a maze of overgrown pits and spoilheaps; further to the south-east along the ridge there is, however, a strong cross-ridge dyke which must have been designed to secure the whole promontory. Cooper's Hill itself has an association with the past which is of a kind that many people find more remarkable than any mere physical remains. It is a centre of local customs perhaps enacted here since prehistoric times: all children of the neighbourhood through the whole of this history, have been brought up to assume these ceremonies should and will take place. Now, when most people unconsciously regret the loss of all such forms and customs, their few survivals exercize a tremendous attraction. To-day the Cooper's Hill wake draws a large crowd of alien sightseers –also it is now run by a committee instead of by instinct.

From our present point of view the only objection to this type of antiquity is that it can only be seen once a year; the wake is celebrated on Whit-Monday. Nevertheless one feature of it is permanent; the immense maypole with a weathercock on top which stands at the extremity of the headland. Maypole dances are no longer danced, but it is decked with flowers for the wake, and these must be allowed to wither where they hang. The great traditional ceremony is the cheese-rolling. The Master of Ceremonies, a villager in white smock and grey, be-ribboned top hat, sits at the top of the steep nose of the headland (it is far too steep to stand easily) with the cheese-roller next to him and the competitors sitting in a line on either side. The Master gives the word, the roller lets the cheese go, and a moment later the racers bound down after it; the winner takes the cheese and (nowadays) there are prizes for the runners-up—if they may be so misleadingly described. A further mark of modern decadence is that a wooden drum with a fragment of cheese let into it is used for the race. A real cheese is sometimes burst by its violent boundings and to-day no one is inclined to provide another. The villagers associate their cheese-rolling with the maintenance of their grazing rights on the common, but the maypole helps to make it certain that the ceremony must originally have been part of a fertility cult, perhaps principally concerned with cattle and horses. I do not know of any other example of cheese-rolling except that already noticed at Uffington, which has long since come to an end.

Next in the remarkable succession of ancient sites along this western edge of the Cotswolds is the fort on Painswick Beacon between Cooper's Hill and Haresfield. This lofty summit on the scarp is enclosed by a strong double rampart and ditch, and from the banks the view is exceptional even among the many fine prospects from the escarpment. The Malverns and the Black Mountains of South Wales show their peaks beyond all the intricate detail and busy life of the wide valley between. Painswick has never been excavated but it need not be doubted that it was built in the Iron Age, probably at much the same time and by the same people as the defences of Bredon Hill. It has a near neighbour in the promontory fort on Haresfield Beacon, just above Haresfield station.

At the end of this line of hills which is partially cut off by the Painswick Valley is Randwick Hill, and here inside the walls of another earthwork are the considerable remains of a long barrow. When excavated in the 1880's it proved to belong to a form which might be thought to be inter-mediate between the full-chambered gallery and the false-entrance type. The main chamber was entered through an opening in the forecourt, but there was no elaborate gallery with side cells, only a single chamber roughly five feet square lying immediately behind the entrance. On the floor the diggers found confused fragments of human skeletons and a number of bird-bones. The report ends: 'By direction of the owner, Mrs. Barrow [an odd coinci-dence], the walls and chambers have been covered up to protect them from damage.' I wish Mrs. Barrow could have been the patron saint of many other barrows dug by this gentleman and his friends, for whereas her fore-sight has preserved the Randwick chamber (even if it is out of sight), most of the other barrows which suffered from their sub-scientific curiosity were left open and have been wrecked by subsidence and the growth of plants and trees.

At this point, the escarpment is cut by the Stroud Valley, and those who are interested in such things should notice how the Frome and its tribu-taries have spread gravels across the valley right to the banks of the Severn. In prehistoric times these firm gravels probably offered an open causeway across the swampy valley bottom which may well have been used by the immigrant long-barrow people on their way to the hills.

There is a concentration of long barrows near the headwaters of the Frome in the triangle between Painswick, Duntisbourne Abbots and Sapperton, but none is distinguished and I propose to leave them to enthusiasts armed with their Ordnance maps. Indeed, if I am going to make any sepulchral recommendations, I should prefer to guide the intelligent traveller to Painswick, where there is an exquisitely-set church, and a churchyard famous for its avenues of Irish yews and elegant eighteenth-century tombs. Before crossing the Stroud Valley to the southern part of the Cotswolds, an area rich in antiquity, I want only to recommend a visit to Cirencester. Here at the crossing-place of Ermine Street, the Fosse Way and Akeman Street was a large Roman town, *Corinium*. The walls, though robbed of their masonry facings, still show well in the very low land near the river, while outside them the embankments of a large amphitheatre deserve to be seen. There is also an unusually good museum, housed in a modern building, where the finds from *Corinium* can be studied in ideal conditions.

Just two and a half miles to the north-west of Cirencester, at Bagendon, are the remains of the ramparts and ditches enclosing an area of some two hundred acres, which formed the defences of the capital of the Dobunni, the Celtic tribe that inhabited much of Gloucestershire in the Iron Age. The most clearly visible remains of the earthworks are at Scrubditch where the bank still stands to a height of almost ten feet. Excavation has revealed the remains of the half-timbered huts, which had foundations and floors of stone. Finds of imported pottery, glass and even wine amphorae show that the inhabitants must have had regular trading contacts with the Roman Empire before the invasion of 43 A.D. At an early period during the Roman occupation Bagendon was abandoned and the new cantonal capital of the Dobunni established at Cirencester.

From Cirencester we are ready to return to the countryside immediately to the south of Stroud, which probably has more spectacular and varied prehistoric remains than any other part of the Cotswolds. The Stroud Valley is itself an open-air museum for the study of early industrial development: in this narrow, steep-sided valley, there are many agreeable stone factories built in the eighteenth century when the tumbling waters of the Frome were still considered good enough to run the mills. The houses, often in small terraces, climb up the steep slopes, roof to door-step, and though nothing could be more English than their architecture, the general effect is charming but decidedly alien   perhaps most like the little towns that one sees in the limestone ravines of southern France.

Returning from Cirencester, we pass the Windmill Tump long barrow which lies south-west of the village of Rodmarton near the Tetbury road, and very close to the source of the river Thames. It is an interesting monument but unfortunately for the passing visitor its most unusual features are now hidden, having been covered in for their better preservation. The mound itself shows clearly enough, outlined as it is by a modern drystone wall. It is of the type with a fine horned forecourt and dummy entrance, but it is the two chambers opening on to the long sides which are of outstanding but invisible interest. The entry to both those cells was through 'port-holes' made not by a single perforation as at Men-an-Tol (p. 180), but by placing together two slabs each with a semicircular bite removed from it. In the southern chamber it was found that the entry was approached by a flight of skilfully laid stone steps and that the port-hole was still closed by a plug of drystone masonry—which must have been fitted in by neat and practised hands after the last burial was made over four thousand years ago. Although such a sealing of the tombs was probably usual, it is a feature which is not known to have survived in any other place.

From Rodmarton it is not far to Avening, the centre of an important barrow group. In a field adjoining the rectory garden a quarter of a mile north of the church are three megalithic chambers which have been taken from a nearby long barrow and re-erected. In one of them is what is among the best examples of a 'port-hole' entrance in all Britain. Although the site of this barrow has not been identified, I am assured that it is not, as has been stated in *Long Barrows of the Cotswolds*, the mound known as Norn's Tump behind the 'Nag's Head Inn'. Norn's Tump may, in fact, be a round barrow.

If now we turn north by the rectory along Step's Lane, we pass on the left the Tinglestone barrow, crowned with beech-trees and with a single massive stone slab projecting high above the larger end. Tinglestone is already within the property of Gatcombe Park, and it is not far along the road to the park gates where an unusually fine long barrow can be seen on a small and heavily wooded ridge just above the lodge. Here again there is a false entrance between the horns, while the only chamber at present known opens on to the north side. Its shadowy opening below a lintel stone has a romantic fairy-book air. Visitors should certainly allow themselves to be lured in, for they will find a perfectly preserved cell, comfortably covered with a thick bed of beech-leaves, where the combination of drystone with megalithic masonry can be studied at ease. The spaces between the megalithic uprights, and frequently between the uprights and the capstone, are neatly packed with drystone masonry of very fine quality. It is a method very widely employed by the architects of the New Stone Age, but in most places the drystone has disappeared leaving the large blocks in misleading isolation.

A short distance further brings us to Minchinhampton which lies at the base of the spur of high ground between the deep valleys of Nailsworth and Chalford. This spur has a number of earthworks: a single straight length of bank and ditch near the tip of Rodborough, a semicircular embankment with a far more powerful line of rampart bisecting it which stands on the edge of the hill above Amberley, and, close at hand, the large and powerful earthwork on Minchinhampton Common which is known as the Bulwarks. The Bulwarks is curved like a bow and it is a little unexpected to find the ditch on the concave side, facing south-east towards the neck of the spur: this position suggests that the earthworks is intended to cut off the whole headland as far as Rodborough, serving as an outer line of defence to the Amberley enclosure. All these earthworks belong to the first century A.D. and it has even been suggested that they formed a stronghold for Caractacus during his flight from the Romans after his defeats in Kent. There is, as yet, no evidence to prove this theory and the earthworks might equally well belong to an earlier date in the first century.

There are several round barrows on the common, and at Amberley a rather poor long barrow known as Whitefield's Tump gains distinction from a persistent and probably reliable tradition that Whitefield preached from its summit in 1743. I know of barrows that support or have supported, signposts, guns, monuments, artillery targets, golf-balls, a gibbet—but this is the only instance I can remember of an evangelical preacher.

About two miles to the north-west of Whitefield's Tump and the same distance south of Stroud, there is a very long barrow on the open common land of Selsey Hill. It belongs to the series which seem to have been built on the escarpment in order to command the outlook over the Vale of Gloucester and the Severn estuary. This barrow, which is known as The Toots, has been severely dug into near the centre; *Long Barrows of the Cotswolds* has this interesting comment: 'The excavation across the middle is so large as to cause it to appear to be *two* mounds; this gave rise to the name "Toots" the plural of Toot, meaning a hill that was used as a look-out post, or thought in later times to have been so used. As this word is now obsolete it seems that this excavation must have taken place a long time ago.'

There is another long barrow with a fine site on Bown Hill near Woodchester, but the next on the escarpment edge is the Nympsfield barrow on Crawley Hill a little further west. This tomb in many ways recalls Notgrove (p. 188), for here, too, we have the skeleton of a chamber of the supposed early type from which the covering mound has largely disappeared; here, too, the site has been carefully re-excavated and restored. The most noticeable difference is that whereas Notgrove has two pairs of side cells opening from the central gallery, Nympsfield has only one, an arrangement which gives it a simple cruciform plan.

Less than a mile south of Nympsfield, the traveller is at last rewarded with a monument which is neither a mound which has lost its chamber nor a chamber which has lost its mound: Hetty Pegler's Tump is so nearly complete that it can give a true impression of what the finest long barrows were like when they were still the religious centres of a living culture. Like Nympsfield, Hetty Pegler's Tump stands on the very lip of the escarpment which is here precipitous; so near that it appears to be in danger of slipping over, or falling, a cloud of slabs, stones and flying ghosts, down to the Severn flats. The key is kept at Crawley Hill Cottage, Uley, and it admits one (unhappily after passing an iron railing) through a low lintelled portal into a twenty-foot long megalithic gallery with two side cells opening off on the left-hand side. Those which must have existed on the right were so severely damaged that they have been sealed off. Here at last it is possible to have the sensation of being closed in a tomb and in the earth; it is dark, and although the chambers are not large the megalithic architecture gives an impression of massive grandeur. It is to me a great regret that the only place in which a worthy rendering of the Mother Goddess of the Stone Age has been found in this country is in the shaft of a flint-mine (p. 249), and not in one of these tombs where to my mind she is most powerfully enthroned. Those who are concerned with architectural detail should again look at the skilful combination of drystone with megalithic masonry and should also notice the pair of inner jamb stones which project into the entrance passage at right angles to its walls.

The last site on this historic stretch of the escarpment brings us to a later age. Less than a mile southwards from the Tump, on a fine natural spur, is the imposing Iron Age fort of Uley Bury. The fort is approached along a narrow neck where the single entrance is protected by earthworks of great size and completeness; the two lines of rampart follow closely the roughly rectangular outline of the spur enclosing its flat summit, while on all sides the ground falls away steeply below them. Nature has rarely provided a more perfect site for a fort of this kind.

To avoid the shame of anticlimax, I should like to leave the Cotswolds here at Uley Bury but there are unfortunately a few places along the southern tail of the Cotswolds which have every right to be named. One more long barrow is included among them—it is just outside the village of Leighterton on the western side, a fine large mound still standing to the unusual height of nearly twenty feet at the east end. Unfortunately it was severely mauled by an antiquary at the very beginning of the eighteenth century and as he left his diggings open all architectural features have decayed.

For the rest, forts continue along the western scarp, and among them Sodbury, overlooking Chipping Sodbury, is a really fine example, comparable to Uley itself. There are other forts on the low hills which here begin to interpose between the face of the Cotswold scarp and the Severn estuary. There is Damery, a good specimen known as Bloody Acre just north of Cromhall, another at King's Weston and several more of less distinction. The Toots, Oldbury, is the most low-lying of them all; even to-day it is not far from Severn bank and when it was built was probably on the waterside.

This journey down the narrowing tail of the Cotswold limestone and the Severn plain has brought us to Somerset and the outskirts of Bath and Bristol, and so to the starting-point of an earlier excursion. From summits and promontories along the whole of the western face of the Cotswolds, we have been able to observe the distant prospect of the Welsh mountains, the Breconshire Beacons and the Black Mountains, with the coastal plain of Glamorgan lying at their feet. It was almost inevitable that immigrants sailing up the Bristol Channel and eager to begin their land-taking should look both to left and to right—to the Welsh foothills as well as to the Cotswolds. Certainly the New Stone Age immigrants did so, and their chambered tombs make a strong cultural link between the two lands. It is now time to follow them to the west, making the crossing further north by way of the intervening uplands of the Malverns and the Forest of Dean.

B. *The Malverns and the Forest of Dean*

Though their area is tiny and their height nowhere more than fourteen hundred feet, the Malverns are for me one of the most dramatic mountain formations of this island. This little spine, some eight miles long and hardly a mile across, is thrust up with such extraordinary abruptness from the flat, heavy plain of southern Worcestershire and the undulating Old Red Sandstone of Herefordshire, that it forces upon even the most time-hardened consciousness a recognition of the reality of geological events, of the catastrophic upheavals that have shaped our country. Running due north and south, the Malverns represent a dimunitive counterpart of the Pennines and were, in fact, folded at the same time—when the Armorican buckling of the crust was forcing the layered rocks of England against the older mountains of Wales.

Approaching between Worcestershire hedges, the traveller can see the road before him suddenly shoot upwards towards the sky as it strikes the mountain wall. He can see, too, the pretty terraces and villas which gathered round the spa when the early Victorians found that the unpleasant waters which flow from the ancient Malvern rocks were good for their polite ills—or good enough at least to justify a break from the daily round of respectable homes.

There is an earthwork on Midsummer Hill above Eastnor Park, but the great mark of prehistoric times upon these hills is the Herefordshire Beacon not very far from Great Malvern. It has become a minor tourist centre, yet the pleasant hotel at its foot and occasional seats and signposts cannot spoil a place which nature has endowed with uncommon beauty and character. The Beacon represents as it were the high, humped shoulder of the Malvern spine; on its summit is the large artificial mound of an early medieval castle, while round it runs a strong enclosing earthwork which I take to be prehistoric work adapted as a medieval bailey. Looking down from the castle mound the main outer ramparts of the prehistoric fort can be seen enclosing the ridge both to the north and south. It is, as now appears, a long narrow contour-fort with this inner enclosure at its central and highest part; in shape perhaps it approaches nearest to Hambledon Hill, with the castle motte taking the place of the long barrow of the Dorset stronghold. The fort was certainly built in the Iron Age, but further excavation is needed to date it more precisely. I do not wish to be one of those guides who must always pause at set points to enjoy the 'view'; the Germanic *blick* is an assault upon our powers of appreciation. Furthermore, with so many prehistoric sites in high places, *blick* follows hotly upon *blick*. Nevertheless, the outlook from the Beacon is so exceptional that it must be added to the more sober attractions of history. On the motte one is enclosed first by the inner ramparts, then to north and south by the outer line of walls; to north and south again stretch the wooded slopes of this slender Malvern island, washed by the varied lowlands of Worcestershire and Herefordshire; these in their turn are enclosed on the east by the Cotswolds, with Bredon showing as their advance guard, and on the west by the Black Mountains and the central massif of Radnorshire.

The plain of Hereford of which one has such a lordly view from the Malverns is a stretch of Old Red Sandstone soils which to-day makes a fertile countryside of farms and cider orchards; in prehistoric times, however, it was very extensively forested and its antiquities are virtually limited to Iron Age hill-forts, and a few minor Roman sites. It is certainly not a county for the earnest pilgrims of prehistory. For those, however, who may be there for other reasons, perhaps to enjoy the enchanting small towns and villages, black and white as magpies with their half-timbered houses, I will give a hasty catalogue of these places, noting those that are worth turning aside for a moment to see. Starting in the extreme north of the county—indeed on the Shropshire border—there is Coxall Knoll camp which is given some individual interest by the two outer enclosures which abut on to the narrow oval of the main ramparts. Still near the border, where names carry echoes of the *Shropshire Lad*, the walls of a small Roman town are visible enclosing the village of Leintwardine. This is *Bravonium* which, standing in the valley of the Clun on the edge of the Welsh foothills, was on the Roman road running south from *Viroconium* (Wroxeter, p. 240).

The triangular fort of Brandon near Adforden hardly deserves to be named, but about eight miles further south, Wapley Hill near Presteigne has a relatively strong fort with as many as five lines of ramparts on the north-east side. A little further east in the parish of Aymestry are Pyon Wood, a small fort, and Croft Ambrey, considerably larger and with three-sided multiple ramparts. Near Leominster there is Risbury to the south-east and Ivington to the south-west—their unusual design makes the Ivington earthworks worthy of study by anyone with special interest in Iron Age military constructions. On the northern side of Hereford, the strong fort of Sutton Walls is among the very few of all these Herefordshire forts to have been excavated; it has been proved to be of about the same age as the first fort on Bredon (p. 190). The name of the village of Kenchester which lies on the western side of Hereford commemorates the Roman town of *Magnae*, the outline of whose walls can be traced on low ground near the river. *Magnae* was the next small place south of *Bravonium* on the route from Wroxeter to Caerwent. Credanhill fort is not far from Kenchester, then, still on the line of the Wye but on the other side of Hereford and east of the river, there is a line of three forts: Ethelbert's Camp, south of Dormington, Cherry Hill, north of Fownhope, and Capler's Camp, in the parish of Woolhope. Back on the west side of the Wye, is Aconbury, a strong hill-fort about five miles south of Hereford.

The last site in the county which I wish to name is one of quite a different kind; King Arthur's Cave near Ross-on-Wye (itself one of the most attractive of all the pretty towns of Herefordshire), plunges us for a moment back into the time of ice-sheets and glaciers. It served as a dwelling for hunters of the end of the Old Stone Age, and was occupied again during the Middle Stone Age.

At Ross we are close to the northern face of the Forest of Dean, a heavily wooded rocky upland that geology, history, custom, have set a little apart —a private realm. Forming the western side of the Severn estuary, the hills of the Forest of Dean make a strong contrast with the Cotswolds on the eastern side. Although their summits are lower than those of the Cotswolds, the hard, dark, Old Red Sandstone surrounding their limestone seems to identify them at once with mountain country—to expose them, indeed, for what they are, outliers from the Black Mountains and Breconshire Beacons. Whilst the Cotswolds belong to the light, with their pale grey and golden limestone, elegant beeches, springing larks, there is something dark and in the romantic sense, 'horrid' about the Forest of Dean. The Forest has, of course, been subtly tainted by mining; iron has been dug since prehistoric times, and small-scale coal-mining still goes on, seeming a little furtive behind its heavy mask of trees. Here and there are titanic tumbles of dark rectangular boulders lying among tree-trunks in the sullen green light filtered through oak and sycamore; here and there, half reverted to this English jungle, overgrown and melancholy spoil-heaps. Of actual antiquities there are virtually none in the Forest; an embanked enclosure at Little Dean near Cinderford and earthworks on Welshbury Hill are all that deserve mention. There is also the Scowles, believed to be Roman iron-diggings; the evidence for this is of the slightest but it is a delicious place to visit in the spring or early summer for its rocky hollows are overhung with brilliant foliage and it seems to escape the pervading sombreness of the country. Although individual sites are so few, the Forest of Dean is interesting in its entirety. It seems to have been the source of the earliest iron of prehistoric Britain; apart from tools and weapons, very many if not all of the long iron bars which were the first British currency were certainly forged from Forest of Dean ores. This clumsy money was being made from the second century B.C.—the flat bar with pinked-up ends perhaps representing what were originally sword blades, but now standardized and converted into a currency. They are found throughout south-western England and extending wherever trade took them, into Wessex, the Thames Valley and the midlands.

The Forest is also made a monument to the past by the survival there of a local society with its own laws and customs going back no one knows how far into antiquity. The foresters inherit the Freedom of the Forest and administer their affairs from the Speech House, a mansion in the heart of the Forest which has now become in part a hotel but still contains the fine Court Room where the foresters hold their meetings.

It is on the south-eastern fringe of the main Forest territory that we reach at last a site of real distinction with much to see and still more to excite the imagination. Above the mouth of the Wye, the hills of the Forest of Dean thrust several long spurs southward towards the Severn estuary, and:

'At Lydney, nine miles north-west of Chepstow along the Gloucester Road, one of these spurs a mile from the present shore and two hundred feet above it, commands a vista of luxuriant forest and spacious estuary which can scarcely be matched for beauty even in a county of pleasant parklands.'

This spur, now included in the great Deer Park created by the Bathurst family, was for a short time, at the end of the Roman occupation, the centre of a cult of the god Nodens, evidently a Celtic divinity, who, with the easy allegiance of his kind, was sometimes equated with the Roman Mars. Already in the Iron Age the Lydney promontory had been defended by building a small rampart across the neck and cutting an entrance in the rock at the point where the main approach road led up to it from the southern point of the spur. This entrance can still be seen, but of the two ramparts on the neck only the inner one is partly prehistoric; the outer line was added and the inner one strengthened after Roman times, probably by demoralized Roman Britons whose architecture like their life rapidly reverted to barbarism when cut off from Rome. We saw another instance of this kind in the rebuilding of the prehistoric ramparts at Cissbury (p. 81).

Behind the ramparts is the shaft of a Roman iron-mine, the marks of the narrow iron-picks still scored on its walls. This, one of the few mines certainly dated to the Roman period, seems to have been worked by poor native labourers during the earlier centuries of Roman rule.

On the spur behind the ramparts the visitor will find a group of later Roman buildings inside a stout precinct wall, all of them probably built in the service of Nodens or his human hangers-on. The place was evidently much frequented by visitors to his shrine and for their accommodation in this isolated place an inn or guesthouse was necessary. To draw yet more money from their purses there seems to have been a line of little shops and stalls where votive figures and other religious knick-knacks were displayed. The largest building is a public bath-house, and although no doubt it had purely secular uses, allowing devotees to combine something of the life of a spa with their religious observances, it is very probable that it was also the scene of ritual ablutions—dippings and bathings ordered by Nodens himself. For it seems that Nodens was in part a healing divinity, one who could help in sickness and the dangers of childbirth. This is suggested by the discovery of many little votive effigies of dogs, an animal which in classical religions is widely associated with healing cults. Perhaps here at Lydney as at the temple of Asklepios at Epidaurus, sacred dogs were kept on the premises to cure the sick by licking the affected parts. Whether or not we are right to imagine the surrounding valleys echoing with the baying of the holy hounds of Nodens, the votive figures are real enough and can be seen in the museum. Most of them are of the poor quality to be expected of pi-art in all times and places, but one is quite exceptional, a figure of a dog resembling an Irish wolfhound, head turned back over its shoulder, vigorous and sincere. One of the votive inscriptions recalls injury and vindictiveness—living emotions of fifteen hundred years ago. A man called Silvanus dedicates to Nodens half the value of a ring, presumably a gold ring, which he has lost. He charges the god not to allow good health to the family he suspects of being the thieves until they have returned it to his shrine.

The temple itself stood towards the southern end of the spur in a place easily reached by the path up the ridge (p. 204) where the prehistoric entrance still gave access to the precinct. It is now reduced to foundations, but it was clearly a basilica temple of the type ancestral to the Christian church. It was first built about 365 A.D. but owing to an unsuspected natural hole in the underlying rock, one of the internal piers collapsed and made rebuilding necessary a few years later. The cult flourished exceedingly during the latter years of the fourth century before it collapsed into the abyss which the Romans left behind them. Then we see this comfortable little world with its piety, superstition, commercialism and its civilized amenities left in the hands of a panicky mob able to do no more than patch up the wretched earthworks built by their prehistoric forbears. Some visitors will find this work of desperate improvization made in the darkness of the fifth century can stir the imagination more deeply than the iron-mine or the walls, mosaics, altars and museum exhibits of the Roman cult centre. Lydney is a place to see whatever one's historical tastes.

Chapter Seven

WALES AND MONMOUTHSHIRE

A. SOUTH AND CENTRAL WALES
B. NORTH-WEST WALES
C. ANGLESEY
D. NORTH WELSH COAST AND THE NORTHERN MARCHES

A. *South and Central Wales*

I BEGIN a new chapter at the mouth of the Wye because history and habit justify treating Wales and Monmouthshire as a unit. On the other hand, it is as well to remember that nature really joins the Old Red Sandstone country of Hereford and the Forest of Dean to the Welsh massif, while the same natural division would make the geologically youthful and low-lying Glamorgan plain a part of lowland England.

We shall find that both the geological structure and the prehistory of the Principality roughly reflect the ancient and endless hostility between south and north Wales. The south is dominated by the magnificent Old Red Sandstone mountains of Breconshire and by the coalfields—all showing a mainly north-south folding left by the Armorican mountain-building. The north has far more ancient rocks, culminating in the worn, volcanically crystallized rocks of Anglesey, originally laid down in the Archaean era, an immeasurable time before the first known stirrings of life on Earth. This north-west corner is further fortified by later volcanic eruptions whose tough igneous rocks have survived to make the highest mountains of the country in the crowding peaks of Snowdonia and Cader Idris. Here there are many marks of north-east-south-west folding that represent the Caledonian period of mountain-building—so much earlier than the Armorican folding of the south. In between the two, the central mountains of mudstones and shales, with no resistant volcanic rocks to form lofty summits, are relatively monotonous and undistinguished.

Antiquities show the same pattern: there is far more that is impressive and interesting in the south and in the north, particularly the north-west.

With the exception of some stone circles of the Bronze Age, the centre has little to show.

As for the nature of the remains, we shall find that the great stone tombs of the New Stone Age are perhaps the most frequent and spectacular. The seafaring peoples who were the masters of this megalithic architecture followed the Atlantic coasts and naturally found attractive land-falls in Wales. Many of their tombs, often recalling those of Cornwall, are still standing in Pembrokeshire, Merioneth and the Caernarvon peninsula. Their rough force and grandeur remains after four or five thousand years as the fitting monument to voyagers who were ready to thrust into these wild and utterly unknown lands. In addition, to the settlements on the western promontories, there was also, as I have said, the incursion of a distinct people—the people responsible for the chambered long barrows of the Cotswolds. We shall encounter similar tombs in Glamorgan, a bond emphasizing the English affinities of this region; later some of them evidently pushed further into the mountains where a local colony left the group of chambered barrows we shall find in Breconshire. More surprisingly, and indeed quite inexplicably, there are a few others in the far north—as though perhaps some leader had broken off from the rest and led a small band to seize land where they could.

Great stone tombs have pride of place among Welsh antiquities, but there are also many marks of the Roman occupation. Just because those Celtic tribes (the Silures and Ordovices) held out so stubbornly among their mountains, the Romans had to build many camps and forts to defeat and then control them. As for remains of the Celts themselves: there are stone hill-forts and villages, often built or at least still occupied long after the Roman conquest.

The remains of prehistoric and Roman Wales cannot rival those of England, yet very many of them are set in places naturally so beautiful, so wild or remote, that their own interest, their own power to attract, is immensely enhanced. The traveller among these mountain valleys and moorlands, where he can still hear a language introduced in the Bronze Age, will feel far closer to the men who built tombs, sanctuaries, forts, than he ever can among mild English hills, where Anglo-Saxon prosperity and domesticity so thickly overlie our barbaric past.

I know of no better way of approach to south Wales than through the Forest of Dean to Monmouth. The Staunton road winds out from the screen of trees and there, with Monmouth and the Usk at one's feet, is the sudden prospect of majestic mountain ranges rising behind the small tossing hills of the Monmouthshire no-man's-land. However, that no-man's-land was forest country in the past, and there are few antiquities to be seen there.

Crossing this pleasant countryside so fertile as farming land and so barren of antiquities, the mountains tower higher until at Abergavenny one reaches the gateway to the natural road through their mass. This is, of course, the valley of the Usk which here opens on to the plain and which men have always used for a way into the interior. Its defence over more than a thousand years is commemorated by the ruined castles and grass-grown castle mounds of medieval lords, by a Roman road with fort and military camps, and by Celtic hill-forts. Before that in less competitive times, the route was obviously followed by migrating long-barrow builders, related to those who settled nearer their landing places in the Cotswolds and on the Glamorgan coasts. Their barrows, of which about a dozen are known, provide the greatest interest of this region. For those gently interested in the pursuit of antiquities, I can think of no more delightful pastime than to visit all these sites during a week or so, making the hunt an excuse for walking, climbing, idling among these delectable valleys.

The geographical key to the whole region lies in the fact that on the west side of the Black Mountains the Usk and a tributary of the Wye flow very close together—separated only by a single narrow spine (along which runs the Roman road). This makes it possible for long barrows built round the foothills of the Black Mountains to form a continuous arc, first along the Usk system and then along that of the Wye. Although I think there can be no doubt that the builders pushed up the Usk, the greater number of their monuments are, as it happens, on the Wye side of the divide. Following the road from Abergavenny to Crickhowell it is justifiable to pause at the first visible antiquity which stands close to the Breconshire boundary. It is a fine example of a menhir, or single standing stone, of which there are far too many in the region for me to name. It stands with an air of melancholy resignation on the right-hand side of the road at Cwrt y Gollen in a spot which was once fine parkland. The first of the long barrows, Carn Goch, is less than a mile further on at Llangattock but it is hardly worth the search necessary to find it, and, for all but the most devoted, it is better to go through Crickhowell and stop to see the second example by peering over the roadside wall just opposite the entrance to Gwernvale House. This long barrow has been violently assailed first by the makers of the turnpike road in the eighteenth century and then in 1808 by Sir Richard Colt Hoare and one Theophilus Jones, a local antiquary. There is very little now to be seen beyond the eight upright slabs which form the surviving walls of a polygonal chamber; the capstone prised off by Colt Hoare has evidently been destroyed. The chamber is very much overgrown with brambles and weeds but is no longer the rubbish dump that it was forty years ago.

The traveller should now be prepared to fork right from the main road along the Rhiangoll, but first he may like to make a rather difficult excursion across the other side of the river to Llangynidr where with good chance he will find the largest of all the Breconshire menhirs. The Rhiangoll road leads past the splendid medieval house of Tretower which with skilful care is being preserved and restored to its original beauty, and so on to the head of the little valley. Here is a spot admirable for the prehistorian. Close on the right side of the lane, though screened from view by a hedge, is the only one of these chambered long barrows to have been scientifically excavated. Ty Isaf proved to have a dummy entrance in the north end, a pair of side chambers just behind it, and a rather oddly placed megalithic chamber with side cells towards the southern end. The diggings have been carefully filled and now only the tops of the uprights are visible, but among them it is easy to distinguish those of the entrance.

Ty Isaf is dominated by a small but steep hill which rises above it immediately to the north; this is Castell Dinas, unquestionably a place to be visited. The summit of the hill, already so well protected by nature, is defended by massive ramparts which reach their strongest and most impressive on the south side above the long barrow. Within their circuit is a Norman motte. Whether the ramparts are Iron Age or were built by the natives during the Roman occupation has never been tested. Castell Dinas is remarkable in itself, but it is perhaps even better worth the climb for the sake of the view which it commands. Standing almost exactly on the watershed between Usk and Wye, it looks down the Wye Valley and also over the broken hilly country, where Brecon lies hidden, to the Mynydd Eppynt. Close at hand on the east the Black Mountains fill the sky. My own only visit to this countryside was made in February in a week of those wonderful pale gold days with which February can sometimes cheat April of the pride of Spring. Hardly even aware that they are an Old Red Sandstone formation, I had expected the Black Mountains to be black. I think I was first shown how wrong I had been when from the banks of Castell Dinas I looked across at them and was enchanted by the ruddy soil on the slopes, last year's still-glowing bracken, and the warm brown of the woods with their haze of February twigs. This is a country where oak-woods abound, woods which a little later in the year must assume that extraordinary yellow, so intense but unlike the yellows of autumn, of the young oak-leaf.

From Castell Dinas it is possible to distinguish the area to the north of Talgarth where the greatest concentration of Breconshire long barrows lies above the bend of the Wye; there are five of them at no great distance from one another, and a sixth, Pen-y-Wyrlod, about two miles further down the valley to the north-east. Of the five I will name only Pipton, which is near the crest of the mild hill above railway and river at Three Cocks Junction. This barrow, when excavated, was shown to have a dummy entrance (similar to the one discovered at Ty Isaf long barrow) and two side chambers, one of which is approached by a passageway, opening out from the north-western side of the forecourt.

This is the point at which I should mention a distant outlier of the Breconshire barrows across the English border about ten miles to the north-east. This is Arthur's Stone in the parish of Dorstone in Herefordshire, a very fine tomb on the summit of a ridge above the 'Golden Valley'. The covering mound now appears to be egg-shaped and the chamber lies near its centre. It is a large one, about eighteen feet by eight, its plan evidently determined by the colossal kite-shaped capstone, split across but not seriously displaced. There are two stones forming the tail of the kite whose real purpose cannot be judged without excavation, but the oddest feature of Arthur's Stone is the entrance passage at the other end of the chamber, an eccentric affair which bends almost at right-angles half-way along its course—unless indeed one prefers to distinguish the two sections as passage and antechamber.

To complete the survey of the south Wales group of chambered long barrows it is necessary to leap from this eastern outlier to its counterpart on the west. The Ty Illtyd barrow lies in the Usk Valley about four miles east of Brecon and is best reached by the lane which here leads over the pass to Llangasty-Tal-y-llyn. It can be seen on the slope towards the top of a pasture field on the left-hand side opposite Manest Farm. Although the long mound is here unusually well preserved, the chamber with its coverstone is visible and appears to have a slab-lined forecourt. The uprights supporting the capstone have at some time been carved with crosses contained within lozenges; they are obviously later than the building of the tomb, but may still be of venerable age. Possibly the scribes also plundered the tomb, or perhaps the cross symbols were intended to counteract the persistent magic of the place—just as iron crosses are sometimes clamped on to megaliths in Brittany.

Westward from Ty Illtyd the balance of interest tilts towards much later periods. As one journeys up this valley, a delightful composition of well-kept farming land within an austere but serene mountain setting, it is not easy to believe that just over the southern range all the little mining valleys of the south Wales coalfield run down towards the coast, deep and narrow grooves filled with the harsh concrete, brick and grime of industrialism.

The citizens of Brecon have wisely kept as an amenity what is perhaps the prehistoric precursor of their small city. To the west of the town on the nose of land between the Usk and the tributary valley of the Honddu is a comely hill crowned by the Crug, a fine more or less circular hill-fort with two strong rings of rampart that multiply to three or four where the natural defences are weakest. There is a footpath up from the outer suburbs of Brecon, a pleasant way first crossing pasture fields which, when I took it, were filled with plump sheep, and then, as such paths should, leading over a last stile on to a green track between deep beds of bracken with the rampart of the Crug looking huge against the sky. The outlook from the fort is pleasing—more domestic, less noble than that from Castell Dinas; one can look up and down the Vale of Usk and watch the country traffic and country activities on its high roads, lanes and fields. The Roman road across the Eppynt came down the Honddu, to join the Usk road at Brecon; about a mile further up the valley it passed Brecon Gaer, a Roman fort which occupies an adjacent and much lower hill just across the road and railway about a mile to the south-west. The Gaer is, indeed, ideally sited; it encloses five acres of a gentle eminence for which the cliché 'cradled by the mountains' seems almost justifiable so truly do the encircling summits seem to bring peace to this large green meadow. When I went there snowdrops were making a huge and dense white shadow under the trees of the farm through which one must approach the fort, and it was hard to think of the place garrisoned with a rowdy regiment of Spanish cavalry—but so we know it was. The Gaer has the usual history of a beginning in the late first century with earthen ramparts and wooden buildings, followed by a rebuilding in stone in the early second century. This remodelling, however, was never completed and the fort seems from that time to have been only intermittently garrisoned.

From the Gaer the Roman road ran up the south side of the Usk and over the watershed to the fort at Llandovery in the Towy Valley. We will follow it, not only for its own sake or the loveliness of the route, which is great, but because it leads to the last group of Breconshire antiquities: the stone circles and standing stones which are distributed in a fan all round the headwaters of the Usk and a little further south over into the head of the Tawe. At first the Roman road approximately underlies the modern road, but just after the village of Trecastell, it climbs up steeply to the left while the new road keeps to the lower ground. At first the Roman line is marked by a lane, then by a cart-track which at last gives way to a pleasant green road running across level moorland. These grassy moors are themselves over twelve hundred feet up, but above them the Brecon Beacons stand regnant, while away to the right is the wide expanse of the Mynydd Eppynt furrowed by many small valleys. The moorland ponies are as soft as puppy-dogs in their deep fur; the calling of the curlew adds a sense of freedom and yet melancholy to the spaciousness of this ancient and exalted roadway. The track swings to the left and can then be seen to drop suddenly out of sight over the edge of the plateau. Just at this point, the highest on the moor, are first two circles of small standing stones, and then the low embankments of two Roman camps, one placed askew within the other. They are difficult to trace, for tile-workings have destroyed their southern side and substituted confusing rows of spoil-heaps. Their history is unknown, but they certainly provided temporary camps for large bodies of troops, and it seems most likely that they were put up during the early campaigns which ended in the subjugation of Wales late in the first century. After passing these camps, known as Y Pigwin, the road zig-zags sharply down to Llandovery in the broad basin of the Towy.

The two circles that stand so near to Y Pigwin belong to a group of seven ranged round the Upper Usk and Tawe. Some miles to the north is one on the Mynydd Eppynt, on the other side of these two Trecastell rings there is first one on Mynydd Myddfai, just over the county boundary in Carmarthenshire, then two more close together at Nant Tarw, Traean-glas, and finally a good example, Cerrig Duon, also in the parish of Traean-glas. This circle has a large menhir (Maen Mawr) and a stone avenue associated with it. Just south-west of Cerrig Duon on the far side of the Tawe from Penwyllt station is the fine stone row known as Saeth Maen, or Seven Stones.

The present distribution of stone circles and alignments in Wales is a strange one; they are relatively uncommon in the areas where the great stone tombs are most frequent, but are found in remote places like this and in areas still more isolated—among the central Welsh mountains where no other megalith-builders ever penetrated. Because the remainder are so cut off from other monuments, I shall choose this place to mention the few circles and rows which stand among the mountains in the extreme north of Breconshire, in Radnor and Montgomeryshire. In the northern tip of Breconshire is another Saeth Maen stone row and a further alignment, Rhos y Gelynen, a little to the west over the Radnorshire boundary. The main Radnorshire group of both circles and stone rows lies among the hills between Builth Wells and New Radnor. Among others in Montgomeryshire, there is a circle on Kerry Hill some miles above the Upper Severn Valley at Newtown, while in the more western part of the county are two close together in the parish of Llanbrynmair. Although it takes us out of what is politically Wales, the Kerry Hill ring cannot historically or geographically be separated from the two Shropshire circles of Marsh Pool and Mitchell's Field which are at no great distance to the north-east, standing even closer to the Severn.

There is no class of prehistoric monument of which less is known than these circles and stone rows; they are assumed to be generally later than the megalithic tombs and are assigned rather vaguely to the Bronze Age. We are ignorant of the people who built them and of the ideas and ritual of which they were an expression. Looking at them in the loneliness and grandeur of the mountain country in which they so often stand, we have to imagine them a centre of movement, colour, vitality and emotion.

While in this area of central south Wales there is one recently excavated site, unique in Britain, that can be visited at Dolaucothi, located three-quarters of a mile south-east of the village of Pumpsaint, halfway between Llandovery and Lampeter. Gold was mined at Dolaucothi during the Roman period, and remains of the opencast and tunnel workings are still to be seen. The mining methods in use here were up to the most advanced technological standards of the time and made use of two aqueducts that supplied water to the site for washing ore and perhaps for powering stone-crushing mills. One of the aqueducts, traversing a distance of seven miles, was capable of supplying some three million gallons of water per day to the mines and the water from both aqueduct channels was controlled by a series of massively constructed reservoirs and sluices that directed the water to the various areas along the mine workings. In the National Museum at Wales is one of the large wooden waterwheels used at the mines for baling out water from the underground workings. Such wheels were worked by slave labour and are a harsh reminder of the darker side of life in Roman Britain. The complexity of the mining techniques in use at Dolaucothi can be paralleled, on a much larger scale, from the rich gold mines worked by the Romans in Spain. It is significant that the auxiliary unit stationed in the nearby fort of Llanio was from Asturia, in north-west Spain where some of the largest of these gold mines were located. It seems likely that it was engineers from this garrison who were responsible initially for developing the Dolaucothi mines.

This excursion to Breconshire and central Wales has resulted from entering the Principality through Monmouth. Another line of entry is, of course, to continue southward from the Wye mouth (p. 204), visiting the varied remains that stand near the banks of the Severn. Almost at the point where the train sweeps one into the daylight after the passage of the Severn tunnel, there is the fort of Sudbrook whose triple and triangular earth-works actually adjoin the river bank. A little to the north near Portskewett and we have reached the easternmost of the Welsh chambered tombs. This monument at Heston Brake is an unusual one; after an entrance between two tall jamb-stones (one now broken) there is what has been described as a parallel-sided passage leading into a rectangular chamber. The passage is, however, both longer and slightly wider than the chamber, and except for a projecting stone which divides them, the two might be seen as a single long gallery. Two of the stones in the chamber wall are perforated, and although the holes seem to be at least partially natural, it is tempting to accept them as a kind of 'port-hole', though they can never have been intended for entries. Human and ox bones were found in both chamber and passage when Heston Brake was excavated in 1888.

We have now edged close to the two greatest Roman sites of south Wales, one a military base, the other a substantial country town. Nearest at hand is the town *Venta Silurum* or Caerwent. First, however, we should notice the powerful, stone-walled fort of Llanmelin which overlooks Caer-went, for it may well be that following the pattern made familiar by many English instances, this Iron Age hill-stronghold was the old tribal centre of the Silures and the prehistoric predecessor of the Roman town.

At *Venta Silurum* itself one is baffled and exasperated by the sense that there is so much more to be seen than is visible. 'Here . . . in the centre of a fertile, hill-encircled plain, the village of Caerwent straggles over the site of the only Roman walled town in the Principality.' The town covers forty-four and a half acres and is roughly rectangular in outline although the north and north-east walls are considerably out of the straight. It seems first to have been built and enclosed by stout earthen walls in about 75 A.D. when, after more than a quarter of a century of struggling against the stubborn resistance of the Silures, the Roman authorities thought fit to establish a town where the example of comfortable and civilized living might do more than warfare to subdue the warlike Celts. Inside the walls the town was divided into twenty *insulae* or blocks by a grid of streets; there were the usual forum and basilica near the centre with fine public baths just across the road, and a temple and rows of shops next door. As a whole the town was more closely built up than *Calleva Atrebatum* (Silchester) one of the few other Romano-British towns to have been excavated on a large scale and once called a 'garden city' because of the amount of open space which occurred within its walls. Indeed, although covering less than half the area of Silchester, Caerwent's population of about three thousand, may have been only a thousand less. Many of the houses were of fair size, especially those in the southern half of the town where the number of private bath-suites, flushed latrines and other amenities enjoyed by the householders suggest that they belonged to the wealthier citizens of *Venta*. About the beginning of the third century lofty stone walls were built outside the old earth ramparts, and later still these were strengthened on the south side by the addition of bastions; the southern wall remains the most striking of the visible remains of Roman Caerwent as only one of the many houses that were excavated earlier in this century is still on view. In the porch of the parish church there are two Roman inscriptions from the town which are worthy of a visit but the other finds from the excavations are now in Newport Museum.

From *Venta Silurum* where, to translate into our own idiom, the Roman Council was conducting propaganda for the Latin Way of Life, it is not many miles to Caerleon, the centre from which Rome conducted her military operations against south Wales. The legionary fortress of *Isca*, which was built close beside the tidal waters of the Usk, near modern Newport, was the southern counterpart of the similar fort at Chester (p. 59). From these two bases a system of lesser forts and outposts linked by roads was successfully established throughout Wales during the last part of the first century. So Wales was subdued, the violent Celtic warriors brought into the *Pax Romana*; yet within that military framework peace, perhaps, was not undivided. We shall see many of the hill-towns where the native peoples continued in their prehistoric way of life, a way which we can be sure included some indulgence in the family and tribal feuds without which life would have been unbearably tame.

Isca was built on the orthodox plan for a legionary fortress laid down in the military handbooks; a rectangle of fifty acres with rounded corners, four gates and a central praetorium or regimental headquarters. As was so often the case in Britain, original earth ramparts and wooden barracks, granaries and other internal buildings were reconstructed in stone early in the second century as part of the improvements inspired by the Emperor Trajan. When in the fourth century the danger was no longer from the Welsh tribesmen but from the barbarian sea-raiders, the foe of Briton and Roman alike, the importance of *Isca* was at an end. Now the defence had to be shifted to the coast, and we shall find a strong fortress established at Cardiff. But until then, for at least two and a half centuries, the Second Legion was stationed at Caerleon as an established part of the countryside, at first unofficially, pleasurably introducing its foreign blood among the native population, later setting up regular married quarters outside the fortress walls. There must always have been much coming and going between fort and town, between *Isca* and *Venta* only eight miles away. Brides and sweethearts might sometimes be found in the town, time-expired veterans retired there, and one can think of the commercial deals, the exchange of profitable information, invitations to shows in the amphitheatre, sporting fixtures which must have united citizens and soldiery.

To-day the best thing to be seen at Caerleon is the amphitheatre, excellently excavated and restored and quite the finest example in the country. There are also some stretches of the fortress walls in places as much as twelve feet high, the foundations of a building which stood next to the praetorium and the ruins of a bath-house outside the walls. In the excavated area known as Prysg Field there has also been uncovered the remains of the barrack blocks in the north-east corner of the fortress showing the fairly confined quarters in which the legionaries lived and the slightly more spacious accommodation accorded to centurions, each of whom had a set of rooms at one end of the barrack block which housed his century. In the angle of the fortress wall is the latrine building which was once flushed by running water although it is not so good an example of its kind as the famous latrine at Housesteads where the arrangements for water supply are still visible. The museum is well worth a visit. When so little of *Isca* remains to be seen to-day, I cannot do better than whet the envy of the modern traveller by repeating an account given by one who described it in the twelfth century—Giraldus Cambrensis:

'The city [*sic*] was handsomely built of masonry, with courses of bricks. Many vestiges of its former splendour may yet be seen, immense palaces, formerly ornamented with gilded roofs, in imitation of Roman magnificence . . . a town of prodigious size, remarkable hot baths, relics of temples and theatres all enclosed within fine walls. . . . You will find on all sides . . . subterraneous buildings, aqueducts, underground passages; and, what I think worthy of notice, stoves contrived with wonderful art to transmit the heat insensibly through narrow tubes passing up the side of the walls.'

Of the 'gilded roofs' it may be observed that one single piece of gilt mosaic is displayed in the museum.

From Caerleon it is easiest and most logical to echo Roman military history by moving to Cardiff. Here, as I have said, a fort was built against the Irish sea-rovers who began to menace this western side of the province at much the same time as the Anglo-Saxon pirates were ravaging its southern and eastern coasts. Cardiff is therefore directly comparable to the Forts of the Saxon Shore which were established between Norfolk and Hampshire (p. 60). This fort, built in about 300 A.D., is much smaller than Caerleon, with the high stone walls and projecting bastions characteristic of such Late Roman architecture. What is unique about it is that the late Marquess of Bute thought fit entirely to rebuild the outer walls, and the visitor may see at least the semblance of the Roman fort right in the heart of the city and housing municipal offices. Within one corner of it is the motte of a medieval castle.

What, however, is least to be missed at Cardiff is the National Museum which contains what is certainly the best displayed collection of antiquities in Britain. Here is a good modern building properly designed for a museum and properly, indeed brilliantly, used. The National Museum also possesses a most notable collection of things from farm and cottage usually classified as 'folk culture'; they help to show how ancient ways and skills lingered among the Welsh mountains far longer than in England. This collection is now shown in the lovely country house of St. Fagan's which is being converted into a 'folk park' on the Scandinavian model.

About five miles out of Cardiff on the south side of the Cowbridge road there is a remarkable concentration of long barrows and other megalithic tombs. The doubtful Coed y Cwm barrow lies closest to the road, but of far greater interest is the well-known chambered long barrow in Tinkinswood just to the south of it. This St. Nicholas tomb is obviously of the Cotswold family—that is at once shown by the long wedge-shaped mound with its containing drystone walls and horned forecourt. The chamber, reached through the forecourt, is a large but plain box-like chamber covered by one colossal rectangular capstone measuring as much as twenty-two by fifteen feet. The entrance is at the side, and not in the centre, of the front wall and therefore lacks the usual architectural formality of jamb-stones; the whole of the front wall is screened by drystone walling of considerable thickness, but with a slab-lined opening leading to the entrance.

About a mile to the south-east is the St. Lythans long barrow; the mound (or rather cairn, for as in the Cotswolds these Welsh examples are of piled stones) has almost disappeared leaving the megalithic chamber with its cover-stone standing naked; there is no question, however, that it was originally very similar to that of St. Nicholas.

From here it is not far to the sea, where a camp known as the Bulwarks abuts on the coast at Rhoose, just west of Barry; further west among the natural hummocks of the wide strip of dunes between Merthyr Mawr and Porthcawl, there are a number of round barrows, some dating from the early part of the Bronze Age, while a short distance inland is the most westerly of the long barrows, Cae Tor in the parish of Tythegston. There are other round barrows together with two later embanked enclosures on Margam Mountain a few miles to the north.

The Gower Peninsula, a charming piece of coast beyond the infernal industrial regions of Swansea, is for its size well endowed with antiquities. Of these the most important and the most spectacular is Parc Cwm, Penmaen, near the centre of the promontory. This monument has a deep forecourt and a gallery with two pairs of side cells very much like the early Cotswold long barrow; the cairn on the other hand is a stumpy oval and appears never to have been long. It has been suggested, therefore, that Parc Cwm is a hybrid architectural form between the Cotswold style and that of the megalith builders of the western Atlantic coasts who, as we shall see, often covered their chambers with round or oval cairns. There are, indeed, two other burial-chambers with rounded covering mounds on the Gower Peninsula—the two Sweyne's Howes, sometimes incorrectly called Swine Houses, on the Rhossili hills near the western extremity. There are two other tombs in the Peninsula which are well worth seeing; one, a gallery with side cells like a smaller version of the Parc Cwm chamber, is masked by the blown sand of Penmaen Burrows behind Oxwich Bay; the second, Maen Cetti or Arthur's Stone, Reynoldston, is an exposed megalithic chamber with an enormous capstone weighing some twenty-five tons. It owes its alternative name to a legend. When one day King Arthur was walking in Carmarthenshire he felt a pebble in his shoe and plucking it out threw it into the air; it landed in Gower and became the capstone of Maen Cetti. So does the historical Arthur become inflated to gigantic stature.

What is perhaps the most famous of all the Gower sites is the Goat's Cave, Paviland. This cave opens on to a deep cleft in the cliffs and care has to be taken about tides. An earnest party working on the film *The Beginning of History* waited so long for the finest possible lighting effects that they were cut off and had to swim for it. It may seem surprising that so inaccessible a dwelling should have been chosen by hunters of the Old Stone Age, but in their day a wide coastal plain lay between the ravine and the sea. It had the advantages of a natural chimney, and a terrace outside facing towards the south. The Goat's Hole, like some of the Mendip caves, was occupied in the earlier part of the last Palaeolithic phase and the animals trapped and hunted included cave bear, hairy rhinoceros, Irish elk, hyaena, large numbers of wild horse and a few mammoth. Among the usual collection of flint scrapers and engravers there were some unusual objects in bone and ivory: two unique bone spatulae, beads made from pierced canine teeth of wolf and reindeer, rods of mammoth ivory, fragments of a ring that may have been a bracelet, and, most remarkable of all, an egg-shaped piece of ivory pierced at the top as a pendant. This had been 'cut from an osseous growth produced by a wound in the pulp cavity of a mammoth tusk'; the deformed tusk from which it was taken had been recovered from the cave a century before the pendant itself was found. It had, in fact, been found by Dean Buckland, and it is chiefly to Dean Buckland that the Paviland cave owes its fame. The Dean combined Holy Orders with the tenure of the first professorship in geology at Oxford; he contrived to be a very useful scientist when his two callings did not come into evident conflict. When they did, it was the Dean who won. At Paviland he made the first discovery of a burial of the Old Stone Age, but finding a human skeleton among bones of extinct animals which he knew must be very much more ancient than the official date of the human creation, his beliefs made him declare it to be a later intrusion, the burial in fact of a Romano-British lady. So this Palaeolithic hunter came to be known as the Red Lady of Paviland, 'Red' because the bones had been covered with ochre, a practice now known to have been frequent in the Old Stone Age and which may have been intended as a symbol of life. Later, when the battles centering round Darwin and Huxley were over and the immense antiquity of man accepted, the Red Lady was disinterred, metaphorically, for a second time. It is an instance of the impossibility of individual discoveries being fully realized until the time is ripe for them. Gower must have been the centre of good hunting territories during the last advance and final retreat of the ice, for there are several other cave-dwellings in the Peninsula—Long Hole, Cat's Hole and Bacon Hole—but none of the others has associations such as those of Dean Buckland and the Red Lady to add imaginative significance to their rock walls.

From Gower the traveller should make his way westward where the estuary of Milford Haven and the many bays and natural harbours of Pembrokeshire attracted the seafarers of the New Stone Age. There they beached their boats and established the communities whose great stone tombs have survived them by so many thousands of years. Nearly all the monuments to be seen are either megalithic tombs, or circles of standing stones, and it would, I think, be unbearably tedious if I were to attempt to name them all—there are nearly forty tombs in Pembrokeshire alone. It will show better manners as a guide if I say where the main concentrations lie, naming only the more important sites—of which, indeed, there are few.

Before turning west, it is worth while to push up the Swansea Valley and climb the hills above Rhyd-y-fro to Mynydd Carn Llecharth on which there stands a ring of upright slabs enclosing a central burial-cist—also slab-built. Monuments of this kind, which are relatively rare outside Scotland, are interesting as a link between the free standing circle which seems to have no original funerary use, and the ordinary round burial-cairn of the Bronze Age. This Llecharth circle is as much as sixty feet across and the slabs are of large size. Nearby there are small stone burial-chambers dug into the steeply sloping hillside.

Towards the west, the first group of sites to be mentioned is in Carmarthenshire—four megalithic burial-chambers and two groups of standing stones on the low hills between the rivers Towy and Taf; on the far side of the Taf beyond the expanse of East Marsh there are the Morfa Bychan tombs in the parish of Marros. These are a line of four round or oval cairns containing small megalithic chambers on the terrace running inland from Ragwen Point. As we enter Pembrokeshire itself, the county which for its size certainly has the most stone monuments of any in Britain, we first encounter a few sites in the relatively low-lying country round Milford Haven. Of these the dolmen of King's Quoit has a fine position near the sea at Old Castle Head, Manorbier, while the names of both King's Quoit and its opposite number, the Devil's Quoit, Broomhill Burrows, at the west end of this southern peninsula of Pembrokeshire, strike the right note for the 'Little England beyond Wales'. There is a group of standing stones near the southern end of the great sweeping curve of St. Bride's Bay, but little else until, passing the romantic landmark of Castle Roch, we reach the northern part of the county where monuments crowd thickly on and between St. David's and Strumble Heads.

This is attractive and interesting country which, like Cornwall, is chiefly renowned for its coasts. Many bays—from long bows of gleaming pale sand, to little pockets with no more than a few yards of sand held among the stones—are recessed between fanged headlands where the sea is always at work, whether it is with a gentle pushing and falling back, or a savage attack with spray streaming out along the cliffs. The inland scenery is more varied than in Cornwall for the plateau of the old sedimentary rocks is broken by abrupt outcrops of the much harder rocks spewed up by volcanoes. These outcrops, looking a little like South African kopjes, have attracted human settlers by offering both building material and good shelter. Each one will be seen to have a little farm with its pretty, dilapidated, out-buildings edged up against it, built of the same rock but most sharply distinguished by a coat of whitewash. It has been noticed that a very considerable number of dolmens have similarly been built against the volcanic

IX Richborough
(*Portus Rutupis*), one
of the four Kentish
Forts of the Saxon Shore.
The stone walls were
added to the earthwork
ramparts and ditches
when the Saxons began
to threaten this coast
in the middle of the
third century.

X Mosaic from the
Roman palace of
Fishbourne in Sussex.

XI The most westerly of the Forts of the Saxon Shore, Porchester in Hampshire.

XII The amphitheatre at Caerleon (*Isca*) in South Wales.

XIII Part of the excavations of the Roman town of St. Albans (*Verulamium*), Hertfordshire.

XIV The Multangular Tower - the western bastion of the fourth-century fortress of York. (*Eboracum*).

XV Hadrian's Wall at
Housesteads
(*Borcovicium*).

XVI The entrance to
the strong room in the
headquarters building
of the fort at Chesters
(*Cilurnum*) on Hadrian's
Wall.

outcrops; their architects certainly made use of the stone, but they would hardly have been interested in the advantages of shelter and one wonders whether these very striking rock masses had been endowed with spirits, local deities, and had, therefore, a sanctity which made them desirable burial-places.

At the base of St. David's peninsula there is a dolmen on each side of the two 'drowned valleys' at Solva. This is a charming village and small harbour, and because it is so charming, it is right to mention the inconspicuous ramparts which defend the headland forming the east side of the harbour.

The traveller, if he is wise, will certainly go to St. David's Head where white-painted boulders will tell him that it is now held on his behalf by the National Trust. All headlands have a strong appeal, for me a much more powerful one than islands; I love to be thrust out into the ocean but not circumscribed. St. David's is among the fairest. The traveller will have had an opportunity to see the tiny cathedral city of St. David's, really a large village curiously built round and *above* the great Norman church—a village where geese gather every morning by the War Memorial in the City Square. Then he will have made his way across the low flat land flanking the little river Alan with the silhouette of the hill behind St. David's Head raised against the sky in front of him. Leaving Whitesand Bay and its bathing to the carefree inhabitants of the present, he will find a surprisingly narrow and little-used footpath which leads to the head, after first dipping to an enchanting small bay which seems to be a secret child of Whitesand. Looking back, the prospect down the immediate cliffs, along Whitesand Bay and past Point St. John to Ramsey Island, is a very lovely one, feelingly enhanced by the soft green of the chequered fields of the inland plateau. Armed with a map, the traveller will seek out the four or five not very notable dolmens, including those of Carn Llidi where one side of the chamber was formed by the natural rocky outcrop. If the rest prove too hard to find he must make for the very nose of St. David where he cannot fail to see the fine stone ramparts, probably of the Iron Age or (native) Roman period which convert it into a promontory fort with conspicuous rings marking the site of huts in the interior. On this ultimate extremity he should also be able to detect the dolmen of Coetan Arthur. Finally the opportunity is offered to this imaginary and happy traveller to climb down onto a lower rock mass, the last spike which land here thrusts against sea. There he can rest watching the bathers in Whitesand Bay, midgets moving on either side of the graceful curved line of the surf, and perhaps looking down on a fishing boat which, as it chugs across the wrinkled skin of the sea, gives him encouragement to think of the craft of the Stone Age voyagers which must have once ridden there. These people may perhaps have carried cattle and sheep with them in their boats, livestock that could have been seen from this vantage-point. But secretly in their heads they must have carried the tradition and the image which would enable them, indeed drive them, to raise those massive stone tombs for their dead which now alone remind us of their voyages.

Between St. David's Head and the second, far greater, concentration of monuments behind Strumble Head and round Fishguard Bay, there is a scatter of tombs among which I should like to single out Carreg Samson or Longhouse in the parish of Mathry. It has a pleasant position near the sea and, with its seven uprights and single large cover-stone, is a good example of the simple dolmen. The crowding of sites round Fishguard Bay shows that four thousand years ago, as to-day, this sheltered inlet was regarded as a good harbour. There are five tombs immediately above it on the west side, and another four not far away on the hills still further west; though none is of special note, nearly all deserve to be sought out by those who enjoy such hunting. Well to the south of Fishguard Bay there is a standing stone row (the only one in the county) at Parc y Meirw, Llanllawer, and near it another dolmen with the name of Coetan Arthur, but the most interesting, because unusual, monuments are further east round Newport. One of them, to the west of the town, is indeed unique; Cerrig y Gof consists of a roughly circular mound with five rectangular cists facing outwards from its circumference. It is a good example of local idiosyncracy in megalithic architecture. Carreg Coetan, which is almost in Newport, is worth seeing precisely because it is *not* uncommon, but a neat and characteristic example of dolmen. The other unusual tomb is among the group inland from Newport on the northern slopes of the Presely Hills. This is Pentre Ifan in the parish of Nevern, a southern representative of a type of tomb which we shall find to be more frequent in north Wales and which has distinguished relatives in Ireland and south-west Scotland. The most striking and characteristic feature is a portal formed of two very tall, pillar-like jamb-stones with a lower one forming, as it were, a half-door between them. Pentre Ifan has the further feature, found in many of the finest Scotch and Irish tombs, of a longish mound with a forecourt leading up to the entry, semicircular in plan and built of upright slabs. Very often the portals are by far the tallest stones in the building, and the capstone therefore slopes back from them, but here the upright forming the inner end of the chamber is equally high. These are the sound archaeological reasons for distinguishing Pentre Ifan, but there are others. It has been mentioned by topographers since the early seventeenth century and in about 1830 it was painted in oils by Richard Tonge of Bath, known as a 'painter and modeller of Megaliths'. The structure is in reality given a slightly fantastic air by the very narrow points of the three uprights on which the capstone rests; it appears improbable that so little can support so much. This impression that the capstone is virtually floating above the burial-chamber is skilfully enhanced by Tonge who makes the supporting stones taller and more slender than they are; they are also slightly twisted and have an appearance extraordinarily reminiscent of Henry Moore's three female figures in Battersea Park. The painter has pricked up the surrounding mild slopes into craggy mountains and has seated a simple shepherd bowed over his crook beside the monument; against a background of piled white clouds he has achieved a brilliant combination of near-accuracy with romantic art.

Another unique grave lies rather over a mile to the south-east of Pentre Ifan in the parish of Meline. This is Bedd yr Afanc, the Dwarf's or Beaver's Grave, a monument which can hardly be described as megalithic as the chamber is built of quite small stones. This chamber is as much as thirty feet long, wedge-shaped in plan, tapering from six feet to three feet, and set down in the centre of a roughly rectangular mound. It recalls a common type of Irish tomb-architecture.

Both Pentre Ifan and the Dwarf's Grave are on the northern slopes of the Mynydd Prescelly or the Presely Mountain and there is a considerable number of dolmens, standing stones and other monuments on the southern spurs which run down on the other side of their long narrow spine. Among these is the stone circle at Meini Gwyr, Llandyssilio East, which is the only circle in south Wales in which the stones are set upon a slightly embanked ring. It can very reasonably be claimed, however, that the Presely Mountain as a whole is of far greater interest in our prehistory than any single monument. We have already seen that the bluestones at Stonehenge were probably quarried from the volcanic dolerite of this ridge, while the larger recumbent 'altar stone' that has the place of honour in the innermost part of the sanctuary is a sandstone which might come from one of several regions of south Wales, but seems most likely to have been taken from the neighbourhood of Milford Haven. Some of the bluestones show marks which suggest they formed part of an earlier building before they were erected at Stonehenge. On the *Megalithic Map of South Wales* the Ordnance Survey authorities have inserted three roads, one the track known as the Fleming's Way which runs east and west along the Presely ridge, and two others leading from it, and following approximately the line of modern roads, down the southern spurs to end on Milford Haven. The implication is that when some existing monument, of what kind we do not know, was dismantled so that its sacred stones might be carried to Salisbury Plain, they were pushed, dragged, levered, rolled down one of these tracks to be embarked in Milford Haven. They may then have been ferried across the Bristol Channel and again transported overland along the parallel ridge of the Mendips. All these speculations will, of course, appear absurd if the geologists are able to prove that the bluestones were transported to the Plain by ice and not by man.

B. *North-West Wales*

Apart from the scattered stone circles and rows in central Wales, there is remarkably little to link the two centres of archaeological interest in south and north Wales. This is particularly true of megalithic architecture; along the whole central span of coast from south of Cardigan to north of Barmouth there is not a single recorded tomb. One can only guess that at the time, over four thousand years ago, when the Stone Age peoples were voyaging along our coasts in search of good landing-places, there may have been some natural barrier of salt marsh or forest fringe which prevented them from beaching anywhere on the shores of Cardigan Bay.

But there is one curious Bronze Age site in the area, at Ysbyty Cynfyn, not far from Devil's Bridge, where within an embanked stone circle has been built a Christian church—thus continuing the sacred associations of the site for some four thousand years. Some of the original stones from the circle have been incorporated in the churchyard wall, while two others now serve as gateposts. Only one of the stones, on the north side of the circle, is still in its original position.

There are a few forts in this otherwise barren region, but they are not of great note and I will name only Pen Dinas near Aberystwyth for this has been excavated and proved to be prehistoric, dating from the end of the Iron Age. In England one confidently expects hill-forts to be pre-Roman but in Wales many seem to have been occupied during the time of the Roman occupation and may even have been built then.

One Roman fort, Castell Collen, just north of Llandridod Wells, has a history reaching from the late first to the early fourth century, and some more than usually visible remains. These consist of the ramparts and the foundations of the headquarters building, the commandant's house and a granary, all standard structures in the average Roman auxiliary fort.

As soon as the traveller has left the volcanic peaks of Cader Idris behind him and crossed over Afon Mawddach, he is back in a territory rich in ancient monuments; the first are in Llanaber parish, a place continuous with Barmouth itself. Leaving the flat coastal strip just before reaching Tal-y-bont, he must make for the solid gloomy old farmhouse of Hendre Eirian and then follow the steep path that climbs up beside the deep gully of the Ceunant Hengwm Egryn. Across this stream and making a fine silhouette above him the toiling traveller will see the ramparts of Pendinas Fort, a place excavated earnestly but without result—it cannot be certainly dated. Towards the shoulder of the hill, he must leave the stream and swing to the right when he will be able to see two long, shapeless masses of piled stone, looking a little like grey disintegrating whales laid out on the hill-side to die. These are the two interesting and important long cairns known as the Carneddau Hengwm. The southern is the larger, nearly two hundred feet long, and the first feature that one is likely to see is a chamber with walls built from the small blocks of the cairn but roofed by a large single capstone. This little cell, near the centre of the cairn, is approached along a short passage; when I visited the site I had covered the last mile in fierce rain, each drop stinging the face like a viper, and I was happy to plunge beneath the shelter of the capstone and to sit, a female Jonah, secure in this relatively comfortable belly. The most striking part of this monument is, however, at its eastern end, hidden from immediate sight by the modern stone wall which rides across the cairn. There are three exceedingly tall uprights with a fallen capstone behind representing the remains of a chamber with a high, blocked portal of the kind we have seen in Cornwall (p. 171) and, after a fashion, at Pentre Ifan in Pembrokeshire. The northern of the two jamb-stones is missing, but I suspect it may be the long block lying half-covered by turf a few yards to the north. The slightly smaller northern whale has less architectural interest; a central chamber with drystone walls similar to its neighbour may perhaps once have been roofed by the slab which now rests on the body of the cairn at the west end; towards the east end there appear to be two rather meagre side cells walled with very thin slabs. Both these Carneddau Hengwm cairns, large and impressive though they are, seem to show an architectural looseness and lack of formality which suggests that they are relatively late monuments built by settlers in whose minds the traditional forms were already growing vague. Not far from the cairns is another pair of adjacent monuments: the Carneddau Hengwm circles; these are now much destroyed but originally the stones stood on a raised ring. I have it on first-hand authority that one well-known archaeologist first met another camped out beside these circles, and that on looking into his frying-pan he found him to be frizzling a mixture of bacon, chocolate and onions. Let me admit, to save all further research, that the circle-digger, camper and original cook was that great and beloved man, Mr. O. G. S. Crawford!

Returning to the coastal road the traveller will find the next site, hardly a mile further north, as easy to visit as the Carneddau Hengwm are strenuous. The Dyffryn long barrow is approached through the iron gates of the village school and will be found alongside the playground not many yards from the highway. The barrow was excavated in the 1960's revealing a long and complex history. It started life in the early Neolithic as a simple dolmen enclosed in a small oval cairn. At a later date a wedge-shaped chamber was constructed to the east of the dolmen and this remained open until late in the Neolithic period when the long barrow proper was raised over the eastern chamber and the original tomb.

Journeying northwards again along the coastal highway, at Llanbedr, about three miles beyond Dyffryn, the road passes two standing stones which are conspicuous in a field on the left-hand side; one is of quite exceptional height and the eye is caught by the railing and trees which surround them. A little further on in the parish of Llanfair is the dolmen of Gwern Einion, an attractive structure which seems to be enhanced by being embedded in a modern stone wall.

I suppose that I have some prejudice against Roman sites as places of pilgrimage, a prejudice due to a conviction that I know the kind of life that went on in barracks and private houses, a rational and commercial kind of life not altogether unlike our own. The monuments left by prehistoric man are attractive partly because they represent ways of feeling and action never fully to be comprehended by ourselves. The best that can usually be expected of Roman remains is that they provoke wonder and admiration for the indomitable *will* of the rational man—an emotion to which I personally am not greatly susceptible. Here, in Merioneth, however, there is a group of Roman antiquities of quite unusual quality—due, I believe, to their extraordinary remoteness, and an imaginative realization of the fear that the alien troops must have felt in a place so exposed to the violence and dark spiritual forces of the barbarians who were at home among these moors and mountains. This place is the fort of Tomen-y-mur. From Llanfair, it is reached by going through Harlech with its fairy-tale castle thrust out above the sea and up the fertile Vale of Ffestiniog, then by lane and gated track to a lonely piece of countryside two miles due north of Trawsfynydd on a finely situated spur. To the west there is an open view down the Vale to the sea; on all other sides magnificent mountain scenery, perhaps the finest to the south where the eye is carried down the high valley of Trawsfynydd with its reservoir lake as far as the distant grey shapes of Cader Idris. The group of monuments which is here enclosed in its own remoteness consists of a fort, an amphitheatre, remains of a bath-house and other buildings, several little square burial-mounds, a parade-ground and a curious artificial platform. The track will lead the traveller first to the amphitheatre, said to be the only one attached to an auxiliary fort: a fact which suggests that special indulgences were needed to keep up morale in a most unpopular station. The path to the fort then leads past a rectangular enclosure which has been partially levelled and embanked and may reasonably be recognized as a parade-ground. The most conspicuous thing in the fort itself is not Roman, but a medieval motte whose pudding-shaped mound rises boldly near the centre of the fortifications. From the vantage-point on its summit, it is easy to distinguish the surrounding ramparts of a first-century fort; it is also noticeable that a cross-wall runs through the motte itself. The explanation is that when Tomen-y-mur was being rebuilt in stone, presumably in the early second century, it was decided to reduce the area and this inner line marks the west wall of the smaller, remodelled fort. The motte therefore stands over the site of the later entrance and it is not at all impossible that the gate may be preserved inside the mound. A Roman track leaves the southeast entrance and leads down to the stream; beside it the foundations of various buildings, one probably a bath-house, are standing open, littered with fragments of brick and tile. This track begins again on the other side of the stream and burial-places can be seen along its course up to half a mile from the fort. As for the large artificial platform, it is to be found between the stream and the parade-ground, but there is little to do there but speculate whether it is a base for a catapult or a pompous monument, and why either a catapult or a monument should have been wanted in the desolate wilds of Tomen-y-mur.

Those who, like myself, have kept their nursery images and still see Wales as a pig's head, will recognize the Caernarvon peninsula as a forward-lopping ear. This ear, then, is marked along its length by warts, or rather by a line of isolated hills which give an attractive profile whether seen from the region we have just left or from the Anglesey side. Three of these hills were used by Celtic tribesmen as the hill-forts for which they are so obviously suited. Before entering the peninsula proper, mention should perhaps be made of Cist Cerig, the high portal stones of a vanished dolmen in the parish of Treflys between Portmadoc and Criccieth, and of two other dolmens in Llanystumdwy parish west of Criccieth. None is of much merit though the interest of Cist Cerig is increased by the 'cup marks', little hemispherical hollows, cut on a natural rock-face twenty-five yards east of the dolmen.

The first and by far the best known of the hill-forts is Tre'r Ceiri which occupies one of the summits of the hill, over eighteen hundred feet high, known as Yr Eifl or the Rivals. Probably the best way to reach it is to scramble up the barren rocky slope between Llanaelhaiarn and Llithfaen, but in so doing the climber winds round the shoulder of the hills in such a way as to enter the camp along the ancient road and through the main entrances on the north-west side. On this side there is an outer rampart running in places as much as two hundred feet from the main wall of the fort; the gateway through it has a massive flanking wall. Tre'r Ceiri is a most remarkable place, perhaps the most interesting spectacle among all the stone-built hill-forts of Britain. It is long and very narrow, running north-east by south-west; the single rampart is entirely built of stones piled loosely but with evident skill—evident because they have kept a fair shape for something like two thousand years. The best stretch is on the north-west side where the wall still stands quite six feet high and has a well-marked rampart walk behind a protecting parapet; a little postern gates opens through its base. From the northern end, which passes fifteen hundred feet, there is a commanding outlook—overland to Snowdon, oversea north to Anglesey with Holyhead Mountain as its chief landmark, the ranges of Merioneth as far as Cader Idris. Readers will, I hope, forgive me for praising yet another view if I confess that I have never seen it, having myself visited the fort in a blinding mist. Tre'r Ceiri is probably best known for the stone-built huts with which it is crowded. These huts are, indeed, most remarkable, some are round and some rectangular in plan, and many of them are approached through well-constructed passages. Outside the wall lie a number of small enclosures, again with dry-stone walls, some of which may be cattle pounds, others gardens; the gate which opens from the narrow south-western end of the fort has imposing flanking walls and leads into a kind of walled roadway with round huts and other enclosures built up against it. One may leave Tre'r Ceiri marvelling at the energy needed to build the rampart and houses from thousands of tons of stones, but also puzzled by the kind of life which could have been led in this high, rocky place, so laborious to approach, so unsuitable, one would have thought, for the management of cattle. As for the period of the occupation, the fort may have been built during the prehistoric Iron Age but it certainly remained in use during the Roman period.

Before going further along the peninsula, it is worth visiting two dolmens on the coast to the north-east, both of them in the parish of Clynnogfawr, famous for its magic well and shrine of St. Beuno. The furthest off is also the least interesting, a neat, orthodox dolmen with faint traces of a circular mound standing in a field just where the road from Clynnog forks to Llanllyfni. The nearer one can be reached by an agreeable path from Clynnogfawr church; it stands in a green meadow very close to the sea within a little railing which seems less offensive than these necessary protections often are. What is most distinctive about this Bachwen dolmen is that the upper side of the capstone is pitted all over with cup-marks, many of them still *looking* very smooth and well rounded.

Returning to push westward along the 'ear' the second hill-fort is Garn Bodfean a mile south of Nevin, which should be approached from a delightfully wooded road on the southern side—very unlike the uncompromising rocky slopes at Tre'r Ceiri. The ramparts here are badly preserved, but there are some excellent examples of round huts; the highest point is occupied by a chaotic pile of stones which may possibly be the ruin of a medieval motte. The skeleton forms of a dead forest on the hilltop make a stricken scene reminiscent of Paul Nash's paintings of the gaunt trunks and angular branches of trees blasted on the Western Front.

From Garn Bodfean the third fort, Carn Fadryn, can readily be seen about three miles away on its sharply isolated, sugarloaf hill.

I will name two megalithic tombs in this extremity of the peninsula, one the Mynydd Cefnamwlch dolmen near the coast just east of Penllech, and the second Tan y muriau near Rhiw, a long cairn with portalled chamber comparable, though far less well preserved, with the Carneddau Hengwm.

At Caernarvon the foundations of part of the walls of Roman *Segontium* are open to the public. *Segontium* was a large auxiliary fort intended to house a garrison of one thousand men. Excavation revealed the usual sequence, of an early timber fort superseded in the second century by more permanent stone buildings. Although the site itself is not one to inspire the imagination, the museum has a fine and well-displayed collection. What is far more interesting than the remains or the museum is to be able to see the successive moves of this settlement down from the hills. On Twthill at the mouth of the Cadnant Valley is the original Celtic Iron Age fort; the Romans built their station on the slopes of Llanbeblig below the hill-fort, and finally Edward III founded modern Caernarvon when he built his magnificent castle right at the water's edge.

C. *Anglesey*

Anglesey is built of some of the oldest rocks of Wales; save for a small pocket in the centre of the east coast, the stuff of the island was almost all laid down in Archaean times. The first, Caledonian, period oᶠ folding has creased it from north-west to south-west; the small valleys and low ridges follow this axis almost with the regularity of pleated paper. Looking at the map it is interesting to see how, except for the modern Holyhead highway and the coastal road, all the country lanes provide a pattern of oblique parallel stripes for the reason that most of them keep to the tops of these regular ridges. Its extreme antiquity has not given the island fine scenery; although it is tilted, sloping gently down towards the south-west from higher ground to the north, there are no hills of any height or distinction, with the exception of Holyhead Mountain which just manages to out-top seven hundred feet. The prospects across the island are uninteresting, but happily it is always possible to look back towards the mainland and see the undulating plateau of Anglesey as no more than a foreground to Snowdonia and the fretted line of the Caernarvon peninsula.

However uninspired the scenery, Anglesey, the ancient Mona, is full of prehistoric interest. It is known, of course, as a late stronghold of Celtic Druidism in Europe and although the priesthood has left no certain visible remains their known presence there adds interest to discovery. For example, when during the war a rich treasure of Celtic Iron Age remains, including a few obviously ritual objects as well as the fragments of many chariots, was taken from a peat bog, it was suggested that it might have been thrown there after the Roman extermination of the Druids in 61 A.D. This Llyn Cerrig treasure is now in the National Museum at Cardiff.

In addition to such half-historical associations, Anglesey can show many prehistoric antiquities, the main interest being divided between megalithic tombs and groups of native Celtic huts of the Roman period.

There is one monument on the western coast of Anglesey that justifies making a detour to Porth Trecastell and thence along to the end of the promontory. This is the megalithic tomb known as Barclodiad y Gawres, recently excavated and splendidly restored. The carved stones are among the finest examples of their kind in Britain. The largest number of megaliths, however, lie along the south-eastern stretch of the island above that magnificent channel, the Menai Straits, which with its swift, quiet water flowing between thickly-wooded banks, has the air of some great river quite beyond the scale of our British Isles. The first important monuments after crossing Menai Bridge are the well-known chambered graves in the grounds of Lord Anglesey's house, on the bank of the Straits hardly more than a mile below the Tubular Bridge. The Plas Newydd dolmen stands at the end of the drive between the mansion and a cricket field where it commands a view across the Straits. In such a place it at once suggests an eighteenth-century folly, an ornament to the house put up by some romantically minded peer. In truth, however, it is a genuine prehistoric monument of a rather unusual kind; there are two adjacent chambers, one larger than the other, with very massive uprights and capstones, separated by a single upright. It is possible, though not to my mind likely, that the smaller chamber was originally a passage or antechamber giving access to the larger. The second monument at Plas Newydd is reached by following a path through kitchen garden and shrubbery to a sloping meadow immediately above the Straits. This is Bryn-yr-Hen-Bobl, a tomb made noticeable by an unusually well-preserved mound, kidney-shaped and surrounded by large trees. A twisted thorn hangs elegantly above the entrance which is of a unique kind. After a forecourt not unlike the horned approach to a Cotswold long barrow, the way into the rectangular chamber is over a slab with two semicircular bites taken out of its upper edge. There can be little doubt that there was formerly an upper slab with corresponding bites which fitted upon the lower, like a pair of stocks, and so formed a double port-hole, the diameter of the holes being unusually small. This grave has been excavated and yielded pottery of the New Stone Age; it also proved to have a long narrow horn projecting from it down the meadow, but it is now very hard to distinguish.

The next site to be visited not much more than a mile away is one of the most famous in Welsh prehistory—the passage grave of Bryn-Celli-Ddu. The imposing tomb is the finest representative in England and Wales of a type of monument well known in Ireland and Scotland, in which a large polygonal chamber is approached along a much narrower passage, the whole being covered by a round cairn or mound. Bryn Celli lies near a farm road just south of Llanddaniel Fab; since its excavation and restoration it has been protected by a Department of the Environment railing, and the key must be fetched from the farmhouse. As now restored a passage and chamber built of large uprights with drystone fillings are covered by a mound with a kerb of quite large stones. Inside the chamber is a pillar stone, almost perfectly circular in cross-section and with an artificially smoothed surface; a monolith of this form and in this position can be assumed to have had a phallic significance. Another most unusual feature is a stone now standing upright immediately beyond the end of the chamber at a point which would originally have been at the centre of the mound. This slab, which the excavator found prone above a ritual pit containing burnt bones, is covered with an incised design of wavy lines and spirals which meander over both faces and the narrow upper edge. The pattern makes one think of the magical maps of the journeyings of the spirit before birth, drawn by some aboriginal Australian tribes. There are many other details to see, but I have described enough to suggest the fascination and importance of Bryn-Celli-Ddu and the hints concerning the religious beliefs and ritual practices of its builders with which it tantalizes us.

One last site is worth visiting in this south-western corner of the isle— the dolmen of Bodowyr in Llanidan parish. This is another neat and blameless dolmen with a regular, almost pyramidal capstone.

The other region rich in antiquities is the high ground along the eastern coast. In the Beaumaris promontory there is plenty of medieval interest, but of prehistoric sites only the hill-fort of Bwrdd Arthur is worth naming. Near the base of the promontory beside the road from Llansadwrn to Pentraeth, the ruined megalith called Hen Drefor Llansadwrn lies in a peaceful meadow with a prospect of the Snowdon peaks. It is now in two parts, with a tall upright portal stone at the east end; probably it was originally a single 'segmental' chamber of the kind to be described at Trefignath (p. 234).

Taking the main coastal road past the wide ruddy stretches of Red Wharf Bay, the traveller should turn left at Red Wharf station; along this lane he will find the not very remarkable dolmen of Glyn on his left and then reach Pant-y-Saer, which stands on high ground above the hamlet of Tyn-y-gongl. This is another of the megalithic tombs of Anglesey which has been scientifically dug   and again the excavation revealed unexpected features. To-day the visitor might not notice more than a large capstone in a sloping position on rather low supporting stones; in fact this chamber is recessed in a kidney mound very much like a smaller Bryn-yr-Hen-Bobl (p. 231), while below the capstone is a rock-cut chamber sixteen by ten feet long which contained the remains of a very large number of bodies. Finds of pottery showed that Pant-y-Saer had been used during the New Stone and Early Bronze Ages.

Rejoining the coast road as far as the village of Benllech, the remains of another megalithic tomb can be seen which were discovered less than a decade ago. It is amazing that this structure could have been overlooked for so long and was only found by accident during the clearance of under-growth. From here it is only a short distance to Llanallgo and there one can take the lane past Lligwy Farm. Close by the roadside the Lligwy dolmen is very noticeable within its ring of iron railings. The colossal rectangular capstone, weighing about twenty-five tons, is supported on a number of disproportionately small uprights; below it a crevice in the natural rock has been utilized to make a shelf. Here, as at Pant-y-Saer, a surprisingly large number of individuals had been buried.

A hundred yards or so further along the lane a signpost and stile show the way to the enclosed settlement of Din Lligwy, the path winding through a wood which in spring is brilliant with flowers. This is a site to which, were I Baedeker, I should give a maximum of stars. Within a stout enclosure wall, there is a group of houses, two of them circular, but the rest rectangular in plan and all spacious, splendidly built and almost intact. Nearly all the walls show a massive construction with an inner and outer facing of large slabs and a packing of smaller stones. Din Lligwy shows signs of having buildings of more than one period, but it is known to have been inhabited during the Roman occupation down to the fourth century A.D.; it must surely have been the stronghold of some chieftain of unusual standing—one would like to think that the lord himself lived in the larger round house, a place quite worthy to rank as a Celtic palace.

After Lligwy, the last monument to be visited on this journey is far away to the north, the Menai Herion near Llanfechell—three tall standing stones set in a triangle. The ruined megalith which lies between them and the sea is excessively hard to find.

Although there are a few other dolmens and standing stones scattered through Anglesey, the only other region to which I should wish to guide the followers of antiquity is that island beyond an island beyond an island —Holyhead. Most visitors are likely to arrive in the town itself and will discover that the advantages of the harbour were already recognized by the Romans. The late Gothic church of St. Gybi stands within a tiny fort, hardly an acre in extent, built on the edge of the harbour. It shows that characteristic Late Roman architecture with projecting bastions at the corners, two of them still standing though badly in need of repair. The place has never been dug, but it is a reasonable guess that Caer Gybi was built during the last hopeless attempt to protect the coast from Irish and other barbarian raiders late in the fourth century.

It is an easy walk through the straggling outskirts of the town to Holyhead Mountain whose modest hump is always to be seen across the level expanse of Anglesey. Once the straggle is left behind, the short climb is delightful; here at last one is made aware of the inestimable age of the rocks: they are highly crystalline and on a bright day glisten with a black-and-white harshness against sea and blank blue sky. It is safe to follow any of the paths which twist up among the tumble of stones for all ultimately lead to one of the entrances of Caer-y-Twr, the fort occupying the summit of this almost sea-girt mountain. The finest entrance, both architecturally and as a look-out place, is the north-eastern, where the stone ramparts turn to make flanking walls very much like those at Tre'r Ceiri. Indeed Caer-y-Twr is like a less imposing Tre'r Ceiri without its huts and enclosures; it has, on the north side, a similar parapeted rampart walk, and the rough but skilful piling of the masonry is very much the same. Towards the southern end ramparts are unnecessary, for the hill falls away in fanged precipices, dangerous and almost impassable; there is, however, a steep path down on the western side. From here a walled track forking left away from the cliff leads to the hut group of Ty Mawr, which, like all such sites in this part of the world, are marked as Cyttiau'r Gwyddelod, or Irish Folks' Houses. It is a long group of huts, nearly all circular, spread down a slope; some have hearths still visible, and at the time of their excavation some were furnished with mortars and grinding-stones. There is no clearly defined enclosure wall like that at Din Lligwy. This settlement seems to have been occupied by the native Celtic population late in the Roman period, probably during the third and fourth centuries. By following the road that zig-zags along the west coast one can reach a smaller but similar settlement against the road junction by the bay of Porth-dafarch; the huts are now overgrown, but there is something appealing in this hamlet set like a seaside resort close beside its pretty bay. This conviction of agreeable living is reinforced by the knowledge that a handsome bronze tankard handle was found among the huts.

The last site to be seen in Holyhead is also the most spectacular. This is the elaborate megalithic burial-chamber which lies beside a lane just beyond Trefignath farm to the south-east of Holyhead town. It is a long narrow structure whose huge angular blocks give an idea of megalithic architecture at its grandest; to-day the tomb falls into three separate sections with the largest and most complete chamber at the east end. Here two tall stones and other outliers suggest a portal with forecourt (a little like Pentre Ifan, p. 222), and it is generally believed that Trefignath represents a type of tomb frequent across the sea in Ulster and south-west Scotland in which a long parallel-sided gallery with high portal and semi-circular forecourt is divided by partition stones into a number of segments. There are two other dubious examples in Anglesey but none other is known in England or Wales and their presence here suggests the sea traffic which must have been carried on round the head of the Irish Sea even at this distant time of the New Stone Age.

D. *The North Welsh Coast and the Northern Marches*

Returning from Mona to the mainland it is impossible to avoid seeing the new and extraordinary profile of Penmaenmawr, the mountain which towers above the cliff road just beyond Llanfairfechan. Here colossal quarries for road metal and other humble purposes have devoured the whole mountain-top including the fine fort which once crowned it. The engineers have left a single column of rock standing to mark the former height of the mountain, and this projects grotesquely above the next line of quarry walls now eating towards it.

Although the fort has gone, there are still sites of great interest to be seen on this hill, and to reach them the visitor should make his way into the back streets which climb up behind the town of Penmaenmawr. Here he can easily find the footpath to Graig Lwyd farm which is comfortably tucked at the foot of a small valley out of sight, and almost out of earshot, of the ugliness and racket of the quarries. The volcanic rock now so much in demand for road metal was found by New Stone Age people to be serviceable for stone implements. Over a wide area of the steep slopes of Penmaenmawr behind and to the west of the farm, the loose scree and surface soil have been found to be thickly littered with stone axes, adzes, and picks in various stages of manufacture—including many broken 'wasters'. This was, in fact, a large-scale factory, and geological analysis has proved that its products were widely traded about the country. There are other such workshops in Westmorland and Antrim, and they are known from their products to have existed in Cornwall. These centres for stone manufactures can be seen as the western counterpart of the flint-mines and factories of eastern and southern England. They seem, however, to have been at their most flourishing at a rather late date.

There is, of course, nothing to be seen above ground of this, one of the most ancient industrial centres in Britain. Indeed, much of the site is now quarried away. Yet we can still imagine the men in their leather clothes squatting at their working-floors, each perhaps with a little hut or shelter round him, equipped with his anvil stone and implements and materials for chipping and polishing. We can recall the sound of hammering and the small rattle of flakes—a faint, faint premonition of the din of the modern quarries.

After a steep climb up the stream to its head the traveller will come out on open moorland and can look back to a marine view bounded by Puffin Island (off the easternmost tip of Anglesey) and the bold form of Great

Orme's Head. Here without much difficulty he will find what is probably the best known of the Welsh stone circles—the Druid's Circle, Penmaenmawr. The stones have stood on a low bank, but many unfortunately have been destroyed, thrown down or moved from their place. A few yards to the west is another group of stones sometimes marked as a smaller circle; it is, however, quite impossible to distinguish an ordered plan. Considerably further west again the path which follows the edge of the moorland towards the summit of Penmaenmawr passes a large round barrow which is said to be of the 'bell' form (p. 51). If such an identification has any significance, this *tumulus* is a freakish outlier of an essentially southern type.

The Roman road from Aber went across the hills up here to the fort of *Kanovium* in the Conway Valley, and mountain-walkers would do well to find it and let it take them past a number of cairns, small forts, standing stones and other minor antiquities until at last they make their way to the riverside at Caerhun, the site of the Roman station. Most people, however, will go by the historic town of Conway and from there up the wide, fertile valley to Caerhun. The fort is easily identified for the parish church stands in one corner, the ramparts actually supporting the churchyard walls. All the barracks and other buildings once uncovered within the fort have returned to meadow and only the strong outline of the walls can now be followed, but it is a place well worth visiting. Its situation on slightly swelling ground with the river winding down between its water-meadows and flanking hills is altogether delightful. The utter peace is disturbed only by the shrieking of peacocks at the Plas—and this, after all, is a distinguished sound.

Higher up, the beauty of the Conway quickens as the mountains draw nearer and the sides of the valley become richly forested. Here there is one site which merits the very considerable efforts needed to reach it. The chambered long barrow of Capel Garmon is across the Conway from Bettws-y-Coed about a mile to the south of the hamlet from which it takes its name. The path leading to it is marked with signposts and very well tended, and the grave itself kept in excellent order—there are few more convincing examples of the care with which we now guard our prehistoric monuments than this one, a monument which cannot be of general interest and in a place so remote. Capel Garmon, together with Maen Pebyll over the next ridge of hills to the west, seem in their plan and construction to be related to the long barrows of Breconshire and Glamorgan—and therefore to those of the Cotswolds—rather than to others in the north. Capel Garmon has the same wedge-shaped mound with horned forecourt leading to a dummy entrance; the chamber, set in the centre of the mound with access by a narrow passage from the south side, is tripartite, a rectangular central 'hall' opening on to a large horseshoe compartment on each side. Only the western portion of the chamber has kept its capstone—a very large one. The few sherds of pottery found at Capel Garmon include both New Stone Age and Early Bronze Age types.

Still further to the south-west, only one and a half miles north-east of Beddgelert, is Dinas Emrys, a place of great natural beauty. It is a steep climb past three sets of ramparts to reach the original west entrance to this hill-fort, but an easier approach can be made from the east. The site was occupied from the Early Iron Age through the Roman period and into the fifth century and the various periods to which the visible remains belong are not immediately easy to distinguish. The most readily recognizable feature is the artificial pool dug during the first century A.D. A medieval legend connects this pool with the fifth century British king, Vortigern, dragons and Merlin the magician. What is perhaps even stranger than the story itself is that finds from the excavations carried out at Dinas Emrys show that it was indeed occupied during the time of Vortigern. The foundations of the stone building close to the pool are also Roman; earlier structures of the Iron Age settlement were of wood and partially underlie the Roman remains. Outside the defences on the slopes of the hillside are traces of field terraces and hut circles, while the tower on the cliff above is medieval and belongs to the twelfth century. In all Dinas Emrys offers a range of remains not be be equalled by many hill-forts.

In returning down-river to the coast, I ought perhaps to name the dolmen with high portal near the Conway mouth at Hendre Waelod, but the main interest of this strip of the Welsh coast will be found to lie in its hill-forts. Indeed the last Welsh megalith which I shall name is Tyddyn Bleiddyn in the parish of Cefn on the west side of the Vale of Clwyd; easterly outlier though it is, it appears to have affinities with the chambered long cairns of Merioneth (p. 225).

The hill-forts are to be found in numbers on both sides of the Vale; perhaps the largest quantity are on the Flint side along the Clwydian range, but the two most remarkable in quality are on the west, not very far from the coast. Both Pen y Corddyn and Dinorben are among the broken hills near the mouth of the Vale behind Abergele, and both show strong ramparts which are not continuous but combined with natural scarps. Pen y Corddyn (nearer the sea) seems to have been built during the first century B.C. and to have been abandoned, like all these forts, immediately after the Roman conquest; it has elaborate defences at its entrances.

Dinorben in places shows colossal ramparts; it began with a single line built well back in the Iron Age, possibly as early as 300 B.C., but later the ramparts were doubled and given a strong inturned entrance flanked by stone guard-chambers.

Iron Age hill-forts in many ways akin to these form the only striking antiquities of the Welsh Marches of Cheshire and Shropshire, a journey which will bring us back to an earlier stopping-place on the northern boundary of Hereford (p. 20). Prehistoric peoples before the Iron Age Celts failed to colonize this border region in any numbers, for it was sandwiched between the almost unbroken forests of the Midland Plain and the inhospitable expanses of the central Welsh mountains. The easiest ways into it were, of course, by the Dee to the north and the Severn to the south. I think it is true to say there is much more evidence of early trade routes through this country than of substantial or prosperous settlement.

Before leaving Wales behind I ought, perhaps, to mention one well-known monument which, although it is not prehistoric in age, has a primitive form. Offa's Dyke still marks fairly accurately the true boundary between English and Welsh and is regarded with some pride—at least by the English. The northern end of this long earthwork rests on the coastal fringes near Prestatyn, the southern on the Severn estuary at Chepstow; the finest portions survive between Presteigne and Montgomery. More than this I will not say, for this great length of bank and ditch is a *historical* monument, having been built in the eighth century almost certainly by King Offa himself—probably a unique example of correct attribution among the names of our pre-Norman monuments. It marked the frontier of the young Anglo-Saxon kingdom of Mercia against the free Britons of the Welsh mountains.

After crossing the Welsh boundary and the Dee we shall find two of the forts we are pursuing on the ridge of sandstone which runs down the centre of Cheshire. The more northerly is Castle Ditch, Eddisbury, in the Delamere Forest area. This is a long oval fort with a double rampart which follows the contour at the edge of the hill; the entrance is elaborately inturned and supplied with guard-chambers, originally built of stone reinforced with wood (though not the true *Murus Gallicus*). The place has had an immensely long history. The hill-top was occupied by the end of the Bronze Age, probably by 600 B.C., and a single rampart was put round part of the hill in the early third century B.C. It was doubled and extended to the whole hill top about two hundred years later only to be dismantled after the Roman conquest by Legionaries from Chester (Roman *Deva*), the fortress housing the famous Twentieth Legion. It was roughly reoccupied in the Dark Ages; Aethelflaeda built a burh there in her struggle against the Norsemen, and finally it was chosen as the site of a little hunting-lodge early in the Middle Ages. Eddisbury has been a stage, though a remote one, for many acts of our history.

The second of the Cheshire camps is Maiden Castle, Bickerton Hill, further south along the same sandstone ridge between Wrexham and Crewe. This camp is more like Bredon Hill in that its double ramparts do not follow the contours but cut off a promontory whose naturally sharp slopes have been further steepened by artificial scarping; the inner of the two walls has a fine inturned entrance and is built throughout in *Murus Gallicus* or stone bonded with timber. Its history is relatively simple, having been occupied for only about a century before the Roman conquest.

Next of these great prehistoric Marcher camps is Old Oswestry, an outstandingly fine and complicated earthwork built on a glacial esker not far from the modern town. Between about 250 B.C. and the inevitable abandonment after the Roman conquest, the walls and entrances were four times reinforced; beginning with two lines of defence, the inner with inturned entrance, a third was then added outside for three-quarters of the total circuit; next the elaborate outworks were built round the west entrance—the intervening space being filled with little clay pens that may conceivably have been used to hold water. Last stage of all—the huge double outer ramparts were built to enclose the entire existing fort, outworks and all. Like Eddisbury, Old Oswestry was occupied by squatters during the Dark Ages, but it had no Christian Saxon or medieval history, and has stood deserted for nearly fifteen hundred years.

Two more forts, both in magnificent natural situations, stand west and east of Shrewsbury—the Breiddin, which is just across the border into Montgomeryshire, and the Wrekin, famous as a beacon hill, and even to-day with a red light to warn aircraft of its abrupt and unexpected presence. In the Welsh site, where the hill is over a thousand feet high, a double line of ramparts with a funnelled entrance at the centre abut on to the sheer cliffs that protect the north-west side. Late Bronze Age people were the first to occupy this defensible hill-top. Early in the Iron Age, a timber-fronted rampart was built, and then replaced by more substantial walls with masonry facings. In the third to second centuries B.C., families were living in substantial rectangular houses; towards the end of the Iron Age there was a change to wattle and daub round houses. For centuries the hill was deserted, only to be refortified in Late Roman times. The Breiddin is a well-known landmark from Shropshire, but the Wrekin must surely be one of the best-known hills in Britain, proclaiming itself a last outlier of the mountain country thrust against the Midland Plain. It is a lovely spectacle to stand on the Long Mynd and look along the line of hills, Hope Bowdler, Caer Caradoc and the rest, to see them end in the sharp, tree-furred spine of the Wrekin, all of them looking like the islands which once in geological time they were. From its first building as early as 200 B.C. this hill-fort had two lines of ramparts, but outworks were added later. Perhaps the most interesting fact in its history is that it may be regarded as the prehistoric precursor of Roman *Viroconium*—which is at Wroxeter, half-way between the Wrekin and Shrewsbury. *Viroconium* was among the larger cities of the Province; it covered a hundred and seventy acres and during the height of its prosperity had a magnificent forum or town hall, and the usual big public baths. Excavation revealed all manner of domestic details—one shop specializing in fine pottery from Gaul, another in kitchen wares, and a third in whetstones; the workshops of blacksmiths and other artisans. Only the baths and the forum colonnade are still visible, together with a few stretches of grass-covered 'earthworks', once the city ramparts of *Viroconium*. The bath site includes the impressive remains of the wall which once separated the palaestra (or exercise hall) from the baths proper and is comparable, but in a more idyllic setting, with the Jewry Wall at the Leicester Roman baths. The history of this cantonal capital of the Cornovii was a long one, stretching into the early decades of the fifth century. It should be looked at as the sequel to the neighbouring British hill-forts, as a symbol of the great power that crushed the resistance which these forts themselves represent; of civilization, with its great advantages and its great losses, bringing an end to the barbarian life of prehistoric Britain.

The two of these Marcher forts that still remain to be named are both to the south of Shrewsbury, where with the Breiddin and the Wrekin they mark the four corners of a quadrilateral. These are Ffridd Faldwyn, which like the Breiddin is just in Wales, half a mile west of Montgomery, and Titterstone Clee six miles east of Ludlow. The Welsh fort seems first to have been put up in the middle of the third century B.C. already with double ramparts, then, like Old Oswestry, to have had various additions made at its entrance gates before being completely enclosed in new outer ramparts. At Titterstone Clee, on the other hand, the first fort (perhaps half a century older than the earliest at Ffridd Faldwyn) was a simple construction with a single rampart of earth and timber which was later doubled and rebuilt in stone.

So now from the north I have reached the border of Herefordshire which formed a stopping-place on the journey from the south (p. 202).

Those who are interested in these frontier forts (of which I have named only the greatest among many lesser strongholds) must picture how Bredon Hill and Llanmelin (p. 190) complete their line down to the Severn estuary. If the reader finds my account of them dry and monotonous, he should remember that I write not for the reader but for the traveller. There can be no dullness for the traveller when he visits these sites in the broken border country, where mountains struggle against lowlands, where Celts struggled against Romans and then again, as Roman Britons, against the Anglo-Saxons whom, except politically, they have ever since held at bay!

Chapter Eight

EASTERN ENGLAND

A. THE CHILTERNS AND EAST ANGLIA
B. THE EAST MIDLANDS AND LINCOLNSHIRE

A. *The Chilterns and East Anglia*

THIS wedge-shaped piece of country running from Buckinghamshire to broaden out in Essex, Suffolk and Norfolk is poorly supplied with anti-quities. Much of it consists of soils that were more or less thickly forested in prehistoric times; even the belt of chalk which bends right across it first as the Chilterns then as the Gogmagog hills and the East Anglian Heights is partially covered with beds of clay and gravel left by the glaciers of the Ice Age and so was more overgrown than the naked chalk of the Southern Downs. It does, however, provide the key to the prehistory of the whole region, for along it ran the ancient trackways which in time crystallized as the Icknield Way.

This part of the English lowlands has been thickly populated and heavily cultivated since Saxon times, while in recent centuries its southern and western stretches have been gripped by London's tentacles, both the villa growth of dormitory settlements and by light and heavy industry. It is true to say of the whole territory that prehistoric man did not endow it with any of his most impressive remains and that historic man has been highly destructive of such remains as there were.

The Chilterns, whose comfortably swelling hills, soft in colour and hung with beech-woods, are always so welcome to the eyes of those who have made the monotonous journey across the Midlands, from Birming-ham, say, or Leicester, have surprisingly little which is worth seeing. The first monument which I wish to mention is something of a joke, for al-though it is an ancient monument, it is not native to the Chilterns, but, of all unlikely places, to the island of Jersey. It is a complex and most unusual example of megalithic architecture which was discovered during the

242

eighteenth century by soldiers levelling a parade-ground outside St. Helier. Wishing to make some show of their esteem for the then Governor of Jersey, Marshal Conway, the grateful islanders dug up their tomb, and embarked it for England, where it arrived by barge up the Thames in 1788, and was re-erected in Conway's grounds close by the Thames at Henley. During the time when the Marshal was rather naturally hesitating over accepting this uncommon gift, his neighbour, Horace Walpole, wrote: 'Pray do not disappoint me, but transport the Cathedral of your island to your domain on our continent.' The incident is a delicious illustration of the romantic antiquarianism of the late eighteenth century—a cult whose tendency towards an exaggerated horror is well expressed by the verses which the Jersey authorities caused to be attached to one of the stones. They begin:

> Pour des Siècles cachés aux regard des Mortels,
> Cet ancien Monument, ces Pierres, ces Autels,
> Où le fang des Humains offert en facrifice
> Ruiffelat, pour des Dieux qu' enfantoit le Caprice;

Since the division of Conway's Park Place estate, the monument now stands in the garden of a house which has been named in its honour 'Templecombe'.

Among the few genuine Chiltern antiquities, there are small forts outside West Wycombe and north-west of Princes Risborough and a more considerable one, Cholesbury, to the south of Tring, which has been dated to the Belgic Iron Age. There is also a New Stone Age long barrow of a sort at Whiteleaf near Princes Risborough—though it is certainly not of a sort that I should have mentioned in Wessex or other prolific areas. The huge chalk-cut cross at Whiteleaf represents a type of hill figure which is characteristic of the Chilterns; I name it here partly because I have named other and even later chalk cuttings, justifying it by their respectable prehistoric ancestry, partly because it stands guard over the Icknield Way, partly because several ingenious antiquaries have tried to argue that the cross has been adapted from a far more ancient fertility symbol.

It is the northern part of the Chilterns near Dunstable which bears the most obvious marks of prehistoric occupation, the reason being that the chalk is less encumbered by glacial clays and gravels than elsewhere and must always have been relatively open and habitable. The fort of Maiden Bower occupies a promontory extending west of Dunstable, and on Dunstable Down itself, at a spot about three miles west of the town, the Five Knolls are a striking group of round barrows. When one of them was excavated the diggers found not only the crouched skeleton of the individual for whom the barrow had been raised early in the Bronze Age—this they expected, or at least hoped, to find—but also a large number of fully-extended skeletons which, from their knives and other odds and ends of possessions, could be identified as those of Anglo-Saxons who lived in the fifth or sixth century. There was clear evidence, too, in the mutilated state of the bones that these bodies had been buried after some violent massacre, and the explanation preferred is that one of the parties of Anglo-Saxon marauders, who in those centuries often swooped upon the disorganized and Rome-forsaken Britons, for once lost the day and suffered the inevitable vengeance. If this is the true story, it may well be that the Britons thought a pagan burial-mound a fitting place to bury latter-day pagans.

The supposed Saxon raiders may have been following Watling Street where it crossed the Dunstable Downs, and it is not impossible that their victorious foes were among the descendants of the citizens of Roman *Verulamium* (St. Albans) which is on Watling Street hardly more than ten miles to the south-west.

It is not for me to play the part of guide to the rich and varied remains to be seen at what is the most spectacular Roman site in southern Britain; it is a place visited by thousands and has its own literature. Roman *Verulamium* was built on low ground in the valley of the Ver, but before the conquest it had been the capital of one of the Belgic princes of the Catevellauni, and the long banks and ditches of this earlier stronghold are to be seen in Prae Wood near, but well above, the Roman city. Because of this earlier importance, almost immediately after the conquest the Emperor Claudius singled out *Verulamium* as the only town in Britain to be honoured with the self-governing constitution of a *municipium*. Together with Colchester and London it was brutally sacked by Queen Boudicca, but soon recovered and prospered during the first and second centuries, the height of its fortunes being marked by the building of its fine theatre in about 150 A.D. Probably this was never used for serious drama, but for singing and dancing and other entertainments suitable for weary officials, merchants and plebs alike; nevertheless it was a true theatre, as distinct from the amphitheatre with its more frankly brutal uses, and very few of these were constructed in Britain. *Verulamium* continued to flourish throughout the Roman period and beyond. Excavations have shown that even in the middle of the fifth century organized urban life persisted with such amenities as the town's public water supply being still maintained. But *Verulamium* could not survive indefinitely either the collapse of the

Roman administration or the advances into southern and central England of the Anglo-Saxon invaders. Like other towns of the lost province it disappeared into the Dark Ages and in medieval times its ruins provided quarries for building materials; the Norman tower of St. Albans shows large red patches where the thin Roman bricks have been incorporated. It is worth anyone's while to make the short journey from London to see the Belgic earthworks, the fine stretch of city wall of Roman *Verulamium*, the many foundations of buildings, tessellated pavements and hypocausts, the excellent museum, and above all the theatre with its colonnaded stage —the only building known to me in Britain where one can experience something of the feeling of the classical ruins of the Continent.

Any visitor who can, should also take the Harpenden road to see on its right-hand side the best length of the Beech Bottom Dyke, a strong boundary probably raised by the Belgic Catevellauni against the other British Celts (p. 57) and beyond it the two sections of earthworks at Wheathampstead, the Devil's Dyke and the Slad, which it is believed formed part of the defences of the Belgic capital (before the successive move to St. Albans and Colchester) from which Cassivellaunus went out to lead his defensive campaigns against Julius Caesar. Only Colchester can compete with St. Albans and Wheathampstead as a place to apprehend in visual form the last days of prehistoric Britain together with the rise, decline and fall of the Roman Province.

Returning now to the ridge of the chalk and the line of the Icknield Way which are to lead us into East Anglia, I will name Ravensburgh Castle, a strong semicircular fort near the Icknield Way west of Hitchin, Willbury on the same side of Letchworth and Arbury Banks near Ashwell. Ashwell has for me as a Cambridge child, a quite Proustian imaginative construction. Hearing of it always as 'the source of the river Cam', the name still creates for me a picture of a clear spring gushing from the chalk and falling into a white basin; round it the trunks of a grove of ash-trees support a pale green canopy. By the roadside at Stevenage are the Six Hills, a line of neat round barrows which have lent their name to a famous nursery garden. As their position and steep-sided form might suggest to the wary, these barrows are not prehistoric in age, but mark Roman burials.

At Royston the Icknield Way takes us to a concentration of antiquities exceptional for this region. On Therfield Heath there is an earthen long barrow, very rare in this part of the world and undoubtedly the work of some community which had followed the line of the chalk from Wessex; the same history several centuries later may account for the group of round barrows, again known as the Five Knolls, on the north-west part of the same Heath. At Royston itself, where the Roman road of Ermine Street (now the Old North Road) joined the more ancient Icknield Way, there is a monument of a very unusual kind which is exceptional, too, in lying beneath one of the main shopping streets of this small town. It is a chamber with beehive roof hewn from solid chalk; it may itself be of far greater age, and indeed seems comparable to the Kentish Dene Holes of the Roman period, but it was evidently made use of in the Middle Ages, for the chalk walls have been carved with low reliefs of Christian subjects —the figures of Saints, the Holy Family and the Conversion of St. Paul. Whether or not this curious little cell, which still holds something remote from the clatter of traffic up above, is older than the twelfth or thirteenth centuries when the sculptures seem to have been made, it has a peculiar interest for all archaeologists. When it was discovered in 1742 the local Member of Parliament, an M.P. less able to conceal his illiteracy than is now normally the case, wrote at once to the eminent antiquary, William Stukeley, to tell him of the find. He wrote that workmen removing a stone 'found it was Hollor' and 'then emadgind that som very Grate Trashur was hid in that Place . . . som think it was a place of Worship in the Earliest times of Chrestyanaty . . . but all think it a Grate Curiosity'. Stukeley, who adored Grate Curiosities, rushed off there and afterwards wrote a pamphlet which involved him in a long dispute about a supposed Lady Roisia de Vere, Foundress of Royston whose oratory he wished the chamber to be. It is interesting to notice that the Member of Parliament reported that nothing was found in the 'Cavaty' except a 'Scull and som Hewman Bones'. Whose could these have been—those of the last hermit to occupy the cell? The Royston Cave shows how monuments of the past depend for their interest not only on their original builders but on all the individuals who much later become involved with them, and the events in which they have a place. It would be by the severance of all such accumulated bonds with its own past that society might, I believe, lose its humanity.

The Roman town at Great Chesterford has of late been excavated, but there is not a great deal to be seen there unless actual digging is in progress; a far more impressive monument of the age are the huge barrows to be seen at Bartlow which must once have stood beside the Roman road from Cambridge to Colchester. They are far bulkier than the Six Hills at Stevenage and may claim to be the largest Roman burial-mounds in the country; it is sad that the fine bronzes and other grave-goods which were taken from them were all lost in a fire.

I am now entering the countryside where I myself grew up and every part of it is alive with sharp, indestructible memories of childhood. There are certainly many of them in wait along the stretch of Roman road, the same Cambridge–Colchester road, which runs as a green track along the ridge of the Gogmagog Hills. For me it is always associated with the smell of hawthorn, falling cascades of wild roses and the nest of a green plover; 'The Roman Road' is a regular Sunday excursion for the more energetic walkers of the university, or used to be in the more leisured days I am recalling. Often I have sat hidden among the branches of a tree and spied at passing dons who were either, if solitary, staring at the ground, or, if in pairs, arguing endlessly, in either condition living in their own skulls and not for a moment seeing the Roman road they had so laboriously sought out. I looked down on them tolerantly over the walls of the world of child-hood—on these alien inoffensive barbarians.

Wandlebury in the parish of Stapleford on the south side of this road is worth seeing in a region where Iron Age camps are relatively few; it has portions of a double rampart and ditch surviving the encroachments of agriculture. The Gogmagogs (or the 'Gogs' as we always called them) can also show a scatter of round barrows, many of them ploughed down and not worth inspection, but interesting as further reminders of the traffic that moved along the chalk thoroughfare throughout prehistoric times. That it continued and was of great importance in the Dark Ages is most forcefully brought home to the imagination by the two boldest monuments of this region. Like Offa's Dyke (p. 238) the two great stretches of bank and ditch known as Fleam Dyke and the Devil's Dyke are post-Roman and therefore beyond my proper range. Nevertheless I cannot altogether ignore the two most familiar field monuments in Cambridgeshire. Both were intended to bar the Icknield Way which passes through them, and both were therefore designed to span the whole of the open ridge of the chalk from fen on the north to forest on the south. They face south-west and are assumed to have been raised by the East Anglians against their neighbours the Middle Angles, perhaps as early as the sixth century. Fleam Dyke runs up from the fenland round Fulborn to the old forest region of Balsham; on how many summer days have I climbed up and down its steep bank enjoying the colour of the wild rock roses, little yellow disks, and the smell of the wild thyme and looking for the purple tents, delicious in their long silky fur, of *anemone pulsatilla*. (As a child of the Cam Valley, I was always conscious of this chalk territory as an alien land, with its own plants and birds, and with its own quite distinctive qualities of light and air.) The Devil's Dyke runs almost dead parallel with Fleam Dyke, climbing up from Reach to Wood Ditton; it is the more massive of the two and is to be seen on a magnificent scale near where it crosses the racecourse on Newmarket Heath.

With the sands of Newmarket Heath we are on the edge of a piece of country of strange individuality. The Brecklands of Norfolk and Suffolk stretch from the edge of the fens between Newmarket and a point north of Brandon down to Thetford and Bury St. Edmunds, two hundred and fifty square miles of barren heathland overlying chalk. Because it is so barren, with harsh grasses, meagre heather and large gashes of bare sand thickly encrusted with black lichens and flints, it has always seemed to me to have an ancient quality of its own, a quality heightened and confirmed by the Norfolk plover that haunt it with their moth-like wings and strident cries. The Breckland was indeed occupied by prehistoric man, but with one exception its antiquities are undistinguished; there are some round barrows and minor earthworks, often riddled with rabbit holes; lake dwellings have been found in West Mere and Mickle Mere at West Wretham while in very many areas the Brecks made a good hunting-ground for humanly worked flints, probably most of them dating from the New Stone and Bronze Ages.

The one exception to the general mediocrity of Breck remains is the famous flint-mining area of Grimes Graves. It may be said that 'folk memory' is badly at fault in identifying disused mine-shafts with the Devil's (Grim's) burial-places, but perhaps after all it is greatly to the credit of that memory to have attached any special significance to the confused terrain of mounds and hollows which is all there was to be seen on the heath at Weeting, near Brandon, before any excavation had been undertaken. Now over many years a number of shafts have been opened and shown to be very like those of Sussex (pp. 82–3) both in their plan and in the equipment of the miners. In some there is a simple shaft, others have side galleries radiating in pursuit of the most prolific layers of flint; the men worked with deer-horn picks, with shoulder-blade shovels and lit the dark galleries with chalk-cut lamps. The period during which the mining went on is also the same as in the south—that is to say, it was in full swing in the New Stone Age and probably continued well into the Bronze Age. Again, here as elsewhere, much of the mined flint was shaped on the spot into axes which must have been traded to agricultural communities throughout the country.

One Grimes Graves discovery is of infinitely greater interest than any made elsewhere, of far greater interest because it is a discovery which gives a quick contact with the emotional life and thought of a remote prehistoric people. The excavators opened a shaft which by some geological chance had not struck the main flint-seam and had therefore been abandoned while still quite shallow. This pit had been chosen for dedication as a shrine. On a projecting shelf was the figure of a goddess carved in chalk, rough, and with the ample thighs and breasts, the corpulence, to be expected of a fertility figure. Below her was an unusually perfect phallus, also carved in chalk, and round both goddess and phallus, a great branchy stack of deer-horn picks—the pick that must have been the badge, as it were, of the miners' trade and itself perhaps of secondary phallic significance. Whether this particular shaft had been chosen for the shrine because it was industrially useless, or because the very lack of flint made them fear for the fertility of other shafts, we cannot guess, but there seems no doubt that the Earth Goddess was being propitiated. This pit has now been roofed and visitors can look down into the shrine with a cast of the cult objects in their original positions. In so doing they will be looking, however darkly, deep into the experience of prehistoric forbears.

As well as the shrine, one of the finest of the other shafts with its galleries has been roofed and made accessible. Thus the traveller who has reached this remote Norfolk heath is rewarded by being able to experience perhaps more accurately than anywhere else the exact physical environment known by people living four thousand years ago. Shrine and flint-mine together certainly make this a place to be visited by all those who hope to establish imaginative contact with the past.

It is well known that the significance of the ancient flint-working at Grimes Graves is magnified by the persistence of the craft at the neighbouring country town of Brandon. I remember as a child being told that the people of Brandon were quite unlike other East Anglians in that they wore very gaudy clothes and had various other characteristics that were supposed to prove them to be the descendants of a special race of prehistoric miners. Probably this is nonsense, but undoubtedly flint-digging and knapping have been carried on in the town from time immemorial and there is a real possibility of continuity with the prehistoric industry. The modern flint-knappers devote themselves to gun flints for which there is a steady demand in Abyssinia, and also in the United States where, I believe, there are clubs that shoot with flint-locks in honour of Wild West days. The craft is now known to cause silicosis and one wonders whether this was an occupational disease among the ancient knappers—shortening still further prehistoric man's meagre expectation of life.

We have now followed the chalk from the Thames Valley into the wilds of Norfolk seeing the various marks left by the prehistoric peoples who used it so freely before us. From this point it bends towards the north coasts where it appears in the Hunstanton cliffs—those marvellous red-and-white-layered cliffs so much like nursery cake. There is little which is important or spectacular to be seen on this low northern extension although a few sites are worthy of mention. At the small Norfolk village of Cockley Cley, to the north-west of Grimes Graves, there is an Icenian village which, thanks to the enterprise of the owner of the site, has now been preserved and partially reconstructed. Still further to the north, at Fring, just five and a half miles south-east of the coastal resort of Hunstanton, is a particularly fine stretch of the Roman road known as Peddar's Way which continues on its notably straight course to Holme-next-the-Sea. To a slightly earlier period belong the Late Iron Age forts at Holkham and Warham; although modest in size they possess something of a rarity value in this particular region. It is possible that both were built by the Iceni against the agressive Belgae in about 1 A.D. The Holkham fort crowns a conspicuous knoll in the level stretches of Holkham Marsh. It can be approached by a track leading north from Holkham church, but it would be wise to obtain the owner's permission before setting out. The Warham fort is not far distant, only a mile south of Wells; its double rampart and ditch are still clearly visible and give a fine view over the flat surrounding countryside. One last site along this stretch of coastline, giving a glimpse of the yet more distant past, is Salthouse, between Cley-next-the-Sea and Weybourne, where a large group of Bronze Age round barrows still cover part of Salthouse Heath. I want now to leave the chalk in order to pick out the few important antiquities to be seen in the country to the south and east of it. They are limited to the end of my range—to the Belgic Iron Age and Roman times—for earlier than that the rich soil of Suffolk and Essex was heavily forested.

If we retreat far enough to advance again from London, I must mention the two Iron Age forts in Epping Forest—Ambresbury and Loughton—though neither is of much merit. Better worth seeing is the fort of Wallbury near Bishop's Stortford whose multiple ramparts are of a kind most uncommon in eastern England. These, however, are small fry: the one really important centre of antiquity is at Colchester. This town stands, as it were, at the junction of British history with prehistory. Cunobelin, or Cymbeline, who united south-east Britain into a single powerful kingdom during the early years of our era, established his capital here in about 10 A.D. He chose a slope above the Colne just to the south-west of the present town at a place where now there is little for the visitor to see beyond a huge notice by which the Corporation have obligingly announced that this is the site of *Camulodunum*, capital of King Cymbeline. The outer dykes defending the settlement—comparable to those we have seen at Chichester and St. Albans (p. 244)—are still visible within the area of Lexden Park. These long lines of bank and ditch are typical of Belgic military ideas in contrast with the enclosed hill-fort of their immediate predecessors. The faint remains of the scattered city of *Camulodunum* are now under fields, houses and roads on the outskirts of Colchester. Excavation showed that Cunobelin, and after him, no doubt, his ill-fated sons ruled there until the time of the Roman conquest. After the defeat of Caractacus, Claudius's armies levelled the place to the ground and there presently established brick and tile kilns and other builders' workshops all busily employed for the new Roman town which was being built nearby, on the site of modern Colchester. This was a *colonia* intended for the settlement of retired soldiers and it seems to have been made the first capital of the province—doubtless with the idea of gaining the tribal loyalty which had belonged to *Camulodunum*. That, one may suppose, was why the Romans chose it for the site of a magnificent classical temple dedicated to the Divine Claudius—the deified Emperor. It was, in fact, the centre of the official Imperial cult. The vaults which supported the platform of this temple are preserved quite unaltered under the Norman castle which now houses the museum. All the rest of the early *colonia* has disappeared, having indeed been the first place to be burnt by Queen Boudicca—whose famous revolt represents, so far as lowland England is concerned, the last uprush of the barbaric energies of prehistoric Britain. We know even the grim detail that the last survivors of the *colonia* were burnt or massacred in this very Temple of Claudius. Of the new town which began to go up after the rebellion had been crushed there are far more striking remains to be seen. There are several stretches of the walls, built probably in the early second century, with a small gate on the north side and the massive remains of the Balkerne Gate on the west. Finally the castle itself contains a good prehistoric collection from Essex as well as a quite outstanding display of Roman material of all kinds. If the visible remains are none of them very spectacular, as the capital of the last free British prince and the first capital of the Roman province, Colchester has powerful claims as a place of pilgrimage.

The remaining places which I wish to name in Essex and Suffolk date from the Roman period. The defences of the Saxon Shore so splendidly preserved in coastal forts in Kent and Sussex (p. 71 ff.) extended up the east coast as far as Brancaster in Norfolk, but there is little to be seen either here or at the more southerly example—Bradwell-on-Sea, west of

Colchester. The one really fine Fort of the Saxon Shore on this coast is Burgh Castle just outside Great Yarmouth. On three sides the walls are almost complete except where the great weight of the external bastions has caused them to topple outwards. One of these fallen drums of masonry still shows on its summit the pit where a catapult was mounted. The north side is now formed by cliffs, with wide stretches of marsh and reed-bed below it. It is almost sure that sixteen hundred years ago when the fort was in use a fourth wall ran along the cliff top, while below it the sea approached so closely that there was space only for a wharf—a wharf where ships of the British fleet, the *Classis Britannica*, would sometimes have moored and sometimes perhaps have brought in captured Saxon pirates.

To the north of Burgh Castle, at Caister-by-Yarmouth, are the remains of a Roman town and port established at the beginning of the second century A.D. The place owed its importance in Roman times to the fact that it provided the shortest sea crossing to the mouth of the Rhine, and it was from the Rhineland that Britain imported an increasing amount of pottery and glassware during the Roman period. The first Roman defences at Caister consisted of a clay rampart and timber palisade, but this was soon superseded by a flint wall ten feet thick. The most substantial building to have been excavated is an inn just within the south gate of the town and surely a popular haunt with the sailors who put into the port. The foundations of this inn, a few fragments of other buildings, a roadway, and the defences, together with traces of the huts of Anglo-Saxon settlers, have been preserved.

To the south of Norwich is Arminghall where a Late Neolithic–Early Bronze Age sanctuary was discovered by air photography and then dramatically revealed by excavation. It had a bank and ditch with a single entrance leading to a horseshoe setting of enormous timber uprights. So little of it can be seen on the ground, no more than traces of the bank remaining, that I am mentioning it only because the place is marked on some Ordnance Survey Maps. Nearby was *Venta Icenorum*, the Roman capital of the former tribal area of the Iceni—the kingdom of Boudicca. The stone and earth walls can be traced, and are at their finest on the east side by the road; no building can be seen in the ploughed field within the walls, but when crops are ripening their plan stands out almost as clearly as on an architect's drawing-board, and, like the neighbouring sanctuary, can be photographed from the air.

At the Norwich Castle Museum which houses a very fine prehistoric collection, the most immediately impressive relics of the East Anglian Iron

Age are a treasure hoard from Ken Hill, Snettisham, hidden by a metal-smith some two thousand years ago. The magnificent gold torcs, or neck-lets, probably belonged to some member of the ruling dynasty of the Iceni. The wealth of this tribe is evident from the number of rich finds that have been made in the area. Was it their riches which eventually brought about the downfall of the Iceni? When their last king, Prasutagus, died during the reign of Nero leaving only half of his estate to the Emperor, and the other half to his own family, the Roman financial officials moved in swiftly to take over the entire wealth of the Icenian royal family and nobility. These exactions roused the implacable wrath of Prasutagus's formidable widow, Boudicca.

To end on a gentler note I will mention the line of barrows at Sutton Hoo, near Woodbridge in Suffolk. One of these humble mounds on being opened proved to cover a ship-burial of some seventh-century king of the East Anglian Royal House. This superb treasure of gold, silver and other rare and precious things is now to be seen in the British Museum. We are solemn about archaeology as a science, but the discovery at Sutton Hoo was the most glorious demonstration there has ever been in Britain of archaeology as pure romance.

B. *The East Midlands and Lincolnshire*

If any reader ever pursued all the chapters of this book, he would notice, or at least might notice, that he had been led round the centre of England and never into it, that a map of its places and routes would leave the Mid-lands unpenetrated. Looked at against the background of prehistory this means, of course, that he has been led round the forests, the forests that were indeed almost impenetrable by early man and fell at last only before the Anglo-Saxons.

That central plain, that territory bounded by the Severn, the Trent and the Avon, which has the young city of Birmingham as its heart, is indeed quite without any prehistoric monuments which any ordinary traveller, anyone, that is to say, who is not an archaeologist, would want to go a step out of his way to see. We now know that there are in fact prehistoric sites along the Avon and other rivers but nothing remains of them above ground. There is an Iron Age fort at Wychbury near Birmingham, but it is a place I should only name in such a desert.

One Roman site, however, of recent discovery and excavation deserves both a mention and a visit. This is the Lunt Roman fort at Baginton near Coventry. It is an early one, belonging to the first century A.D., and was abandoned before any stone defences or internal buildings were erected. A stretch of the turf and timber defences, including one of the wooden gateways with its guard towers has been reconstructed, partly in order to test how such structures stand up to the effects of weathering. At the same time they make an unusual and impressive sight, giving form and substance to the normally shadowy traces of such early semi-permanent forts.

To the east of the Trent there is a little more to be seen, though it is Roman and Iron Age with nothing from earlier times. First there is Leicester, the Roman *Ratae Coritanorum*, where not far from the station visitors can see the so-called Jewry Wall, the only massive piece of Roman masonry standing above ground, and part of the palaestra, or exercize hall belonging to the public baths of *Ratae*. Here the would-be bathers could first work up a sweat before proceeding to the baths themselves, the foundations of which can be seen in front of the Jewry Wall beside Leicester's splendid new Archaeological Museum. The baths at Leicester are one of the few examples still visible in Britain of a type of public building once common to all Roman towns of any size.

One other interesting, if enigmatic, archaeological site known as the Raw Dykes is visible just to the south of Leicester on the Rugby road, sandwiched between the power station and the gas works. This large dyke or ditch has been the subject of much speculation concerning its date and function. One of the most plausible explanations yet advanced is that it represents part of the aqueduct that was built to supply the Roman town at Leicester (and its public baths) with water from the Knighton Brook, only a mile and a half away.

Far more striking though little known are the remains of the Roman town of *Durobrivae* at Water Newton, close beside the Nene a few miles to the west of Peterborough. The motorist driving along the Great North Road should be sharply reminded that he is driving on the foundations of the Roman Ermine Street when he sees the massive earth bank that once formed part of the town wall of *Durobrivae* rising conspicuously beside the road. What has been excavated, and is indeed far better known, is the potteries which formed a kind of industrial suburb of *Durobrivae*, lying partly on the northern bank of the Nene at Castor (just across the river from Water Newton). It was the most highly organized pottery centre in Britain and supplied the province with much of its most popular wares. The products of its kilns, broken in fragments by kitchen-maids or even more violent agents of history, have been laboriously excavated at hundreds of sites up and down the country. Though there is practically nothing to be seen at Castor to-day, I cannot resist giving this description of its former life.

'Well-to-do manufacturers lived in houses resembling the villas of prosperous farmers, surrounded by the smaller but still romanized houses of their work-people and by kilns of an unusually elaborate and efficient type. Here the industry was evidently worked on a capitalist basis with highly organized methods of production and distribution . . . there are indications of the way in which it was shipped in barge-loads by river from the pottery wharves.'

For a moment one seems able to see it all there by the Great North Road, the compact town in the foreground, the river traffic where no doubt the boatmen talked and swore in their Celtic tongue with some dog Latin for educated masters; the crates of the rather fragile and finicking Castor ware stacked on the wharves or being embarked; smoking kilns, huddled cottages and the pleasant gardens and verandas of the manufacturers' houses.

We can follow Ermine Street (which leaves the line of the Great North Road after Costerworth) as it drives straight up the limestone belt of Lincoln Edge (p. 39) towards Lincoln itself. At Ancaster we drop down to a natural break in the limestone of Lincoln Edge, a gap through which the Witham flowed for centuries before it changed to its present course. Both Celts, and after them Romans, thought it worth while to command this gap. The Iron Age fort of Honington on the Edge to the south-west of Ancaster is roughly rectangular in plan; small, but strongly defended with three lines of ramparts. Forts with multiple defences of this kind are rare in eastern England, and Honington seems to invite excavation—'weapons and bridles', almost certainly Celtic, were found there in the seventeenth century but now, naturally but unhappily, are lost. The Roman site under-lies the present village of Ancaster; it has been described as 'a small but substantial rural township or village, serving as a posting-station on the main Roman route to Lincoln and the North'. The defences can best be seen surrounding the open ground opposite the church known as Castle Close, while a single bastion, much overgrown, survives to the north of Ancaster Hall. They seem to have consisted of an outer ditch, stone wall with bastions and an inner earthen bank; this construction, borne out by the evidence of the coins dug up by the villagers, suggests that the defences were put up late in the Roman period, probably in the fourth century.

Another seventeen miles along Ermine Street brings us to Lincoln, which as *Lindum* was a Roman town of dignity and importance. The site of a legionary fort, it was established as a *colonia* designed primarily for retired soldiers from the armies; at first the walls, bounded by an immense ditch, enclosed an area on the top of the hill including the site of the medieval castle and cathedral; later it was more than doubled, the walls being extended down as far as Guildhall Street within a hundred yards of the river Witham. There are some fragments of the wall and outer ditch still to be seen, most conspicuously in the Castle and also in modern Eastgate, where the northern tower of one of the Roman gateways has been uncovered in the car park of the Eastgate Hotel. But the great glory of Roman Lincoln is the Newport Arch, through which traffic up the Bailgate still passes. Nowhere else in Britain, I believe, can motor-cars be seen driving through an archway, the stones of which are still as the Roman masons laid them. In addition to the central arch with its sixteen-foot carriageway, there is a low side gate for a seven-foot pavement; the corresponding footway which must have existed on the other side of the road is now marked only by the first stone or so of its arch. The Newport Arch was formerly the inner side of the great North Gate of *Lindum*, a gateway which projected beyond the walls on its outer side—where presumably the main architectural embellishments would have been.

From this gate the Ermine Street drove northward towards York following the limestone of Lincoln Edge with the kind of ruled straight line which we like always to attribute to Roman roads. I do not, however, propose to pursue it, for often though we are told that this was a much used prehistoric thoroughfare, the counterpart to the Icknield Way to the east, the truth is that there is nothing to be seen on its course. Instead I must shift eastward, where the Lincoln Wolds form the continuation of the chalk belt which we left where its broken edge forms the cliffs of Hunstanton (p. 250). These pleasant chalk uplands of Lincolnshire were populous in prehistoric times from the New Stone Age onwards, but because they are relatively low and fertile they have been more intensively cultivated than some of the Sussex and Wessex downland, the ancient marks have been obliterated. Many, indeed, have gone since the nineteenth century.

Among the monuments which have been destroyed or flattened by ploughing are earthen long barrows which seem unquestionably to have been raised by New Stone Age farming communities who had slowly made their way here from their earlier settlements on the southern chalk. Almost all are now wretched places to visit, but their historical interest is so great that I should like to name the least wretched—in the south the pair known (correctly enough) as the Dead Men's Graves which lie between Skendleby station and Claxby, and a little further north, the largest surviving on the Wolds, a long barrow between the villages of Swaby and Walmsgate by the Louth road. Another few miles along this road it is worth noticing a group of seven round barrows on Balby Hill near Haugham; they are good specimens of their kind, representing a few survivors out of the many which have been ploughed out of sight.

It remains only to mention two Roman sites on the Wolds. One is the small walled town which is now engulfed by its modern successor—the country market town of Horncastle in the valley of the Bain in the south-west corner of the Wolds. The little Roman settlement was in the north-west sector of Horncastle, with the present market-place near its centre; among surviving fragments of wall, the best is just off Lawrence Street where the bastion and walls of the northern corner are easily visible. They were probably built in about 300 A.D. The citizens of Horncastle, however, have been made more conscious of their 'Roman Heritage' by the discovery from time to time of funerary urns and lead coffins under the southern part of their town.

The second Roman station is away towards the northern extremity of the Wolds at Caistor. Here the remains are even poorer, a stretch of the south wall and one bastion just west of Fountain Street and a fragment of the west wall adjoining the grounds of the grammar school. These walls, too, probably date from the turn of the third and fourth centuries. It is right to regard both Horncastle and Caistor as civilian 'towns', but in that troubled time they must also have served as minor military centres playing their part in the defence of the east coast against Anglo-Saxon pirates.

Chapter Nine

THE NORTH OF ENGLAND

A. North Staffordshire, East Cheshire and Derbyshire
B. The Yorkshire Wolds
C. The North York Moors and the Vale of York
D. The Yorkshire Pennines
E. The Four Northern Counties

A. *North Staffordshire, East Cheshire and Derbyshire*

JUST as London shows a contrasting patchwork of fashionable quarters and slums, shopping or industrial areas and spacious parks, with abrupt transitions from one to another, the north of England has black industrial conurbations ending abruptly on the edge of wild moorland; spas and great country houses within a short journey of squalor. Not even in Yorkshire is this medley more striking than it is here in north Staffordshire, east Cheshire and Derbyshire, where some of the most splendid houses, loveliest dales, wildest moors in Britain are held between Stoke-on-Trent and Derby, Manchester and Sheffield. So, too, the marks left by the sparse communities of hunters, pastoralists, primitive farmers, survive in the neighbourhood of the hundreds of square miles of brick and concrete, the swarming millions of modern industrial populations.

We can start in country which is no great distance from the region already surveyed on the Welsh Marches, but which, because it forms continuous upland with the Pennines, belongs essentially to the sterner world of the north. In the southern part of this upland area, the Carboniferous Limestone is cut by the beautiful dales of Manifold and Dove, and between Dove Dale and the valleys of the Wye and Derwent the countryside is scattered with the disused shafts and open scars of lead-mining, an industry which has been carried on there since Roman times. It is a region richest in Bronze Age remains (it may indeed have been made attractive by its copper deposits) but the first, most westerly, site I want to name is of a very different kind. This is Thor's Cave at Wetton above the Manifold, a naturally romantic place which is given an historical interest through having been inhabited during the Iron Age. One is inclined to think of cave-dwellings as belonging essentially to the Stone Age hunters, but in fact, as we have seen at Wookey Hole (p. 153), Iron Age Celts and even their immediate descendants, the Roman Britons, were always glad to become troglodytes where good limestone caves were available.

There are already some fine round barrows between Manifold and Dove, but they are more abundant east of the Dove in Derbyshire, where we are at last again in country which allows the lover of antiquity to walk from site to site through the course of a day. Some of these round cairns have central cists made of stone slabs, as for example the two on the long smooth limestone hill of Minning Low west of Ardwark, where they lie below its conspicuous crest of wind-blown trees. The larger of these Minning Low cairns is exceptional in containing stone cists. Minning Low is made more worth a visit by the stretch of Roman road which runs up to it from the north-west, the road, in fact, from Buxton which as *Aquae* was already known as a spa in Roman times. Other round cairns of outstanding interest are on the west side of the Buxton–Matlock road on the Liffs and Endlow, but it is perhaps misleading to select one or two where almost every summit has its *tumulus*.

From End Low the traveller need only cross the modern Buxton road to regain the line of the *Aquae* Roman road and follow it to Gib Hill, an unusually large round barrow, which is already within sight of the most famous of all prehistoric monuments in this part of the world—Arbor Low. This is one of the 'hĕnge' sanctuaries in which a circle of stones is enclosed within a bank with a ditch intervening, and with one, two or four entrances (p. 107 ff.). Arbor Low is, indeed perhaps the best example in the country of the variety of sanctuary which has two openings through the embankment; with so fine a monument it would seem justifiable to excavate while at the same time restoring to their original sockets the stones which at present, unhappily, all lie prone on the ground. If we take the Long Rake Lane westward we pass many barrows, built here so that the dead might lie near Arbor Low, and can then cross the river Bradford at Youlgreave and strike up on to the well-wooded Harthill Moor. Here there is a small earthwork, Castle Ring, a stone circle (much damaged and with no enclosing bank), and the Hermit's Cave, a perfectly natural feature which, however, adds to the romantic charm of Harthill. The traveller should now push on eagerly into the lovely country above the Derwent where within two miles he will find on Stanton Moor another varied group of antiquities including a stone circle with an outlying menhir known as the King's Stone. It is a little entertaining to find that this circle is known not, as is so usual, as Nine Maidens, nor yet anything so rough as Long Meg or the Bridestones, but Nine Ladies, a refinement which, so far as I know, is unique. The Cork Stone on the south side of the Moor is a natural boulder which has been rigged for climbing, but it serves as a useful pointer to an interesting antiquity lying about four hundred yards to the east. This is a round barrow which after excavation has been enclosed in a railing and left open so that the curious can see its internal construction—concentric stone rings built round the central cist.

We have now reached the nearest point on the uplands to an archaeological site of great scientific importance away on the east side of Derbyshire between Chesterfield and Worksop—the limestone gorge of Creswell Crags whose cliffs are pierced with caves occupied by Old Stone Age hunters. Creswell Crags may indeed be recognized as the Cheddar of the North. What is so remarkable about these cave-dwellings is that their occupation covered (not of course continuously) an immense range of time. Between them the Pinhole and Mother Grundy's Parlour span the time from the middle phase of the Old Stone Age when Neanderthal Man was the dominant species through the days of high hunting late in the Old Stone Age, to the early part of the Middle Stone Age. During this last phase the surviving hunting communities developed their own local ways of making flint implements which have now been honoured with the archaeological name of the Creswellian Culture. This is a span which could cover fifty thousand years and which saw many fluctuations in the climate; when hunters first took up residence in the Pinhole the ice had not yet made its last advance across Europe, before the last family left Mother Grundy's Parlour it had finally retreated and forests were beginning to spread in its wake. During the height of the arctic climate the ravine was probably untenanted, choked with glacier ice.

Although the lovely heather moors of the Peak District are scattered with the remains of prehistoric man and make magnificent walking country, there is nowhere again the concentration which encourages the guide to recommend an itinerary like that from Minning Low by Arbor Low to Stanton. Instead, I will pick out a few places which are outstanding and leave the traveller to reach them how he will.

First there is the well-known round barrow, Hob Hurst's House, worth seeking out for its position alone: it stands overlooking the woods, lakes and parkland of Chatsworth House where the broad belt of Bunker's Hill wood runs up to Harland Edge. Due west from here on high bare country between Taddington and Chelmorton is the Five Wells Farm *tumulus*, another round cairn whose now roofless central cist, divided into two compartments, comes nearer to the traditions of megalithic architecture (p. 48) than is usual in these Bronze Age graves. The view from here northward across the vales of the Wye to Kinder Scout has been described with less originality than truth as 'one of the loveliest in England'.

The two remaining sites take us from the Bronze Age with its predominantly religious inspiration, and bring us back into the martial world of more recent times. The first of them is certainly the most spectacular prehistoric monument within walking distance of a great industrial town. Carl Wark is about three miles from the south-western outskirts of Sheffield on a moorland summit overlooking the Derwent Valley near Hathersage. Its position is magnificent, and so, too, are its defences. Walls standing six feet high are built of huge blocks of Millstone Grit, dark and stark as that rock, the material of many of our industrial towns, so often appears. Carl Wark had long been presumed to belong to the Iron Age. Recent investigation, however, has shown it to be post-Roman, perhaps a stronghold of the days of the Anglian settlement.

The fort on Mam Tor due west of Carl Wark, is itself far less spectacular, but the natural position is even more impressive. The ramparts defend the hill at the extremity of the high narrow spine of Rushup Edge which forms the southern wall of the Vale of Edale; on the north the hills mount straight to Edale Moor and Kinder Scout, the two-thousand-foot plateau which makes the climax of the Peak.

Here on this precipitous ridge, looking over a fertile vale to naked moors, we are standing midway between Manchester and Sheffield, and the Yorkshire border runs a mile or so beyond the summits of the Peak.

B. *The Yorkshire Wolds*

If politically Yorkshire is divided into three ridings, so also archaeologically it falls into three parts—but the two systems do not correspond. The three distinct regions which are well or even abundantly supplied with the remains of early man correspond, as we have come to expect, with upland areas: the chalk wolds in the south, the North York Moors made up of the eastern moorlands, the Hambledons, and the Cleveland Hills, and thirdly, the great, broken mass of the Pennines all the way from the river Tees to Sheffield. The Vale of Pickering which separates the Wolds from the northern moors, and the Vale of York whose wide expanse cuts off both from the Pennines, were both alike in prehistoric times in being exceptionally swampy, overgrown and generally difficult and unpleasant to cross. They therefore discouraged intercourse between the three upland areas, and were themselves virtually uninhabited before Roman times.

It is my intention as a guide to deal first with the Wolds (together with the long nose of Holderness), then with the northern moors where the antiquities are thickest, and finally work up the Pennines from the Derbyshire boundary.

The prehistory of Holderness is interesting, but has left no visible remains on the ground. For example one can see nothing, unless one is uncommonly lucky in finding tiny flints, of the Middle Stone Age sites of this low-lying, peaty area, nor are there any marks of the remarkable successive New Stone Age, Bronze and Iron Age lake-dwellings at West Furze, Ulrome.

As for the Wolds, the attractive chalk upland was ideally suited to early man, and he did not fail to take advantage of its openness and good pastures. There are a dozen long barrows, suggesting substantial New Stone Age communities; round barrows and other finds prove a quite exceptionally thorough settlement by the invaders of the Early Bronze Age (p. 49) which continued through the rest of the period; some of the most important of the Celtic invaders of the Iron Age first established themselves on the Yorkshire Wolds, and left their mark upon them in the chariot-burials and humbler cemeteries. Nevertheless, because the Wolds are very largely under cultivation, many remains have been destroyed, others made unimpressive—perhaps no more than swellings slightly distorting the regularity of the plough-furrows. This agricultural destruction has taken place mainly during the last two centuries, for until the Enclosures the monuments were being preserved for us, held safely below the turf and furze that pastured huge flocks of sheep.

Very many of the long and round barrows on the chalk were excavated by those doughty Victorian antiquaries, Mortimer of Driffield and Canon Greenwell of Durham. The Canon's spoil is in the British Museum, but Mortimer's collection went to the museum in Hull which bears his name.

The Wolds curve round Holderness in a wide crescent that ends in Flamborough Head and if we mount on to the southern end where it rises gently above the Humber, we shall find the site of a famous Celtic Iron Age barrow group, now largely destroyed, which lay at Arras west of Market Weighton. This was an exceptionally rich cemetery; one privileged old man had been buried with his chariot, a pair of horses (or rather ponies) and the heads of two pigs. Here at Arras a woman had been given a chariot-burial; as well as her whip and horse-harness, a mirror had been laid with her in the grave. Here was a woman indeed!

Passing Huggate Pasture where there are remarkable entrenchments— five lines of bank and six of ditch, with a total width of two hundred feet, we come to the famous round barrow of Howe Hill near Duggleby, at the foot of the southern slopes of the opening through the chalk known as the Great Wold Valley. This is a huge mound still standing twenty-two feet high and with a diameter of one hundred and twenty-five feet, which was found to have been raised over a circular pit sunk over eight feet deep into the chalk, and over a second, shallower, grave. In the deep hole there were four crouched skeletons with a polished axe, leaf-shaped arrowhead and a round-bottomed pot, in the shallower two bodies had been buried, one that of a very tall old man who is said to have lain with his head over the edge of the pit 'as though contemplating the occupants'; in the body of the mound, but apparently buried at the same time, were other skeletons, including two of young children, and from forty to fifty cremation-burials. If the excavators were right in believing all these interments had been made at one time, then we are certainly here in the presence of a ritual holocaust celebrated by our forbears with all extravagance of life which has horrified some observers of the Royal Graves at Ur or among the nomads of the Kuban. The grave-furniture at Duggleby is of a kind that one would expect to belong to a New Stone Age community, yet this type of round barrow normally belongs to the Bronze Age; among the skeletons some had long heads, some short. It has been suggested that this extra-ordinary monument represents an admixture of Early Bronze Age invaders with native Stone Age inhabitants of the Wolds. About a dozen miles eastward along the Great Wold Valley, Willy Howe is another colossal round barrow.

It is not very far south from here to a most remarkable site near Mortimer's own home at Driffield. This is the great Iron Age barrow cemetery known as the Danes' Graves, which stretches over a wooded slope about four miles north of the town; formerly there were at least five hundred mounds, from ten to thirty feet across and seldom of much height; even now two hundred survive, closely packed together. Most of these barrows covered quite humble burials—crouched skeletons with odds and ends of poor ornaments—bronze brooches and armlets, a few beads and pins— and a pottery vessel sometimes containing a leg of pork. One large grave held the skeletons of two men who had been interred with their battle chariot, whose metal parts—iron tyres, hub-bands, lynch-pins—survived. There were horse-bits, but no remains of horses, doubtless because the tribe could not afford their sacrifice.

We are now approaching the end of the chalk, the tip of its longest finger which thrusts here so far to the north; it is crowded with ancient monuments. Perhaps the most dramatic is at Rudston, west of Bridlington, where a colossal monolith stands among the cast-iron palings, the flimsy crosses and other headstones in the village churchyard. It is a column of gritstone, rectangular in section and tapering towards the top; at twenty-five feet six inches it is taller than any of the uprights at Stonehenge, taller than the Devil's Arrows at Boroughbridge and indeed is believed to be the tallest standing stone in England. Grit of this kind does not outcrop nearer than Cayton Bay, ten miles to the north, and the labour of dragging a block of this size up on to the Wolds must have been prodigious.

One of the finest of a number of mysterious earthworks of unknown date which are common on the Wolds, is the triple Argam Dyke which runs northward from Rudston to Reighton. More striking still is the Danes' Dyke, probably constructed during the Iron Age between 300 B.C. and the first century A.D., which runs across Flamborough Head about two miles from the tip; it is two and a half miles long and cuts off about five square miles of that enchanting headland where the cliffs are so full of columns, arches, vaulted caves of chalk, that they seem like the ruins of some strange marine cathedral. The bank of the Danes' Dyke is in some places as much as eighteen feet high and an immensely wide ditch fronts it on the landward side.

Just to the east of these dykes, at Staple Howe, a mile south-east of Knapton is a welcome occupation site amongst so many monuments erected for the dead. Here, on the hill known as Staple Howe in Knapton plantation, has been excavated an Iron Age farmstead dating back to 500 B.C. The 'farmhouse' was a large stone-built oval hut surrounded by a palisade enclosing the hilltop. At a later date this main hut was replaced by two smaller timber-built huts and a building, perhaps a granary, that was set on a wooden platform. Inside the huts were found hearths and ovens and in one the remains of an upright loom. A path has been constructed to the site and the positions of the buildings within the enclosure marked out so that the visitor can appreciate the layout of this early farmstead.

On Flotmanby Wold between Hunmanby and Folkton is one of the largest and most conspicuous long barrows in Yorkshire, and a place very pleasant to visit with its downland scenery and the outlook across the Vale of Pickering to the oddly assorted shapes of the northern moors. Folkton itself is a name famous in archaeology, for in one of the round barrows on Folkton Wold there were found three chalk-cut idols of the Early Bronze Age. These squat, cylindrical objects had been laid in the grave of a five-year-old child, the smallest touching its head, the two larger at the hips. There is nothing else in the world at all like them, although we can find parallels for some of their individual designs. In very shallow relief they show a curiously composed arrangement of zigzags, lozenges and other geometric designs, all unquestionably with magical significance; on the raised disk at the top of each idol are circular patterns which can be recognized as eye symbols, while each bears on its side a pair of eyes below heavy arched eyebrows. These unique idols are now in the British Museum where they will have lost their magical powers, but it is still satisfactory to reflect (though not perhaps very relevant) that they were found at the very northernmost limit of the substance of which they are carved—the chalk which is so dear and characteristic a part of our island.

C. *North York Moors and the Vale of York*

In crossing from the chalk wolds to the Jurassic sandstone plateau of the North York Moors, even the least geologically minded must be a little astonished to see the young Derwent river coming down from the moors behind Scarborough and turning sharply away from the sea which waits to receive it only three miles off, to flow, as it were, backwards along the Vale of Pickering, joining the Ouse a long way south of York, and finally reaching the sea by way of the Humber. This curious diversion took place as late as the Old Stone Age when the ice in the Vale of Pickering blocked the escape of the water south of Scarborough, piling up the great mass of boulder clay that shows in the rather messy cliffs of this piece of coast. The waters of the glacial lake which ponded up behind in the Vale broke through in the westerly direction between the Wolds and the Howardian Hills, making the valley which the Derwent still follows.

Scarborough no longer encourages one to think of glaciers or of Stone Age hunters, but is not without its early antiquities. The Castle Hill is a remarkable natural formation, an outlying block of limestone rising nearly three hundred feet sheer out of the sea. It seems first to have been occupied by invading Čelts in the very earliest phase of the British Iron Age; their hearths and rubbish pits and the pottery and bronzes which came from them are famous in archaeology—this can claim, indeed, the rank of a 'classic' site, but nothing remains to be seen on the ground. On the other

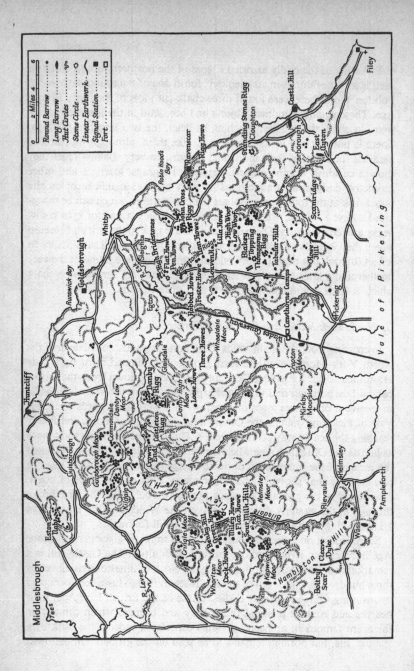

hand when some eight hundred years later, in the fourth century A.D., the barbarian raids on these coasts were becoming desperately menacing, the Romans built guard-towers, and one was placed, unknowingly, of course, right on top of the remains of the Early Iron Age settlement. These coast-guard stations consisted of an outer ditch, a square walled enclosure about a hundred feet across, with corner turrets, and at the centre square stone foundations that seem to have supported a lofty wooden signal tower. The ruins at Scarborough are worth seeing, but the finest example is on the northern edge of the moors in Goldsborough Pasture near Runswick Bay. These towers were placed at intervals of from six to ten miles: there were others at Filey Brigg, at Ravenscar, and Huntcliff in the north. At Golds-borough a discovery was made that recalls some violent moment of the bitter struggle for a shore now given over to holiday resorts. Three skulls, one of them a woman's, were found in a well, then:

'In the south-east corner of the tower there had been an open hearth over which the skeleton of a short, thick-set man lay face downwards. . . . Near his feet lay the skeleton of a taller man, also face downwards, and beneath him the skeleton of a large and powerful dog, the head against the man's throat, the paws across his shoulders. Near the feet were two silver coins of Eugenius (392–4) and Honorius (395–423).'

Baffling, anonymous but most poignant history held in matter—a few bones and pieces of money. Here, on a pin's head, one is privileged to see the fall of the Roman Empire.

From Scarborough the moors rise gently and gradually round the head-waters of the Derwent towards the rugged top of this sandstone plateau with its many small fertile valleys, West Riding Dales in miniature, which run down towards the Vale of Pickering to the south and the Esk to the north. I feel here, just as I felt in the isolated moorland masses of Exmoor and Dartmoor, that what as a guide I should wish to do is to recommend the thousand square miles of the North York Moors as a single monument to prehistoric man, one of those small areas where his handiwork is often still dominant over that of his descendants. There are still ten thousand round barrows and cairns up here among the heather and coarse moorland grass; Bronze and Iron Age hut clusters, dykes and defences of all kinds, standing stones and stone circles, long barrows. They are all there, part of the moorland scene, tales of a day when man fitted himself into a country-side, embellished it a little, but did not hack it into alien shapes.

Yet I feel as a guide I must pick out some of the best to see of all these remains of the past, hoping as I do so that they will be visited only as the pleasant savouring of a walk, places to serve as a nominal goal, halts for food, drink or a cigarette; relics to move the imagination of the living by sudden thoughts of all those who have been there before. Only by providing for such spacious days could so crabbed a catalogue be justified.

In the area of the ancient Royal Forest of Pickering round Troutdale there is an immensely complicated series of lines of dyke—single, double, triple, multiple—of which the best known are the Scamridge Dykes. They are far too intricate to describe in detail, and may very well have been built not in prehistoric times but by Anglian communities in the Dark Ages. Perhaps the most interesting antiquities hereabout are Roman, the Cawthorn camps—four embanked military camps which lie on the edge of the plateau (sometimes known as the Tabular Hills) four miles north of Pickering. Two seem to have been used as quarters for troops, who built the other two as training exercizes; all may have been connected with the laying of the paved road known, most misleadingly, as Wade's Causeway, which runs past the camps to strike north-easterly across the moors. On Wheeldale Moor a length of a mile and a half has been uncovered to show a road about sixteen feet across, with culverts and gutters and a raised kerb containing the central way with its pavement of flat slabs. It is a fine spectacle, and there is no need to be prevented from enjoying it by our ignorance of its route, destination or military purposes.

There have been at least eight long barrows along this southern side of the moors (they are rare further north), two are to be seen not very far from the Cawthorn camps at Crapton, while Howe Hill is the only survivor of three which formerly lay near the Scamridge Dykes. These are the principal monuments to be seen along the southern edge of the moors above the Vale of Pickering and I want now to return to the Scarborough neighbourhood in order to follow up the coast and then swing westwards again along the higher ground. On the coastal part of the moorland, where one walks with the North Sea always at one's elbow, there is a small circle on Standing Stones Rigg just west of Cloughton; although only thirty feet across it is well marked with twenty stones still in position. If the traveller pushes on in this direction, he will pass a number of round cairns, or barrows, large enough to have their individual names—Three Howes near Falcon Inn, Pye Rigg Howe and Stony Marl Howe both within a mile or so of the Roman coastguard station at Ravenscar—but on reaching John Cross Rigg he will find the first of the vast groups of tiny round cairns which are a feature of these moors. Here the necropolis numbers thirteen hundred and a strong dyke system runs through it. The stretch of country to the west from John Cross, that is to say Sleights and Goathland Moors, the Whinstone Ridge, down as far south as the freakish-looking natural hill of Blakey Topping, is so crowded with antiquities that it is possible to feel that one is looking at a prehistoric landscape from which only human life has drifted away. At the northern end, on Sleights Moor, the High and Low Bridestones offer an interesting contrast; the latter are natural formations, curious weathered blocks of sandstone, some of which look like huge toadstools, raised as they are on narrow stems. The High Bridestones, on the other hand, though hardly so fine to look at, are human handiwork, a stone circle of the Bronze Age; the individual monoliths are many of them very large, and although to-day more than half have fallen, this remains easily the best sanctuary of its kind in this part of the country.

South of the Bridestones, the spine of Whinstone Ridge and beyond is knobbed with a continuous line of round cairns—I will give their names for they have a certain charm. These Howes then are called Pen, Broken, Robbed, Foster (two of these), Ann, Louven, Lilla, High Woot and Low Woot. I should like to know what are the incidents, the eponymous heroes responsible for all these names, which now cling to them and have become part of the map, part of the verbal landscape which every countryside possesses. Following their line has brought us down to the neighbourhood of Blakey Topping which has three standing stones on its southern side, and beyond them another cairn necropolis on Thompson's Rigg.

The magnificent high moors which form the core of all this upland area, the deeply furrowed ridge running from Goathland Moors right across to the Cleveland Hills, is fine walking country and shows no decrease in antiquities. On the watershed where Glaisdale Moor adjoins Danby High Moor a conspicuous landmark is Loose Howe, a round cairn which proved to cover a Bronze Age burial of an unusual kind. The excavators struck suddenly on an oaken timber near the base of the mound, and from it gushed gallons of water. This had been contained in, and was helping to preserve, a boat-shaped coffin with neatly fitting lid, which had contained a body extended at full length, wearing clothes and shoes and with the head resting on a straw-stuffed pillow. Oak coffin-burials are known elsewhere; what was unique at Loose Howe was the presence beside the coffin (itself carefully carved to suggest a craft) of a dug-out canoe, perhaps a ritual vessel, perhaps one which had been made for practical use. The symbolism of the Boat of the Dead coming, perhaps, from Egypt, made itself felt in Europe during the Bronze Age, and it may be assumed that in some indirect way the concept found expression in this burial on a remote Yorkshire moor. But it also probably expressed something more direct, more personal. The Bronze Age people of Britain had their wide overseas trade and here in the north they were much concerned with a traffic across England in Irish gold. It is not at all impossible that the individual buried below Loose Howe was himself a seafarer with knowledge of Irish and Scandinavian ports. Such discoveries as this help to put some imaginative life into other of these moorland monuments, these heather- or grass-covered piles of stones, turf and soil, places which have fallen slowly out of memory since the funeral crowds dispersed and the ghosts themselves were forgotten.

There are many other cairns in the immediate neighbourhood: the three Western Howes and Cock Howe within two miles to the north-east, Flat Howe and Shunner Howe a little further in an easterly direction. From the high ground on which Loose Howe still rides conspicuously, though robbed now of its secret, two spurs, Danby High Moor, and Castleton Ridge, thrust down towards the Esk. The tip of the Danby spur, known as Danby Rigg, is occupied by a cairn cemetery with a single large standing stone not far from the centre; this stone is the survivor of a circle which was found to enclose an urn-burial dating from the middle of the Bronze Age. On the south the necropolis is bounded by a single wall running across the ridge; on the other side, there is an extraordinary stony area entirely free of cairns which is protected by two strong ramparts running parallel with the cemetery wall some seven hundred yards further south. This stony area, it is believed, is the site of the Bronze Age settlement to which the cemetery belonged—the stone circle perhaps being the chief sanctuary of the whole community.

On the neighbouring Castleton Rigg and the lower spur beyond known as Crown End are other settlements with walls, huts, enclosures and cairns. Anyone who enjoys an excuse to linger on the moors and who is not exasperated by the confusing pattern of these Bronze Age villages can take Danby Rigg and its neighbours as a model for puzzling out many other similar sites, less extensive or complete perhaps, that throng the moors, giving an impression of an unusually dense prehistoric population.

From Danby Rigg one can look across the Esk Valley to the northern part of the moorland where similar settlements flourished, their remains being found throughout Danby Low Moor, Commondale, and Guisborough Moors, with a great concentration of small cairns on the headland between Sleddale and Kildale. The most interesting excursion, however, is to the small out-lying Eston Moor which lies on the extreme north immediately above Middlesbrough, Stockton and all the black industrial spread of the Tees basin. This rises to its highest point at Eston Nab where sandstone crags overhang the Tees Valley; it is made conspicuous for many miles by a stone beacon tower built at the time of the Napoleonic wars. Against the crags of the Nab is a powerful semicircular rampart with a circumference just large enough to include the beacon; this fort, which in the south would be assumed to belong to the Iron Age, was built by a people who still had a Bronze Age way of life—what, however, this means in actual dates, it is hard to say.

Returning now to the south of the Esk, I want to complete this survey of the North York Moors by passing down the western side formed by the Cleveland and Hambledon Hills whose steep scarps rise like cliffs above the flat green country of the Vale of York. The Cleveland Hills have for me a special quality for the reason that during the second glaciation of the Great Ice Age when almost the whole of the north and central England was buried beneath ice, they alone emerged above it, dividing one vast glacier grinding down the Vale of York from the other, yet vaster, which covered eastern England. However warm and prinked with skylarks the moors, however green and peaceful the Vale, I see behind it the image of a hulk of crags showing intensely black within the harsh embrace of the glaciers.

On the Cleveland Hills the most prolific area for antiquities lies in the wedge of country running from the escarpment between Whorlton Moor and Hasty Bank and the junction of Reydale and Bisdale. Along the high and sometimes narrow central ridge of this territory is a line of large round cairns like that on Sleights and Goathland Moors (p. 268); starting in the north from Whorlton Moor they are Stone Rock, Benky Hill, Green Howe, Cock Howe, Miley Howe and Flat Howe, while after a gap of a mile or so, two mounds delightfully named the Sour Milk Hills are surrounded by spurs thickly scattered with smaller cairns. Away across Bilsdale near Chop Gate there is a standing stone circle with the common name of the Bridestones.

The south-west corner of the North York Moors is formed by the Hambledon Hills, cut off by the fertile trough of Rydale with Rievaulx Abbey held gently in a bend and the neat, comfortable town of Helmsley with its castle guarding the entrance. Here we again find the long barrows of the New Stone Age peoples, the best being in a fine lofty position on Kepwick Moor. The strong semicircular earthwork abutting on to the cliffs of Boltby Scar recalls Eston Nab; near it the Cleave Dyke runs along the edge of the escarpment. Further down towards Ampleforth there is the small enclosure of Studford Ring, and the Double Dyke which cuts off the whole of the remaining headland. Within this headland on Pry Rigg is an unusually large round barrow still standing twelve feet high; it covered an urn-burial of the Bronze Age.

So, with something of a whimper, ends my overcrowded tour of the North York Moors; overcrowded, no more than a catalogue, it has still failed to give more than a hint of the riches of this lovely moorland territory. There is nothing magnificent, perhaps; nothing even which is individually spectacular, yet there is no other territory where the remains left by prehistoric man have been less disturbed or where one gets a clearer impression of a countryside which once belonged to him.

Before advancing on the third and greatest upland area of Yorkshire, the Dales and other Pennine country of the West Riding, I ought to name the few places of interest to be seen in the intervening lowlands of the Vale of York. We are now far enough to the north to be entering the military area of the Roman Province; because, first, of the resistance of the native Celtic tribe of the Brigantes, who proved even harder to crush than the Ordovices and Silures of Wales, and then of the need to hold the northern frontier against the undefeated barbarians of Scotland, this northern territory remained in the hands of the soldiers and had little of the normal civil life of a Roman province. Aldborough, in the heart of the Vale of York, was, as *Isurium Brigantum*, the northernmost administrative tribal city. York itself, founded as a legionary fortress in 71 A.D., remained the great military base for the north, just as Caerleon and Chester were for Wales. Beyond it a network of military roads, camps and forts, lies behind the famous frontier of Hadrian's Wall. It is quite impossible for me to act as a guide to a system which is so complicated and has left so many remains; I can only name a few places where there is most to see.

At York, *Eboracum*, there is a Roman collection in the Yorkshire Museum (as well as an abundance of prehistoric material, including chariot-burials from the Wolds) but architectural remains are disappointing, the best show-piece being the Multangular Tower, the surviving western bastion of the fortress as it was rebuilt early in the fourth century. After York, interest follows the line of the Roman road running from Aldborough northwards up the Vale—a road which as far as Scotch Corner just beyond Catterick is familiar to us as A.1 of our own road system. At Aldborough, *Isurium Brigantum* has been recalled most attractively by its mosaic pavements for which the present village may be said to be noted. Some have been reburied, some carried off to Leeds and other distant museums, some are in Aldborough's own museum, and two are where I think Roman antiquities should more often lie—in the premises of an inn, the 'Aldborough Arms'. If prehistoric relics should always be on downs or moors or sea cliffs, I prefer my Roman domesticity somewhere near a comfortable drink.

At Catterick some traces of a large Roman station of *Cataractonium* are to be seen on the south bank of the Swale at Thornborough, and just to the north where the Roman road forked at Scotch Corner the road itself is visible with a ridge eight yards wide and five feet high. Here A.1 parts company with the work of the Roman engineers, for while it swings east to Darlington, one Roman thoroughfare went straight northwards to cross the Tees at Piercebridge while the other turned due west for the Stainmore Pass on the line still followed by the Carlisle road. Forts on its line are to be seen at Greta Bridge (behind, but I fear not close beside the 'Morritt Arms'), at Bowes, and then, a really fine spectacle, just on the county boundary before dropping steeply to Brough and the Eden Valley, the road cuts through the legionary camp of Rey Cross. This camp lies nearly fifteen hundred feet up and covers twenty acres; the ramparts are of limestone and the entrances protected by external barriers. It was probably put up to house a legion quite early in the campaign; it is certainly a temporary camp and may be supposed to have been succeeded by the permanent stations at Bowes and Brough.

I passed Aldborough with an eye only for its Roman remains. But I must return, for close to it is one of the most famous prehistoric monuments in Yorkshire, the Devil's Arrows at Roecliffe, now a suburb of Boroughbridge. These are three colossal monoliths, of Millstone Grit curiously fluted by weathering, standing in a line running north and south; the northernmost is eighteen feet high, the others, standing at intervals of two hundred and three hundred and seventy feet, are both twenty-two feet in height—out-topping the Stonehenge uprights, but still just beaten by Rudston (p. 264). They are almost certainly of Bronze Age date, yet one need not doubt that as an ancient centre of tribal sanctities they had some part in the Brigantian settlement at Aldborough and so with the Roman foundation of *Isurium Brigantum*. Something of their old power remained with them until the other day, for they stood in open fields and their presence was still to be felt; now, however, they have become involved in a Boroughbridge building estate—and the pagan gods fly from English back gardens.

The importance of this region in the Bronze Age is emphasized by the quite plentiful remains on the low-lying sandy moorland a little further north. On Hutton Moor near Ripon are the many barrows and two 'henges' of a peculiar type, with two circular ditches and the bank on the berm between them. Three similar sanctuaries are less than five miles away on Thornborough Moor near West Tanfield. These three stand in a straight line with their entrances all opening in the same direction; they are nearly six hundred feet across and it is thought that the banks were once crowned by a ring of standing stones. The Thornborough Rings must surely have been used by a great concourse of people on days of festival, and they seem to prove a substantial population pasturing their flocks and herds on this relatively sheltered and well-drained upland.

D. *The Yorkshire Pennines*

Western Yorkshire possesses some of the sternest industrial areas and some of the fairest and most satisfying country in England. For myself, if I were to live in the country, it would be in the Yorkshire Dales, Upper Wharfedale or Wensleydale for choice, or some of the smaller valleys tributary to them. I love them for the reason that they seem to me to have attained the perfect balance between man and nature; each valley has its abundantly fertile lower stretches, adorned perhaps by castle and abbey, then, as one penetrates deeper among the hills, it narrows, bare, dark moors appear on the summits, the number of fields making the span from side to side of the valley grow steadily less, small towns give way to villages. In these higher parts of the valley, man—who has had it all his own way nearer to the mouth—must begin to fight against his surroundings; defended by their lovely drystone walls, the fields can be seen along the top of each slope trying to maintain their greenness, their good pasture, against the brown floods of heather and bracken pushing down from the moors. So at last one reaches the point at which the fields are defeated; it is the head of the valley, with nothing in front but becks rushing down from moorland and mountain.

It is, I only dimly know why, a delight and a happiness to walk over from one dale to the next—to leave the compact grey inn by the river, to follow a lane past farms and fields, barns and perhaps a spinney or two, until a gate through the last, embattled, stone wall admits the traveller on to the moors. Here man has no stake beyond a few sheep and perhaps a line of beehives where his small henchmen make the heather pay tribute. So for a few miles the traveller crosses untamed upland, before reaching an outlying field reclaimed beside a beck, then another gate and a return to pasture, coppice, cottages and another inn beside another river.

It is, of course, between gate and gate, as it were, that the traveller can expect to find the marks of early man, and in making the passage from valley to valley he must wonder how far the life which raised huts, earth-works, barrows, drained down into the valleys and provided the ancestry of the present dalesmen. There have been many newcomers pushing up the Dales since prehistoric times, Scandinavians as well as Anglo-Saxons, but there is no question that the Celts and earlier prehistoric people who formed the strong and martial tribe of the Brigantes have a large share in the blood of the dalesmen, and indeed of the whole formidable breed of Yorkshiremen which survives to thicken the blood and stiffen the back-bone of the English nation.

Before stopping short on the Derbyshire boundary on the edge of the Peak, I urged the spectacular quality of Carl Wark, a fort only a short distance outside Sheffield to the south-west; on the north-east side of that great steel town, about three miles up the valley of the Don, is another fort which is better known though far less imposing than Carl Wark. This is Wincobank, a fortification whose double ramparts enclose an oval of between two and three acres on the summit of a spur above the river. The ramparts are of earth over well-built drystone walling, and excavation has shown that they were raised not long before the Roman conquest, prob-ably during the first half-century of our era. Another oval fort with a lofty bank still standing is in Scoles Wood some two miles nearer to Rotherham. Those who see Wincobank can also see the linear earthwork known as Roman Riggs for it runs below the fort on its way along the north-west side of the Don Valley to Swinton and Mexborough. At the Sheffield end there is a single bank, but further down the valley it is doubled; in some stretches the banks are still thirteen feet high, always with the ditch or ditches on the riverside. Formerly it was believed that Roman Riggs was post-Roman, a defensive boundary dug by the Britons of the kingdom of Elmet against their Anglian neighbours among whom they held out for so long in the obscurity of the Dark Ages. More recently, however, there has been an inclination to allow a greater antiquity and to recognize it as a barrier thrown up by the Brigantes in their fierce struggle to check the advance of the Romans.

In general the Millstone Grit moorland which continues up to the famous gap through the Pennines made by the Aire and Ribble was less well peopled in early times than the limestone of the Dales which is fully exposed north of the gap. That is why the next monument to which I should wish to guide any traveller is at some distance—on the southern outskirts of Huddersfield. Castle Hill, Almondbury, is a most impressive place, though one just reached by the tentacles and grime of industry. It is an elaborate construction rare in this part of the country, and in many ways comparable with the forts of the Welsh Marches (of which it can indeed be taken as a northern outlier). When it was first established in about 300 B.C. a single stone rampart with rock-cut ditch defended only the southern end of the narrow oval hill on which it stands. In the next phases the walls were doubled and extended right round the summit, and at the northern end a deeply sunk track led past an outer enclosure to the strongly defended entrance. In the last stage of all, just as at Old Oswestry (p. 239), a vast outer rampart was added enclosing the whole place and running quite low near the foot of the hill. Inevitably Almondbury was abandoned when at last the Romans were able to overcome the resistance of the Brigantes and it stood vacant for about a millennium. Its history was not, however, at an end. In the reign of Stephen a mighty ditch was dug across the main inner part of the fort and the material from it piled up into the motte for a stone keep—the prehistoric walls serving as an outer bailey. This stronghold was promptly dismantled under Henry III and the hill was left in peace except for the building of a house up there in the fifteenth century; now it is a favourite walking and courting ground for the citizens of Huddersfield.

On the other side of the town there are traces of the Roman fort at Slack which defended a road running up from Manchester, but they are less worth seeing than the next camp on this same road which lies about eight miles to the south-west at Castleshaw below Saddleworth. Road and camps were made late in the first century during the campaigns against the Brigantes, but at Castleshaw the outline of a smaller and later work can be seen inside the original banks. About fifty years later the Slack road was abandoned in favour of a more northerly route running from Manchester to Ilkley over Blackstone Edge. This road where it is exposed on Blackstone Edge above Littleborough is one of the finest Roman spectacles in the county; it climbs on to the moors as a sixteen-foot track, its paved surface held between deeply sunk kerbstones and with a sunken central channel also held between vertical slabs. This shallow trough down the centre is noticeably worn on the steepest slopes and it has been suggested that this may have been done by the skid-pans of descending carts; a more convincing explanation is that the trough was filled with turf to make the going easier for horses dragging loads uphill.

The road crossed the Calder near Sowerby and the Aire near Keighley on its way to Ilkley where the remains of a Roman fort underlie the parish church. This fort was established in the last quarter of the first century and remodelled in stone within fifty years—but to this chill statement one touch of individual life can be added. A civil settlement grew up outside the fort and there, either in the first or second century, there lived a Briton who kept the native Celtic name of Conicilli. His name has escaped the oblivion which closed over those of all his fellow citizens from the chance that he threw away a broken bone spatula on which in some idle and possessive moment he had scratched those nine letters. Chance is the salt of history! Ilkley has famous carved Anglian cross-shafts in the church-yard, but more legitimately within my range are the Bronze Age carvings which have been brought down from the moors and placed opposite the church. These are specimens of the 'cup-and-ring' carvings, which include a great variety of patterns but most commonly show a circular central hollow surrounded by incised rings, sometimes with radial lines cutting through them to the centre. The designs, which were certainly religious and magical in their significance, were cut by Bronze Age peoples on to natural rock faces or boulders on the moor; occasionally they are found on cist-graves of the period, and they are related to the simple cup-marks already seen here and there on a megalithic tomb. Many more are to be seen still in position above Ilkley and Burley on Rombald's (or Rumble's) Moor—there is a famous example of swastika form on Addington High Moor—while others are carefully kept free from heather on Baildon Moor, much used as a Sunday parade and picnic ground by Bingley and Bradford people.

One can be sure that the men who made the cup-and-ring markings were already pasturing their sheep on this moorland well over three thousand years before wool began to make the fortunes of the towns that now hedge them round. Rombald's Moor is sown with minor antiquities— cairns, hut sites and enclosures—and in the Twelve Apostles between Ilkley and Bingley can show a stone circle which is deservedly well known locally. Probably the richness of this whole region is largely due to the importance of the Aire Gap which has been a much-used thoroughfare from the Stone Age to our own.

At Nesfield, a little way up the Wharfe from Ilkley, there is a strong semicircular camp with its rampart ends resting on a cliff edge in a manner so reminiscent of Eston Nab (p. 270) that it has usually been allowed a Bronze Age rather than an Iron Age date. It is a good moorland walk from this fort to the fine exposure of Roman road on Blubberhouses Moor; this is another of the roads built during the first-century campaigns against the Brigantes and it comes up from Ribchester in Lancashire, with other good stretches visible just north of Barnoldswick and east of Thornton, before it passes the fort now known as Burwen's Castle at Elsack.

If the traveller pushes on up Wharfedale—and there are few better things which a traveller can do—he will find a number of sites that deserve to be seen round Grassington, the town where the railway has its terminus and the greatest delights of the Dale begin. First near Thorpe is the Elbolton Cave, distinguished by having been made a dwelling for a New Stone Age community, then on the north side of Grassington follows the 'Druid's Circle', an oval enclosure about one hundred and fifty feet long and half that in width, its bank showing a coping of flat-topped stones. It has been suggested that this 'arena' might have been the meeting-place of the peasants living in the huts whose foundation can be seen in the neighbouring Grass Wood and who cultivated barley in the 'Celtic' fields just visible at High Close Pasture. This settlement was probably of native Brigantes, but while they may already have been living there during the Iron Age one can be sure that the place was still inhabited during the Roman period—it is as well to remember that the Romans mined lead between here and Pateley Bridge and native labour would have been in demand.

The Grassington settlement with its huts and fields is one of the best of many similar remains to be seen on the West Riding Moors. Another outstanding example is on the plateau of the Great Scar Limestone south of Arncliffe, a charming village in Littondale, where the small, lively Skirfare hastens down to join the Wharfe. Here Celtic fields are adjacent to a very solidly built hamlet with circular and rectangular buildings ranged round a yard with two entrances. Such places whether occupied in Iron Age or Roman times, make one think both of the villages in north Wales (p. 233 ff.) and some of the hut-circle groups on Dartmoor. At any time in history it has been possible to live in many manners—not more than five miles from Arncliffe a family were living as troglodytes in the well-known Dowkerbottom Cave in the limestone scar between here and Kilnsey.

If instead of keeping to the more easterly Dales one turns along the western edge of the limestone, there is a variety of antiquities to be found round Ribblesdale. This is North Craven, the finest country of the Great Scar Limestone, with splendid cliffs and ravines shaped by water into columns and flutings, sometimes soft grey, sometimes appearing almost white. The water has also filled them with caves, but although these offer endless opportunities for modern men craving adventure, most of them were too inaccessible to appeal to prehistoric men for whom life was already difficult enough. One well-known exception, however, is the Victoria Cave near Settle which was inhabited by Middle Stone Age hunters who left there, as well as some characteristic little flints, a single tanged harpoon head of a kind exceedingly rare in Britain. It stood empty for millennia, blown soil, roof-peelings, and other silts accumulated above the

Stone Age litter to a depth of six feet, then, after something like five thousand years, a community of Roman Britons moved into the cave and lived unknowingly on the new earth floor above the relics of their remote predecessors.

By far the noblest site in Craven is Ingleborough, a mountain whose summit of over two thousand three hundred feet has a tough cap of Millstone Grit overlying its limestone bulk. It seems to have been a great Brigantian stronghold and we can legitimately imagine the tribesmen holding out here against the Romans—it may well have been one of the last strong points to fall before their superior efficiency, their military and engineering science. The summit is protected by sheer crags, but these were most powerfully reinforced by a rampart built from thousands of blocks of Millstone Grit, sometimes lined on the inside by very large slabs. This wall, now much tumbled, encloses what, thanks to the Millstone Grit, is a level grassy plateau of about fifteen acres, an ideal situation for the many round huts whose outlines can still be traced in the turf. Ingleborough, then, was not a mere fort and place of refuge but a true hilltown, a place which had known birth as well as death and all the enjoyment and labour of everyday life. It is perhaps the most moving monument to prehistoric man in all Yorkshire, and it is sad that much has been mutilated to supply material for a huge and senseless modern cairn.

Running up the Ribble Valley below Ingleborough is one of the roads of the Roman conquerors, the so-called Craven's Way which, coming up from Settle, skirts round the north shoulder of Whernside and drops to Dentdale. For the energetic and leisurely (when will society realize that these two states are inseparable?) it is well worth tracing its course—which on the high moorland is said to show as a heavily cambered and kerbed road, twenty feet wide and with flagged culverts, some of which still carry water.

Another well-defined Roman road crosses the Craven's Way and will serve to lead us back to the eastern Dales. This is the route which underlies the modern road from Ingleton to Ribblehead, where it makes the crossing, then appears in its own right as a fine track across the high moorland of Cam Fell and Wether Fell, before running straight down to the fort at Bainbridge which is still to be seen on a grassy mound above the Ure in Wensleydale. This fort seems to have been established in the first century, when it was provided with clay ramparts and wooden parapets and gateways; it had a long subsequent history and was in use through most of the Roman occupation.

I must now lead the traveller to some remarkable earthworks which are so far on the lower eastern edge of the Dale that they might equally well have been included with the Vale of York (p. 272). They may be said to lie in the general neighbourhood of Richmond. The first is Maiden Castle at Grinton in Swaledale, a curious place with a roughly circular bank and ditch approached from the east by a stone avenue. There are round barrows in the vicinity, and although the ditch lies outside the bank, it seems very probable that Maiden Castle is not a fort but some kind of sacred enclosure or meeting-place.

It is quite near here that there begins a long line of dyke which is comparable with Roman Riggs and at least equally obscure in its history and purpose. Though it is said to have an extension to Grinton the main part of the ten-mile-long earthwork of Scot's Dyke appears to start at Hindwath-on-Swale whence it ran, facing east, to Barforth-on-Tees. The eastern end is largely destroyed, but here on the higher ground it shows well at Kirklands north-east of Gilling and at Olliver Duckitt; where they are well preserved, its twenty-five foot bank and deep ditch make an impressive spectacle.

The Scot's Dyke passes to the east of an even more remarkable earthwork in Stanwick Park near Forcett. This is known locally as Jackdike Arches and comprises an enormous triangular enclosure of nearly seven hundred acres, the bank and ditch being almost unbroken over their course of four and a half miles. The history of the Stanwick earthworks as revealed by Sir Mortimer Wheeler's digging leads into the Roman conquest of Britain at a point where the protagonists are known by name, thanks largely to the writings of Tacitus. Having conquered the lowlands, the Roman army was now thrusting into the highland zone. At this time the Brigantes, probably the largest of all the British tribes and occupying much of northern England, were ruled over by Venutius and his queen, Cartimandua. Friendly policy towards the Romans had brought them the status of a client kingdom. In 51 A.D. when the heroic leader of the British resistance, Caractacus (son of Cunobelin, Shakespeare's Cymbeline) asked for asylum at the court, Queen Cartimandua handed him over to the Romans in chains.

Already before this the Brigantes had been in turmoil, with the pro-Roman policy still maintained by Cartimandua but now opposed by her husband and the elite of his warriors. The royal pair separated in violent hostility. Venutius succeeded Caractacus as leader of the resistance, while Cartimandua took his squire Vellocatus as her consort for bed and throne.

It was probably at the date of his break with the queen in about 57 A.D.

17. The Roman bath at Bath (*Aquae Sulis*).

18. The Roman villa at Chedworth, Gloucestershire.

19. Remains of walls from Caerwent (*Venta Silurum*), once a substantial Roman town in South Wales.

20. The Fort of the Saxon Shore at Burgh Castle, just outside Great Yarmouth.

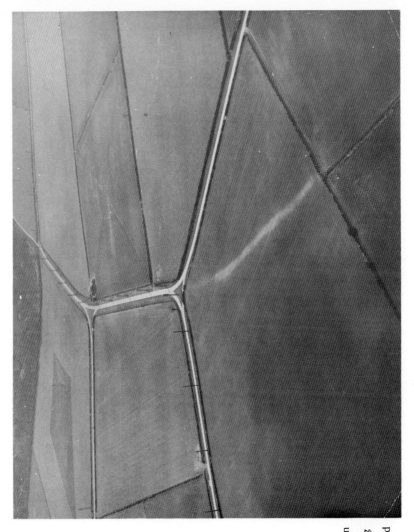

21. The Roman road at Barnock, near Stamford in Lincolnshire: the original road can be traced passing through a field, as the modern road swings round to avoid field boundaries.

22. Part of the Roman
paved way on Blackstone
Edge, on the borders of
Yorkshire and Lancashire.
In the centre of the way is
a sunken channel, which
may well have been filled
with turf to give horses
foothold when climbing
uphill.

23. The bath house of the fort at Chesters (*Cilurnum*), on Hadrian's Wall.

24. The latrines at Housesteads (*Borcovicium*), on Hadrian's Wall.

(or possibly as early as the betrayal of Caractacus) that Venutius moved northward beyond the easy reach of the Romans and built the first of the defences at Stanwick—the strong, seventeen-acre fortress on Tofts Hill towards the centre of the site. With Roman support Cartimandua was able to hold out in the old Brigantian capital (possibly Almondbury, p. 275) but further forces rallied to Venutius and before long he fortified a much larger area to the north of Tofts. These ramparts, built before 60 A.D., were exceptionally strong; for long stretches the ditch was cut deep into the limestone while the huge bank behind was faced with stones.

Hearing of the struggle for the succession in Rome that followed the death of Nero, Venutius attacked Cartimandua with so much success that she had to be rescued by her imperial allies. As Tacitus put it on behalf of Rome, 'The throne was left to Venutius, the war to us.'

The king was not allowed long to enjoy his victory. The energetic general Vespasian won the Imperial crown and posted a new Governor to restore the situation in Britain. More fighting men were crowding to Venutius at Stanwick, and the third phase of building added the immense fortifications to the south. It seems, however, that the work was not quite finished when at some time between 71–74 A.D. the Romans attacked with all their disciplined force. As the excavator says 'We can almost see the tribesmen toiling vainly at their gate, almost hear the Ninth Legion tramping up from its new fortress at York to one of its rare victories.' So ended the great Brigantian resistance, leaving the Romans free to carry their frontier yet further to the north.

With these earthworks we are back in the neighbourhood of Scotch Corner and the Roman roads and forts which we followed up the Vale of York (p. 272). We are also on the county boundary and have finished the survey of Yorkshire, a county which perhaps has more survivals from prehistoric and Roman Britain than any other outside Wiltshire.

E. *The Four Northern Counties*

The superb mountain masses with their core of volcanic rocks which dominate Cumberland and Westmorland made barriers too formidable for prehistoric man to pass them freely. Unexpectedly enough their higher valleys seem first to have been fully penetrated by Norsemen sailing down from the north by way of the Scottish coasts hardy settlers used to lands even colder, darker, more mountainous. Nevertheless early man, with his slow persistent land-taking, pushed round their flanks and up the more accessible valleys, while the Romans cut roads and planted forts where military necessity dictated. The counties can show practically nothing of the Old or Middle Stone Age hunters; of the first farmers of the New Stone Age not very much, though the lakeside dwellings of Ehenside Tarn near St. Bees illustrate a thriving community settled on the coast where the crafts of carpentry and potting were practised with skill. There was also the trade in stone axes conducted from Langdale Pikes in the very heart of the Lake District. By the Bronze Age we shall find settlement had been widely extended, leaving its mark mainly in round cairns and stone circles. By the Iron Age there must have been a considerable scattered population, but it was poor and backward, following a way of life hardly to be distinguished from that of earlier centuries.

The Barrow peninsula, which was neither mountainous nor heavily forested, seems to have been relatively populous; near Urswick there are a number of Bronze Age round barrows and the small fort of Urswick Stone Walls which was certainly occupied by native tribesmen during the Roman occupation and perhaps before. One of the three best stone circles is that of Swineside, which stands folded between the fells of Black Combe and the Duddon estuary near Millom. The blocks rise from poor, rather boggy grassland, redeemed in spring by bluebells which flourish inside the circle. Smaller rings once standing on the coast at Annaside and at Hall Foss by Bootle have been destroyed.

At Ravenglass we again encounter the Romans. A port was early established here, apparently intended as a naval base for an attack on Ireland projected before the Romans realized that even the conquest of Scotland was beyond their strength. From it a road can be traced up Eskdale to the fort of Hardknot which occupies a magnificent position below Hardknot Pass; it has a stone wall with earth embankment and has been shown to date from the early second century. From here the road goes by way of the Wrynose Pass to Ambleside where the larger fortress of *Galava* occupied a pleasant slope, in strongest contrast to the austerities of Hardknot, looking down Lake Windermere from the outskirts of Ambleside. At *Galava* the stone walls of the fort with those of its barracks and granaries built in the reign of Hadrian overlie an earlier station of earth and wood.

Returning now to Eskdale, troops using the valley road to and from Hardknot must often unknowingly have passed below an unusual Bronze Age funerary monument. This is a stone circle enclosing five round cairns each itself enclosed in a peristalith, which stands to the north of Boot. Eskdale was evidently attractive country, for there are long cairns and hut sites between Raven Crag and Latterbarrow, and an extensive settlement probably occupied during the Iron Age at Barnscar, by Devoke Water. Debouching once more on to the coast I will name the Singlen Stones, a destroyed circle once standing to the west of Egremont.

In the Lake District itself works of early man are so few that it seems a kind of idiocy to single them out in a world where nature has worked on so heroic a scale. Yet just as a small painting from the hand of a Stone Age hunter can bring sudden life to the monotonous and empty magnificence of some vast limestone caverns in the Dordogne, so in places where nature has been left almost to herself, some fragment of ancient human handiwork may quicken and add feeling to the land. There is pitifully little: a stone circle, unremarkable, on Elva Plain near Bassenthwaite, a line of small forts down the south-east side of Derwentwater, and then at Keswick something worthy of description, something with power enough to kindle the scene. This is the circle of standing stones near Keswick, familiar as Castlerigg or the Keswick Carles. It has a noble situation on a little rise against Castlerigg Fell, itself in a hollow closed by a vast rim of mountains, with Skiddaw and Saddleback close at hand. There are now thirtynine Carles, standing and lying in a circle a hundred feet across and with the remains of some stone structure at the centre. It is known that John Keats went to look at Castlerigg, and as in his life he had little chance to see moorland circles, it is surely safe to assume that he was possessed by an image of the Keswick Carles when in *Hyperion* he saw the gods:

> . . . like a dismal cirque
> Of Druid stones, upon a forlorn moor,
> When the chill rain begins at shut of eye,
> In dull November, and their chancel vault,
> The heaven itself, is blinded throughout night.

Beyond the Lake District where the broad Eden Valley separates the mountains round Shap from those leading up to Cross Fell we find another region where antiquities can be found by their more diligent pursuers. The Roman road from Brough (p. 273) ran down this valley with a fort at Kirkby Thore (*Bravoniacum*) and another at Old Penrith (*Voreda*); generally it is obliterated by the modern road but a stretch can be seen north of Appleby. On the southern flank of the valley between Ravenstonedale and Ullswater round barrows and circles, at Orton, Shap and Mayburgh, are enough to prove a substantial population in the Bronze Age; the Iron Age is represented by an extensive settlement area south of Crosby Ravensworth, and (probably) by small forts north of Ullswater. More of these small forts appear on the east side of the Eden beyond Penrith, but the one proud monument of this valley is the circle and outlying menhir, Long Meg and her Daughters, which stand near Little Salkeld. Long Meg herself is the menhir; she still has fifty-nine daughters ranged in a ring three hundred and fifty feet across in mild meadowland, not comparable in grandeur with the site at Castlerigg.

At Penrith the Roman road left the Eden to run by an upland route now exactly followed by the modern road to Carlisle—and Carlisle, as *Luguvallium*, was an important station behind the western end of Hadrian's Wall. This, however, is not the place to approach this most famous of our Roman monuments; it is traditional and wise to guide the traveller first towards its eastern end.

In Durham the ancient rocks are thickly overlaid with glacial clays which even to-day make it a land where mining is curiously intermingled with surviving patches of forest. In early times the trees were everywhere and effectively prevented settlement. Almost its only antiquarian interest, and that is very slight, follows the lines of the two Roman roads running up to the Wall, an eastern through Chester-le-Street to Newcastle and western through Binchester (*Vinovia*) near Bishop Auckland through Ebchester (*Vindomora*) and Lanchester (*Longovicium*) to the great supply base of *Corstopitum* which is at Corbridge on the east side of Hexham a mile or so behind the line of the wall. At Corbridge there is much to be seen, including among the buildings armourers' workshops and temples. The museum has one of the best collections of Romano-British sculpture in the country, the most famous piece being the Corbridge Lion in which something of the native Celtic spirit has given a new force and vitality to a classical form.

Here on the Tyne we command Hadrian's Wall, perhaps the most famous pre-Christian monument in Britain after Stonehenge. Fame has made it the centre of a vast literature—popular, middling and learned— and it would be folly for me to try to act as guide to this great and complex barrier with which the Romans protected the northernmost frontier of their Empire. Nevertheless, as excavation has of late modified that history, I propose to quote the story as it is now, more correctly, known. It will be remembered that late in the first century the Romans had defeated and expected to subdue the tribes of Scotland, and had occupied its lowlands as far as Strathmore beyond the Tay. But it proved untenable; after 100 A.D., when even the Tweed was abandoned, a frontier had to be found between the Tyne and Solway. Fierce attacks followed; the Emperor

Hadrian then in person came here, and the continuous fortification of the frontier was begun.

When the project was started in 122 A.D., the plan was to build a stone wall ten Roman feet wide and some fifteen feet high running from Newcastle to the Irthing. From there the frontier was continued as a turf wall, twenty Roman feet wide, as far as the Solway. A large ditch ran in front of these ramparts, except in certain stretches where they followed the edge of the crags, or where the bedrock resisted cutting. At mile intervals, fortlets, known as milecastles, were built. They were designed both to provide accommodation for the patrolling garrison and also to give passage through the Wall—which was never intended to sever communications between north and south, 'barbarians' and Romano-Britons, but merely to control them. Between the milecastles at intervals of one third of a Roman mile were watch towers twenty feet square and up to twenty-eight feet high.

Such was the original plan of the Wall, but before the building, carried out by contingents from the three legions garrisoned in Britain, the Twentieth, Second and Sixth, had been long under way the plan was radically altered. The first change seems to have been the decision to build forts along the line of the Wall itself instead of maintaining fighting garrisons to the rear. Only one explanation makes sense of this alteration: that the construction of the frontier caused considerably more hostile reactions among the tribes to the north than had been expected. With the advancement of the forts came the second major change which was the construction of another ditch, this time to the *rear* of the Wall. This Vallum Ditch, twenty feet wide, was itself flanked by large berms or platforms and then by banks twenty feet wide. There seems little doubt that the Vallum must have been intended to demarcate the military zone which was the frontier of the province and also to act as a deterrent to surprise attack from the rear.

Among other changes was the narrowing of the stone wall to eight Roman feet or even less, presumably in an effort to speed up the building rate. Another was the replacement of the turf wall in the western sector by a narrow gauge stone wall which in places followed a different line to that taken by the turf frontier. Although the Wall itself ends at Bowness on Solway in the west, its system of forts and towers is continued along the Cumberland coast down to St. Bee's Head.

The most unexpected feature in the early history of Hadrian's Wall, considering the effort that had gone into its construction, was that in the time of Hadrian's successor, Antoninus Pius, the Roman frontier was moved forward again to the Forth-Clyde line where a turf wall and fort system, known as the Antonine Wall, was constructed. The move was not a great success and in about 181 A.D. this northern wall was overrun by the Scottish tribes. Soon afterwards Hadrian's Wall again became the northern frontier of Roman Britain and was to remain so for a further two centuries.

In 196 the garrison was withdrawn to take part in civil war on the Continent, and the Celtic tribes, long pent behind the Wall, swarmed over it, pillaging and destroying as far south as York and Chester. In about 200 A.D. under the Emperor Severus the frontier was restored, the forts on the Wall were strengthened, while many of the turrets and lesser works were suppressed as a part of a new policy that included the use of mobile light cavalry patrolling far in advance of the actual fortifications (p. 287). Though this policy was long successful, further withdrawals of troops and barbarian attacks took place in the third and fourth centuries. At last in 383 A.D. when the whole Western Empire was falling in like an empty house the Roman troops were marched away for a last time and this stout frontier, too, was allowed finally to collapse.

The Roman Wall is an ideal place for pilgrimage; how many thousands of people of all ages, nationalities, interests, must have walked along its course, enjoying it as a companion through country which is sometimes charming, occasionally magnificent. Such pilgrims will, I suppose, have found most to interest them in the fort and bridge of Chesters (*Cilurnum*) at the Chollerford crossing of the North Tyne, in the grandeur of the fort at Housesteads (*Borcovicium*) and its neighbour at Great Chesters (*Aesica*), and finally the elaborate bridge abutment which carried the military road over the Irthing near Gilsland. But all will have been most stirred by the continuous line of the wall itself, the sight of a frontier which is certainly the finest surviving in the Western Empire—an emotion which must reach its strongest in the stretch beyond Housesteads where this defiant masonry crests the wild and precipitous scarp above Crag Lough. Here one can stand and experience something of the meaning of Rome, of that philistine Empire which we so often abuse. Here one can put oneself in the place of the Roman sentry staring out apprehensively to the lonely hills beyond, where prehistoric life went on in its darkness and strength.

Into that last triangle of England I must now lead the way. In it we shall find the remains left by the Roman armies, the remains left by their native allies and enemies and the remains of their Bronze Age ancestors.

One route in particular invites the traveller—Dere Street, the Roman road which drives northward from Corbridge to cross the Scottish border and reach Melrose. There is also the Devil's Causeway, a second Roman road which keeps closer to the east coast, heading for Tweedmouth, but it does not offer so attractive a route. Dere Street passes a fort near Woodburn, then runs up a few miles of Redesdale to the fort of *Bremenium* at High Rochester. There was an Agricolan fort here and reconstruction in the Antonine period, but most of the visible defences date from the time of Severus. During the third and early fourth centuries it was distinguished in being the most northerly fort anywhere garrisoned by the Roman army. The fort with massive masonry walls had stone-throwing machines (*onagri*) on strong emplacements and outer earthworks of such depth that no native missiles could pass them. So *Bremenium* commanded the course of the beck up which the Roman road itself ran northward and which formed one of the best routes by which the northern tribesmen could rush down from their fastnesses on and beyond the Cheviot Hills. It served as a garrisoned outpost, from which cavalry could patrol a wide no-man's-land north of the Wall. The last site before Dere Street enters Scotland is that of the camps and other Roman earthworks at Chew Green, Makendon. In its more southerly reaches Dere Street passes vast numbers of little hill-forts dotted all along the North Tyne, most thickly between Chollerton and Wark and round Elsdon. These were probably mostly built at different times during and after the Roman occupation; perhaps a few are earlier. The Bronze Age, too, has left its remains here; on one side of the Tyne there is an unusually fine menhir or standing stone in the grounds of Swinburn Castle—a block twelve feet high and weathered into curious grooves; on the other there are the Goatstones, the remains of a stone circle on Ravensheugh Crags at Simonburn. Away to the north-west another area of interest is formed by the Coquet Valley with a great concentration of antiquities round Rothbury. Here on both sides of the river we find the cup-and-ring carvings which are among the most distinguished archaeological possessions of this part of Northumberland. Here they are relatively simple, round depressions with surrounding rings carved on boulders very much like those of the West Riding (p. 277). On the north side of the valley there are plenty of round barrows and standing stones—the latter most numerous on Debdon Moor. To the south of the river, Witchy Neuk is a remarkable semicircular fort abutting on a crag and approached by a dyke. There are groups of cairns scattered round it and lines of small standing stones on the east side. The whole of this complex probably dates from the Roman period—Witchy Neuk itself was certainly occupied during the third century A.D. At Lordershaw, further up the

Coquet, the Five Kings standing stones are worth seeing and easily accessible.

For our last region I must lead the weary traveller still further north towards the apex of this triangle, to the west and north of the Cheviot in the country between Breamish and Till. Here the Cheviot foothills are studded with round barrows and almost every little hill is crowned with fortifications—so numerous, so conspicuous, that they form an important *motif* within the pattern of the landscape. Among these countless small fry, a few stand out. There is the curious fort at Old Bewick where two adjacent crescents of strong ramparts with stone-cut ditches abut on to a cliff edge; there is Greaves Ash near Linhope on the upper waters of the Breamish, where on a platform below Greenshaw Hill double ramparts enclose an inner line of defences, with the foundations of round huts and other enclosures visible inside. Broughheur due north of the summit of Yeavering Bell near the junction of the Glen and Till at Wooler is crowned by strong polygonal ramparts. These are only a few out of a vast number of sites which would be more interesting if excavation had told us more of their history.

Perhaps the Bronze Age has pride of place even above these crowding forts of later centuries. These are circles up the Glen Valley and along the Till—the finest in the country being at Duddo not far from the place where Till flows into Tweed. But the chief glory of the Bronze Age in this region are the cup-and-ring carvings which abound on either side of Wooler and Doddington; from Hunter's Moor they follow the high moorland for seven miles—at Wrangham, Doddington, Dod Law, Gledlaw, Whitsunbank, Simonside, Weetwood and Fowberry. This group of symbols is certainly the most numerous and most varied in England, including many designs far more bizarre than those of the Rothbury group. The most remarkable examples of this magical art appear on the slab of Routing Lynn north-west of Dod Law, its whole surface staring with incomprehensible, haunting symbols. Looking at them we can wonder for a last time what the images meant to the man who squatted here carving them, what tides of ritual, what magical acts took place round these forsaken holy places. We look at what was written to express the mind of prehistoric man, and cannot read.

So here, where the Devil's Causeway points to Berwick, with Otterburn not far behind and Flodden close at hand, I shall leave the traveller in this once troubled border country between Saxon and Scot. I have led him far from Surrey sands and Wessex chalk over mountains and up dales to these remote Cheviot Hills, and in doing so have journeyed to and fro over the past hundred thousand years. It has been a long way to go in both time and space, but I think we have seen all the finest of our ancestral monuments, all the places where the past stirs the imagination; the places where formerly we were and from which we have come.

GAZETTEER OF SITES DESCRIBED IN THE GUIDE
(Sites only mentioned by name are not included)
Ordnance Survey One-inch (New Popular Edition) Sheet No.

A = Age; B = Bronze; I = Iron; O = Old; S = Stone; Meg. = Megalithic

NAME OF SITE AND PAGE REFERENCES	COUNTY AND 1″ O.S. SHEET NO.	TYPE OF MONUMENT	NATIONAL GRID REF.
Abinger Common, 66	Surrey 170	Mesolithic pit dwelling	TQ/112459
Aconbury, Hereford, 202	Herefordshire 142	I.A. Fort	SO/503331
Aldborough (*Isurium Brigantum*), 272, 273	Yorkshire 91	Roman Town	SE/406666
Alfred's Castle, Lambourn, 106	Berkshire 157	I.A. Fort	SU/277827
Alfriston, 76	Sussex 183	Long Barrow	TQ/509034
Almondbury, Huddersfield, 275–6, 281	Yorkshire 102	I.A. Fort	SE/153141
Ambleside (*Galava*), 282	Westmorland 88	Roman Fort	NY/372034
Ambresbury, Epping Forest, 250	Essex 161	I.A. Fort	TL/438003
Ancaster, 255	Lincolnshire 113	Roman Fort	SK/983437
Annaside, 282	Cumberland 88	Stone Circle	SD/092866
Anstiebury, 66	Surrey 170	I.A. Fort	TQ/153440
Arbor Low, Buxton, 259	Derbyshire 111	B.A. Sanctuary	SK/161636
Arbury Banks, Ashwell, 245	Hertfordshire 147	I.A. Fort	TL/260387
Argam Dyke, Rudstone, 264	Yorkshire 93	Earthworks	TA/112717
Arminghall, 253	Norfolk 126	B.A. Sanctuary	TG/240061
Arncliffe, Littondale, 278	Yorkshire 90	I.A. Settlement	SD/931717
Arras, Market Weighton, 262–3	Yorkshire 98	I.A. Cemetery	SE/925418
Arthur's Stone, Dorstone, 210	Herefordshire 142	Meg. Long Barrow	SO/318431
Avebury, 24, 25, 52, 53, 55, 107–111	Wiltshire 157	B.A. Sanctuary	SU/103700
Aveline's Hole, Burrington Combe, Mendip, 157	Somerset 165	O.S.A. Cave	ST/475586
Avening, 197	Gloucestershire 157	Meg. Long Barrows	ST/887984
Aylesford, 69	Kent 171	I.A. Cemetery	TQ/729591

NAME OF SITE AND PAGE REFERENCES	COUNTY AND 1″ O.S. SHEET NO.	TYPE OF MONUMENT	NATIONAL GRID REF.
Buckland Rings, Lymington, 100	Hampshire 180	I.A. Fort	SZ/315968
Bullsdown, Bramley, 92	Hampshire 169	I.A. Fort	SU/671583
Bulwarks, The, Rhoose, 217–18	Glamorgan 153	I.A. Fort	SS/838886
Burford Down, Dartmoor, 169	Devonshire 187	Stone Row Stone Circles	SX/637604
Burgh Castle, Yarmouth, 252	Suffolk 126	Roman Fort	TG/475046
Burwen's Castle, Elsack, 277	Yorkshire 95	Roman Fort	SD/929493
Bury Castle, Selworthy, 162	Somerset 164	Earthwork	SS/918472
Bury Hill, 97–8	Hampshire 168	I.A. Fort	SU/346436
Butser Hill, Petersfield, 88	Hampshire 181	Round Barrows I.A. Earthworks	SU/712201
Butterdown Hill, Ivybridge, 169	Devonshire 187	Stone Row	SX/656594
Buxton (Aquae), 259	Derbyshire 111	Roman Town	SK/060730
Buzbury Rings, Cranborne Chase, 133	Dorset 179	I.A. Fort	ST/919059
Bwrdd Arthur, Beaumaris, 232	Anglesey 107	Fort	SH/588816
Cadbury Camp, Bristol, 151	Somerset 177	I.A. Fort	ST/454725
Cadbury Castle, 159–160	Somerset 176	I.A. Fort	ST/618246
Cae Tor, Tythegston, 218	Glamorgan 153	Meg. Long Barrow	SS/850790
Caer Gybi, Holyhead, 233	Anglesey 106	Roman Fort	SH/247826
Caerhun (Canovium), 236	Caernarvonshire 107	Roman Fort	SH/777374
Caerleon (Isca), 59, 215–16	Monmouthshire 155	Roman Fortress	ST/339906
Caernarvon (Segontium), 229	Caernarvonshire 115	Roman Fort	SH/485625
Caerwent (Venta Silurum), 19, 214–15	Monmouthshire 155	Roman Town	ST/469905
Caer-y-Twr, Holyhead Mountain, 234	Anglesey 106	I.A. Fort	SH/218829
Caesar's Camp, Aldershot, 92	Hampshire 169	I.A. Fort	SU/835150
Caesar's Camp, Wimbledon, 65	Surrey 170	I.A. Camp	TQ/224712
Caister-by-Norwich (Venta Icenorum), 252	Norfolk 126	Roman Town	TG/231034
Caister-by-Yarmouth, 252	Norfolk 126	Roman Port	TG/517123
Caistor, 257	Lincolnshire 104	Roman Town	TA/118013

NAME OF SITE AND PAGE REFERENCES	COUNTY AND 1″ O.S. SHEET NO.	TYPE OF MONUMENT	NATIONAL GRID REF.
Canterbury (*Durovernum Cantiacorum*), 70–1	Kent 173	Roman Town	TR/151579
Capel Garmon, Bettws-y-Coed, 236–7	Denbighshire 107	Meg. Long Barrow	SH/818544
Cardiff, 216–17	Glamorgan 154	Roman Fort	ST/181766
Carisbrooke Castle, 101	Isle of Wight 180	Roman Fort	SZ/487878
Carlisle (*Luguvallium*), 284	Cumberland 76	Roman Town	NY/400570
Carl Wark, Sheffield, 261, 275	Derbyshire 111	Dark Age Fort	SK/260815
Carn Brea, Redruth Moors, 176	Cornwall 189	Fort	SW/686407
Carn Euny, Land's End, 181	Cornwall 189	I.A. Settlement Fogou	SW/142283
Carn Fadry, 229	Caernarvonshire 115	I.A. Fort	SH/280352
Carn Goch, Llangattock, 208	Brecknockshire 141	Meg. Long Barrow	SO/212177
Carn Llidi, St. David's Head, 221	Pembrokeshire 151	Meg. Tomb	SM/735279
Carneddau Hengwm, Llanarber, 225	Merionethshire 116	Meg. Long Barrows	SH/614205
Carreg Coitan, Newport, 222	Pembrokeshire 138	Meg. Tomb	SN/055390
Carreg Sampson, Mathry, 222	Pembrokeshire 138	Meg. Tomb	SM/846334
Castell Collen, 224	Radnorshire 128	Roman Fort	SO/055628
Castell Dinas, 209	Brecknockshire 141	I.A. Fort	SO/178302
Casterley Camp, Upavon, 117	Wiltshire 167	I.A. Fort	SU/116535
Castle-an-Dinas, Penzance, 178	Cornwall 189	I.A. Fort	SW/485350
Castle-an-Dinas, St. Columb Major, 175	Cornwall 185	I.A. Fort	SW/945624
Castle Ditch, Eddisbury, 238	Cheshire 119	I.A. Fort	SJ/553694
Castle Ditches, Swallowcliffe, 127–8	Wiltshire 167	I.A. Fort	ST/963283
Castle Dore, Fowey, 176	Cornwall 186	I.A. Fort	SX/103548
Castle Hill, Scarborough, 265	Yorkshire 93	I. A. Settlement Roman Signal Station	TA/052982
Castle Ring, Harthill Moor, 259	Derbyshire 111	Stone Circle	SK/225625

296

NAME OF SITE AND PAGE REFERENCES	COUNTY AND 1″ O.S. SHEET NO.	TYPE OF MONUMENT	NATIONAL GRID REF.
Castleshaw, Saddleworthy, 276	Yorkshire 102	Roman Fort	SE/002097
Castleton Rigg, 270	Yorkshire 86	B.A. Settlement	NZ/684062
Castor (see Water Newton), 254–5	Northampton-shire 134	Roman Town Roman Fort	TL/125984
Catterick (*Cataractonium*), 273	Yorkshire 91	Roman Fort	SE/220990
Cawthorne, Pickering, 268	Yorkshire 92	Roman Camps	SE/784900
Cerne Abbas Giant, 141–3	Dorset 178	Hill Figure	ST/666016
Cerrig Duon, Traen-glas, 212	Brecknockshire 140	Stone Circle Standing Stone	SN/852229
Cerrig y Gof, Newport, 222	Pembrokeshire 138	Meg. Tomb	SN/040390
Chactonbury Ring, 81	Sussex 182	I.A. Fort Roman Temple	TQ/139121
Chalbury, Weymouth, 137	Dorset 178	I.A. Fort	SY/695839
Chapel Carn Brea, Land's End, 181	Cornwall 189	Round Cairn	SW/386282
Chapman Barrows, Exmoor, 162	Devonshire 178	I.A. Fort	SY/695839
Charterhouse-on-Mendip, 155–6	Somerset 165	Roman Town Roman Mines	ST/506561
Chastleton Burrow, Chipping Norton, 187	Oxfordshire 144	I.A. Fort	SP/258283
Cheddar Gorge, Mendip, 156–7	Somerset 165	O.S.A. Caves	ST/467538
Chedworth, 191	Gloucestershire 144	Roman Villa	SP/053135
Chesters (*Cilurnum*), Chollerford, 286	Northumberland 77	Roman Fort	NY/912701
Chestnuts, The, Trottiscliffe, 69	Kent 171	Meg. Tomb	TQ/653592
Chichester (*Noviomagus*), 58, 85	Sussex 181	Roman Town	SU/860050
Chichester, 85	Sussex 181	I.A. Dykes	SU/850070
Chiselbury Camp, Compton Chamberlayne, 127	Wiltshire 167	I.A. Fort	SU/018281
Cholesbury, Tring, 243	Buckinghamshire 159	I.A. Fort	SP/930072
Chun Castle, Land's End, 56, 181	Cornwall 189	I.A. Fort	SW/405339
Chun Quoit, Morvah, 181	Cornwall 189	Meg. Tomb	SW/402339
Church Hill, Findon, 83	Sussex 182	Flint Mines	TQ/113083
Churn Knob, Blewbury, 102	Berkshire 158	Long Barrow	SU/520835

NAME OF SITE AND PAGE REFERENCES	COUNTY AND 1″ O.S. SHEET NO.	TYPE OF MONUMENT	NATIONAL GRID REF.
Cresswell Crags, 260	Derbyshire 112	O.S.A. Caves	SK/535742
Crickley Hill, Birdlip, 193	Gloucestershire 144	I.A. Fort Roman Barrow	SO/927161
Croft Ambrey, Aymestry, 202	Herefordshire 129	I.A. Fort	SO/444668
Crown End, 270	Yorkshire 86	B.A. Settlement	NZ/683075
Crug, The, Brecon, 211	Brecknockshire 141	I.A. Fort	SO/225206
Culliford, 138	Dorset 178	Long Barrow Round Barrows	SY/700857
Cursus, The, Stoneghenge, 124	Wiltshire 167	Earthwork	SU/120430
Cwrt y Gollen, Crickhowell, 208	Brecknockshire 141	Standing Stone	SO/236167
Damerham Knoll, 131	Dorset 179	I.A. Fort	SU/099186
Damery, Severn Estuary, 200	Gloucestershire 156	I.A. Fort	ST/707944
Danby Rigg, 270	Yorkshire 86	Cairn Cemetery Standing Stones B.A. Settlement	NZ/710065
Danebury, Nether Wallop, 56, 98	Hampshire 168	I.A. Fort	SU/323377
Dane's Dyke, Flamborough Head, 264	Yorkshire 93	Earthworks	TA/213732
Dane's Graves, Driffield, 263	Yorkshire 99	I.A. Cemetery	TA/097633
Dawse Castle, Watchet, 161	Somerset 164	I.A. Fort	ST/070430
Dead Men's Graves, Claxby, 256	Lincolnshire 114	Long Barrows	TF/445719
Debden Moor, 287	Northumberland 71	Round Barrows Standing Stones	NU/070050
Dere Street, Woodburn, 286–7	Northumberland 77	Roman Road Roman Fort	NY/890860
Devil's Arrows, Boroughbridge, 273	Yorkshire 91	Standing Stones	SE/391666
Devil's Bed and Bolster, Rode, 152	Somerset 166	Meg. Long Barrow	ST/808535
Devil's Dyke, Brighton, 80	Sussex 182	I.A. Fort	TQ/259111
Devil's Dyke, Newmarket Heath, 247	Cambridgeshire 135	Saxon Earthworks	TL/569658
Devil's Humps, Bow Hill, 87	Sussex 181	Round Barrows	SU/823122
Devil's Jumps, Monkton Down, 84	Sussex 181	Round Barrows	SU/825173

NAME OF SITE AND PAGE REFERENCES	COUNTY AND 1″ O.S. SHEET NO.	TYPE OF MONUMENT	NATIONAL GRID REF.
Devil's Quoit, Manorbier, 220	Pembrokeshire 151	Meg. Tomb	SS/075967
Devil's Quoits, Stanton Harcourt, 184	Oxfordshire 158	B.A. Sanctuary	SP/409049
Dinas Emrys, 237	Caernarvonshire 116	I.A. Fort	SH/606492
Din Lligwy, 233	Anglesey 106	Settlement	SH/496862
Dinorben, Abergele, 237–8	Denbighshire 108	I.A. Fort	SH/967757
Ditsworthy Warren, 169	Devonshire 187	Stone Rows Stone Cist Standing Stone Hut Circles	SX/590670
Dolaucothi, 213	Carmarthenshire 140	Roman Gold Mine	SN/665405
Dorchester (*Durnovaria*), 141	Dorset 178	Roman Town Roman Aqueduct	SY/693907
Dorchester, 184	Oxfordshire 158	N.S.A. Rings I.A. Earthworks Roman Town	SU/577493
Dover (*Dubris*), 71, 72–3	Kent 173	Roman Fort and Lighthouse	TR/326418
Dowkerbottom Cave, 278	Yorkshire 90	I.A. and Roman Cave	SD/952688
Dowsborough, Quantocks, 161	Somerset 164	I.A: Fort	ST/160392
Drew, Stanton, 150	Somerset 166	Stone Circles	ST/601633
Druid's Circle, Grassington, 278	Yorkshire 90	I.A. Earthworks	SE/005651
Druid's Circle, Penmaenmawr, 236	Caernarvonshire 107	Stone Circle	SH/723747
Duddo, Till Valley, 288	Northumberland 64	Stone Circle	NT/931437
Dunkery Beacon, Porlock, 161, 162	Somerset 164	Stone Circle	SS/887467
Durrington Walls, 52, 125	Wiltshire 167	Henge Monument	SU/150438
Dyffryn, 226	Merionethshire 116	Meg. Long Barrow	SH/587233
East Mynne, Minehead, 162	Somerset 164	I.A. Fort	SS/932483
Ebchester (*Vindomora*), 284	Durham 78	Roman Fort	NZ/102556
Ebor Gorge, Mendip, 154–5	Somerset 165	O.S.A. Cave	NT/528490
Eggardon, 144–5	Dorset 178	I.A. Fort	SY/541947
Elbolton Cave, Thorpe, 278	Yorkshire 90	N.S.A. Cave	SE/010618
Elva Plain, Bassenthwaite, 283	Cumberland 82	Stone Circle	NY/177318

302

NAME OF SITE AND PAGE REFERENCES	COUNTY AND 1″ O.S. SHEET NO.	TYPE OF MONUMENT	NATIONAL GRID REF.
Haresfield Beacon, Haresfield, 195	Gloucestershire 156	I.A. Fort	SO/820088
Harrow Hill, Storrington, 83	Sussex 182	Flint Mines	TQ/082100
Harroway, 92	Hampshire 168	Ancient Road	SU/500510
Hascombe Hill, 65–6	Surrey 170	I.A. Fort	TQ/005386
Hell Stone, Portisham, 144	Dorset 178	Meg. Tomb	SY/605867
Hembury, Honiton, 46, 148–9	Devonshire 176	Causewayed Camp I.A. Fort	ST/112030
Hendre Wealod, 237	Denbighshire 107	Meg. Tomb	SH/772765
Hengistbury Head, Christchurch, 100	Hampshire 179	Round Barrow I.A. Earthworks	SZ/169908
Herefordshire Beacon, Great Malvern, 201	Herefordshire 143	I.A. Fort	SO/760400
Heston Brake, Port Skewett, 214	Monmouthshire 155	Meg. Tomb	ST/506887
Hetty Pegler's Tump, Uley, 199	Gloucestershire 156	Meg. Long Barrow	SO/790001
Heyshott Downs, 84	Sussex 181	Round Barrows	SU/895166
High Bridestones, Sleights Moor, 269	Yorkshire 86	Stone Circle	NZ/851046
High Rochester (*Bremenium*), 287	Northumberland 86	Roman Fort	NY/833986
Hoar Stone, Enstone, 186–7	Oxfordshire 145	Meg. Long Barrow	SP/377237
Hob Hurst's House, Bunker's Hill, 260	Derbyshire 111	Round Barrow	SK/287692
Hod Hill, Cranbourne Chase, 133–5	Dorset 178	I.A. Fort Roman Camp	ST/856106
Holkam, 250	Norfolk 125	I.A. Fort	TF/875447
Hollingbury, 79–80	Sussex 182	I.A. Fort	TQ/322078
Holmbury Hill, 66	Surrey 170	I.A. Fort	TQ/104430
Holtye, 66–7	Sussex 171	Roman Road	TQ/461391
Horncastle, 257	Lincolnshire 114	Roman Town	TF/258696
Housesteads (*Borcovicium*), 286	Northumberland 77	Roman Fort	NY/790688
Howe Hill, Duggleby, 263	Yorkshire 93	Round Barrow	SE/880668
Huggate Pasture, 263	Yorkshire 98	Earthworks	SE/860560
Huntcliff, 267	Yorkshire 86	Roman Signal Station	NZ/693216
Hunter's Burgh, Windover, 77	Sussex 183	Long Barrow	TQ/549037

NAME OF SITE AND PAGE REFERENCES	COUNTY AND 1″ O.S. SHEET NO.	TYPE OF MONUMENT	NATIONAL GRID REF.
Long Meg and her Daughters, Little Salkeld, 284	Cumberland 83	Stone Circle Standing Stone	NY/571373
Longhouse, 222	Pembrokeshire 138	Meg. Tomb	SM/846334
Loose Howe, Danby High Moor, 269–270	Yorkshire 92	Round Cairn	NZ/703008
Lowbury Camp, Goring, 102	Berkshire 158	Roman Farm Saxon Barrow	SU/540823
Lullingstone, 67	Kent 171	Roman Villa	TQ/529651
Lunt, The, Baginton, 253–4	Warwickshire 132	Roman Fort	SP/342746
Lydney, 22, 204–5	Gloucestershire 156	I.A. Earthworks Roman Temple Roman Iron Mine	SO/615026
Lyneham, Sarsden, 187	Oxfordshire 145	Meg. Long Barrow	SP/297208
Maen Cetti (Reynoldston), 218	Glamorgan 153	Meg. Tomb	SS/491195
Maen Pebyll, 236	Denbighshire 107	Meg. Long Barrow	SH/845566
Maesbury, Mendip, 153	Somerset 166	I.A. Fort	ST/610472
Maesknoll, Dundry, 150	Somerset 156	I.A. Fort Round Barrow	ST/600660
Maiden Bower, Dunstable, 243	Bedfordshire 147	I.A. Fort	SP/996225
Maiden Castle, Bickerton Hill, 239	Cheshire 109	I.A. Fort	SJ/498529
Maiden Castle, Dorchester, 18, 56, 138–9	Dorset 178	Causwayed Camp I.A. Fort	SY/669885
Maiden Castle, Grinton, 280	Yorkshire 90	Stone Row Round Barrows Earthworks	SE/023982
Maumbury Rings, Dorchester, 132, 140–1	Dorset 178	B.A. Sanctuary Roman Amphitheatre	SY/693907
Mam Tor, Rushup Edge, 261	Derbyshire 111	I.A. Fort	SK/128837
Margam Mountain, 218	Glamorgan 153	Round Barrows Earthworks	SS/810890
Martinhoe, 163	Devonshire 163	Roman Signal Station	SS/663493
Martin's Down, Kingston Russell, 144	Dorset 178	Long Barrow Earthworks	SY/572912
Mayburgh, Ullswater, 283	Westmorland 83	Stone Circle Round Barrows	NY/519284

306

NAME OF SITE AND PAGE REFERENCES	COUNTY AND 1″ O.S. SHEET NO.	TYPE OF MONUMENT	NATIONAL GRID REF.
Meare, 158–9	Somerset 165	I.A. Settlement	ST/445422
Meini Gwyr, Llandyssilio East, 223	Pembrokeshire 139	Stone Circle	SN/142266
Meini Herion, Llanfachell, 232	Anglesey 106	Standing Stones	SH/364917
Membury, 106, 148	Dorset 177	I.A. Fort	ST/283028
Men-an-Tol, Penwith Peninsula, 180	Cornwall 189	Meg. Tomb	SW/426349
Meon Hill, 190	Gloucestershire 144	I.A. Fort	SP/177453
Merdon Castle, 98	Hampshire 168	I.A. Fort	SU/421265
Merrivale Bridge, Dartmoor, 169	Devonshire 187	Stone Rows Stone Circle Standing Stones Hut Circles	SX/548751
Metherall, Dartmoor, 168	Devonshire 175	Stone Row	SX/673842
Midsummer Hill, Eastnor Park, 201	Herefordshire 143	I.A. Fort	SO/760374
Minning Low, Ardwark, 259	Derbyshire 111	Stone Cist and Round Cairn	SK/209573
Minchinhampton Common, 198	Gloucestershire 156	Round Barrows I.A. Earthworks	SO/863012 SO/850010
Morfa Bychan, Garness Mountain, 220	Carmarthenshire 152	Stone Cist and Round Cairn	SN/210080
Mounsey Castle, Dulverton, 162	Somerset 164	I.A. Fort	SS/886296
Mount Caburn, 78	Sussex 183	I.A. Fort	TQ/444089
Mulfra Quoit, 180	Cornwall 189	Meg. Tomb	SW/452354
Mynydd Carn Llecharth, 220	Glamorgan 153	Stone Cist and Round Cairn	SN/689075
Mynydd-Cefnamwlch, Penllech, 229	Caernarvonshire 115	Meg. Tomb	SH/227339
Mynydd Myddfai, 212	Carmarthenshire 140	Stone Circle	SN/280290
Nant Tarw, Traean-glas, 212	Brecknockshire 140	Stone Circles	SN/818258
Nesfield, 277	Yorkshire 96	Fort	SE/093496
Nine Barrows Down, Isle of Purbeck, 136	Dorset 179	Round Barrows	SY/995816
Nine Ladies, Stanton Moor, 260	Derbyshire 111	Stone Circle Standing Stones	SK/249635
Nine Maidens, Bodmin Moor, 173	Cornwall 186	Stone Circle	SX/237782

NAME OF SITE AND PAGE REFERENCES	COUNTY AND 1″ O.S. SHEET NO.	TYPE OF MONUMENT	NATIONAL GRID REF.
Nine Maidens, Boscawenun, Land's End, 181	Cornwall 189	Stone Circle	SW/413274
Nine Maidens, Penwith Peninsula, 180	Cornwall 189	Stone Circle	SW/435352
Nine Maidens, St. Columb Major, 174	Cornwall 185	Stone Row	SW/937675
Nine Stones, Bellstone, Dartmoor, 168	Devonshire 175	Stone Circle	SX/612928
Nine Stones, Winterbourne Steepleton, 144	Dorset 178	Stone Circle	SY/613904
Normanton Down, 121	Wiltshire 167	Round Barrows	SU/115413
Norn's Tump, Avening, 197	Gloucestershire 157	Round Barrow	ST/889985
Norton Bavant, 119	Wiltshire 167	Long Barrow	ST/924442
Notgrove, 188–9	Gloucestershire 144	Meg. Long Barrow	SP/096211
Nottingham Hill, Cheltenham, 190	Gloucestershire 144	I.A. Fort	SO/981284
Nympsfield, Crawley Hill, 198–9	Gloucestershire 156	Meg. Long Barrow	SO/794013
Oakhill, Mendip, 152	Somerset 166	Roman Crossroads	ST/638462
Ogbury, Durnford, 125	Wiltshire 167	I.A. Fort	SU/143383
Old Berry Castle, Dulverton, 162	Somerset 164	I.A. Fort	SS/910283
Old Bewick, 289	Northumberland 71	Fort	NU/075210
Old Burrow Walls, Glenthorne, 162	Devonshire 163	Roman Signal Station	SS/788493
Old Oswestry, 239	Shropshire 118	I.A. Fort	SJ/295304
Old Penrith (*Voreda*), 283	Cumberland 83	Roman Fort	NY/525327
Old Sarum, Salisbury, 126	Wiltshire 167	I.A. Fort Roman Settlement Saxon and Medieval Town	SU/130730
Old Winchester Hill, 88	Hampshire 181	I.A. Fort	SU/641206
Oldbury Castle, Chippenham, 113	Wiltshire 157	I.A. Fort Hill Figure	SU/048695
Oldbury Hill, 67	Kent 171	O.S.A. Cave I.A. Fort	TQ/582562
Oliver's Castle, Roundway Hill, 113	Wiltshire 167	I.A. Fort	SU/002647
Osmington, 137	Dorset 178	Hill Figure	SY/716843
Painswick Beacon, 195	Gloucestershire 143	I.A. Fort	SO/869119

NAME OF SITE AND PAGE REFERENCES	COUNTY AND 1″ O.S. SHEET NO.	TYPE OF MONUMENT	NATIONAL GRID REF.
Pant-y-Saer, Tyn-y-gongl, 232	Anglesey 107	Meg. Tomb	SH/510825
Parc Cwm, Parc le Breos, Gower, 218	Glamorgan 153	Meg. Long Barrow	SS/537899
Parc y Meirw, Llanllawer, 222	Pembrokeshire 138	Stone Row	SM/999359
Paviland, Gower, 218–19	Glamorgan 152	O.S.A. Cave	SS/437859
Pawton, St. Breoke Downs, 174	Cornwall 185	Meg. Long Barrow	SW/968683
Paynim Way, Wittenham, 184	Oxfordshire 158	Ancient Road	SU/582920
Pembury Knoll, 131	Dorset 179	I.A. Fort	SU/039171
Pen Hill, Mendip, 153	Somerset 166	Long Barrow Round Barrows	ST/564487
Pen y Corddyn, Abergele, 237–8	Denbighshire 108	I.A. Fort	SH/915764
Pendinas, Aberystwyth, 224	Cardiganshire 127	I.A. Fort	SN/585804
Pendinas, Llanarber, 225	Merionethshire 116	I.A. Fort	SH/607209
Penmaen Burrows, Gower, 218	Glamorgan 153	Meg. Tomb	SS/530880
Penmaenmawr, 235	Caernarvonshire 107	Axe Factory	SH/720760
Pennance, 180	Cornwall 189	Meg. Tomb	SW/450375
Pentre Ifan, Nevern, 222–3	Pembrokeshire 139	Meg. Long Barrow	SN/099370
Pentridge, Cranborne Chase, 130	Dorset 179	Roman Road	SU/011153
Pevensey (*Anderida*), 75	Sussex 183	Roman Fort	TQ/644048
Piddinghoe, 79	Sussex 183	Round Barrows	TQ/425037
Piercebridge-on-Tees, 273	Yorkshire 85	Roman Fort	NZ/210157
Pilgrim's Way, 23, 68, 70	Kent 171	Ancient Road	TQ/650612
Pilsdon Pen, Broadwindsor, 147	Dorset 177	I.A. Fort	ST/412013
Pimperne, Cranborne Chase, 130–1	Dorset 179	Long Barrow	ST/917104
Pipton, Three Cocks Junction, 210	Brecknockshire 141	Meg. Long Barrow	SO/160373
Plas Newydd, Menai Bridge, 231	Anglesey 107	Meg. Tomb	SH/521697
Portchester, 99	Hampshire 180	Roman Fort	SU/625046
Port Way, 97	Hampshire 167	Roman Road	SU/260415
Porth-dafarch, Holyhead Island, 234	Anglesey 106	Settlement	SH/234802

NAME OF SITE AND PAGE REFERENCES	COUNTY AND 1″ O.S. SHEET NO.	TYPE OF MONUMENT	NATIONAL GRID REF.
Pound, The, Winterbourne Abbas, 144	Dorset 178	Long Barrow	SY/625908
Poundbury, Dorchester, 141	Dorset 178	I.A. Fort Roman Aqueduct	SY/682912
Priddy, Mendip, 154–5	Somerset 166	Long Barrow Round Barrows B.A. Sanctuary	ST/541530
Pry Rigg, 271–2	Yorkshire N.R. 92	Round Cairn	SE/593484
Pyon Wood, Aymestry, 202	Herefordshire 129	I.A. Fort	SO/423663
Quarley Hill, 96–7	Hampshire 167	I.A. Fort	SU/262423
Randwick Hill, 195	Gloucestershire 156	Meg. Long Barrow I.A. Fort	SO/825069
Ravenglass, 282	Cumberland 88	Roman Fort	SD/087959
Ravensburgh Castle, Hitchin, 245	Hertfordshire 147	I.A. Fort	TL/099295
Ravenscar, 266	Yorkshire 93	Roman Signal Station	NZ/970010
Reculver (Regulbium), 71–2	Kent 173	Roman Fort	TR/227693
Redhill, 151	Somerset 165	Long Barrow	ST/516649
Rey Cross, 273	Yorkshire 84	Roman Fort	NY/900124
Rhos y Gelynen, 212	Radnorshire 128	Stone Circle	SN/905631
Richborough (Portus Rutupis), 71, 72	Kent 173	Roman Fort	TR/325602
Rillaton, Linkinhorne, 172–3	Cornwall 186	Stone Cist and Circle	SX/260719
Rockbourne Down, 131	Dorset 167	Round Barrows I.A. Settlement Roman Earthwork	SU/110213
Rodborough Common, 198	Gloucestershire 156	I.A. Earthworks	SO/850038
Rollright Stones, 184–6	Oxfordshire 145	Meg. Tombs Stone Circle	SP/296309
Roman Riggs, Don Valley, 275	Yorkshire 103	Earthworks	SK/430986
Rombalds Moor, Ilkley, 277	Yorkshire 96	Rock Carvings	SE/090470
Rothbury, Coquet Valley, 287	Northumberland 71	Standing Stones Rock Carvings	NU/057017
Rough Tor, Bodmin Moor, 173–4	Cornwall 186	Fort Hut Circles	SX/145800
Routing Lynn, Dod Law, 288	Northumberland 64	Rock Carvings	NT/984367
Rudston, 264	Yorkshire 93	Standing Stone	NY/100682

NAME OF SITE AND PAGE REFERENCES	COUNTY AND 1″ O.S. SHEET NO.	TYPE OF MONUMENT	NATIONAL GRID REF.
Saeth Maen, Penwyllt, 212	Brecknockshire 153	Stone Row	SN/833154
St. Albans (*Verulamium*), 19, 58, 59, 244–5	Hertfordshire 160	Roman Town	TL/136071
St. Catherine's Hill, Winchester, 91	Hampshire 168	I.A. Fort	SU/484276
St. George's Hill, Weybridge, 65	Surrey 170	I.A. Fort	TQ/086618
St. Lythans, 217	Glamorgan 154	Meg. Long Barrow	ST/101723
Salthouse Heath, 250	Norfolk 125	B.A. Barrows	TG/075423
Scamridge, Pickering, 268	Yorkshire 93	Long Barrow Earthworks	SE/490860
Scoles Wood, Rotherham, 275	Yorkshire 103	I.A. Fort	SK/395953
Scotch Corner, Catterick, 273	Yorkshire 85	Roman Road	NZ/210057
Scots Dyke, Hindwith-on-Swale, 280	Yorkshire 91	Earthwork	NZ/187020
Scowles, The, Forest of Dean, 203	Gloucestershire 155	?Roman Iron Mines	SO/605047
Scratchbury, Warminster, 118–19	Wiltshire 166	Round Barrow I.A. Fort	ST/911443
Seaford, 77	Sussex 183	I.A. Fort	TV/494978
Sea Mills (*Abonae*), 151–2, 163	Gloucestershire 155	Roman Settlement	ST/533775
Segsbury, Wantage, 102	Berkshire 158	I.A. Fort	ST/384845
Seven Barrows, Kingsclere, 94	Hampshire 168	Round Barrows	SU/462553
Sibdury, Tidworth, 125	Wiltshire 167	I.A. Fort	SU/216506
Sidbury Castle, Sidmouth, 148	Devonshire 176	I.A. Fort	SY/128913
Silbury Hill, Avebury, 55, 111–12	Wiltshire 157	Artificial Mount	SU/100685
Silchester (*Calleva Atrebatum*), 60, 92–4	Hampshire 168	Roman Town	SU/640625
Singlen Stones, Egrement, 283	Cumberland 82	Stone Circle	NX/998112
Six Hills, Stevenage, 245	Hertfordshire 147	Roman Barrows	TL/237237
Slack, Huddersfield, 176	Yorkshire 102	Roman Fort	SE/084174
Smacam Down, Sidling St. Nicholas, 141	Dorset 178	Long Barrow	SY/657994
Smay Down, Tidcombe, 96	Hampshire 168	Long Barrow	SU/309593

NAME OF SITE AND PAGE REFERENCES	COUNTY AND 1″ O.S. SHEET NO.	TYPE OF MONUMENT	NATIONAL GRID REF.
Sweynes Howes, The, Rhossili, 218	Glamorgan 152	Stone Cists and Round Cairns	SS/148898
Swinburn Castle, 287	Northumberland 77	Standing Stone	NY/936755
Swineside, Broughton-in-Furness, 282	Cumberland 88	Stone Circle	SD/172883
Table Men, Land's End, 181	Cornwall 189	Meg. Tomb	SW/364259
Tan y Murriau, Rhiw, 229	Caernarvonshire 115	Meg. Long Barrow	SH/227280
Templecombe, Henley, 242–3	Buckinghamshire 159	Meg. Tomb	SU/785814
Therfield Heath, Royston, 245	Hertfordshire 147	Long Barrow	TL/341402
Thomspon's Rigg, 269	Yorkshire 92	Cairn Cemetery	SE/880925
Thornborough Moor, West Tanfield, 274	Yorkshire 91	B.A. Sanctuaries	SE/285795
Thor's Cave, Wetton, 259	Staffordshire 111	I.A. Cave	SK/099549
Three Brothers of Grogith, St. Keverne, 178	Cornwall 190	Stone Cist	SW/767196
Three Howes, Falcon Inn, 268	Yorkshire 93	Round Cairns	SE/966981
Tidcombe, 96	Hampshire 168	Long Barrow Roman Road	SU/293576
Tinglestone, Gatcombe Park, 197–8	Gloucestershire 156	Meg. Long Barrow	ST/882982
Tinkinswood, St. Nicholas, 217	Glamorgan 154	Meg. Long Barrow	ST/902733
Titsey, 67	Kent 171	Roman Villa	TQ/407544
Titterstone Clee, Ludlow, 240	Shropshire 129	I.A. Fort	SO/592779
Tomen-y-Mur, Trawsfynydd, 226–7	Merionethshire 116	Roman Fort	SH/707387
Toots, The, Oldbury, 200	Gloucestershire 156	I.A. Fort	ST/613927
Toots, The, Selsley Hill, 198	Gloucestershire 156	Meg. Long Barrow	SO/826032
Trescastell, 212	Brecknockshire 141	Stone Circles Roman Fort	SN/883291
Trefignath, Holyhead Island, 234	Anglesey 106	Meg. Tomb	SH/259805
Trefor, Llansadwrn, 232	Anglesey 107	Meg. Tomb	SH/548776
Tregear Rounds, St. Kew, 174	Cornwall 186	I.A. Fort	SX/033800

NAME OF SITE AND PAGE REFERENCES	COUNTY AND 1″ O.S. SHEET NO.	TYPE OF MONUMENT	NATIONAL GRID REF.
Tre'r Ceiri, Caernarvon, 228	Caernarvonshire 115	I.A. Fort	SH/374447
Trethevy, St. Clare, 171	Cornwall 186	Meg. Tomb	SX/259688
Trevelgue Head, Newquay, 175	Cornwall 185	Round Cairns I.A. Fort Iron Mines	SW/825630
Trippett Stones, Bodmin Moor, 173	Cornwall 186	Stone Circle	SX/130750
Trowlesworthy Down, Dartmoor, 169	Devonshire 187	Stone Rows Stone Circles	SX/573644
Trundle, The, Goodwood, 85, 86, 87	Sussex 181	I.A. Fort Causewayed Camp	SU/877111
Twelve Apostles, Bingley, 277	Yorkshire 96	Stone Circle	SE/137447
Twthill, Caernarvon, 229	Caernarvonshire 115	I.A. Fort	SH/483631
Ty Illtyd, Manest Farm, 210	Brecknockshire 141	Meg. Long Barrow	SO/098263
Ty Isaf, 209	Brecknockshire 141	Meg. Long Barrow	SO/182291
Ty Mawr, Holyhead Mountain, 234	Anglesey 106	Settlement	SH/217818
Tyddyn Bleiddyn, Cefn, 237	Denbighshire 108	Meg. Tomb	SJ/020720
Uffington Castle, 102	Berkshire 158	I.A. Fort	SU/299863
Uley Bury, 199	Gloucestershire 156	I.A. Fort	ST/785989
Urswick, 282	Lancashire 88	Round Cairns and Row I.A. Fort	SD/263744
Valley of the Rocks, Lynton, 163	Devonshire 163	Hut Circles Standing Stones	SS/706497
Victoria Cave, Settle, 278–9	Yorkshire 90	M.S.A. and Roman Cave	SD/839650
Wade's Causeway, Wheeldale Moor, 268	Yorkshire 86	Roman Road	SE/806977
Walbury, 95	Berkshire 168	I.A. Fort	SU/374618
Wallbury, Bishops Stortford, 250	Essex 148	I.A. Fort	TL/492178
Wandlebury, Stapleford, 247	Cambridgeshire 148	I.A. Fort	TL/494534
Wansdyke, Marlborough Downs, 20, 96, 113–14, 150	Wiltshire 157	Post-Roman Dyke	SU/050660
Wapley Hill, Presteigne, 202	Herefordshire 129	I.A. Fort	SO/346625
Warham, 250	Norfolk 125	I.A. Fort	TF/944409

NAME OF SITE AND PAGE REFERENCES	COUNTY AND 1″ O.S. SHEET NO.	TYPE OF MONUMENT	NATIONAL GRID REF.
Windrush, 192	Gloucestershire 144	I.A. Fort	SP/181123
Winkelbury, Cranborne Chase, 128	Dorset 167	I.A. Fort	ST/953217
Winklebury, Basingstoke, 92	Hampshire 168	I.A. Fort	SU/613528
Winterbourne Stoke, 120	Wiltshire 167	Long Barrow Round Barrow	SU/100417
Witchy Neuk, 287	Northumberland 71	Fort	NY/993993
Wittenham Clumps, 184	Oxfordshire 158	I.A. Fort	SU/569925
Woodbridge, 253	Suffolk 142	Saxon Barrows	TM/283489
Woodhenge, Durrington, 124–5	Wiltshire 167	Late Neolithic Sanctuary	SU/150434
Woodyates, Cranbourne Chase, 129	Dorset 179	Roman Village	SU/028194
Wookey Hole, Mendip, 153–4	Somerset 166	O.S.A. Cave I.A. Cave	ST/531480
Worlebury, Weston-super-Mare, 157	Somerset 165	I.A. Fort	ST/314625
Wrekin, The, 239–40	Shropshire 118	I.A. Fort	SJ/630082
Wroxeter (*Viroconium*), 19, 240	Shropshire 118	Roman Town	SJ/565087
Wychbury, Birmingham, 253	Warwickshire 130	I.A. Fort	SO/918817
y Pigwin (see Trecastell), 212	Brecknockshire 140	Roman Camps	SN/828312
Yarnbury Castle, Amesbury, 120	Wiltshire 167	I.A. Fort	SU/035404
Yeavering Bell, 288	Northumberland 71	Fort	NT/927293
Yellowmead, Dartmoor, 169	Devonshire 187	Stone Circles	SX/575677
York (*Eboracum*), 60, 272	Yorkshire 97	Roman Fortress Roman Town	SE/603523
Ysbyty Cynfyn, 224	Cardiganshire 127	Stone Circle	SN/752791
Zennor Quoit, Penwith Peninsula, 179–80	Cornwall 189	Meg. Tomb	SW/454385

GENERAL INDEX

(All individual monuments are indexed in the Gazetteer)

All Sphere Books are available at your bookshop or
newsagent, or can be ordered from the following address:
Sphere Books, Cash Sales Department,
P.O. Box 11, Falmouth, Cornwall.

Please send cheque or postal order (no currency), and allow
19p for postage and packing for the first book plus 9p
per copy for each additional book ordered up to a
maximum charge of 73p in U.K.

Customers in Eire and B.F.P.O. please allow 19p for
postage and packing for the first book plus 9p per copy
for the next 6 books, thereafter 3p per book.

Overseas customers please allow 20p for postage and
packing for the first book and 10p per copy for each
additional book.